# Something Extra

*The Brigade Tie*
*Worn with pride.*

# Something Extra
# 28 Commonwealth Brigade
# 1951 to 1974

Compiled by
H. B. Eaton

| Korea | 1951 to 1953 |
|---|---|
| Malaya | 1955 to 1960 |
| Malay Peninsula | 1964 to 1966 |

The Pentland Press Limited
Edinburgh · Cambridge · Durham

First published in 1993 by
The Pentland Press Ltd.
1 Hutton Close
South Church
Bishop Auckland
Durham

ISBN 1 85821 049 6

Typeset by Elite Typesetting Techniques, Southampton.
Printed and bound by Antony Rowe Ltd., Chippenham.

# Something Extra

This is the story of the life of an infantry brigade told by the soldiers who served in that rather special brigade. It is, therefore, a story about soldiers, related by soldiers in the language of soldiers and makes no pretence at being a work of literary merit nor an official history. The contributions of former brigade members in Australia, Canada, Great Britain, Malaysia and New Zealand provide the 'meat' of the account, together with extracts from regimental histories and other national sources.    The account traces the life of the 28th Commonwealth Infantry Brigade during an interesting period of military history which deserves some recognition and publication. From its inception in 1951 to its disbandment in 1974, 28 Commonwealth Brigade was active in Korea, Malaya, Thailand and Singapore and brigade units undertook operations in Borneo, Laos and Mauritius.

The account was first suggested by members of the British Korea Veterans Association who considered that the Commonwealth Brigade's achievements had been neglected in most historical accounts of that war. As the project took shape, former members from the nations concerned requested that the account should be extended to cover the complete period of the brigade's existence. With the assistance of many of those who served in Korea and thereafter – in particular the major contribution made by the late Brigadier Peter Moore – it has been possible to record the full story of the 28th Commonwealth Infantry Brigade.

The account has been compiled by a former regular soldier who served two tours of duty in the Commonwealth Brigade: the first as an infantryman in Hong Kong and Korea and the second on the staff of Brigade Headquarters in Malaya. Such a return for duty with the brigade was not uncommon; many of the brigade's units and members – from Australia, Great Britain and New Zealand – returned for second and third tours of duty with a formation which gave its members 'something extra'.

# Contents

|  | Page |
|---|---|
| List of Illustrations | ix |
| Forewords | xvii |
|  |  |
| What is a Brigade? | 1 |
| Origins | 3 |
| 28 Commonwealth Brigade | 11 |
| The Imjin Line | 22 |
| The Commonwealth Division | 29 |
| Kowang-San | 38 |
| Maryang-San | 61 |
| Hill 227 | 77 |
| Winter 1951-1952 | 85 |
| The Static War | 95 |
| The Last Battles | 124 |
| Truce | 145 |
| Renaissance | 159 |
| Deployment | 168 |
| North Malaya | 178 |
| Terendak | 234 |
| Confrontation | 251 |
| Peace | 280 |
| ANZUK | 300 |
| In Retrospect | 322 |
| Commanders of 28 Commonwealth Brigade | 325 |
| Units of 28 Commonwealth Brigade | 327 |

viii                    *Contents*

Contributors                          331
Bibliography                          333
Index                                 337

# List of Illustrations

Frontispiece:    The Brigade Tie

|  | Page |
|---|---|
| The Far East. (N. England) | 5 |
| 1st Bn. King's Own Scottish Borderers disembark at Inchon, greeted by pipers of the Royal Ulster Rifles, 23rd April 1951. (IWM) | 8 |
| West-Central Korea. (N. England) | 9 |
| Maj. Richard Webb, 16 Fd. Regt. R.N.Z.A., with Maj. William Farthing, 955 Fd. Arty. Bn. U.S.A., recall their experiences at the Fort Still Artillery School, Oklahoma, as classmates in 1948–1949. In the IX Corps area, Central Front. 10th May 1951. (IWM) | 15 |
| The Imjin Area. (N. England) | 24 |
| Soldiers of 3rd Royal Australian Regiment crossing the Imjin River on a Centurion tank, June 1951. (IWM) | 25 |
| C Company, 3rd Bn. Royal Australian Regiment, move up to new positions North of the Imjin River, 8th June 1951. (IWM) | 26 |
| Cpl. Tucker, K.S.L.I., instructs members of the 3rd R.A.R. on the Vickers Medium Machine Gun, July 1951. (AWM) | 27 |
| The 60th Indian Field Ambulance, Indian Army Medical Corps, commanded by Lt. Col. A. G. Rangaraj, on left. (IWM) | 30 |
| Brig. G. Taylor, D.S.O. and Lt. Col. F. G. Hassett, O.B.E. leave A Company, 3rd Bn. Royal Australian Regiment, after watching a fire power demonstration in the reserve area, August 1951. (IWM) | 31 |
| Maj. Robertson, Salvation Army, and his jeep with the 3rd R.A.R. (AWM) | 33 |

Page
Op. Commando Area. (N. England)                                    39
3rd Battalion, Royal Australian Regiment moving forward for        42
    Operation 'Commando', October 1951. (AWM)
60th Indian Field Ambulance evacuating casualties on an Ameri-     44
    can helicopter. (AWM)
Hill 355 'Kowang-San' – under fire. (IWM)                          45
Operation 'Commando', October 1951. Medium Machine Gun of          46
    3 R.A.R. giving covering fire. (AWM)
Lt. Ballenden, M.C., K.S.L.I., convalescing in Japan after being   48
    wounded in Operation 'Commando', October 1951. (AWM)
Operation 'Commando', October 1951. A casualty being evacu-        49
    ated from a company jeep-head of 3rd R.A.R whilst Korean
    porters bring up rations, ammunition, water and fresh bread.
    (AWM)
Brig. G. Taylor, D.S.O., commander 28 Commonwealth Brigade,        53
    at a forward command post, October 1951. (IWM)
Pte. William Speakman, V.C. 1st Bn. King's Own Scottish Bor-        68
    derers. (*Soldier*)
25-pounder gun of 16 Fd. Regt., Royal New Zealand Artillery.       71
    (IWM)
Lt. Gen. William Bridgeford, C-in-C British Troops Japan and       75
    Korea, visits H.Q. 3rd Bn. Royal Australian Regiment. Left
    to right: Lt. Col. J. F. Macdonald, K.O.S.B., acting comman-
    der 28 Bde.; Lt. Col. F. G. Hassett, C.O. 3 R.A.R.; Gen.
    Bridgeford; Maj. Gen. J. Cassels, commander 1 COMWEL
    Div. (IWM)
Sole Survivor, Hill 227, 18th November 1951. (Capt. Eaton)         81
Soldiers of B Coy., 1st Bn. King's Shropshire Light Infantry,      96
    guarding communist prisoners at the Koje-do P.O.W. Camp,
    May 1952. (IWM)
F.M. Lord Alexander, British Minister of Defence, visits 28 Com-   97
    monwealth Brigade, May 1952. (AWM)
Mortar pit, 1st Bn. King's Own Scottish Borderers, 1952. (IWM)     99
The Samichon Area. (N. England)                                   101
Shields made by 16 Infantry Workshops R.E.M.E. in June 1952.      102
Gen. Lawton Collins, U.S. Army Chief of Staff, with Brig.         103
    Thomas Daly, commander 28 Commonwealth Brigade; Maj.
    Gen. A. J. Cassels, commander 1 COMWEL Div., in the rear,
    16 July 1952. (IWM)

Page

A patrol of 2 Platoon, A Company, 1st Bn. King's Shropshire 104
Light Infantry, enjoy a last smoke before going out; 2lt. J. D.
Parry, Pte. J. Norris, Pte. G. Hodson, Sgt. B. Skelton, July 1952.
(IWM)

B Coy., 1 D.L.I., Christmas Dinner 1952. (Lt. Col. Atkinson) 116

Presentation of the Birthday Cake to Brig. Daly, Camp Casey, 120
19th March 1953, with the Bugles of the D.L.I., Band of the
R.A.R. and Drums of the R.F. (Gen. Daly)

Senior Officers of 28 Commonwealth Brigade, March 1953. (Gen. 121
Daly)

A mortar pit of the 1st Bn. Royal Fusiliers, Hill 210, May 1953. 125
(Mr. Kirley)

The Sharp End – forward trenches on Hill 210 occupied by the 126
Royal Fusiliers, May 1953. (Mr. Kirley)

The Durham Light Infantry hand over their positions to the 3rd 130
Royal Australians, May 1953. (AWM)

'No mate – the Light Infantry.' (Capt. Eaton) 131

Chinese shell exploding forward of D Company, 3rd R.A.R., on 132
Hill 355, May 1953. (AWM)

New Zealand gunners, Royal Fusiliers and pipers of the Black 134
Watch, Coronation Day, 1953. (IWM)

Lt. Col. Stevens presents the flag of the Royal Fusiliers, flown on 138
Hill 355, to Maj. I. H. McBride, Brigadier-Major, for the 6th
Bn. of the Royal Melbourne Regiment. (AWM)

Pte. G. E. Rose, B Company, 2nd. Bn. Royal Australian Regi- 139
ment, with a Browning machine gun on The Hook, 18th July
1953. (IWM)

Armistice – a New Zealand gunner and an Australian infantry- 142
man, 28th July 1953. (AWM)

Soldiers of the 3rd. Bn., Royal Australian Regiment, retire from 143
the demilitarised zone after the armistice, July 1953. (IWM)

Vickers machine gun team of the 1st Bn., The Essex Regiment, in 151
winter clothing. 1953. (IWM)

Brigadier Wilton inspects the Royal Warwickshire Regiment. 152
February 1954. (AWM)

Pte. Moody, Essex, Pte. Harvey, R.A.R., Lcpl. Hunter, Essex, 153
Pte. Kim, Katcom, Pte. Potts, R.A.R. (Essex Regt.)

Brig. J. G. N. Wilton, O.B.E., inspects the Essex Regiment. Feb- 153
ruary 1954. (Essex Regt.)

Page

ANZAC Day, 25th April 1954; representatives of the 1st and 3rd   155
Battalions of the Royal Australian Regiment, the Royal New
Zealand Artillery and the Essex Regiment. (AWM)

Brigadier Murdoch, March 1954. (AWM)   156

North Malaya. (N. England)   160

Formation Sign, 28 Commonwealth Infantry Brigade Group   164
Malaya.

Major Peter Oxley (Brigade Major) and Brig. Moore (Com-   172
mander 28 Commonwealth Brigade), March 1956. (Brig.
Moore)

1st Battalion Royal Scots Fusiliers, on patrol in a tin mine, June   175
1956. (*Soldier*)

The Chief of the General Staff meeting officers of 28 Common-   179
wealth Independent Brigade Group at Ipoh, 1957. (Brig. Bogle)

Perak (N. England)   180

C Coy., 1 Loyals, in the Pari Valley, Malaya, June 1958. (Brig.   196
Collins)

Tracker Team, 1 Loyals, North of Sungei Siput, Malaya, Decem-   196
ber 1958. (Brig. Collins)

Lt. Gen. Sir James Cassels with Pte. Sigai Anak Jugam, Sarawak   197
Rangers, and Lt. Jim Barlow, 1 Loyals, at Ipoh, 9 September
1958. (Gen. Mogg)

Gen. Sir Cecil Sugden, Quartermaster-General, inspects the Com-   198
monwealth Provost Coy with Brig. Mogg at Taiping, 8th February 1959. (Gen. Mogg)

3rd Royal Australian Regiment; left to right: Pte. F. K. O'Brien   200
who shot a terrorist – the third 'kill' by 3 R.A.R., Pte A.
Clauson and Sergeant R. Moyle, with shotgun. (AWM)

HQ 28 Commonwealth Infantry Brigade Group and North Malaya   207
Sub-District.

C Coy. patrol, 1 Loyals, Perak River, Malaya January 1959.   208
(Brig. Collins)

Brig. Mogg at a Bde. T.E.W.T. at Sungei Kuang, Malaya, 5th   209
August 1959. (Brig. Collins)

Lt. Col. J. C. Johnson, 1 Loyals, with the Loyals' tiger cub at   210
Grik, 28th November 1959. (Gen. Mogg)

Brig. Mogg fires 75,000th shell delivered against the terrorists by   211
100 'A' Field Battery, Royal Australian Artillery, 5th September 1959. (AWM)

Page

B Company, 1/3 East Anglian Regiment, on jungle patrol, Perak, 213
Malaya. (*Soldier*)

Lady Mountbatten and Brig. Mogg at the new hospital at 215
Kamunting, 8th February 1960. (Gen. Mogg)

Lt. Gen. Manuel F. Cabal, Chief of Staff of the Philippine Army, 218
visiting 28 Commonwealth Brigade at Taiping with Brig. Mogg
and Maj. East, Brigade Major. (AWM)

The Victory Parade, Kuala Lumpur, 2nd August 1960. The New 219
Zealand Regiment. (Gen. Mogg)

Sgt. Harris, East Anglian Regiment, instructs Sgt. Pullen, Royal 222
Australian Regiment, on the 7.62mm Self Loading Rifle.
(AWM)

Brig. Hassett serves Pte. Schneider's Christmas Dinner, Taiping, 225
Christmas Day, 1960. (Capt. Eaton)

Brig. F. G. Hassett, Brigade Commander, and Maj. R. D. P. 226
Hassett, Royal New Zealand Artillery, Brigade Major. (AWM)

Commonwealth and Thai signallers, Exercise Rajata, Ubon, Thai- 228
land, March 1961. (Capt. Eaton)

Brigade Command Post on exercise, Malaya, 1961. (Capt. Eaton) 229

Terendak Camp, Malacca. (*Soldier*) 235

Cpl. Ray Folbigg, Royal Australian Signals, and family in their 235
quarters, Terendak Camp. (*Soldier*)

The New Zealand Regiment on the Sungei Perak, April 1962. 237
(*Soldier*)

Cpl. Noel Freeman, 1st Battalion The New Zealand Regiment, 247
August 1963. (*Soldier*)

'A' Company, 1 K.O.Y.L.I., February 1964. Bareo Airstrip, Sara- 252
wak, with an R.A.F. Whirlwind helicopter and a Beaver. (LI)

Borneo. (N. England) 253

Mortar Team, 1 K.O.Y.L.I., July 1964. (LI) 254

Malaya. (N. England) 262

Brig. R. B. Dawson, Maj. J. M. Church (Brigade Major), Maj. L. 263
A. Eyles (D.A.A. & Q.M.G.) and Lt. Col. R. N. W. Lydekker,
R.A., Exercise 'Raven', Bahau, Malaya, 16th July 1964. (Brig.
Lydekker)

Sgt. Borley, Queen's Royal Irish Hussars, and Sgt. Keith Payne, 264
3rd Royal Australian Regiment, at a ceremonial parade to commemorate the affiliation of the two regiments during the Korean
War. Ipoh, August 1964. (AWM)

Page

Brig. T. D. H. McMeekin, Lt. Col. R. N. W. Lydekker and Mr. T.    267
C. Critchley, Australian High Commissioner to Malaysia.
Terendak, 12th November 1964. (Brig. Lydekker)

Lt. Col. A. I. D. Fletcher (left) listens as Maj. Sir Gregor    268
MacGregor briefs two patrol commanders on the Malay-Thai
Border. (SG)

105mm Pack Howitzer of 176 (Abu Klea) light Battery, Sarawak,    269
December 1964. (Brig. Lydekker)

5.5 inch Medium Gun of 170 (Imjin) Medium Battery being    270
winched up a 1:2 hill at Batu Lintang, Sarawak. (Brig.
Lydekker)

Gdsm. J. Singler, 1st Scots Guards, meets the headman of a    271
longhouse in Sarawak. (SG)

102 Field Battery, Royal Australian Artillery, in action in Sarawak.    272
(Brig. Lydekker).

Lt. Col. A. I. D. Fletcher, R.S.M. J. Grant, H.R.H. The Duke of    278
Gloucester, 1st Bn. Scots Guards, Kalabakan, Sabah, 13th
January 1966. (SG)

Gen. Tunku Osman bin Tunku Mohd Jewa and Lt. Col. East, C.O.    282
4 R.A.R. Terendak, 1st February 1967. (Col. East)

Lt. Col. East with the villagers of Kampong Pantai Merah. (Col.    283
East)

Air Platoon, 1st King's Shropshire Light Infantry, Terendak,    284
1967. (3 LI)

The advance party of the 1st K.S.L.I. arrive at Connor Park Aero-    288
drome, Australia, by Argosy aircraft, 15th September 1967, for
Exercise 'Piping Shrike'. (3 LI)

Lt. Col. Ballenden at Shoalwater Bay, Australia, 1967. (3 LI)    289

Senior Officers, 28 Commonwealth Brigade, November 1967.    291
(Col. East)

Drum Major Holland, 1st Royal Australian Regiment, and Brig.    297
R. M. Gurr, commander 28th Commonwealth Infantry Brigade.
Selarang, Singapore, 1971. (AWM)

Senior Officers – ANZUK Force – Singapore 1971. (Gen. Walsh)    301

'My dear chap, we can hit a matchbox at 5,000 yds.' (Gunner)    302

'You've got defensive fire – it's simulated!' (Gunner)    302

Brig. M. J. H. Walsh with Cpl. Harris and Pte. Klein, 6 R.A.R., on    303
exercise at Mersing. (AWM)

Formation Sign, 28 ANZUK Infantry Brigade.    304

Page

W. O. Pipe Major Alec MacLeod-Lee, 6th Battalion, Royal Aus- 306
tralian Regiment, with pipers and musicians of the Royal Highland Fusiliers and the 6th R.A.R., Singapore. (AWM)

Royal Review 28 ANZUK Bde. Kangaw, Singapore 5th March 307
1972. (Gen. Walsh)

Royal Review 28 ANZUK Bde. Kangaw, Singapore 5th March 308
1972. (Gen. Walsh)

H.R.H. The Princess Margaret visits The 1st Bn. Royal Highland 309
Fusiliers (Lt. Col. I. MacKay, M.B.E., M.C.), Nee Soon, Singapore 18th October 1972. (Gen. Walsh)

The Marae (Maori Meeting House) 1st Bn. Royal New Zealand 310
Infantry Regiment Dieppe Barracks, Singapore. (Gen. Walsh)

Brig. M. J. H. Walsh receives a Maori greeting during the dedica- 310
tion of the Marae; 2nd November 1972. (Gen. Walsh)

Final Parade of 28 ANZUK Brigade, Kangaw Airfield, Singapore 315
October 1973. (AWM)

Brig. Kennedy presents a plaque bearing the badges of the units 319
of 28 ANZUK Brigade to Brigadier Russell on the formation of
28 Infantry Brigade, Singapore, February 1974. (Brig.
Kennedy)

# Forewords

## Australia

The Commonwealth Division was a first class fighting formation. It was highly regarded by other U.N. troops and deserved to be. I believe all five Nations sent good people to represent them but its first commander, Major-General Cassels, was an outstanding leader who built the fledgling organisation into the harmonious whole which performed so well for the duration of the Korean conflict.

The 28th Commonwealth Brigade in Malaya, with its British, Australian and New Zealand units and close relationship with Gurkha and Malay troops, was a small Commonwealth Division. It also was a highly efficient formation which carried out its many diverse tasks with distinction.

It was an honour to be part of these formations which demonstrated, in a practical way, the ability of various nations to operate harmoniously and efficiently in what were often very testing times.

General Sir Francis Hassett, A.C., K.B.E., C.B., D.S.O., M.V.O.

## Great Britain

I regard it as the greatest honour and privilege to have been lucky enough
to have had the opportunity to command the 28th Commonwealth Brigade
for two years during the time of the final defeat of the Communist Terrorist Organisation in North Malaya. This unique formation comprising
Australian, New Zealand, British, Gurkha, Malayan and aborigine forces
proved itself to be highly professional, well trained and effective particularly in the difficult jungle conditions of the Emergency. Their success
produced a healthy rivalry between the different National units and developed a unique and powerful Commonwealth spirit which overcame
national or political differences. This spirit fostered a close comradeship
throughout the Brigade and made it a special family of which all ranks felt
proud to belong.

Hamish Eaton's history is not only a record of the successful exploits of
the Brigade and its close relationship with Police and the Civil Administration, providing a unique contribution to the stability in Malaya, but
throughout there runs a tale of courage, endurance and humour. There is
also a common thread of determination to work together combined with
stern dedicated service and belief in the cause by a devoted band of
warriors in the comradeship of arms.

I am deeply proud to be a member of this team.


General Sir John Mogg, G.C.B., C.B.E., D.S.O., D.L.

## New Zealand

New Zealanders who served in Korea and Malaya will be grateful to Hamish Eaton for the feast of facts and memorabilia presented in this book about 28 Commonwealth Brigade. Korean gunners will be particularly grateful for the manner in which the contribution made by 16 Field Regiment R.N.Z.A. has been recognised. Although not an integral part of the Brigade the very nature of its close support role gave the Regiment intimate contact with all the units of the Brigade and the Regiment can therefore claim, if not membership, the strongest possible affiliation.

It was a special experience to have been associated with the Brigade and to have had the opportunity of working so intimately with officers and men from Australia and the United Kingdom. Although we came from different ends of the earth the common threads between us were remarkable. Language, customs, systems, attitudes, national pride and above all the common bond of the profession of arms made for a unique relationship. Is it too much to hope that at some future date soldiers of another generation will have the opportunity of serving in a similar formation? Friendships too were formed particularly among the families; friendships which have survived the vicissitudes of time and in many cases rejuvenated during the course of visits abroad.

Pre-eminently, however, there was a fierce pride in 'our' Brigade, we all believed that it was a unique formation and that it was a privilege to belong to it. Hamish Eaton has admirably encapsulated the intangibles of that privilege. This history will help fill the void of literature about a very special formation which really did give its members 'something extra'.


Major-General R. D. P. Hassett, C.B., C.B.E.

# What is a Brigade?

Before relating the story of the 28th British Commonwealth Infantry Brigade it may be advisable to establish what a brigade is. The dictionary defines a brigade as a sub-division of an army, varying in different countries and times but usually consisting of three battalions (frequently with a regiment of field artillery) and forming part of a division. However, in larger foreign armies the same definition could apply to a regiment or an American regimental combat team. Even military readers might find the distinction somewhat confusing. To understand the difference between a brigade and a regiment it is necessary to delve into military history.

Regiments, comprising ten companies of 100 foot soldiers each, were raised originally by Colonels. Regiments were known by the names of their Colonels but were later identified by numbers, indicating their seniority in the Army. Such numbered regiments earned honorific or territorial titles in the course of time. As the need to enlarge the army arose, the Colonels took it upon themselves to double the size of their regiments by raising a further ten companies; the two halves of these enlarged regiments were called battalions (bodies in battle array) and command was delegated to Lieutenant-Colonels who deputised for the Colonel of the Regiment. The battalions were identified as the 1st and 2nd Battalions of the Regiment. In most Continental armies, these additional battalions remained under the command of their Colonel and served together as integral parts of the complete regiment.

In the British Army, however, the battalions of regiments were often detached to serve in the Americas or the East and rarely remained together as a whole regiment. A typical British infantry regiment might have had one battalion serving at home, one battalion in India and, in later years, two or more battalions of Territorial Army soldiers available for

1

mobilization in war. This peculiarly British system was adopted by the Indian Army and the armies of the British Commonwealth nations. To command and manage these assorted battalions in various parts of the world, brigades were created and were commanded by Brigade-Colonels, later to be known as Brigadier-Generals and, latterly, Brigadiers. To support these collections of battalions, an artillery element of battalion size was often placed under command. To add to the confusion, cavalry and artillery 'battalions' of the British Army are still known as regiments!

The brigade structure developed to include necessary support and service units and a complete brigade group was capable of deploying as an independent command if required. Battalions from British, Indian and Gurkha regiments were mixed in brigades and, since the armies of the Commonwealth nations were based on the British system, it was possible to incorporate battalions from the various nations.

The 28th Commonwealth Infantry Brigade was the supreme example of an integrated and international formation formed of elements from five independent nations, something which could not have been achieved in a Continental-type regiment of similar size and composition.

# Origins

The original 28th Infantry Brigade was formed in August 1914, as part of the 9th (Scottish) Division to cope with Lord Kitchener's first 'hundred thousand'. 9 Division consisted of 26, 27 and 28 Brigades which were composed of 'K1' Service Battalions, manned entirely by eager volunteers. 28 Brigade, commanded by Brigadier-General S. W. Scrase-Dickins, comprised the 6th Battalion of The King's Own Scottish Borderers, the 9th Battalion of The Scottish Rifles (The Cameronians) and the 10th and 11th Battalions of The Highland Light Infantry. The brigade mustered at Bordon Camp, in Hampshire, and went to France in March 1915. 28 Brigade was involved in the Battle of Loos in September 1915 but was broken up in May 1916; the 6th K.O.S.B. and the 9th Scottish Rifles were transferred to 27 Brigade and the two battalions of the H.L.I. joined the South African Brigade.

28 Brigade was reformed in September 1918 and was composed of the 2nd Battalion of The Royal Scots Fusiliers, the 9th Scottish Rifles and the Royal Newfoundland Battalion. Thus, in 1918, the brigade contained a 'Commonwealth' element. 28 Brigade moved into Germany as part of the occupation force after the armistice and was disbanded in March 1919.

In 1939, 28 Brigade was embodied as a second-line Territorial Army brigade of the 9th (Highland) Infantry Division but had a short life since its component battalions were transferred to reform 154 Infantry Brigade on 7th August, 1940. The remnants of 154 Brigade had been evacuated from Cherbourg in June after the 51st (Highland) Division's stand at St. Valery-en-Caux.

Another 28 Brigade was activated on 9th July 1941; the 28th East African Brigade. This 28 Brigade fought with the 1st and 2nd African Divisions in Abyssinia and moved to India in 1943, where it was disbanded on 1st June 1945.

On 1st December 1943, yet another 28 Brigade was formed from the old 2nd Gibraltar Brigade. This new brigade joined the 4th Infantry Division and was shipped to Egypt, arriving on Christmas Eve. From Egypt the brigade went to Italy, landing on 16th March 1944. Thereafter, 28 Brigade fought its way up Italy via the second battle of Cassino (11th-18th May), Trasimene (20th-30th June), Arezzo (4th-17th July), the advance to Florence (17th July-10th August) and the Rimini Line (14th-21st September). From Italy the brigade moved to Greece in December 1944 where it remained until demobilization on 31st August 1945.

28 Brigade reappeared in the New Territories of Hong Kong on the formation of the 40th Infantry Division in 1949. The Chinese Communists had gained the upper hand in the civil war against the Kuomintang and were sweeping victoriously Southwards – towards the Crown Colony of Hong Kong. 40 Division was raised to defend the colony's land border with China and was commanded by Major-General G. Evans. The divisional sign was the bantam cock, worn originally by the 35th and 40th 'Bantam' Divisions in the 1914-1918 war. The new division consisted of 26, 27 and 28 Brigades. 26 Brigade was primarily a Gurkha Infantry Brigade with the 1st Battalion of The Cameronians (The Scottish Rifles), the 2nd 6th and the 2nd 10th Gurkha Rifles; 27 Brigade consisted of the 1st Battalion of The Royal Leicestershire Regiment, the 1st Battalion of The Middlesex Regiment and the 1st Battalion of The Argyll and Sutherland Highlanders. 28 Brigade, commanded by Brigadier D. R. Morgan, D.S.O., M.C., was composed of the 1st Battalion of The King's Own Scottish Borderers (one of the regiments to have served in the original 28 Brigade), the 1st Battalion of The South Staffordshire Regiment and the 1st Battalion of The King's Shropshire Light Infantry. During 1949 and 1950 the division constructed defensive positions along the border with China and trained hard and realistically on the hills of the New Territories.

In June 1950 the North Korean People's Republic invaded the Republic of Korea, the Communist North attacking the American-supported South. An appeal was made to the United Nations to counter this unprovoked aggression and the member nations began to respond. Great Britain placed naval units at the disposal of the United Nations Command and it was decided to send a token land force to Korea. Hong Kong was the nearest military garrison and it fell upon two battalions of 27 Brigade to undertake the task, the Middlesex and the Argyll and Sutherlands. However, even these two battalions were not up to strength; national service was still in operation and some sixty per cent of most units were two-year

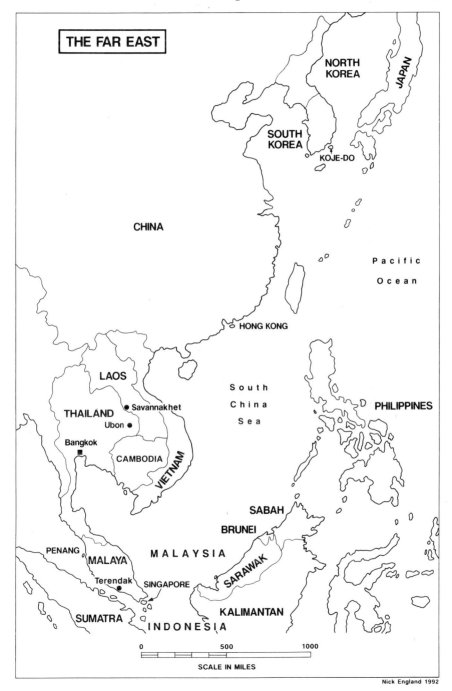

**THE FAR EAST**

NORTH KOREA

JAPAN

SOUTH KOREA

KOJE-DO

CHINA

Pacific

Ocean

HONG KONG

LAOS

South

China

Sea

Savannakhet

THAILAND

PHILIPPINES

Ubon

Bangkok

CAMBODIA

VIETNAM

SABAH

BRUNEI

PENANG

MALAYSIA

MALAYA

SARAWAK

Terendak

SINGAPORE

SUMATRA

KALIMANTAN

INDONESIA

0          500          1000

SCALE IN MILES

Nick England 1992

conscripts, who came and went as they served their time. To fill the ranks of the two battalions, a call was made to the other units of the division and men from all the British battalions volunteered for service in Korea.

27 Brigade Headquarters, under Brigadier B. C. Coad, together with the Middlesex and the Argylls, sailed from Hong Kong and reached the port of Pusan in Korea on 29th August 1950 – there to be plunged into a bitter war which took the brigade from the perimeter around Pusan to the far North of Korea and back to South Korea. The story of 27 Brigade's exploits has been told in several excellent accounts already published. The official battle honours awarded are evidence of the range of the brigade's actions – the Naktong Bridgehead, Chongju, Pakchon, Chongchon, Chuam-Ni, Kapyongchon and Kapyong – fierce little battles like the Middlesex capture of 'Plum Pudding Hill' and the Argylls' defence of Hill 282, where a posthumous Victoria Cross was awarded to Major Kenneth Muir.

Brigadier Coad's two battalions were always regarded as the 'Cinderella Brigade', dependent upon the goodwill of their American allies for most of the necessities of life in Korea. On 30th September 1950, Coad's brigade was enlarged by the arrival of the 3rd Battalion of The Royal Australian Regiment, Lieutenant-Colonel C. Green, volunteers to a man, representing Australia's contribution to the land forces of the United Nations. Thus 27 Brigade was transformed into the 27th Commonwealth Infantry Brigade and the Royal Australians soon earned their share of the battle honours. The 'Cinderella Brigade' was further strengthened when it was joined by the 60th Indian Parachute Field Ambulance of The Indian Army Medical Corps, under Lieutenant-Colonel A. G. Rangaraj, who joined the Commonwealth Brigade on 4th December 1950. The Indians reached Pyongyang in North Korea just as the great retreat to the South began; the field ambulance was almost stranded – but for the ingenuity of two members of the unit who managed to 'activate' a derelict locomotive in the railway sidings. 60th Field Ambulance have the distinction of being the last train across the Taedong River bridge before its demolition by U.S. Army engineers. The brigade was heartened to receive its own artillery support with the arrival of the 16th Field Regiment of The Royal New Zealand Artillery, Lieutenant-Colonel J. W. Moodie, on 22nd January 1951. Within a month, Coad's growing command became 'four-square' when it gained the 2nd Battalion of The Princess Patricia's Canadian Light Infantry, Lieutenant-Colonel J. R. Stone. The Commonwealth Brigade then contained representative units from six different nations – including Scotland. During all this time, 27 Brigade had been almost continually in action.

By April 1951 the Middlesex and the Argylls had been fighting in Korea for the best part of eight months, including a very harsh winter, and plans were afoot to relieve the British battalions of 27 Brigade. The Commonwealth Brigade was relieved in the front line by the 6th Republic of Korea (R.O.K.) Division and withdrew to the U.S. 9th Corps reserve area where it was hoped to effect the change of British battalions with fresh troops from Hong Kong. Brigadier George Taylor (who had assumed command of 28 Brigade from Brigadier Morgan in September 1950) with elements of 28 Brigade Headquarters joined the Commonwealth Brigade in readiness for the exchange of units – but the Chinese People's Volunteers upset the plan. On 22nd April the Chinese launched their Spring offensive along the front; to the West, the 29th British Infantry Brigade bore the brunt whilst on the central front the 6th R.O.K. Division were heavily attacked north of the Pukhan River. The South Koreans suffered heavily and the New Zealand gunners were rushed North to assist the battered division. By 23rd April the Republic of Korea division was withdrawing in the face of overwhelming enemy attacks. Brigadier Burke (then commanding the Commonwealth Brigade) sent the 2nd P.P.C.L.I. and the 3rd R.A.R. to block the end of the valley through which the South Koreans were retreating. Hardly had the two battalions occupied positions on Hills 677 and 504 than it became apparent that the Korean withdrawal had become a rout and, but for the prompt and close support of 16 Field Regiment, R.N.Z.A., all might have been lost. The Kiwis engaged the enemy over open sights and slowed their advance. The Australians tackled the Chinese as they infiltrated amongst the fleeing Koreans but small parties of the enemy succeeded in reaching the brigade's reserve battalion, the Middlesex. The Chinese advance was checked but by first light on 24th April the Chinese had massed for further assaults on the Australians on Hill 504. 3rd R.A.R. faced continuous attacks throughout the day and, at one stage, were surrounded until a company of the Middlesex, supported by 'A' Company of the 72nd U.S. Tank Battalion, broke through to re-establish communications and reinforce the Australians' right flank. During the afternoon of the 24th it was decided to withdraw the Australians to a position behind the Middlesex; this was successfully accomplished by midnight despite harassment from the enemy. During the night the main weight of the Chinese attack fell upon the Patricias on Hill 677 who, after being partially overrun, called upon the New Zealand gunners to deliver defensive fire on the hill. George Scott, a Scot serving as a signaller with 'D' Company of the P.P.C.L.I., remembers that he had to convince the Kiwis that the map co-ordinates sent over the radio were correct. 'But that's your own position!' objected a disbelieving gunner. 'Correct,' replied Scott, 'and my Sunray wants that fire now.' The fire was laid as requested and the Canadians held their ground. By the morning of 25th April the Chinese had been stopped in their tracks at Kapyong, a battle honour richly deserved by the Commonwealth Brigade. The New Zealand gunners had fired some 10,000 rounds and the enemy suffered heavy losses. The 5th U.S. Cavalry Regiment (three infantry battalions and two artillery battalions) were placed under Brigadier Burke's command and moved up on the brigade's left flank to support the 24th U.S. Infantry Division, who had been stripped of their right flank protection by the retreat of the R.O.K. division.

Meanwhile, as the battle raged, the 1st Battalion of The Argyll and Sutherland Highlanders, left in reserve, had been quickly and efficiently relieved by the 1st Battalion of The King's Own Scottish Borderers. The

*1st Bn. King's Own Scottish Borderers disembark at Inchon, greeted by pipers of the Royal Ulster Rifles, 23rd April 1951.*

(IWM BF 10204)

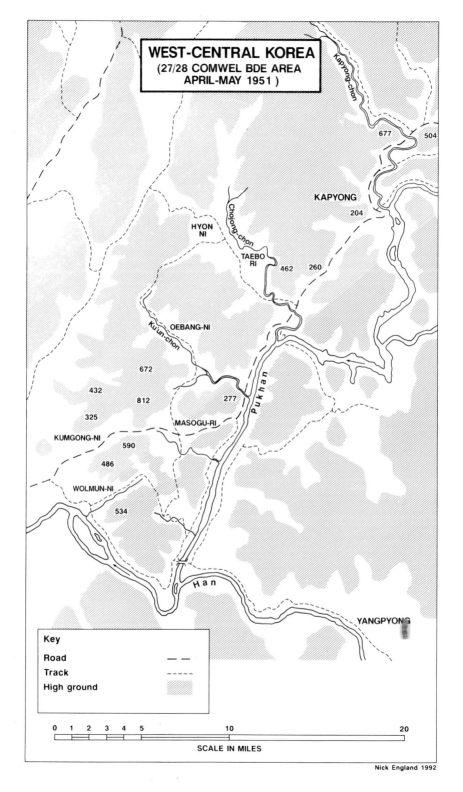

# WEST-CENTRAL KOREA
## (27/28 COMWEL BDE AREA APRIL-MAY 1951 )

Kapyong-chon

677        504

KAPYONG

204

Chojong-chon

HYON NI

TAEBO RI        462        260

OEBANG-NI

Ku'un-chon

672

432        812        277        Pukhan

325

590        MASOGU-RI

KUMGONG-NI

486

WOLMUN-NI

534

Han

YANGPYONG

| Key | |
|---|---|
| Road | — — |
| Track | ----- |
| High ground | |

0  1  2  3  4  5          10                    20

SCALE IN MILES

Nick England 1992

K.O.S.B. had travelled out from Hong Kong on the U.S.S. *Montrose*, disembarking at Inchon and then driven up to the Han River in a fleet of American trucks. The lightly equipped Borderers absorbed the later reinforcements to the Argylls, drawn from all regiments of the Highland Brigade, and took the Argylls' place as brigade reserve. With the arrival of the first of his 28 Brigade battalions, Brigadier George Taylor and his headquarters staff took over from Brigadier Burke and, at midnight on 25th April 1951, Brigadier Taylor assumed command of the 28th Commonwealth Infantry Brigade.

# 28 Commonwealth Brigade

The 28th Commonwealth Infantry Brigade came into existence in the front line. Although the main thrust of the Chinese attack had been blunted at Kapyong, the brigade still faced a determined enemy. The newly arrived King's Own Scottish Borderers, Lieutenant-Colonel J. F. M. MacDonald, were brought forward on 25th April to form a close defence perimeter around brigade headquarters whilst the other battalions, veterans of the old 27th Commonwealth Brigade, still held the ground to the North. As he relinquished his command to Brigadier Taylor, Brigadier Burke presented the 27 Brigade flag (the three-nines triangle) to Lieutenant-Colonel I. B. Ferguson as a mark of the esteem in which his battalion, the 3rd Royal Australian Regiment, was held by the brigade. The newly arrived 28 Brigade personnel still wore the 40 Division bantam cock flash – and were to do so until their jungle green shirts wore out. 28 Brigade had no distinctive flash of its own and later wore the Commonwealth Divisional insignia. However, there was little time for heraldry or ceremonial, Brigadier Taylor's command was in contact with the enemy.

By noon on 26th April 1951, the situation on the brigade's left had deteriorated. The 24th U.S. Infantry Division was forced to give ground and the Chinese had infiltrated to threaten the American division's artillery lines and 28 Brigade's communications route which ran Southwestwards down the course of the Pukhan River. To protect this vital route, Brigadier Taylor decided to move the brigade to cover the flank and the rear on the high ground North of Chojong-Chon. The 5th U.S. Cavalry (under command of 28 Brigade) was ordered forward to replace the Commonwealth battalions for the night and cover their withdrawal before retiring through the brigade at 6.00 a.m. on 27th April. General Van Fleet, commander-in-chief of the Eighth United States Army in Korea, paid a fleeting visit to the brigade and agreed with Brigadier Taylor (who quoted Wellington's adage that the test of generalship was to know whether to retreat or not) that the 24th U.S. Division and the Commonwealth Brigade should 'roll with the punch' and withdraw to a firm defensive line. Ammunition and supplies were running short by this time and, over in the West, Brigadier Brodie's battered 29 Brigade and the U.S. I Corps were still in contact with the Chinese. The battalions of 28 Brigade moved during the night to positions seven miles Southwest of Kapyong and began to dig in. The 5th U.S. Cavalry followed very early in the morning of the 27th, sooner than expected. In answer to a query from the K.O.S.B. an American officer observed: 'These guys always beat the gun.' As the tail of the U.S. Cavalry passed through the King's Own Scottish Borderers, Lieutenant-Colonel MacDonald gave the order for his platoons to draw in their horns. The K.O.S.B. filed down from their hills and embussed in waiting trucks to drive some 20,000 yards to their next position East of Hill 277, blocking any movement by the enemy down the Kuun-Chon valley to the Pukhan River. Following the Borderers came the 1st Battalion of the Middlesex Regiment (Lieutenant-Colonel A. Man) who joined the traffic to take up position on the West side of the Pukhan River.

By 3.00 p.m. on 27th April only the Australian and Canadian battalions were left holding the high ground above the Chojong-Chon. Time was now an important factor and, fortunately, the Chinese had been slow to take advantage of the brigade's withdrawal. Even so, the forward observers of the Royal New Zealand Artillery with the Patricias on Hill 462 called for covering fire as the first ant-like groups of Chinese swarmed over the hills. The withdrawal continued like clockwork and an eyewitness later recalled: 'It was indeed heartening to see the splendid Diggers filing down from the hills in the pouring rain. They had been fighting for four days and continually scaling heights in the most inaccessible country, yet their morale was inspiring as they trooped past loaded with belts of ammunition, heavy weapons, musical instruments and the inevitable sooty brewing can. But indeed all the troops of the Brigade had behaved in a calm and disciplined manner.' Brigadier Taylor and General Blackshear Bryan, commanding the 24th U.S. Infantry Division, stood on the inter-formation boundary line to ensure a simultaneous withdrawal and, as the King's Own Scottish Borderers marched past in column of platoons, General Bryan commented: 'Having seen some of your men, I have no fears about the flank.' By 5.00 p.m. the last battalions had left the high ground and were moving to their new positions in the Kuun-Chon/Pukhan River area, leaving two troops of tanks of the 72nd U.S. Tank

Battalion, under Lieutenant Koch, to cover the Chojong-Chon and Kapyong valleys. Despite the heavy rain, waterlogged roads and darkness, the American tanks successfully completed the rearward journey without mishap. Meanwhile, the Canadians and Australians were occupying their new positions in the soaking gloom of a Korean night.

Thirty minutes after midnight on 28th April the brigade received orders to move, this time back to the IX Corps reserve. Early in the morning of the 28th the troops vacated the trenches they had dug and occupied during the night. It had been raining steadily for two days and this precluded any air cover but the Kiwi gunners again rose to the occasion, firing off some 1,800 rounds of surplus shells into the advancing enemy. Added to the misery of the rain was a lack of transport. A dump of some 16,000 gallons of petrol, left forward of the Middlesex Regiment by the 5th U.S. Cavalry, had to be destroyed because it could not be transported to the rear. The King's Own Scottish Borderers were dismayed to see their heavier kit, dumped before they moved up to the brigade area, being burnt. The battalion's sea kitbags, regimental stores and even kilts were thrown on the bonfire and, but for the timely intervention of Brigadier Taylor (who happened to be passing by), ten sets of bagpipes might also have been lost. The Princess Patricia's Canadian Light Infantry also had problems on the march to the rear. Lieutenant-Colonel Stone was waylaid by a staff officer of the 24th U.S. Division who was intent on deploying the Canadians on the hills to the West to protect the flank of the American division. Colonel Stone objected strongly, pointing out that he did not know the terrain and it was too dark to reconnoitre the area. Fortunately, Brigadier Taylor – 'complete with red tabs' – was again on hand and quickly persuaded the American that a widespread deployment of the P.P.C.L.I. was 'not on'. Nevertheless, 28 Brigade moved back in good order and arrived at the reserve area of Yangpyong by 9.00 p.m.

The brigade was given two days to get its breath, a welcome break – especially for the Australians and New Zealanders who had spent ANZAC Day (25th April) on the hills above Kapyong. For their heroic stand at Kapyong, the 3rd Battalion of The Royal Australian Regiment and the 2nd Battalion of The Princess Patricia's Canadian Light Infantry – as well as 'A' Company of the 72nd U.S. Tank Battalion – were to receive the United States Presidential Unit Citation, the highest collective award to be bestowed. The 16th Field Regiment of The Royal New Zealand Artillery later received the Republic of Korea Presidential Citation for their gallant efforts in support of the 6th R.O.K. Division. However, news of these awards was still in the future as the brigade received orders to move on 1st May. The initial Chinese advance had spent itself along the front but the enemy were regrouping for the second phase of the offensive. To meet this threat the U.N. Commander decided to let the massed infantry attacks of the Chinese throw themselves against prepared positions. Having withdrawn from immediate contact with the enemy, the U.N. forces were able to establish a new line over favourable terrain with time to construct adequate defences. 28 Brigade, under the command of the 24th U.S. Infantry Division, moved forward to defend the ground between the Han and Pukhan Rivers. Brigadier Taylor, after an air reconnaissance of the area, issued an order of the day:

> 'The British Commonwealth Brigade has been given the most
> important job in the big battle of Seoul. We are to hold the high
> ground to the East of the city; as long as this is held the enemy
> cannot break into Seoul from the Northeast. On our right and in
> reserve will be troops of the 24th Division. General Van Fleet has
> decided to destroy the enemy on grounds of our own choosing. In
> our strong positions we can hold on for weeks (in similar posi-
> tions the Italians at Keren kept at bay two crack British and Indian
> Divisions for long time). Don't forget concealment and surprise,
> and work like beavers to strengthen our positions. As men and
> soldiers you have the full measure of our ant-like opponents. The
> menace of the urgent hour is upon us. I am confident that we will
> not fail. Now is the time for leadership and guts.'

Brigadier Taylor had leadership and guts galore in his command and, as those who had served under him in Hong Kong knew only too well, his exhortation to work like beavers was no idle threat. The Canadians promptly nicknamed him 'Old Wire and Mines Taylor' – pronounced with an exaggerated English upper class accent. The brigade responded enthusiastically, almost welcoming the opportunity to fight the enemy from well-prepared positions. For the next ten days, construction of defences across the 'peninsula' occupied by 28 Brigade was given top priority, although all units also carried out aggressive patrolling on a large scale. The Middlesex held the left of the line, around Hill 534 and the Han River; The King's Own Scottish Borderers were in the centre with the Patricias on the right, flanked by the 19th U.S. Regimental Combat Team on the West bank of the Pukhan River. The 3rd Royal Australians were held in brigade reserve. Every sub-unit was surrounded by wire entanglements; sections, platoons, companies and battalions to a depth of seventy

*Major Richard Webb, 16 Fd. Regt. R.N.Z.A., with Major William Farthing, 955 Fd. Arty. Bn. U.S.A., recall their experiences at the Fort Still Artillery School, Oklahama, as classmates in 1948–1949. In the IX Corps area, Central Front, 10th May 1951.*

(IWM MH 28031)

yards in many places with trip flares, mines, booby traps and burning barrel devices interspersed amongst the coiled wire. In contrast, the 19th R.C.T. on the brigade's right favoured taut, geometrical wire fences. Suddenly in the small hours of 11th May, General Hoge, commander of IX Corps, issued plans for an advance timed to commence at 7.00 a.m. These unexpected orders caused a considerable flurry until a further signal from Corps H.Q., later confirmed at 11.00 a.m., announced 'No move today' and the advance was postponed indefinitely. This rapid change of orders was a bit confusing but it did give battalion commanders the opportunity to fly an aerial reconnaissance of the ground the brigade had been ordered to take. General Van Fleet visited the brigade on 12th May to clarify the situation. A full-scale Chinese offensive was expected within the new few days and the General was determined that such an attack should be met by a defended line and not by troops advancing in the open. After General Van Fleet's visit, the brigade intensified its work on the defensive line.

Meanwhile, the 3rd R.A.R., which had been held in brigade reserve, relieved the Middlesex Regiment on the left of the line. On 13th May the 1st Battalion of The King's Shropshire Light Infantry, Lieutenant-Colonel A. S. Shaw-Ball, landed at Inchon after travelling from Hong Kong on the American troopship the U.S.S. *Montrose* – which had brought the K.O.S.B. to Korea and returned the Argylls to Hong Kong. The Shropshires were driven to the brigade reserve area and there effected an immediate exchange with the Middlesex Regiment; the Middies boarded the same trucks to be delivered to Inchon and the *Montrose* for the passage to Hong Kong. Thus, after some nine months in Korea, the last of the original 27 Brigade battalions left to be replaced by another 28 Brigade unit. Late arrivals and replacements to the Middlesex Regiment were absorbed by the K.S.L.I., exchanging their blue berets for the rifle-green headdress of the light infantry. Like the K.O.S.B., the K.S.L.I. were acclimatized and fit, having served their apprenticeship in George Taylor's realistic school of the hills of the New Territories in Hong Kong.

On 17th May intelligence reports of large scale enemy movement were received and, by last light of the same day, some 6,000 Chinese were observed moving South to threaten the right flank of 24 Division. The 19th Regimental Combat Team was subjected to battalion-size probing attacks during the night and the forward battalions were compelled to give ground as the Chinese sliced through their neat wire fences. The third battalion of the 19th R.C.T., finding the ground in their area to be too rough for wire fences, had spread coiled barbed wire haphazardly amongst the undergrowth. The attackers became hopelessly entangled in this obstacle and the battalion held firm, inflicting many casualties on the trapped Chinese, throwing more than 9,000 grenades in what the battalion commander described as 'great sport'. After repulsing the attacks the 19th R.C.T. was able to re-occupy the lost ground by first light of 18th May.

Meanwhile, 28 Brigade was standing to in force, expecting a 'Banzai Attack' which did not materialize. 'D' Company of the 3rd Royal Australians did come under some light enemy fire during the night but suffered no casualties. The brigade continued to patrol its front and 'A' and 'D' Companies of the K.S.L.I., now in brigade reserve, operated with American tanks as an armoured 'task force' on the brigade's left. The New Zealand gunners, together with the brigade's mortars and machine guns, laid heavy harassing fire which deterred the enemy from concentrating on the brigade's front. On 18th May, Second-Lieutenant Foulis's platoon of 'A' Company, the K.O.S.B., flushed twenty Chinese on a hilltop but were engaged by a further party of the enemy on a nearby spur. After a fierce hand-to-hand tussle, in which Private Johnstone killed two Chinese with a hand grenade and seized a 'burp gun' (a Russian submachine gun), the patrol was threatened by some 200 Chinese working their way around the hill. The machine gunners of the 3rd Royal Australians engaged the target and the platoon commander called for the New Zealand gunners to assist. Another group of about 100 Chinese was seen in front of the Patricias but was dispersed when the Canadians called for defensive fire from the Kiwi guns. During the late evening of 18th May a further attack was launched on the 19th R.C.T. but fizzled out in the face of heavy and concentrated defensive fire. This ended the expected full-scale attack by the Chinese on the 24th Division. Further to the East, however, the Chinese mounted a major assault and the 7th Republic of Korea Division had suffered heavy casualties – to the extent of being declared non-operational. The 2nd U.S. Infantry Division was also under heavy attack and the situation was worsening.

On the morning of 19th May IX Corps ordered 24 Division to advance in accordance with the plans made on 11th May. A general offensive was considered to be necessary to relieve the pressure on the Eastern front. 28 Brigade, all set for a period in defence, prepared to mount a hurried attack, probably one of the most difficult operations of war. The brigade was to advance on the left flank of 24 Division, over undulating country punctuated by steep hills rising some 400 to 800 metres. The advance began on 20th May with patrols moving forward across the lower ground on the left of the brigade's axis of advance. Brisk little fights took place along the brigade front as infantry patrols encountered spirited opposition from enemy groups of up to 100 strong. Mines, laid indiscriminately upon the crowns and shoulders of the few roads in the area, were found and cleared without delaying the tank and foot patrols moving Northwards.

The two main features of Hills 590 and 486 presented a formidable threat to the advance. For want of recent information on these obstacles, Brigadier Taylor decided to probe with fighting patrols. The Royal Australians secured Hill 590 without opposition and a platoon of 'D' Company of the Borderers, led by Lieutenant Innes, scaled Hill 486 in the morning mist of 20th May and surprised the Chinese at breakfast. However, the hill was occupied by a company of the enemy and the Borderers, their initial task completed, withdrew in good order. The Shropshires – at one stage with the Intelligence Officer, his sergeant and the author in the van – were clearing the smaller hills to the Southwest efficiently, meeting fairly light opposition from snipers and 'stay behind' parties. 'A' and 'D' Companies of the K.S.L.I. (Majors Heard and Cottle respectively) were called forward to execute a classic pincer attack on Hill 486, complete with airstrike, artillery barrage, 4.2 inch mortar support and the machine guns of the Royal Australians on the neighbouring Hill 590. A 'D' Company participant recalled the attack:

'We panted up that last lump of rock, occasionally eyeing the undergrowth and firs which sprouted all over it, but really too hot and out of breath to worry about Chinese. Just when we were beginning to reckon that our objective was to fall into our hands like a ripe plum, small arms fire came from a small knoll some 700 to 800 yards away, rattling amongst the trees and rocks. 12 Platoon, who were nearest, soon had answering fire brought down on some rat-like creatures who could be seen skulking among the diggings on the knoll. Soon our gunner friends were making life very unpleasant for the unfortunates who were foolish enough to give their position away. 'A' Company finished them off. We dug in and prepared for an unpleasant night.'

The Shropshires took the hill by 4.00 p.m., killing some sixty to seventy of the enemy although Lance-Corporal Yapp was killed and Lance-Corporal Hanlon was to die of wounds. The Chinese launched a counter-attack but the Shropshires held firm and repulsed the enemy. During the evening it began to rain again and the brigade dug in for another wet night on the barren hills of Korea.

On the morning of 21st May the 3rd Royal Australians led the advance and clambered up the 812 metres of Chonma-san, securing the hill with no opposition. On the left, the King's Own Scottish Borderers moved through the K.S.L.I. to meet mortar and sniper fire as they fought their way along a spur leading to Hill 432 whilst the Patricias protected the Borderers' flanks. The Americans on the brigade's right were making good progress over somewhat easier ground but the 25th Division, to the West of 28 Brigade, were some 2,000 yards behind the brigade's left flank, The heavy rain, together with anti-tank mines laid on the East-West road through the brigade area, increased the difficulties of supplying the advancing battalions and some vehicles and men were lost in this rear area. Communications between brigade headquarters and the K.S.L.I. were lost as the Shropshires followed the Australians up and over Chonma-san and North to Hill 672. Having secured the high ground, the battalions again dug in – 'it rained all day and poured the following night, everyone was soaked to the bone, but on the 22nd the sun came through followed by the porters.'

Thus heartened, the advance continued with the Australians on the right and 'A' and 'D' Companies of the Shropshires moving forward to occupy two small hills north of 672. During the day mines were cleared from the road in the brigade area and supplies of ammunition and rations were brought forward. The K.S.L.I. were attacked at 3.00 p.m. on 22nd May but the Chinese were beaten off, Lieutenant Grundy captured three of the enemy although Corporal Richardson was killed in the fight. With communications re-established, the Australians and the Shropshires consolidated for the night. The King's Own Scottish Borderers fought a long and gallant battle for Hill 432 during 22nd May. Two platoons of 'D' Company, Major MacKenzie, made the initial assault on this veritable rock fortress and rabbit warren. Lieutenant McMillan Scott's platoon led on the left and, although meeting stiff opposition, gained the summit of the hill but were forced to withdraw after some close fighting and a fierce counter-attack. Running short of ammunition, Major MacKenzie withdrew his platoons as airstrikes and artillery fire struck the hilltop. 'A' Company, Major Duncan, moved round the East of the hill during the night and early in the morning of 23rd May, 'A' and 'D' Companies attacked the hilltop – to find only twenty dead Chinese, the rest having escaped during the hours of darkness. The K.O.S.B. suffered fourteen casualties during this action but gained the grudging admiration of the New Zealand artillery observers with the battalion who admitted that the Borderers were up to the standard of the New Zealand Division in the last war.

With the fall of Hill 432, 28 Brigade's main objectives had been attained. The enemy were withdrawing before the brigade and only small parties of Chinese were encountered. A K.S.L.I. soldier, who celebrated his twenty-first birthday in a water-logged slit trench on the slopes of Chonma-san with a tin of ground meat and spaghetti (C7 American combat rations) and a tot of rum, recalls: 'The advance to the North was pure infantry work, marching, climbing and digging – very much like the training the battalion had practised on the hills of the New Territories, except that now and again the "exercise" was enlivened by small parties of Chinese who had to be chased from the hilltops.' One of the Borderers endorsed this impression: 'The lads did splendidly. Our Hong Kong training showed up well.' These little actions in which the brigade suffered some casualties were typical of the Chinese tactics in retreat. The small groups left behind were determined and brave; they dug themselves in extremely well, making good use of the boulders with which the hills were strewn by digging away most of the earth beneath and leaving only the smallest aperture. In this way they made themselves impervious to artillery, air and small arms. Flame throwers would have been useful but porterage up the precipitous and rocky hills would have been hazardous. Almost all the heights had razor-edged ridge lines behind which the enemy hid, unassailable by artillery and perfectly positioned for any immediate counter-attack. Even so, the Chinese faded before the well-trained soldiers of 28 Brigade and the New Zealand gunners caught them as they retired. Air strikes interdicted the enemy's lines of communications and the Shropshires once advanced up a valley littered with the bloated carcases of mules, used to carry ammunition and support weapons, particularly mortars which the Chinese used extensively.

The Chinese offensive on the Eastern front had been contained and the U.N. counter-attack in the West had trapped the enemy. The Communists suffered heavy casualties and, for the first time in the campaign, large numbers of Chinese prisoners were taken. In retrospect, it is interesting to speculate on the reasons why the Chinese did not launch the heavy assault expected on the brigade's positions. Although there was a considerable build-up and several probing attacks were made on both flanks, the enemy never got to actual grips with the Commonwealth Brigade. It may be that the Chinese intended nothing more than to contain the West Central front whilst the full weight of the offensive was concentrated in the East. The general opinion at the time was that the brigade's positions were too strong and the enemy had no wish to face determined resistance. In the event, 28 Brigade was able to advance more than fifteen miles – as the crow flies but considerably longer when climbing up and down the hills – and attained all its objectives by 24th May.

On 25th May the brigade was allowed to rest for two days in the Hyon-Ni/Taebo-Ri area. Padre Phillips and a party from the 3rd Royal Australians took the opportunity to revisit Kapyong on 26th May and conducted a funeral service for sixteen of their comrades who had been killed in the battle. After the successful advance, the brigade was sorry to lose the other 'Kapyong' battalion – the 2nd Princess Patricia's Canadian Light Infantry. The 25th Canadian Infantry Brigade had recently arrived in Korea with two of its infantry battalions: the 2nd Battalion of The Royal Canadian Regiment (Canada's Finest) and the 2nd Battalion of The Royal 22e Regiment (*Vingt-Deuxieme*). The Patricias left the Commonwealth Brigade on 27th May to become the third battalion of the newly arrived brigade which was moving to the Western front. Meanwhile, 28 Brigade's three battalions, The King's Own Scottish Borderers, The King's Shropshire Light Infantry and the 3rd Royal Australian Regiment, enjoyed the luxury of living in pup tents set in idyllic valleys in which the call of the cuckoo could be heard. However, they were not allowed to make themselves too comfortable and were ordered to move on 27th May. The brigade marched to the East on 28th May and were collected by a fleet of American trucks to follow the Patricias to the Western front. The long and dusty journey was made memorable only by the passing sight of the nurses of the Norwegian Mobile Army Surgical Hospital who were also *en route* for the West. The move involved a complete change of command, from the 24th U.S. Infantry Division of IX Corps to the 1st U.S. Cavalry Division of I Corps.

General Blackshear Bryan was sorry to lose the Commonwealth Brigade from his division and told a press reporter:

> 'I've never been prouder of any unit I have commanded. I have known and admired the Canadians for many years. The Australians proved themselves when they were with 27th Brigade and they remind me of Texans with their absolute confidence in themselves and their delight in tackling tough jobs. The new English and Scottish battalions of the K.O.S.B. and K.S.L.I. seem as excellent as the Middlesex and Argylls and I cannot give them higher praise than that.'

# The Imjin Line

The Commonwealth Brigade arrived in its new area, to the South of the River Imjin on the Western Front, on 29th May 1951. On the brigade's left was the 29th British Infantry Brigade, occupying positions around the site of the Battle of the Imjin the previous month. The 25th Canadian Brigade was in the rear as an immediate reserve. 28 Brigade had occupied its new positions by 30th May and, of course, it rained. The commander of the 1st U.S. Cavalry Division, General Palmer, had placed the brigade forward to relieve some of his battalions which were to be used the following week in a planned offensive. 28 Brigade's immediate task was to dominate the area in front of the 'Kansas Line' (which followed the course of the Imjin) by aggressive patrolling to a depth of some 6,900 yards, well to the North of the river.

'C' Company of the K.S.L.I., Major Evans, supported by Centurion tanks of the 8th King's Royal Irish Hussars (from 29 Brigade), attempted the first river crossing on 1st June. The river current was unusually strong after heavy rain, and, by 4.00 p.m., only two platoons had gained the Northern bank, 8 Platoon under Lieutenant Whitamore being the first across. The supporting tanks had become bogged down in the mud and Brigadier Taylor ordered that no more infantry should attempt the crossing. The two platoons made contact with the enemy and Lieutenant Whitamore pinpointed Chinese locations for the New Zealand gunners to engage. Having completed their primary task, the Shropshire platoons broke contact to withdraw but received heavy and accurate fire as they returned to the river. Major Evans was wounded, Privates Clifton and Miller killed and eight men wounded, of whom Private Davey was to die of his wounds. The patrol was ferried back in assault boats under fire and Sergeant Raison, the Shropshire's pioneer sergeant, was recommended

22

for the Military Medal for successfully evacuating the platoons to the Southern bank of the Imjin.

This foray demonstrated that it was necessary to establish a secure bridgehead from which to mount patrols in the territory North of the Imjin. An assault river crossing was planned and the 2nd Princess Patricia's Canadian Light Infantry was borrowed from the reserve brigade to operate with their old friends, the 3rd Royal Australians. A crossing point was selected at the confluence of the Hantan and Imjin, just North of the 38th Parallel (the line of latitude which marked the division between North and South Korea) and the operation was scheduled for 4th June. 3rd R.A.R. were to make the initial crossing and establish a perimeter before the 2nd P.P.C.L.I. would move through to take Hill 194 to the north. On the eve of the operation, heavy thunderstorms broke and the river rose considerably during the night. The crossing was postponed. The Royal Engineers made a reconnaissance and selected a better site some 3,000 yards upstream, to the North of Hill 194 in the Cavalry Division's area, and the crossing was replanned for 6th June – the seventh anniversary of 'D Day'.

The initial phases of the crossing went well, two companies of the Patricias secured the far bank without meeting opposition, the Chinese had apparently disappeared from the area. The sappers moved in to construct a Class 50 bridge over which two armoured task forces, each consisting of a company of the 3rd R.A.R. and a troop of the 8th Hussars, would cross to probe forward of the secured bridgehead. As the Royal Engineers began to position the pontoons the Chinese laid heavy mortar fire. The work was delayed but the bridge was completed by the early afternoon on 7th May and the tank-borne Australians rolled across to strike deep into no-man's-land North of the Imjin. Private Pat Knowles was aboard one of the tanks and recalls: 'We went across the Imjin, with armour support, ran across a few pockets of Chinese machine gunners, they fired on us waist high – from about 300 yards – and never hit a soul. The Besa machine guns soon fixed them. Those Centurions were a fantastic tank, made the Yank tanks look like tin cans.' Having established a secure bridgehead, the brigade's offensive patrolling programme was stepped up; patrols from all the battalions, supported by the tanks, made daily forays from the 'Kansas Line' into Chinese territory. At first the patrols encountered light opposition from scattered machine guns and mortars but these small outposts were soon mopped up and later patrols were able to dispense with tank support. The strengths of patrols were later reduced as less enemy activity was encountered and often the only sign of the Chinese were prominently displayed propaganda messages and leaflets intended for the U.N. forces.

24

*Something Extra*

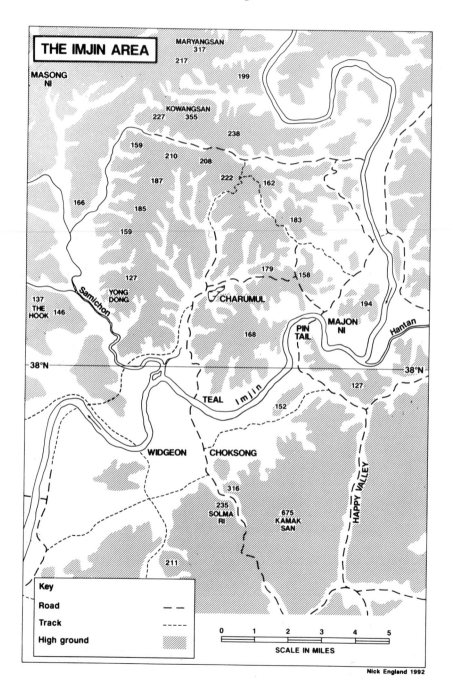

THE IMJIN AREA

MARYANGSAN
317
217

MASONG
NI

199

KOWANGSAN
227    355

238

159

210

208

187    222    162

166    185

159    183

127    179    158

YONG
DONG    CHARUMUL    194

137
THE    146    168    MAJON
HOOK    PIN    NI    Hantan
TAIL

38°N    38°N

TEAL    Imjin    127

152

WIDGEON    CHOKSONG

316

235
SOLMA    675
RI    KAMAK
SAN

211

Key

Road    —  —

Track    - - - -

High ground

0    1    2    3    4    5

SCALE IN MILES

Nick England 1992

Whilst the brigade occupied the 'Kansas Line' positions, Brigadier Taylor's policy of digging defences, laying mines and spreading wire continued along the 12,000 yard front. Another task undertaken by the reserve battalion was the search for the bodies of those who fell in 29 Brigade's battles of the previous April. The New Zealand gunners, and other support weapons, engaged in daily harassing shoots and parties of Korean refugees were passed through the brigade lines for processing as they escaped to the South. A Shropshire officer recalls those days:

'There followed a period of relative quiet, during which the Kiwi gunners amused themselves at innumerable targets, real and imaginary. Patrols were limited to standing and fighting patrols by 'A' and 'B' Companies along the South bank of the river by day and occasional recces by 'D' Company in some untenanted ground to the flank by day. It was a quite safe and normal practice for a company commander to sit on top of an OP with his gunner

*Soldiers of 3rd Royal Australian Regiment crossing the Imjin River on a Centurion tank, June 1951.*

(IWM BF 10289)

and various hangers-on discussing what to shoot up next; a pair of Vickers twenty yards below for opportunity targets added to the general bank holiday air (and noise). Nothing ever came back.'

With one of its battalions deployed to protect the bridgehead, the brigade had no immediate reserve. Should a major Chinese attack materialize, the 1st U.S. Cavalry (on the brigade's right) would consolidate on the 'Kansas Line' and the bridgehead guard would withdraw to become the brigade reserve. The 2nd P.P.C.L.I. were relieved at the bridgehead by another battalion 'borrowed' from the Canadian Brigade, the 2nd 'Van Doos' (Royal 22e), who crossed the river on 11th June. The Chinese remained strangely inert during this period, possibly because the first tentative peace talks between the Communists and the United Nations had begun in Kaesong, to the west of the brigade's area. During this 'lull' several changes of command were effected; Lieutenant-Colonel 'Bill' Barlow assumed command of the Shropshires from Lieutenant-Colonel

*C Company, 3rd Bn. Royal Australian Regiment, move up to new positions North of the Imjin River, 8th June 1951.*

(IWM MH 28032)

Shaw-Ball and Lieutenant-Colonel Frank Hassett replaced Lieutenant-Colonel Ferguson as commanding officer of the 3rd Royal Australians on 6th July.

Patrol activity continued across the Imjin. One patrol of the K.S.L.I. found a Sherman tank and two Oxford carriers left by 29 Brigade during the April battles – but the recovered vehicles were quickly reclaimed by their owners. The 3rd Royal Australians mounted several patrols to the North but lost some men in the river when their assault boats foundered. 'A' Company of the 3rd R.A.R. struck as far North as Hill 222 but suffered two casualties when they were mistakenly engaged by American tanks on their return journey. 'B' Company of the same battalion managed to reach the area Northwest of Hill 222 on 23rd June without making contact with the enemy. 'B' Company of the K.S.L.I. did meet some of the enemy on 9th July when a patrol led by Sergeant Rudd chased a small party of Chinese who escaped to the North. By this time the Shropshires

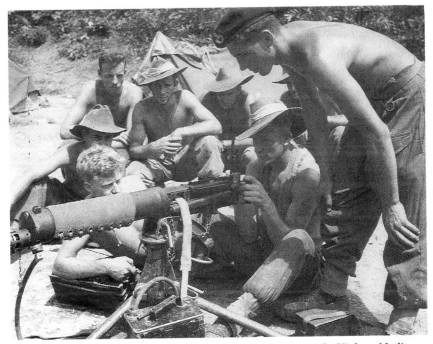

*Cpl. Tucker, K.S.L.I., instructs members of the 3rd R.A.R. on the Vickers Medium Machine Gun. July 1951.*

(AWM HOB 2372)

had moved up to replace the 'Van Doos' on 18th June; 'C' and 'D' Companies were across the river defending the bridgehead whilst the rest of the battalion occupied a bluff overlooking the Imjin. It was during this period that the brigade was entertained by the veteran British actor Jack Warner who brought his small concert party up to the banks of the Imjin to stage a series of shows. 'A' and 'B' Companies of the K.S.L.I. were later withdrawn from the riverside to construct defensive works to the rear of the Australians whilst the front remained comparatively quiet.

With the United Nations firmly in occupation of the territory to the South of the 38th Parallel and the Chinese and North Koreans removed from the Republic of Korea, the stage seemed to be set for the commencement of the initial truce negotiations. At this 'peaceful' juncture of the Korean War, the Commonwealth Brigade was withdrawn to the reserve area on 17th July 1951.

# The Commonwealth Division

Although 28 Brigade was nominally in reserve by 18th July 1951, the 3rd Royal Australians, supported by 'A' Company of the K.S.L.I. remained in their 'Kansas Line' positions on the South bank of the Imjin. The rest of the brigade retired to bivouac in the valleys South of Hill 127, relaxing in the pleasant warmth of the Korean summer – although always on call for many of the patrol tasks and the construction of defences.

On 28th July 1951, the Commonwealth forces in Western Korea were combined to form the 1st Commonwealth Infantry Division under the command of Major-General 'Gentleman Jim' Cassels. On a levelled padi field in the reserve area, the buglers of the Shropshires sounded a fanfare as the flag of the new division was broken out above the divisional headquarters, code-named 'Fort George' in honour of its commander's regiment, The Seaforth Highlanders. The new division incorporated the 25th Canadian Infantry Brigade, the 28th Commonwealth Infantry Brigade and the 29th British Infantry Brigade together with its own supporting arms and services. The creation of the Commonwealth Division was a welcome change of command for the brigades which had served in a selection of American divisions. 25 Canadian Brigade, code-named 'Northland', sported a brigade flash featuring the maple leaf on red; 29 Brigade, code-name 'Newmarket', had a flash with a white circle on black but 28 Brigade, code-name 'Newcastle', had no distinctive flash. On the occasions when uniform was worn, all divisional units wore the pale blue shield bearing the crown, the insignia of the new division. The formation of the division brought the supporting arms and services under divisional control, thus the 16th Field Regiment R.N.Z.A. came under the divisional Commander of Royal Artillery and the 60th Indian Field Ambulance under the Director of Medical Services. In practice, however, these units remained with the brigade.

*The 60th Indian Field Ambulance, Indian Army Medical Corps, commanded by Lt. Col. A. G. Rangaraj, on left.*

(IWM MH 28033)

*Brigadier G. Taylor, D.S.O. (left) and Lt. Col. F. G. Hassett, O.B.E. (right) leave*
*A Company, 3rd Bn. Royal Australian Regiment, after watching a fire power*
*demonstration in the reserve area, August 1951.*

(IWM MH 28034)

Sartorially it was easy to identify the component units of the division.
Unlike the Americans, none of the Commonwealth troops wore steel helmets; the Canadians had distinctive khaki combat caps and the British wore
berets or the ubiquitous cap-comforter. In 28 Brigade, each battalion had its
own stylish headgear: the Australians clung to their slouch-hats, usually with
the brim let down, the New Zealanders wore a khaki beret with a black
diamond patch sewn behind the cap-badge, the Indians were always im-
maculate in maroon turbans or paratroopers' berets, the King's Own Scottish
Borderers wore jungle hats with a patch of regimental tartan attached and the
King's Shropshire Light Infantry kept their rifle-green berets. Uniform, as
such, was practically non-existent in the line. British pattern jungle greens
were issued but many of the troops had obtained, by bartering or other
means, various items of American army clothing to supplement the issue
and, in addition, some had managed to equip themselves unofficially with
American weapons. International bartering flourished, mainly because the
American soldiers were denied access to alcohol (due to the efforts of The

Daughters of the American Revolution to protect their boys from the evil of drink) and the NAAFI/E.F.I. imported large quantities of Japanese beer for the troops and spirits for the officers and senior N.C.O.s. Many extravagant claims for business acumen were made – such as the subaltern who gained an American jeep for a bottle of whisky. Others traded for dollars in anticipation of their five days R. & R. (rest and recuperation) leave in Tokyo. In theory, every soldier was entitled to five days leave every four months but this much desired temporary escape from Korea depended on the unit's strength and operational situation. In the British battalions the leave roster was further complicated by the continual arrival and departure of drafts of National Servicemen. The other units of the Commonwealth Brigade – the Australians, Indians and New Zealanders – were composed of seasoned volunteers; the Australians served for eight months in Korea, the New Zealanders volunteered for eighteen months and the Indians were all regular soldiers. As the war dragged on, many of the Australian and New Zealand 'K Force' soldiers returned voluntarily for further tours of duty with the brigade. The difference between the younger men of the British battalions and the older volunteers of the other units was often remarked upon. A visiting British gunner general was impressed by the 'old men':

'The brigade was supported by its own 16th Field Regiment, Royal New Zealand Artillery, under Lieutenant-Colonel Moodie, the wartime soldier who, like most of his officers and men, had come to Korea as a volunteer. The regiment is composed by no means entirely of ex-gunners. They tell me it could man a tank squadron or a bomber squadron. None the less its performance with its 25 pounders has won it the confidence of all it has supported.'

The New Zealand gunners were held in high esteem by their infantry colleagues. Major Hassett of 16 Field Regiment notes:

'Although 16 Field Regiment was not specifically part of 28 Brigade it did act as the close support regiment, hence whenever 28 Brigade was in the line the regiment provided battery commanders and observation post officers for each of the battalions. The commanding officer with his Tac HQ was always collocated with the brigade commander at Brigade HQ. As a consequence the regiment and its officers had a much more intimate contact with all units of the brigade than did individual battalions.'

This 'intimacy' fostered a 'family' feeling between the infantrymen and their supporting gunners, each battalion had what it considered to be its own battery: 161 (Peter) Battery with the Middlesex and the K.S.L.I., 162 (Queen) Battery with the Argylls and the K.O.S.B. and 163 (Roger) Battery with the 3rd Royal Australians.

The mixture of older, experienced soldiers and the younger British conscripts worked extremely well. Brigadier Taylor confirmed this in an interview with the press:

> 'This brigade has been successful in its short career here due to the men's excellent teamwork. Right from the word go they have worked together like clockwork and although they have fought on the retreat, on the defensive and on the attack in mud and dust over terrible terrain, they have performed all their tasks efficiently. I am proud to command this Commonwealth Brigade and I think I shall be prouder yet.'

*Major Robertson, Salvation Army (extreme left), and his jeep with the 3rd R.A.R.*

(AWM RANK 221)

The next operation was to prove Brigadier Taylor's words. A deep probing patrol in strength was planned to discover the elusive Chinese in the
hills North of the Imjin River. Three battalions from three divisions were
to push forward some seven miles – one battalion of the U.S. Cavalry
Division, the Belgian Battalion of the 3rd U.S. Infantry Division (the
Belgians had previously served in the British 29th Brigade until the
formation of the Commonwealth Division) and the 1st Battalion The
King's Shropshire Light Infantry from the Commonwealth Division. On
4th August a ferry was installed forward of the Royal Australian positions
and a bridgehead screening party was established on the North bank of the
Imjin. The Shropshires moved up into the Australian lines and at first light
of 5th August were ferried across the river. The other two battalions
committed to the operation crossed simultaneously, further to the North.
The Shropshires advanced without meeting any opposition and had covered some 3,000 yards by 2.45 p.m. when it began to rain heavily. The
K.S.L.I. slithered up and down the hillsides as the storm gathered in
intensity, reducing visibility to a few yards, and managed to reach their
objective, Hill 222, by nightfall. Having gained the hilltop, the
Shropshires were informed by radio that the river had flooded and the
battalion would have to stay on the hill until further notice. Meanwhile,
the Belgians and the U.S. Cavalry had also attained their objectives,
meeting some enemy opposition, and were on the way back to their own
lines. The sodden Shropshires dug in for the night and maintained constant vigilance. The battalion had gone out carrying one day's American
combat rations per man – the 'C7' pack. By nightfall this individual ration
had been consumed. The Chinese seemed to be just as cowed by the
torrential downpour and the Shropshires spent a safe, but extremely wet,
night on Hill 222. The river was in full spate the next morning, 6th
August, and one sapper, one Belgian and two Koreans were drowned
whilst attempting to cross the flood. The rain abated gradually during the
day and a helicopter appeared to drop a load of tommy-cookers and
ammunition amongst the hungry light infantrymen. Another helicopter
landed some combat rations during the afternoon but at 4.00 p.m. the
Shropshires were told to stay on Hill 222 for a second night. Fortified by
the welcome rations the K.S.L.I., stood-to throughout the night, fully
expecting the Chinese to make an attack now that the rain had stopped. At
one point, 'A' Company were convinced that they could hear enemy
movement to their front and called for defensive fire. Firing at extreme
range, using American reprints of old Japanese Imperial Survey maps, the
Kiwis laid their guns on the forward (Northern) slopes of Hill 222 and

delivered a brief barrage exactly on target. Unfortunately, one shell fell slightly short, killing Corporal Fellows and wounding three of his men. No enemy attack ensued and at 7.00 a.m. on 7th August the wounded men were evacuated by helicopter. Small patrols searched the forward slopes of 222 but no sign of the Chinese was discovered. A further helicopter drop of rations was received at 9.30 a.m. and at 10.30 a.m. the Shropshires were ordered to withdraw. The battalion retired in good order, reaching the Australian covering screen and the river by 2.25 p.m. The Shropshires were ferried back to be greeted on the South bank by Major Robertson, the Salvation Army officer attached to the 3rd Royal Australian Regiment, who dispensed tea from his jeep. One of the Shropshires remembers the patrol:

> 'Although we did not meet the enemy we were all very conscious of being deep into enemy territory, about four and a half miles North of the Imjin, and accordingly that much more alert – especially at night. It rained most of the time and we had a miserable stay on top of Hill 222 – especially when the rain eased and we heard that we could not get back across the river. We had set out with one day's combat rations each and had to eke the remnants out until an airlift could be organized. During the patrol we cleared a few civilians from the area and brought them back. We could get no valid information from them, they spoke no English and we spoke no Korean. The consensus of opinion was that the Chinese probably knew what we were doing but preferred to hold back, either to see how far we would go or to entice us to go too far.'

Since this small operation was the first mounted by a unit of the new Commonwealth Division, it received attention from the press and the American Army newspaper *The Stars and Stripes* reported: 'At no time were the men depressed although they were wet, hungry and under constant threat of attack. It says much for the morale of the British soldier. After the ferry was repaired they marched clean shaven and smiling to board vehicles waiting to take them back to their areas and their first good meal and uninterrupted sleep in days.' Further patrol activity followed and on one such patrol – Operation 'Boomerang' mounted by the 3rd Royal Australians – the elusive enemy was encountered and suffered about fifteen casualties during a brief fight.

As a result of the patrol programme and the scarcity of Chinese in the hills North of the Imjin, it was decided to take advantage of the situation and establish the 'Wyoming Line' some four to five miles forward of the 'Kansas Line'. The 25th Canadian Brigade was detailed for Operation 'Minden' with elements of 28 Brigade to assist. On 8th September the King's Own Scottish Borderers established a bridgehead to protect an American engineer unit as they built a bridge over the Imjin at the site known as 'Gloucester Crossing'. The 3rd Royal Australians and the King's Shropshire Light Infantry crossed in support of 25 Brigade and the K.S.L.I. found themselves faced with their old friend, Hill 222.

'Point 222 was our objective and 10 Platoon of 'D' Company, K.S.L.I. were given the "baby" to hold. The Chinese did not make themselves known until we were within 500 yards when they started to use a 60 mm mortar. The gook behind the weapon would probably have failed his TOETs – anyway, he did us no harm and wasted twenty or so bombs. The next phase began when they turned a MMG on 3 Section who were leading and Lance-Corporal McCabe and his men were obliged to bite the dust. The rest of the platoon found themselves in a similar situation when they tried to manoeuvre and so there was a brief wireless conference between the platoon commander, company commander, FOO and other supporting representatives and they all had a crack at Point 222. Meanwhile, 10 Platoon had emptied a few Bren mags at the gooks and they were able to make a few corrections, which soon brought the Kiwi 25 pounder shells where they were wanted. The American 155s had, by this time, taken up the tune on the other side of the hill and the C.O. ordered 'D' Company to withdraw. Next day the Canadians were on Point 222 and found it deserted except for seven dead gooks.'

'D' Company suffered two killed and nine wounded during the attack and another Shropshire remembers:

'The wounded had to be brought down from 222 and carried a good mile and a half across open padi fields to the Regimental Aid Post at battalion headquarters. The journey was rather perilous since the Chinese mortars were then ranged over Hill 222 and their bombs were falling in the open fields. One longed to jump behind the nearest padi-bund but dared not drop the suffering man on the stretcher, it was a desperate haul carried out at a shambling trot until out of mortar range.'

The Indian Field Ambulance crossed the Imjin in support of the operation and the wounded were quickly treated and evacuated. 'B' Company of the K.S.L.I. also suffered a casualty the next day when Lieutenant Chidwick's platoon was pinned down by machine gun fire.

The 3rd Royal Australians were advancing to the West and Lieutenant-Colonel Hassett was eager to push forward to Hill 187 but Brigadier Taylor restrained the ebullient Australians to the brigade plan. 'D' Company of the 3rd R.A.R. occupied a small hill to the Southeast of 187 but were driven off, losing two men killed and four wounded. The Canadians and 29 Brigade occupied the new 'Wyoming Line' on 11th September and the Commonwealth Brigade returned to the reserve, except for 'A' Company of the 3rd Royal Australians (Captain J. Shelton) who were detached to support the Royal Northumberland Fusiliers (of 29 Brigade) on the left of the new line in the Samichon area.

In view of the amount of patrolling which had been the mainstay of the brigade's activities during this period, the King's Own Scottish Borderers formed a special platoon which they called the Battle Patrol. This platoon was blooded on 19th September when it successfully carried out a long range patrol and killed five of the enemy. Autumn was drawing in and the troops in reserve enjoyed the unexpected luxury of roast chestnuts which were gathered from the trees around the derelict Korean villages. As the front line was pushed Northwards, any Korean civilians still living in the area were evacuated to the rear and their homes and farms demolished to deny shelter to guerillas or infiltrators – and to provide timber and materials for defence works. The only Koreans legally allowed in the divisional area were the porters of the Korean Service Corps, those who were too old or too young for military service in the R.O.K. army. Each battalion had a 'company' of such porters who brought all the necessities of life to the forward companies on their backs, using the ancient Korean 'A' frame. It was from these hard-working porters that the troops learned their pidgin Korean, including the word 'gook' which really meant a person but came to be applied to all Asians and the general purpose cry of 'idiwa' – which could be used to command, exhort or berate. The Korean porters also acted as laundrymen, barbers and cooks and became very loyal and dedicated to the units they worked with. Several Korean orphan boys, abandoned in the war, were unofficially adopted by units and found some security serving with these generous foreigners and were loath to part from their temporary 'foster parents' when they became old enough for military service.

# Kowang-San

The truce talks were still underway in the early autumn of 1951 and it became evident that the Communists were seeking to bargain from a position of strength. Such an advantage was unacceptable to the United Nations and plans were made to establish a more commanding balance of power. The commander of I Corps, Lieutenant-General John W. ('Iron Mike') O'Daniel, received orders to push the front line Northwards. The Western front was directed to advance to occupy more commanding positions with the 1st British Commonwealth Division on the left of the Corps front, to the West of the Imjin; the 1st U.S. Cavalry Division in the centre, to the East of the Imjin and the 3rd U.S. Infantry Division on the right. The Commonwealth Division's sector of the 'Wyoming Line' was particularly vulnerable. The highest point, Hill 222, was overlooked by the dominating feature of Hill 355 and the hills to the North; the division's left flank was also overlooked by higher ground and offered no natural line of defence. In September, taking advantage of the enemy's apparent lack of activity, plans were laid for the move forward. Two brigades of the Commonwealth Division were detailed for the advance: 25 Canadian Brigade to push the left flank Westwards to the Samichon River line and 28 Commonwealth Brigade to take the high ground to the North.

On 23rd September Brigadier Taylor gave his battalion commanders details of their tasks in Operation 'Commando'. Intelligence on the enemy's dispositions indicated that 28 Brigade would be faced by a Chinese division, the 191st which had recently relieved the 192nd in the line. The Chinese were believed to have one regiment on the hills to the North of the Un Dong road and another regiment to the South of the road, both with two battalions forward and a third in immediate reserve. Aerial photography showed an elaborate system of trenches and dugouts, probably with

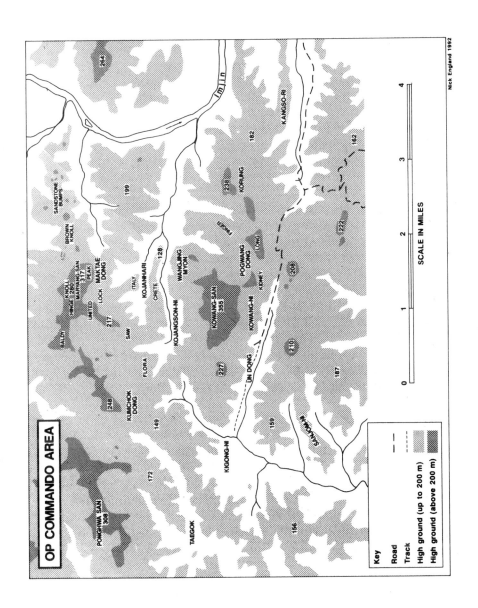

OP COMMANDO AREA

Key
Road
Track
High ground (up to 200 m)
High ground (above 200 m)

SCALE IN MILES

Nick England 1992

living quarters dug into a depth of about twenty feet. It was estimated that 28 Brigade would encounter some four or five battalions supported by artillery.

The brigade commander's plan for the advance was for the King's Own Scottish Borderers to take Hill 355 (Kowang-San), the King's Shropshire Light Infantry to take Hills 210 and 227, the 3rd Royal Australian Regiment to take Hills 199 and 317 (Maryang-San) and the 1st Battalion of the Royal Northumberland Fusiliers, on loan from 29 Brigade, to take Hill 217. The Royal Northumberland Fusiliers were the last of the original 29 Brigade battalions, the other two having been replaced by fresh battalions from Hong Kong and Great Britain. The battalion attacks were designed to run in sequence, thus providing flank security and enabling the artillery to provide maximum support to each successive phase of the brigade offensive. It was recognised that the terrain would limit armoured support and the Un Dong road was probably mined; since this was the best approach route for tanks a troop of sappers was allocated to the K.S.L.I. to clear the road during the attack. The battalion and company commanders were given an opportunity to make an aerial reconnaissance of their objectives and routes in artillery spotter planes. The commanding officers of the K.O.S.B. and the K.S.L.I. had some reservations on the plan presented by the brigade commander, concerned that if the offensive did not run to schedule they might suffer heavy casualties in the attacks. Colonel Hassett, of the 3rd R.A.R., considered that the further objective of Hill 317 would be harder to take and even harder to hold.

'I tried to see it from their viewpoint,' Brigadier Taylor later noted, 'I was ordering the K.O.S.B. to attack and capture a most formidable position. It looked like the Rock of Gibraltar and they knew they could not have close tank support because of the ground. Barlow rightly realised that unless the Scots on the high ground made steady progress, the K.S.L.I. would have to try to advance under the shadow of 355. I felt they were in very great danger of taking counsel of their fears and I had to try and reassure them, making the following points strongly: we had a very fine brigade that had trained hard in Hong Kong and also in Korea, we had been nearly six months in the field with light casualties and we were in fact veterans by now – particularly the Australians – and we had put some 240 N.C.O.s through the battle course at our brigade school in Korea; we would have excellent air, artillery and armoured support; the plan was a sound one based on concentration of fire and surprise, economy of force and flexibility – and no one made any suggestions to change it. The two British commanding officers with good sense had not disclosed their doubts to their splendid company commanders. I think that I persuaded them to become more confident.'

The element of surprise was essential to the operation. The attackers had to cross almost three miles of no-man's-land to close on Hill 355. A night attack was rejected because of the difficulties of the terrain, the fatigue factor and not being able to make full use of the Centurion tanks, even if they could negotiate the ground. It was decided to mount two initial predawn attacks on Hills 208 and 199 by the K.S.L.I. and the R.A.R. and for the main attacks to follow through immediately afterwards in the early morning.

The battalion commanders issued their orders on 1st October and on 2nd October the battalions moved up to their start lines. The men of the forward companies moved singly, fifty yards apart and each carrying a blanket in addition to their fighting order equipment. This careful movement took most of the daylight hours and the enemy were deluded into believing it to be minor patrol activity. By nightfall the attacking companies were on their start lines, laying up under their blankets on the scrub-covered hills, the K.S.L.I. near Hill 222 and the K.O.S.B. and two companies of the 3rd R.A.R. to the east of Hill 238 – all completely undetected by the Chinese.

At 3.00 a.m. on 3rd October, 'B' Company of the 3rd Royal Australians, Captain Nicholls, moved out on the right of the brigade front and, just before dawn, rushed Hill 199 to overwhelm a small party of unsuspecting Chinese, killing five, wounding ten and taking one prisoner for the loss of three Australians wounded during the attack. At 5.00 a.m. over 120 guns and mortars began to lay heavy fire on known enemy gun and mortar positions. Under cover of the artillery barrage, the leading companies rose from their cover, refreshed after the night's rest, and struck out on their lines of advance. 'D' Company of the K.S.L.I., Major Cottle, moved forward on the left of the brigade and in the half light of dawn occupied its first objective, Hill 208, with no serious opposition. At 6.00 a.m., despite some light mortar fire, 'D' Company gave the signal for the rest of the Shropshires to advance. Meanwhile, 'A' Company of the 3rd R.A.R., Captain Shelton, with the Machine Gun Platoon and a troop of the 8th King's Royal Irish Hussars in Centurion tanks, followed 'B' Company and were in position on Hill 199 by daybreak, ready to give covering fire for the next stage of the attack on Hill 355 by the K.O.S.B.

*3rd Battalion, Royal Australian Regiment moving forward for Operation
'Commando', October 1951.*

(AWM HOB 2534)


'B' and 'C' Companies of the K.O.S.B., Majors Harrison and Little
respectively, advanced at 7.15 a.m., 'B' Company to attack 'Finger' on
the right and 'C' Company 'Long' on the left. By daylight the Chinese
were aware that an attack had been launched and by 8.35 a.m. 'C' Company encountered fierce resistance on the lower slopes of 'Long', coming
under heavy fire from the objective and also mortar fire from 'Kidney'.
'B' Company – despite enemy artillery and mortar fire – assaulted and
captured 'Finger' and were in position to render supporting fire for the
attack on 'Long'. By noon 'C' Company was ordered to withdraw and

re-group for a further attack on 'Long' supported by 'A' Company, Major Duncan. Concerned that the programme for the offensive might be delayed by the enemy's resistance on 'Long', Brigadier Taylor hurried forward from his command post on Hill 238 to urge that the attack be mounted as soon as possible. 'C' Company of the 3rd R.A.R., Major Gerke, was called from the brigade reserve to give further support for the attack on Hill 355. The Borderers launched the assault on 'Long' at 2.15 p.m., supported by covering fire laid by 'B' Company on 'Finger' together with artillery, mortar and machine gun fire directed at 'Long' and Hill 355. The effectiveness of this combined barrage was evident in a later report of a wireless intercept of a Chinese observation post on 355. 'I cannot see anything. All my signallers and mortarmen are dead,' reported the Chinese observer before he went off the air – never to be heard again. 'A' and 'C' Companies, accompanied by a lone piper, stormed and took 'Long' by 3.30 p.m. Taking advantage of the situation, Lieutenant-Colonel MacDonald ordered 'A' Company and the Battle Patrol, supported by the Centurions intended for the Shropshires, to press on and attack 'Kidney'. After a brisk and decisive fight the Borderers gained the hill by dusk and set about consolidating their position.

On the brigade's left, 'B' Company of the K.S.L.I., Major Taitt, had moved up through 'D' Company on Hill 208 but were dismayed to learn that the supporting tanks of 'A' Squadron, 8th Hussars, were unable to negotiate the swampy padi and steep gradients in the area. With covering fire from 'D' Company, 'B' Company pushed forward and attacked a defended hillock to the West of Hill 208 but were halted by a hail of grenades and small arms fire. The company withdrew and made a second determined attack which drove the Chinese from the hillock by 1.00 p.m. although seven men of 'B' Company were wounded in the assault. At 3.15 p.m. 'C' Company of the K.S.L.I., Captain Houghton-Berry, moved through 'B' Company to attack another Chinese held hill to the immediate North. Ten to fifteen Chinese were killed and eight prisoners taken in a desperate fight which cost the Shropshires two dead and Second-Lieutenant Moore and five men wounded. For this sharp action Captain Houghton-Berry was mentioned in despatches, Corporal Wade recommended for the Distinguished Conduct Medal and Corporal Pendlebury for the Military Medal. Four Centurion tanks caught up with the Shropshires eventually and the Mortar Platoon and Battalion H.Q. joined 'D' Company on Hill 208.

As night fell on 3rd October the leading companies dug in for the night and the faithful Korean porters carried up ammunition, water and rations for the following day. After the first day of Operation 'Commando', the

*60th Indian Field Ambulance evacuating casualties on an American helicopter.*

(AWM HOB 3538)

Royal Australians were on Hill 199, the King's Own Scottish Borderers on 'Finger', 'Long' and 'Kidney' and the Shropshires on Hill 208 and the two smaller hills to the west of 208. The 60th Indian Field Ambulance had evacuated fifty-one casualties and, inevitably, the bodies of ten men killed in action.

Before dawn on 4th October the divisional artillery began to pound Hills 210 and 355. 'D' Company of the K.S.L.I. were ordered forward by Lieutenant-Colonel Barlow and advanced toward Hill 210 at 5.00 a.m. with elements of 'C' Company and three Centurion tanks commanded by Lieutenant Butler. The tank guns were brought to bear at almost point-blank range and blasted the Chinese emplacements. Despite a brave defence the enemy were overwhelmed by 10.15 a.m. and eleven prisoners were taken by the light infantrymen. Forty-one Chinese dead were counted on the hilltop and seven machine guns and eight mortars captured. 'D' Company lost Private Ford and suffered seven wounded. For this exemplary action Major Cottle received the Distinguished Service Order, Lieutenant Borwick the Military Cross, Private Norton the Military Medal and a mention in despatches for Private Wells.

*Hill 355 'Kowang-San' – under fire.*

(IWM BF 10426)

*Operation 'Commando', October 1951. Medium Machine Gun of 3 R.A.R. giving covering fire.*

(AWM HOB 2433)

Whilst the Shropshires were battling for Hill 210, 'D' Company of the K.O.S.B., Major Robertson-MacLeod, and the Battle Patrol advanced for the assault on the Southwestern slopes of Hill 355. As 'D' Company launched its attack from the West, 'B' Company moved forward from 'Finger' to make a co-ordinated attack on the Southeast side of Kowang-San. 'C' Company of the 3rd R.A.R., Major Gerke (ordered forward in support of the K.O.S.B.) made a simultaneous attack on the Wangjing-Myon feature from the East. The Australians took Wangjing-Myon by 9.00 a.m. after killing nineteen of the enemy and taking three prisoners. Major Gerke led his men on to launch a further attack on the next small hill below 355; Private Burnett of 7 Platoon headed the assault with his Bren gun and, despite ten men wounded, the Australians took the hill by 12.15 p.m. Private Burnett earned the Distinguished Conduct Medal for his gallantry in this action. Leaving 8 and 9 Platoons to hold the hills captured by 'C' Company, Major Gerke took 7 Platoon up the steep Eastern face of Hill 355 and, by 2.00 p.m., had gained the summit of Kowang-San. On the South and West sides of the hill, supported by covering artillery fire and the machine guns and tanks on Hill 199, the Borderers fought their way up the slopes of Kowang-San. By 3.00 p.m. the K.O.S.B. had cleared the half-mile long crest of the hill, driving the Chinese down its Northern side leaving 26 dead, 14 prisoners and many wounded. The capture of Kowang-San cost the Borderers 7 killed and 34 wounded and the Royal Australians had 11 men wounded.

As the battles raged for the hilltops, a section of 12 Field Squadron Royal Engineers under Captain Pollard cleared the road between Hills 210 and 355 ('The Mad Mile') to allow a troop of Centurions to move forward for the attack on Hill 227. 'A' Company of the Shropshires, Major Heard, made the assault:

'On the afternoon of the second day we reached our company objective, the now famed Hill 227 on the flank of 'Little Gibraltar' (Hill 355 alias Kowang-San). The position was extremely wooded and impassable to tanks. It was also very heavily fortified with bunkers and communicating trenches. Support was given by the 8th Hussars from 210 but nevertheless heavy fighting took place. 3 Platoon went forward to take a small hill on the right of the main objective – 9 Section (Corporal Proctor) leading – successfully dealing with a tricky line of trenches and claiming the company's first enemy dead – a burp-gunner who was too slow off the mark. 2 Platoon's task was to secure a position half-way up the wooded slopes of 227, allowing 1 Platoon to pass through and assault the top. Until that time the enemy had chiefly relied on recoilless rifle and mortar fire, but as 1 Platoon closed to within a few yards of their forward positions, the Chinese opened up with small arms and grenades. Lieutenant Ballenden was hit but stayed with his platoon until 3 Platoon were able to take over (for which he subsequently received the Military Cross). We gained the top – and a prisoner – shortly before dusk, the main body of the enemy having by that time retreated along the ridge Northwards. During the night, however, small parties of the enemy came back to make a nuisance of themselves, particularly around 2 Platoon's area – although Private Clarke frightened some of them off after literally holding his fire until the last minute. Early next morning the position was finally cleared and several enemy wounded discovered.

*Lieutenant Ballenden, M.C., K.S.L.I., convalescing in Japan after being wounded in Operation 'Commando', October 1951.*

(AWM HOB 3033)

The morning led to the capture of two more prisoners, one walking into our positions complete with all his kit and with such abandon that he was almost mistaken for a porter!'

Private Leggett was killed during the battle for Hill 227.

With the dominating features of Hills 355 and 227 taken successfully, the victorious companies consolidated for the night. The 25th Canadian Brigade had also moved forward during the day, delaying their attacks until 11.00 a.m. in response to Brigadier Taylor's request for artillery to support the K.O.S.B. attack on 355. Thereafter the divisional artillery's 'milk round' of supporting fire was switched to the Canadians' targets, enabling 25 Brigade to secure most of their objectives without encountering

*Operation 'Commando', October 1951. A casualty being evacuated fom a company jeep-head of 3rd R.A.R. whilst Korean porters bring up rations, ammunition, water and fresh bread.*

(AWM HOB 2446)

any serious opposition. As night fell the Chinese brought their artillery to bear on the captured hills and supply routes, delaying the delivery of supplies to the forward companies. Communications were maintained by platoon 88 wireless sets as new defences were dug on the hilltops.

The 5th October dawned with an autumnal mist which covered the lower slopes of the hills. This was the third day of the operation and the Chinese were reacting to the attacks, calling up their reserves and heavier artillery. The Royal Northumberland Fusiliers moved out from their forming up point to advance on their objective, Hill 217. The companies made good progress, 'Y' Company reached the Western end of 'Crete' and 'Z' Company were within 500 yards of Hill 217 by 10.00 a.m. but the mist, which had covered their advance, also necessitated a halt for the Fusiliers to get their bearings. The mist cleared by 11.00 a.m. and 'Y' Company quickly took 'Saw' whilst 'Z' Company clambered up to surprise the enemy on Hill 217, taking ten prisoners. After the initial success of the Fusiliers' assault on 217 the Chinese rallied and 'Z' Company was subjected to a hail of small arms fire and grenades from a well-entrenched and determined enemy. The Northumberlands fought back a succession of minor counter-attacks but were hard-pressed to hold their ground against a numerically superior enemy.

At the same time the Australians advanced from Hill 199, also under cover of the morning mist. 'C' Company had returned to the battalion after their action on 355 and 'D' Company, Major Hardiman, had also rejoined after supporting the Canadian Brigade. 'B' Company, Captain Nicholls, crossed the valley towards the ridge North of Hill 199, closely followed by 'D' Company. 'B' Company encountered the enemy on a small hill at 9.30 a.m. and took the position after a quick attack in which one man was killed and another wounded. 12 Platoon of 'D' Company, led by Lieutenant Young picking his way by compass bearing through the mist, bumped the enemy at 9.15 a.m. The Chinese opened fire and threw grenades but the mist precluded any artillery or mortar support so 'D' Company halted to return fire at the invisible enemy. The mist began to clear at 10.30 a.m. and the Chinese could be seen on three sandstone bumps about 200 yards in front of the Australians. Major Hardiman sent 10 Platoon, Lieutenant Leary, to make a left-flanking attack and 11 Platoon, Lieutenant Clark, to the right. The Chinese were thoroughly confused by this pincer movement and 'D' Company fell upon the disorganized enemy. Twenty-two Chinese were killed and ten taken prisoner although 'D' Company suffered seven casualties, including Major Hardiman and Lieutenant Leary. Lieutenant Young took command of the company with Sergeant Rawlinson leading 12 Platoon. The company's radio had lost its aerial during the attack and Lieutenant-Colonel Hassett could only locate his advancing troops when they waved their fluorescent air recognition panels. A small patrol contacted 'B' Company and communications were re-established. 'Can you go on?' asked Colonel Hassett. 'Give us fifteen minutes of artillery and we'll be ready to move,' replied Lieutenant Young and passed targets for the New Zealand gunners and Centurion tanks to engage. The Machine Gun Platoon was sent forward to give covering fire and, after ten minutes of intensive fire from the artillery, tanks and machine guns, 'D' Company launched an attack on 'Brown Knoll'. Lieutenant Clark's 11 Platoon led the assault but a Chinese rocket launcher caused casualties; Corporal Black was wounded but took his section into the assault and 'Brown Knoll' was taken by 2.15 p.m. As 12 Platoon swept through the objective to tackle a small green hillock beyond they were halted by machine gun fire. 10 Platoon relieved 11 Platoon on 'Brown Knoll' and 11 Platoon joined Sergeant Rawlinson's 12 Platoon in a bayonet charge supported by the battalion's machine guns. The eighteen inch bayonets accounted for 68 Chinese and 30 prisoners were taken by 4.00 p.m. 'D' Company suffered 2 men killed and 13 wounded, although 2 of the wounded remained in action. In passing, it is worth noting that the Australians were still armed with the splendid Lee-Enfield rifle of 1914-1918 vintage whereas the British and the Canadians had the later Second World War Number 4 Lee-Enfield.

As the other companies of the 3rd R.A.R. were at grips with the Chinese on the Eastern approaches to Maryang-San, 'A' Company was diverting the enemy's attention by mounting an attack from the South towards Maktae-Dong. Private Pat Knowles:

'We made our way up towards 317 until we reached the first line of trenches, where we were held up by a Centurion tank of the 8th King's Irish Hussars and a Chinaman with a bazooka having a quiet little duel. The shells from the tank were exploding about fourteen feet from us, the rockets from the bazooka were scoring direct hits on the tank but to no effect. We called out to the tank commander to cease fire so we could flush out the Chinaman but he probably couldn't hear us and rightfully attended to his own front. After about five minutes the Chinaman ran out of ammunition, dropped his bazooka, came out of his hide and took off down the track – for about six paces anyway. Later, after we took our part of the hill, one of the boys spoke to the sergeant tank

commander and asked what damage the bazooka had done to the
Centurion. The sergeant replied: "No damage. The Chinaman
saved us the trouble of scraping off the mud".'

'A' Company's attack drew the enemy's fire whilst the other companies
were attacking from the East and also gained valuable ground for the final
assault on Hill 317. Meanwhile, 'B' Company reported that the Chinese
were leaving 317 and the bare hill to its East. Colonel Hassett sent 'C'
Company up through 'D' Company to take advantage of the situation and
attack the high ground under cover of supporting artillery fire. Climbing –
sometimes even crawling on all fours – the Diggers of Major Gerke's 'C'
Company raced up the steep hillside of their objective. Lieutenant
Pembroke of 9 Platoon was in the attack:

> 'In the attack on 317 the Chinese were "beaten for pace" – we were
> moving too fast for them. I shall never forget the sight of wild, red-
> eyed, blackened Jim Young (of "D" Company) giving us some
> quick information as we moved through; the tremendous bombard-
> ment of 317 as we advanced; small groups of dazed Chinese moving
> down past us. Strangely, we ignored each other – they were intent
> on avoiding our murderous shelling; we were conscious of our own
> orders not to let anything hold us up. We finally scrambled up the
> last precipitous few yards and 317 was ours.'

Maryang-San was taken by 5.00 p.m. and 'C' Company of the 3rd R.A.R.
gained the distinction of being first on 355 and first on 317 and Major
Gerke the Distinguished Service Order for his company's achievements.

To the Southwest, desperately short of ammunition and sustaining
heavy casualties, the Royal Northumberland Fusiliers were still faced by a
resolute enemy well dug-in along the ridgeline North of Hill 217. In view
of the deteriorating situation – two platoons of 'Z' Company had been
reduced to half strength – it was decided to withdraw the Fusiliers to
'Crete'. 'Z' Company was literally down to its last few rounds as they
retired, evacuating their wounded under the cover of an artillery barrage.
The Northumberlands' dogged fight had at least drawn the Chinese fire
and reinforcements, thus easing the Australians' task in taking Hill 317.

As night fell, Chinese artillery laid harassing fire on the newly occupied
hilltop positions and the forward companies prepared to receive counter-
attacks. The problem of gaining the last objective, Hill 217, was reconsid-
ered. Brigadier Taylor suggested that the Northumberland Fusiliers send

one of their reserve companies up through the 3rd R.A.R. on the higher ground to attack 217 and this was agreed. However, because of the long and difficult climb during the hours of darkness and the dilemma of supplying both the Australians and the attacking company in time for a dawn assault, Lieutenant-Colonel Speer (commanding the R.N.F.) reported to the Brigadier at 4.00 a.m. that he was unable to move his company in time. Brigadier Taylor was bitterly disappointed to realise that unless the Fusiliers' company was on, or near, the forming-up point it was too late to exploit the Australians' success from the higher ground. It was decided, somewhat reluctantly, that the 3rd R.A.R. should continue to harry the Chinese from their vantage point on Maryang-San whilst the Royal Northumberland Fusiliers mounted another attack from the South.

The morning of 6th October was again misty and 'W' and 'Y' Companies of the Fusiliers advanced to take up positions for a further attack on Hill 217. 'Y' Company, although subjected to artillery and small arms fire, secured a

*Brigadier G. Taylor, D.S.O., commander 28 Commonwealth Brigade, at a forward command post, October 1951.*

(IWM BF 10429)

firm base on 'Saw' and 'W' Company moved through to attack 217 at 10.50 a.m. 'W' Company dealt efficiently with minor opposition as they climbed the hill but were halted by four machine guns skilfully sited to enfilade the approaches to the objective. Flanking attacks were mounted by the Fusiliers, to the right and to the left, but met strong enemy resistance. The Chinese were well entrenched and showered the attackers with grenades, machine gun and small arms fire. Enemy artillery and mortar defensive fire was brought down on the southern slopes of 217 and the Fusiliers suffered many casualties. 'X' Company was sent up to assist 'W' Company but attempts to storm the ridge were repulsed by a determined and fierce Chinese defence.

On the higher ground, above 217, the Royal Australians set about attacking the Chinese. Lieutenant Pembroke of 'C' Company took part:

'Jack Gerke briefed me to secure at first light a heavily wooded knoll about half way to the "Hinge". This was not an attack but rather an expansion of the Company's defended area. As usual a heavy fog covered the area as we moved down the slope of 317 and then up the steep incline to the wooded knoll. Corporal Danny Powell's section was in the lead. I sent him forward to reconnoitre the "Knoll" while the remainder of us went to ground. After some time he reported back that there was a large number of enemy on the "Knoll", some cooking breakfast, apparently feeling safe because of the thick fog. In whispers we quickly decided a plan of attack, with one section left of the track and the other right. We decided on a grenade assault with Danny Powell, who knew the exact location, to give the signal for all to throw grenades. The result was devastating for the main part of the Chinese force huddled over their cooking fires. We then charged forward firing rifles and Owen guns. Almost immediately a Chinese sentry emerged from thick scrub right beside Platoon Headquarters, firing a machine gun from the hip. Poor Lance-Corporal Yeo fell dead, shot through the head. Further machine gun fire came from another position up the "Knoll" towards the "Hinge". I sent a section forward and after a brief fire fight the enemy was eliminated. Meanwhile the remainder of the platoon moved through to clear the enemy position. We found nineteen enemy dead and many more badly wounded and took seven totally shocked and bewildered prisoners. I asked Company Headquarters to send forward men to escort the prisoners back and help with the wounded. The platoon prepared a defensive position covering the main dangers – the saddle leading up to the "Hinge" and the Northern spur running down to the valley. Most of the Chinese bodies were pushed into the steep wooded re-entrants leading off the spur. The rest of the day was a confused picture of digging in, reorganising, coping with the many enemy dead, repelling small counterattacks, all under constant shelling, mortaring and small arms fire.'

From the high ground, the Australians aided the Fusiliers by bringing machine gun fire to bear on Hill 217 and the Shropshires' machine guns on Hill 227 sprayed the hills to the West of 217 to deter the enemy from bringing up reinforcements. Nevertheless, the Chinese mounted several forays against the Fusiliers which were beaten off, despite further casualties. In the late afternoon, permission was given for the Northumberland Fusiliers to withdraw at their own discretion. A strong Chinese attack from the North and West decided the day. 'W' and 'X' Companies made a fighting withdrawal through 'Y' Company on 'Saw' and the enemy were engaged by all available artillery.

During the evening, Colonel Hassett sent 'B' Company of the 3rd R.A.R. forward for an attack on 'Hinge' the next morning. The Royal Australians' tactical headquarters moved up to Hill 317 so that Lieutenant-Colonel Hassett could control the following day's action. This was not an unusual situation since all the battalion commanders moved forward to control their companies as they advanced. Brigadier Taylor's tactical brigade headquarters also kept well forward with the battalions and even the divisional commander, Major-General Cassels, accompanied by a small 'rover' group, moved amongst the battalions during the operation. It had been decided not to press the attack on Hill 217 from the South but to harass the enemy with probing attacks and intense fire from the higher ground occupied by the Australians.

The 7th October was another misty morning and, from his vantage point on Maryang-San, Colonel Hassett watched a barrage of fire from the artillery, tanks, mortars and machine guns sweep the 'Hinge'. At 8.00 a.m. 'B' Company of the Royal Australians advanced from the 'Knoll'. Lieutenant Pembroke with his 9 Platoon on the 'Knoll' were reinforced by the Anti-Tank Platoon during the night and describes the events:

'At first light "B" Company moved through in preparation for its attack on the "Hinge". The successful but costly attack by "B" Company took the pressure off 9 Platoon but the enemy quickly realised that the way to defeat "B" Company – who had taken the

"Hinge" after a bitter fight and had repulsed several local counter-attacks – was to interdict the route from 317 through 9 Platoon's "Knoll" to the "Hinge". All day he kept up a barrage of shells and mortar bombs on this lifeline. Towards afternoon the battle faded. It seemed the worst was over and all were congratulating themselves on having survived. Then came the moment of Operation "Commando" which is sharpest in my memory. I was in my weapon pit hoping for a quiet night. I glanced at my watch, it was exactly 21.00 hours. Suddenly in a great arc to the front the sky lit up with an incredible series of flashes. Some thirty seconds later the area from 317 to the "Hinge" received an immense concentration of shells and mortar bombs which lasted for what seemed an eternity. Movement was impossible and for the first time I understood what artillery neutralisation of an area really meant.'

During the day airstrikes had been called to hit Hill 217 and the ridges to the west of Maryang-San, the Chinese suffered terrible casualties but brought heavy artillery to bear on the brigade's positions. One result of the increased shelling was the disruption of the essential porter trains trudging up the hills to keep the Australians supplied. The K.O.S.B., the K.S.L.I. and the Royal Engineers diverted their own Korean porters to the help of the Royal Australians and necessary supplies were delivered by nightfall. As the night fell, however, the Chinese heavy artillery and self-propelled guns from adjacent hills renewed their bombardment of 'B' and 'C' Companies of the 3rd R.A.R. before the enemy launched an attack on the 'Hinge' and the 'Knoll'. Lieutenant Pembroke:

'The main Chinese regimental counter-attack struck 'B' Company but 9 Platoon also received its share of attention. It was dark and the 'Knoll' was heavily wooded with the sections relatively dispersed; control was therefore difficult, particularly with shells and mortar bombs constantly bursting amongst the trees. Opportunities to get a group of the enemy clearly in one's sights and fire effectively were few and far between. This emphasised the importance of clearly appreciating lines of approach and sticking to the pre-determined fire plan.'

'B' Company was attacked on three sides but managed to repulse the enemy. A call for defensive fire was made but, as Brigadier Taylor recalls:

'The brigade signal officer came to me and said "The Australians are trying to get through to us on the radio but owing, I think, to atmospheric disturbance I can not make any sense of it!" I realised that 3rd R.A.R. were probably being counter-attacked and told the young N.Z. artillery officer left at Brigade H.Q. by his C.O. than I wanted an Uncle Target (a concentration of divisional artillery) to be fired. He could not take the responsibility of getting through Divisional Artillery H.Q. so I did it, and after some argument, they agreed.'

Three further attacks were mounted during the night, as well as harassing patrols, but helped by the divisional artillery, the mortars and machine guns of the other battalions of 28 Brigade, the 3rd Royal Australians held their precarious positions. One Australian, his personal weapon blown away in the confusion, was reported to have kicked at least one Chinese to death during the desperate struggle.

'The effectiveness of our own artillery and mortar fire was paramount,' says Lieutenant Pembroke, 'I have no doubt that "B" Company and 9 Platoon would have been overrun that night if the many hundreds of Chinese who died in the re-entrants and the spur lines from our artillery and mortar fire had been able to reach the forward section positions. However, in war things are never one sided. Amongst the many tribulations from the Chinese fire, 9 Platoon's morale was visibly shaken for a while when a shell scored a direct hit on a weapon pit killing all three occupants. Throughout that long night, from the radio and those passing through to "B" Company, I learned of the hazardous situation of "B" Company and the incredible bravery of those parties who struggled forward to keep "B" Company supplied. Then, after a night of feverish activity, it was dawn and Operation "Commando" was over.'

By 5.00 a.m. on 8th October the Chinese had withdrawn from the 'Hinge', leaving at least 120 dead and many wounded piled in front of the battered Australian trenches. That morning, in one of the very few examples of humanity displayed during the Korean War, the weary Royal Australian Regiment allowed the Chinese to collect their wounded under a flag of truce. After three days of continuous fighting it was evident that the Australians needed a rest. The divisional front was hastily readjusted:

25 Canadian Brigade extended its front Northwards and the Princess Patricia's Canadian Light Infantry moved across to relieve 'D' Company of the K.S.L.I. on Hill 210; 'D' Company relieved 'C' Company of the K.S.L.I. on Hill 227; 'C' Company moved East to relieve the K.O.S.B. on Hill 355 and the Borderers moved up to take over from the Royal Australians on Maryang-San and the neighbouring hills. 3rd R.A.R. withdrew wearily to occupy the positions around Hill 199. Even Colonel Hassett had to admit that his men needed a break – 'Their sheer guts is beyond belief,' he is reported to have commented as his companies came down from the Maryang-San hills. Colonel Hassett's own part in the battle was recognised by Brigadier Taylor in his recommendation for the Distinguished Service Order: 'I consider Lieutenant-Colonel Hassett's conduct and handling of this brilliant battalion action outstanding in every way.'

As the front was reshuffled, pressure was maintained on the Chinese by the artillery and from the air, providing effective cover for the move of the infantry companies. Airstrikes blasted Hill 217 and the Chinese-occupied hills to the West, the Mustang aircraft of No. 2 Squadron of the South African Airforce, 'The Flying Cheetahs', making a particularly telling contribution. Between airstrikes, the artillery continued to pound the enemy hills and air observation posts located Chinese gun positions for counter-battery tasks. Whilst the King's Own Scottish Borderers relieved the Australians on Maryang-San, their leading patrols reported that the Chinese had left the battered summit of Hill 217. 'D' Company of the Borderers advanced cautiously to occupy the bitterly contested hill without opposition. The final objective of Operation 'Commando' had been secured.

So ended the last successful advance into North Korea – in fact the last brigade action of its kind until the taking of Port Stanley in the Falklands Campaign some thirty-one years later. The five-day battle had secured the dominant hills commanding the territory to the North of the Imjin River and had driven an arrowhead deep into the Chinese main defence line. The enemy had suffered heavy losses, the 191st Division was practically non-operational and had to be relieved in the line. The Indian Field Ambulance treated 262 Commonwealth casualties during the operation, 5 of whom later died to add to the 58 killed in action. The battalion 'borrowed' from 29 Brigade, the Royal Northumberland Fusiliers, had lost at least 10 men killed and 85 wounded. The Fusiliers were then the 'veteran' British battalion in Korea and were about to be relieved, a bitter conclusion to their year in the front line.

Brigadier Taylor issued a letter to all the members of the 28th Commonwealth Infantry Brigade on the 9th of October:

'I wish to congratulate ALL RANKS on their splendid achievement in the Battle of KOWANG-MARYANG SAN. You have badly mauled the 191 CCF Div. and stormed and taken defensive positions of very great natural and artificial strength and beaten off counter-attacks with great resolution.

'You have again proved your superiority over an enemy who fought with considerable determination and some skill.

'The Brigade achieved a good measure of surprise in its skilful deployment for battle under the noses of the enemy and by bold manoeuvre, but success above all came from the fine combination of all arms which enabled the infantry to close with the enemy, which they did with the greatest skill and dash and in other cases they were able to get to grips by bold use of the early morning mist.

'None of the above could have been achieved without a high standard of training, which we must always maintain by training when we can on the job.

'I would especially like to thank those officers and other ranks who laboured long and hard to maintain the flow of ammunition and supplies to the fighting companies and to rescue the wounded. Last but not least I would like to thank the Brigade Battle School for the training of 250 N.C.O.s; whose good standard of training enabled fine officer leadership to exert its maximum effort. This meant that we won decisively all the little actions without undue loss which finally added up to victory.

'Thank you all.

'From now on the Motto of the Brigade will be:-
"ORGANISED SPEED"

George Taylor'

The Corps Commander, Lieutenant-General John W. O'Daniel, also expressed his appreciation of the Commonwealth Division's successful part in 'Commando':

'It was a masterful manoeuvre, skilfully combining aggressiveness and complete detailed planning, resulting in the taking of key terrain features with a minimum cost in manpower and with the exploitation of firepower. The capture of critical terrain was conducted in a manner fully in keeping with the finest traditions of the military service and is a tribute to the courage and professional skill of the officers and men of the Division.'

Operation 'Commando' had been a predominantly infantry battle in which company, platoon and section commanders had played a decisive role. Nevertheless, the artillery also proved its value in the attack and in defence. The firepower of the corps and divisional artillery was a major factor in the brigade's success – although the other divisions of I Corps also required considerable artillery support during the offensive. 16 Field Regiment, Royal New Zealand Artillery, in close support of 'its' brigade, fired some 72,000 rounds during the five-day battle. General Hassett (then Lieutenant-Colonel commanding the 3rd R.A.R.) recalls:

> 'the good planning and support given in these attacks both at divisional and brigade level. I thought at the time that these were admirable and am still of that opinion. 1 Commonwealth Division under General Cassels was a first class fighting formation. The employment of divisional and corps troops, in support of the battalions, was so phased that they had the maximum timely support. All the supporting arms were good, particularly as we saw a lot of them. The Brigade plan was also a good one and George Taylor was a most able tactician.'

The Chinese proved themselves to be a formidable foe; the infantry showed stubborn determination in their defence of the hills and, at times, a reckless disregard for human life. They also brought their artillery into effective action, introducing their newly acquired Soviet-made 152 mm howitzers, self-propelled guns and multiple rocket launchers to the battlefield – probably brought into Korea during the false lull of the initial truce talks period. After Operation 'Commando' the nature of the Korean War underwent a complete change, becoming a static conflict between entrenched opponents in which artillery power was to become a decisive factor.

For the capture of the hills to the North of the Imjin River, the battalions of 28 Commonwealth Brigade, together with the 8th King's Royal Irish Hussars and the 1st Battalion of The Royal Northumberland Fusiliers, were awarded the proud battle honour 'Kowang-San', an honour which was earned by the brigade as a whole.

# Maryang-San

The success of Operation 'Commando' established the 'Jamestown Line' to the North of the Imjin and 28 Brigade had secured and occupied a vital sector in the new line with the King's Own Scottish Borderers at the 'sharp end'. The Chinese had suffered considerable loss of face – and life – during the operation and were determined to regain the lost ground. To this end, the enemy built up his artillery and brought fresh troops to the front to regain the initiative in the interminable truce negotiations. From 8th October onwards Chinese artillery regularly bombarded the hills occupied by the brigade.

The King's Own Scottish Borderers on the hills taken by the 3rd Royal Australians were in a particularly vulnerable location. The K.O.S.B. positions formed a Northward pointing arrowhead with 'C' Company, Major Little, as the forward tip on 'Hinge'; 'B' Company, Major Harrison, was the left barb on Hill 217 and the adjacent ridge; 'D' Company, Major Robertson-MacLeod, the right barb on Hill 317 (Maryang-San) and the 'Knoll' (Hill 280); 'A' Company, Major Duncan, in immediate reserve in the Maktae-Dong area and the Battle Patrol on 'Lock'. The forward companies were under constant Chinese observation, especially from the bare hill known as 'Baldy' to the West of the 'Hinge', and had great difficulty preparing their defences under regular mortar bombing. Artillery fire was brought to bear on the slightest movement and the daily support by porter train was a hazardous undertaking. Casualties amongst these companies was now a daily occurrence. Lieutenant J. B. Henderson commanded 11 Platoon of 'D' Company on the 'Knoll':

'During the month we occupied these positions we were by no means idle. Wiring and mining (by Sappers) went on continuously.

61

These positions were, however, under constant observation from Chinese OPs, with the result that there could be no "swanning" from one platoon to another. It was due to this that our first difficulty arose. Wiring had to be carried out and the men never grumbled at having to do it. However, every time anyone was skylined we could hear the ominous plop, plop of a mortar followed by the unfriendly screaming of the bomb. As wiring was being done from anything up to thirty yards away from the trenches, it was impossible to reach one's trench before the arrival of the bomb. To counteract this we dug shallow trenches, actually in amongst our wire, so that the obvious action could be taken. A trench only a foot deep was sufficient to save us from splinters. All was well while the front slopes were being wired because we could hear the telltale "plop". However, the rear slopes presented a new problem (learnt and solved unfortunately at the cost of an excellent section commander and one other soldier), that of being unable to hear the "plop" from the mortar. After a very short time, we had a couple of men sitting on the top of the ridge, whose only job was to listen for the mortar and, on hearing it, to shout to the others who were wiring, of the coming danger. Neither of these methods was of course foolproof, but knowing that they were there, the men worked much better and in far better heart. By the end of October the wire perimeter round the "Knoll" was considerable and no Chinaman was envied a journey through it. Wiring tasks had also been started between company positions. Only at night were the platoon positions not a hive of activity. Wiring and digging went on throughout daylight in shifts. While one shift worked, two others were sleeping or seeing to their personal administration. Owing to the chance of sleepless nights each man was given during daylight as much time off as could be afforded to sleep or at least rest. Our trenches housed three soldiers and were themselves sited as close together as was sensibly possible. Each one had ingenious overhead cover and space for sleeping. The arcs of fire of every trench were very carefully worked out so that there was no ground left which did not come under fire. Pits for ammunition, water and food were dug and provided with overhead cover. This proved of great value in our battle. Stores of ammunition and food and wire were brought up every day by the company second-in-command and his team of Korean porters. These gallant little men carried no weapons and worked ceaselessly all day at whatever job they were presented with. It was quite uncanny the way in which the Chinese sensed the approach of porters. Even though they were kept, where possible, to dead ground, their approach was usually heralded by a score of 80 mm mortar bombs. Eventually stores were brought up during darkness or semi-darkness. Preventing the Koreans from chattering was by no means easy!'

Conditions were much the same all along the brigade front. On the evening of 12th October the heaviest Chinese artillery barrage yet encountered fell on Hill 227 and the neighbouring positions, a prelude to an enemy battalion attack which was launched at 11.00 p.m. 'D' Company of the K.S.L.I. fought bravely and the enemy attack was beaten off by 2.30 a.m. the following morning. During this action Corporal Whitmore won the Military Medal and Captain Miller, the Royal New Zealand Artillery forward observer with the company, was awarded the Military Cross. 'D' Company lost Private Land killed and one man wounded but sixteen enemy dead were found at first light on the 13th and one prisoner was taken.

Patrol activity was increased during the latter part of October with fighting patrols from the K.S.L.I. ranging as far as Hill 149 and the hills to the North of 227. Second-Lieutenant Whybrow of 'D' Company was wounded near 'Check Point George', to the North of 227, when his patrol came across an area festooned with booby-trapped potato masher grenades hung from trees. Second-Lieutenant Isaacs, of 'B' Company, killed two Chinese with hand grenades and Second-Lieutenant Adams, of 'A' Company, bumped a Chinese patrol near Hill 149. The enemy artillery was continuously active during this period and was engaged by the U.N. artillery firing counter-battery tasks. On one such task an American 155 mm 'Persuader' howitzer was accidentally driven out along the 'Mad Mile' towards the Chinese lines. It was believed that the battery commander confused the map references of the target he was to engage and the gun position he was to occupy. The howitzer was recovered but the battery commander in his jeep disappeared and was never seen again. On another occasion, a party of twenty Korean refugees, accompanied by two cows, managed to pick their way through the Shropshires' mortar platoon's double-apron wire fence. The only supply route to Hill 227 was a dirt road fully exposed to enemy view from the West, movement along the 'Mad Mile' was extremely hazardous and traffic inevitably drew Chinese fire. Since this track not only served 'A' Company on 227 but also the

Mortar Platoon and Battalion Headquarters, it was decided to reduce traffic by moving the K.S.L.I. headquarters to the reserve company area some 2,000 yards to the East – to the jeers of the forward companies! To support patrol activity from Hill 227, Centurion tanks of the 8th King's Royal Irish Hussars were driven up to a spur on the West side of 227 to bring their guns to bear on Chinese bunkers across the valley; after a good day's shoot the tanks were withdrawn at last light. The new battalions of 29 Brigade were brought forward to provide reserve support and a company of the Royal Norfolk Regiment occupied 'Kidney' as an immediate reserve for the K.S.L.I.

On 25th October Brigadier Taylor relinquished command of 'his' brigade – 'I doubt if there was a better brigade in the Army,' he claimed with justifiable pride – to Lieutenant-Colonel J. F. M. MacDonald, former commanding officer of The King's Own Scottish Borderers who passed command of the battalion of Major D. H. Tadman. Brigadier Taylor returned to England to command the strategic reserve brigade, 49 Brigade, which he was later to take to Kenya to play an important part in quelling the Mau Mau uprising.

On 3rd November Lieutenant Henderson of 11 Platoon of the K.O.S.B. on the 'Knoll' remembers that

'the activity around us increased and although patrols had as usual been sent down the various ridges towards the Chinese, no reports of meeting any enemy in strength had come in. However, that night we could hear movement all around our positions. We heard tracked vehicles moving towards us and stopping and at the same time a large amount of banging and scraping. This we took to be digging, which later proved to be right. All these "night noises" were reported to battalion H.Q. and the bearings taken on the areas we considered the various sounds to be coming from. Our 3-inch mortar platoon had a busy night with harassing fire.

'The dawn of the 4th was, to say the least, rather foreboding and our breakfasts and morning shaves were very hurried affairs. To all intents and purposes the surrounding countryside was unchanged, all except for two things – a large sign had been painted on a white board and stuck firmly in the ground on "Baldy" by means of two large poles, and on it, for all to see were the words "GO HOME BRITISHERS OR THIS WILL BE YOUR GRAVEYARD". A great joke everyone thought and agreed that the Chinese had a sense of humour. Secondly, stretching from "Baldy" for 200 yards towards "Hinge" we saw a freshly dug trench, which had not been there the day before. At 10.00 hours, just as the porters and the familiar face of the company second-in-command appeared, there came a report from the sentry on duty in the lookout trench at the West end of the "Knoll", that the enemy in large numbers were coming out from behind "Baldy" and moving towards a small copse to the right of it, using their freshly dug communication trench as cover. This information was at once passed to the company commander who had, in fact, just received the news from battalion headquarters as "C" Company on the "Hinge" had already reported having seen the Chinese moving towards them from "Baldy".

'At 10.15 hours an airstrike warning was passed to us from company H.Q. and we made our aircraft panels as obvious as possible. The airstrike was going to go on "Baldy" and the copse. Along with this information came the news that 1,500 Chinese had been seen massing behind the feature that was to be the target for the airstrike. It seemed only a moment later that four Sea Furies appeared and circled over our position. The rather slower spotter plane, which always accompanied the Sea Furies, flew noisily over us and placed a well aimed yellow smoke canister near the summit of "Baldy". It was greeted by a hail of small arms fire from the Chinese. The Sea Furies followed one after the other. Each plane appeared to attack in a different manner. One would have a long shallow approach and another a steep screaming dive. Napalm, rockets and machine gun bullets tore and rent "Baldy" into a flaming mass and we little envied our enemy on that hill. The Sea Furies got a well earned cheer as, their lethal loads discarded, they flew away to the South.'

Two further airstrikes hit the enemy concentration and the artillery engaged Chinese gun positions in counter-battery fire as the bombardment increased in tempo and volume. Self-propelled guns were seen firing from the mouths of tunnels driven through the hills opposite and the enemy poured shells on the brigade front. Lieutenant Henderson:

'From the moment the airstrike was over the entire battalion position came under intense artillery and mortar fire. We on the "Knoll" could see 217 and "United" suffer from accurate Chinese concentrations. Dust and smoke rose from the positions and they

were soon engulfed in a pall of smoke. Only by the explosions did
we know that they were still getting the "Full treatment" (as our
Kiwi gunner friends had always called it). Then the guns would
switch to the "Knoll" and 317 and we weren't much interested in
what was happening elsewhere! This bombardment went on almost continuously until 4.00 p.m., during which time our platoon
position changed shape considerably. The precious trees which
had afforded so much cover were uprooted and lay strewn around
each trench. Due to the dust visibility was nil. Tins, cardboard,
webbing, paper and filth were everywhere. Our Bazooka rocket
launcher had been twisted into a U-like object seen only in a
school laboratory. The water cans, altogether well dug in, were
punctured, torn and useless. Telephone communications between
companies had long since been severed and the 88 sets of our two
platoons had been smashed by shell splinters.'

Shells were falling at the rate of 6,000 per hour – 100 a minute – on the
K.O.S.B. hills but heavy concentrations were also falling on the neigh-
bouring battalions.
Lieutenant Henderson continues:

'Fortunately we had a 31 set and it still functioned. The 11
Platoon signaller managed to make contact with company H.Q. on
Point 317 at 16.15 hours and was informed that they were being
attacked by enemy infantry but that their wire was holding. We
gathered that "C" and "B" Companies were also under attack.
This was the last information we got until 03.30 hours on 5th
November. Chinese burp guns could be heard from the "Hinge"
and although we could not see "United", fighting was also going
on there. At almost the same moment the left hand section of 7
Platoon and the right hand two sections of 11 Platoon were engaged by Chinese soldiers, who appeared from what must have
been dugouts and bunkers dug the night before under our very
noses. Now the many hours wiring paid its dividend and our Bren
gunners had a field day. Thirty-six grenades proved a most significant infantry weapon (each man had six grenades). During this
entire attack enemy mortar fire fell not only on us but amongst
Chinese troops themselves. Now we suffered another setback; 11
Platoon's ammunition trench was reported to be on fire. As this
contained 100 reserve grenades and many thousands of reserve

.303 SAA it was indeed a danger spot. What remained of our drinking water was used by 11 Platoon sergeant in a gallant effort to extinguish the flames. To ensure that this would not happen again all the spare ammunition was issued out to sections and, during a lull, the grenades were primed and the Bren gunners given full cases of .303. As there were twelve Bren guns on the position this issue exhausted our central dump. Time passed quickly and it was soon dark. From all round came the noise of Vickers, Bren, Burp and rifle, plus, of course, the continuous roar of our supporting artillery.'

'C' Company of the K.O.S.B. on the 'Hinge', were attacked by waves of Chinese at 4.15 p.m. and savage hand-to-hand fighting soon ensued. Major P. F. King, the Royal New Zealand Artillery observer with the company, called down defensive fire around the position until the Chinese were in amongst the company and his radio set was destroyed. The gunner major armed himself with grenades and led counter-attacks against the enemy on the hill. Although wounded three times, Major King fought relentlessly and his wireless operator, Gunner Rixon, stayed with him and made numerous trips to and from company headquarters to fetch supplies of grenades and ammunition. In the end, Gunner Rixon, already wounded in the head, helped to evacuate his officer and, in the process, was himself wounded a second time. For their part in this desperate battle, Major King was awarded the Distinguished Service Order and Gunner Rixon the Distinguished Conduct Medal. Despite the gallantry of the defenders, 'C' Company was ordered to withdraw at 6.15 p.m. to join 'A' Company in the battalion reserve area.

'B' Company of the K.O.S.B. on Hill 217 and 'United' were subjected to a heavy bombardment which included rockets and high velocity shells from self-propelled guns. At least 1,500 Chinese spearheaded the attack, advancing through their own shellfire and defensive fire to lay nets and bangalore torpedoes over the surrounding barbed wire. 'They walked through our D.F.s until we almost had it coming down on us and then they walked through their own barrage. I swear they were drugged,' commented one officer of the Borderers. Sheer weight of numbers forced the forward platoons to retire to the ridgeline after fierce fighting. Firing Bren guns from the hip, hurling grenades and grappling hand to hand, 'B' Company fought desperately. Private William Speakman, at company headquarters, heard that the section on the left of the company position had suffered heavy casualties and was being overrun. Speakman collected piles of grenades and gathered six men to drive the Chinese back, Speakman led his party in ten grenade charges through machine gun and mortar fire to repel successive waves of Chinese as they reached the crest of the hill. The forward platoons held out until 5.30 p.m. when the survivors crawled back to the Battle Patrol's position on 'Lock'. The attackers swarmed over Hill 217 and concentrated their assault on 'United'. Speakman had been wounded in the leg and was ordered to have a field dressing applied to the wound. Once bandaged, the big soldier returned to his party to lead them in further attacks. 'B' Company fought a bitter battle under the light of flares and amongst the smoke of continuous explosions but, despite their determined efforts, 'B' Company was eventually ordered to retire at 8.45 p.m. Speakman gathered his little party for one last charge and, under withering machine gun, mortar and small arms fire, they cleared the enemy from the crest and held it with showers of grenades whilst the rest of the company effected a withdrawal. Short of

*Private William Speakman, V.C.*
*1st Bn. King's Own Scottish Borderers.*

Soldier Magazine

ammunition and depleted in numbers, the remnants of 'B' Company fell back and consolidated on 'Italy' by midnight. Lieutenant Brooks of 6 Platoon was despatched to obtain ammunition and radio sets from battalion headquarters and successfully completed the return journey under constant fire, thus earning himself the Military Cross. Private Speakman was to receive the Victoria Cross, Major Harrison the Distinguished Service Order, Sergeant-Major Murdoch the Distinguished Conduct Medal, Corporal Wood and Lance-Corporal Buchanan the Military Medal.

'D' Company of the K.O.S.B., on Hill 317, was reduced to the company headquarters and one platoon by 9.00 p.m. on 4th November and were forced fall back to the reserve platoon position on 'Peak' at 10.00 p.m. The two platoons on the 'Knoll' were still holding their precarious position at midnight. Lieutenant Henderson:

'Twice while it was dark we were attacked again. Our 2-inch mortar flares were worth their weight in gold. By 03.00 hours, when we eventually made contact with battalion H.Q. and learnt that the "Knoll" was the one remaining position in the arrowhead held by ourselves, ammunition was running very short. It was assessed afterwards that the two platoons had fired 200 mortar flares as well as 150 HE bombs from a captured Chinese 60 mm mortar. Our casualties included one killed and eighteen wounded; five of the latter were stretcher cases. One of the walking wounded was blinded. Two stretchers only were available and so three others had to be found. The best that could be done was to use beds made by the men out of thin saplings and signal wire; a poor substitute for men whose legs and thighs were smashed and yet better than merely being carried. At 03.30 hours we were given the order to withdraw by battalion H.Q. Surely it must have been our lucky day for the withdrawal from "Knoll" was a complete success. Not only did we manage to evade the enemy all round our position, but no sooner had the position been abandoned than what seemed to be a real "banzai" took place on it. Bugles and screams split the now quiet night and the "Knoll" fell to the Chinese. 7 and 11 Platoons had, however, the supreme satisfaction of knowing that while they had remained no enemy managed to break through the wire perimeter.'

The complete success of the withdrawal from the 'Knoll' was due to Second-Lieutenant Purves, of 7 Platoon. Lieutenant Henderson was

amongst the wounded who were carried out. Second-Lieutenant Purves
conducted a fighting withdrawal, evacuating all the wounded and equipment under fire and brought them safely out to join the remnants of 'D'
Company on 'Peak'. For this action Second-Lieutenant Purves has the
distinction of being the only national serviceman to be awarded the Distinguished Service Order; he later became Chairman of the powerful
Hong Kong and Shanghai Bank in 1986.

Meanwhile, the Borderers' neighbours were also under attack. The left
hand company of the Royal Australians, 'D' Company, received a Chinese attack and their outpost on 'Brown Knoll' was forced to withdraw.
The feature was retaken by last light but further Chinese assaults drove
the Australians off by 5.40 a.m. on 5th November. 'B' Company of the
K.S.L.I. lost their company commander, Major Taitt, and his signallers –
Privates Holder, Jones and Pring – when the company headquarters
received a direct hit during the bombardment. At last light, 'D' Company
of the Shropshires on Hill 227 was attacked. The main weight of the
Chinese assault fell upon 11 Platoon, Second-Lieutenant Blyth, and
communications were maintained by wireless, the telephone lines having
been ripped to pieces by the shelling. Despite heavy enemy fire 'D'
Company, temporarily commanded by Captain Evison, held their positions and the Chinese did not succeed in penetrating the company's
perimeter. Continuous defensive fire was laid around 227 during the night
and the enemy attack was blunted by 11.30 p.m. Small spurts of activity
continued around the company through the night until 6.00 a.m. the next
morning. 'D' Company lost Sergeant Wilson killed and three men
wounded. A platoon of 'A' Company was sent forward to clear the area
around 227 at first light on 6th November and found twenty-two dead
Chinese and two wounded who were taken prisoner, the attackers had
been carrying rudimentary bangalore torpedoes and nine of these were
found near the wire. Translation of a captured document later revealed
that the attack on Hill 227 had been ordered by P'eng Hsien-chieh, commanding officer of the 569th Regiment of the 190th Division with the
intent 'to recover the lost positions, annihilate a large number of the
enemy, give the enemy a fatal blow and create a favourable situation
for the peace talks.' The plan was to 'coordinate with our friendly units
which are to wipe out the enemy, battalion size, at MARYANG-san and
recapture that position. 569 Regiment, according to division order, is to
wipe out the enemy on Hill 227; it is also to dispatch a contingent to
deliver a feint attack on the enemy at KOWANG-san to contain the
enemy.' The 1st Battalion of 569 Regiment was detailed for the attack on

*25-pounder gun of 16 Fd. Regt., Royal New Zealand Artillery.*

(IWM KOR 618)

227 with two companies in the assault. The Chinese also launched three night attacks on the Princess Patricia's Canadian Light Infantry, to the left of 28 Brigade on Hill 159, but these attacks were successfully repulsed. The gunners were also subjected to enemy artillery fire. One Kiwi gunner was killed and one wounded by 152 mm shells which fell upon the gun positions of 16 Field Regiment, R.N.Z.A. The Kiwis fired 10,387 rounds during 4th November and the 25 pounder guns were blistered and smoking hot, the gun crews almost exhausted by their strenuous efforts.

Support Company of the K.O.S.B. also played a vital part in the night's battle. The Mortar Platoon, Second-Lieutenant Rooke, laid continuous defensive fire, lobbing some 5,000 bombs in four hours, and the carriers of the M.M.G. Platoon, Second-Lieutenant Lyal, evacuated the wounded whilst under heavy artillery and mortar fire. By midnight the battle had died down and the Chinese swarmed victoriously over the hilltops around Maryang-San. During the hours of darkness, the 1st Battalion of The

Royal Leicestershire Regiment (who had recently arrived from Hong Kong to relieve the Royal Northumberland Fusiliers in 29 Brigade) came under the command of 28 Brigade and moved forward to support the K.O.S.B.

At 2.00 a.m. in the morning of 5th November Chinese artillery fire lifted to engage the Borderers' battalion headquarters and 'A' Company. Tracer rounds were fired down the valley to the East of 'Italy' and the Scots braced themselves for another attack – which did not materialize. By dawn the K.O.S.B. were holding their new positions: 'A' Company still in its reserve position near Maktae-Dong, 'B' Company and the Battle Patrol on 'Italy', 'C' Company alongside battalion headquarters to the South of 'A' Company and the remnants of 'D' Company on the higher ground of the 'Peak'. The Royal Leicesters were ordered forward in the morning, retracing the route taken by the Northumberland Fusiliers for the attack on Hill 217. The enemy was relatively quiet during the morning but could be seen clearly in occupation of Hills 217 and 317, Maryang-San. Thirteen airstrikes were mounted during the day and the artillery battered the Chinese-occupied hilltops. As the Leicesters advanced cautiously towards the hills, the Royal Australians on Hill 199 made preparations for a diversionary attack on Hill 317. At 2.00 p.m. the Leicesters and the Australians, supported by the Centurion tanks of the 8th Hussars and the divisional artillery, launched their attacks. The Chinese responded with intense and accurate defensive fire delivered by their artillery, mortars and small arms. By last light on 5th November the Australians had retaken 'Brown Knoll' after a fierce fight, killing eighteen enemy and capturing five prisoners, but the Leicesters were still held up short of their objective by the sustained and heavy Chinese fire. The fighting fizzled out by 11.30 p.m. leaving the Chinese in possession of Maryang-San and its neighbouring hills.

Corporal A. G. Applin served in 'D' Company of the Royal Leicesters and won the Military Medal during this action. He later recalled the attack:

'The attack went in. A green company advancing over open terrain for over a mile and subjected to mortar fire as intense and concentrated as any World War II provided. The first casualty. A signaller with a mortar splinter in his head that sliced off the back of it. The young medic, first time in, but with the presence of mind not to remove the hand he had placed behind the dead man's head because the hand was full of brains. Then surreptitiously wiping his hands on a clump of grass. The stench of cordite. The crump of falling mortars. Passing through the K.O.S.B. positions, still littered with the debris of close-quarter battle and unrecovered dead. Moving over the first of several crests and seeing our own wounded streaming, crawling back. And then the shouts of the indomitable who had forced their way out along a flank. Impassive Korean porters, carrying packs of reserve ammunition, crouching down behind the packs, afraid to move either forward or back. Confusion, everywhere confusion but the organised confusion of men, no longer boys, determined to get the job done. No-one will ever know for certain how many 'D' Company ever reached the Assault Line – but the attack went in. The gallant "Firpo" (Sergeant Phillips, M.M.) leading his platoon up the second crest, rifle slung, arms spread wide, keeping his troops in extended line as they went forward at the Point. "Bullets! Bullets! Bullets!" "Firpo" could well have been back in the New Territories on an exercise. When they recovered his body it was riddled. The Chinese could always pick out a leader. On the other flank, just as light was failing, an N.C.O. from another platoon was racing forward to throw grenades into the enemy slits over the crest. Hill 317 saw more than its share of desperate and foolhardy deeds that day, but the entrenched enemy were too strong. As night fell "D" Company was forced to withdraw, the last off the hill. Sergeant Millhouse gave covering fire while the survivors carried their wounded and their weapons down the hill. We heard the moaning of the wounded who had no-one to carry them. The long trek back, still under sporadic mortar fire, through the minefield that no-one had told us about. The hot tea and the two Padres working at the R.A.P. The stretchers covered with blankets, bodies covered from head to toe. Some ours. Some K.O.S.B. Some 3rd R.A.R. Major Bob Docker – soldier and gentleman, refused to have his own wounds treated until the other ranks had been attended to. And over it all, like a sorrowful benediction, the memory of boys who a few short hours before had sung the "hit" of the period: "They tried to tell us we're too young . . ."'

On 6th November, the brigade front was realigned and consolidated. The Royal Leicesters relieved the K.O.S.B. in their forward positions and the Borderers withdrew to the Hill 238 area as brigade reserve, there to re-organize and recoup after their exhausting battle. The fight for Maryang-San had cost the brigade 18 lives, 174 wounded and 56 missing of which 7 dead, 87 wounded and 44 missing were from the K.O.S.B. The Chinese casualties for the battle will probably never be known, some prisoners were taken but thousands must have been killed and wounded. The battle had called for close air support and extensive artillery defensive and counter-battery fire. During the thirty-six hours ending at 6.00 p.m. on 5th November the divisional artillery had fired 30,829 rounds in support of the hard-pressed rifle companies.

At the close of the battle the Chinese had retaken the arrowhead of hills to the North of Hill 355, sacrificing hundreds of their infantry but using their artillery to great effect. The King's Own Scottish Borderers had borne the brunt of the onslaught and had fought gallantly until their positions were untenable. The other battalions of 28 Brigade had also suffered artillery bombardment and infantry attacks but had retained their positions on the other hills.

The commander of the 28th British Commonwealth Brigade issued a special order of the day on 7th November 1951:

'Special Order of the Day by Lieut.-Colonel J. F. M. MacDonald, D.S.O., O.B.E., Commander 28th British Commonwealth Infantry Brigade.

'Sunday 4th November 1951, will be remembered and revered for all time in the annals of The King's Own Scottish Borderers.

'On this day, you stood your ground from early dawn in the face of intense and accurate enemy bombardment, and as the afternoon wore on, you met and held a major Chinese Communist attack and dealt the enemy a deadly blow. The actions fought by you all, both collectively and individually on this day, were beyond praise, and it is true to say that your gallantry and sacrifice saved the divisional front from being penetrated.

'Your adversary was clearly confident that his intense bombardment and human mass attack, in which he used one division (6,000 men), would overwhelm the defenders of the now famous Point 217 – Point 317 ridge line. He had failed completely and utterly, however, to appreciate that he was opposed by men, whose courage, tenacity and fighting skill was second to none – The 1st Battalion The King's Own Scottish Borderers. Your magnificent exploits on this fateful Sunday have, therefore, given him further proof, if such be needed, that such tactics against you are doomed to disaster.

'Higher commanders, both Commonwealth and American, have spoken in glowing terms of your splendid action. No finer tribute can be paid to the esteem in which you are held, than the words spoken to me by your Corps Commander, General O'Daniel, who said, "When I first heard of this major attack and learnt that it was directed at The King's Own Scottish Borderers, I had no doubt of the outcome of the battle – your boys are magnificent and know how to fight."

'As a Scottish Borderer, your late commander and commander of the brigade during the battle, I was filled with intense pride, admiration and emotion at your gallantry and skill. I also recalled to my mind the famous regimental motto – *Nec Aspera Terrant* (nor do they fear danger).

*Lt. Gen. William Bridgeford, C-in-C British Troops Japan and Korea, visits H.Q. 3rd Bn. Royal Australian Regiment. Left to right: Lt. Col. J. F. Macdonald, K.O.S.B., acting commander 28 Bde.; Lt. Col. F. G. Hassett, C.O. 3 R.A.R.; General Bridgeford; Maj. Gen. J. Cassels, commander 1 COMWEL. Div.*

(IWM MH 28035)

'During the battle the Battalion covered itself with glory and honour and I congratulate you all on an outstanding and heroic achievement.

Korea. 7th November 1951.'

The battle honour 'Maryang-San' was awarded to The King's Own Scottish Borderers and The Royal Leicestershire Regiment. In later years, a survivor of the battle, recalling those hectic and frightening days, commented: 'It took a lot to take Maryang-San and the Chinese lost even more taking it back.' General Hassett agreed: 'We knew from past American experience that 317 would be hard to take and that its loss would cause the Chinese to react strongly.' Nevertheless, the feature had been taken successfully after a bitter battle and had held for some twenty-seven days before the Chinese were able to regain some of their lost territory – at a great cost in human life.

# Hill 227

As the brigade drew breath after the fierce battle of Maryang-San, the Chinese artillery continued to pound the positions occupied by the 3rd Royal Australian Regiment and the other battalions on the brigade front. True to form, the enemy launched an attack on the Australians on 7th November but the diggers stood firm and repulsed the Chinese. Chinese gunnery had improved since the introduction of the heavier weapons and the daily 'stonk' by enemy artillery was to become a regular feature of life in the front line.

During the month of November, the Korean autumn was advancing with morning frosts and chilly nights. The seasonal change was initially welcomed by soldiers who had spent the previous two years in the semi-tropical climate of Hong Kong. The brigade was still wearing the jungle green tropical clothing in which they had arrived in Korea and an issue of woollen pullovers came as a necessary addition to the soldiers' meagre wardrobe. Soon after the issue of pullovers, the Commonwealth Division's logistics branch began to issue battle-dress to all ranks, closely followed by supplies of windproof smocks. Although their clothing was warmer, the soldiers' diet remained the same: American combat rations issued daily to each individual and supplemented by tea, tinned milk, sugar and the occasional loaf of bread – spartan fare for young men who were expending enormous amounts of energy on the construction of defence works and enduring sleepless nights.

On 10th November 'A' Company of the King's Shropshire Light Infantry replaced their 'D' Company on Hill 227. Lieutenant Chambers was a platoon commander in 'A' Company and describes the position:

'Point 227 was a relatively small knoll about the size of three tennis courts. It had originally been heavily wooded but Chinese and our own artillery had reduced it to a bare knoll. The Chinese had defended it with a ring trench about ten metres down from the top and, as this was virtually the only way it could be defended, the K.S.L.I. had taken over the trench system, improving it and pointing the other way. There was really only room for two platoons and the third platoon was on a small knoll to the East, with company headquarters about half way between. The trench had quite large bunkers set into the rear of it each holding three to four men. Between 6th October and 4th November large quantities of barbed wire had been carried up by the Korean porters so that there were no less than eight barbed wire fences circling the top. In some places there were twelve. In addition to this, in the wire large pits had been dug and filled with jerricans of napalm with an explosive charge which could be detonated electrically from the platoon positions, using wireless batteries. The position therefore resembled a scene from World War I.'

Another Shropshireman remembers occupying one of these former Chinese bunkers with two friends. After some time they became aware of a foul stench and began to wonder whether one of their number had lost control of his bowels. This caused some tension amongst the occupants until, in the course of enlarging and strengthening their accommodation, they uncovered the remains of a Chinese soldier who had been buried by shell fire during the capture of the hill.

The enemy's harassing fire continued and increased and patrols were sent out to screen the brigade's front. One such patrol, mounted by 'A' Company of the K.S.L.I. reconnoitred as far as Hill 149 on 14th November and found the Chinese occupying newly dug positions. The following day a platoon of 'A' Company, accompanied by a party of sappers, set out to destroy the new trenchworks. On approaching 149 the platoon discovered that the enemy had occupied the trenches in strength and, after a brisk fire fight, the demolition party withdrew. On 16th November persistent shelling of Hill 227 began to increase to the rate of one shell every five minutes. Privates Eadsforth and Jackson were killed during the bombardment and, with hindsight, the defenders realised that the Chinese gunners were probably ranging in on their target.

The shelling ceased at dusk but recommenced at dawn on 17th November, rising to a fierce crescendo by 4.30 p.m. Lieutenant Chambers recalls that day:

'A terrific bombardment of Point 227 took place with a great weight of artillery of all types taking part including mortars and direct fire from self-propelled guns. The shells came down at the rate of about three a second and within five to ten minutes most of the communication trenches had collapsed and were blocked; all the telephone lines had vanished and the barbed wire entanglements became almost non-existent. The napalm fougasses also failed to work due to cut wires. Most of the rest shelters collapsed and the whole hill was hidden in a cloud of dust. The Chinese forces followed hard on the concentration which lasted about half an hour and, when it slackened, were about fifty yards from the trenches. The platoon commanders tried to get hold of their platoons but due to the blocking of the trenches, collapsing of the bunkers and the proximity of the enemy this proved more or less impossible. The Chinese had obviously assembled around Point 149 and along the ridge running West from 227. The main part of the attack started up the spur, but meeting opposition from 2 Platoon, sheered off left and came in between 2 and 3 Platoons. Most of 2 Platoon had now been killed or trapped under debris but platoon headquarters and half a section were holding the little spur. Whilst they were holding, the Chinese had crossed over the top of the hill and reached company headquarters. At this time the company commander (Major K. A. Heard, M.C.) had left to try and contact his platoons without success and some of his headquarters were taken prisoner. 3 Platoon, meanwhile, had engaged in hand-to-hand fighting and several had been taken prisoner, including the platoon commander, Second-Lieutenant J. Adams, and the New Zealand artillery observer, Captain Hector MacLean. These prisoners, together with those from company headquarters, were assembled and marched off down the spur of 227 towards 149. Within minutes a D.F. from our guns came down upon them and, in the resulting confusion, led by the two officers they made their escape down the re-entrant, across the road to the P.P.C.L.I. positions on the ridge at Point 159. The Chinese meanwhile started to clear 227 and on their way from company headquarters came to the rear of the remaining section and H.Q. of 2 Platoon. Three men were taken prisoners. The other three, including the platoon commander (Lieutenant Chambers himself), fought their way back over the top of the hill to company headquarters which they found occupied by Chinese and then managed to reach the rear slopes of 227. Here they stayed for a short while and gathered another four stragglers from company headquarters before making their way by a circuitous route to the M.M.G.

Platoon and reporting by radio to battalion headquarters. 1 Platoon, Second-Lieutenant Clough, on their little knoll, although subject to bombardment, had not received an infantry attack and it was clear that they would be next as the Chinese hoped to roll up to 355. The stragglers from 2 Platoon and H.Q. joined 1 Platoon and awaited attack, whilst calling down fire on 227 itself. Throughout the long night fire was directed on 227 from the New Zealand battery and, indeed, regimental artillery and the M.M.G. Platoon. The Mortar Platoon, Lieutenant C. B. Grundy, did a magnificent job and fired forty tons of bombs during the night. So effective was this fire that although digging was heard on 227 no attack developed on the knoll.'

Eight survivors managed to escape from the Chinese in the darkness, including Corporal Parsons, the mortar platoon observer with the company, and the two officers – although Gunner Garland, Lieutenant MacLean's radio operator, was marched away by the Chinese to become the only New Zealand prisoner of war in Korea. Lieutenant Chambers took command of a scratch 'platoon' of survivors and established a defensive position to the East of Hill 227 near the Machine Gun Platoon, Lieutenant Cleaver. From this position Lieutenant Chambers was able to report on the state of the hill to battalion headquarters. As a result, 'D' Company was ordered forward from the battalion reserve and approached Hill 227 at 11.15 p.m. but, despite the constant barrage, the Chinese were still alert and active and 'D' Company took four casualties. Lieutenant-Colonel Barlow ordered 'D' Company to withdraw and await first light before mounting their attack.

Early in the morning of 18th November, Hill 227 was subjected to a fifty-minute barrage before 'D' Company, supported by tanks, counter-attacked at 7.00 a.m. On gaining the summit, they found that the Chinese had fled and the hill was unoccupied. 'On trying to re-organize the position, which was by now a complete shambles, about six members of "A" Company were discovered trapped in their bunkers having survived both enemy and "friendly" artillery in massive quantities. "A" Company commander, Major Keith Heard, was also discovered wounded in one of the bunkers originally belonging to 3 Platoon.' There were many dead Chinese littering the blasted hilltop and one wounded Chinaman who was taken prisoner. 'D' Company spent a very uncomfortable day on the hill, making the best of what little cover remained and keeping to the reverse slopes with only observation posts forward to watch for the enemy; even so, they suffered considerably from enemy shellfire. Supplies were brought up along the 'Mad Mile' and R.S.M. Knight and a party of buglers from battalion headquarters came to evacuate the wounded, recover the dead and assist 'D' Company in repairing defence works. A composite platoon of 'A' Company survivors was brought forward to occupy a defensive position at the West end of Hill 355, coming under the command of 'C' Company. 'D' Company of the Royal Norfolk Regiment was also moved forward to come under the command of the K.S.L.I. as the immediate reserve company and took up position just before nightfall. During the day, airstrikes were delivered on the Chinese-occupied hills and artillery exchanges continued. The two troops of the 8th Hussars who had supported 'D' Company's early morning attack raked the enemy's entrenchments with their guns and machine guns whilst Lieutenant Cleaver's Vickers machine guns and Lieutenant Grundy's 3-inch mortars maintained steady harassing fire throughout the day. In the early evening the Chinese artillery bombardment of Hill 227 increased in quantity. Defensive fire tasks were called down around the hill but, in the fading light of dusk, the first wave of Chinese infantry advanced, trotting through their own and the defensive fire to clamber up 227. 'D' Company were faced with a numerically superior enemy and were soon grappling hand to hand. Major Cottle informed battalion headquarters that the hill would soon become untenable and was given the order to withdraw. In the chaos of the close quarter fighting it was impossible to relay orders and only Major Cottle with thirty-two of his men, including seventeen wounded, managed to get off the hilltop. Lieutenant Borwick's 10 Platoon were still occupying the position

*Sole Survivor*
*Hill 227, 18th November 1951.*

previously held by 1 Platoon of 'A' Company and they also remained undamaged and intact. Survivors of 'D' Company later escaped to join Major Cottle's party during the night. After the evacuation of the hill, the Chinese fired tracer over the Machine Gun Platoon's position towards Hill 355, normally the signal for the next phase of an attack but no such assault was made. The artillery, mortars and machine guns concentrated their fire on 227 throughout the night.

At 5.00 a.m. on 19th November 10 Platoon ventured out from their position to patrol the hilltop and found it clear of the enemy. A message was sent quickly to battalion headquarters and the prepared counter-attack for the morning was cancelled. 10 Platoon made a hasty search of the area but failed to find a large number of Chinese dead who had been caught by the defensive and harassing fire tasks laid on 227. The hill was so blasted and devoid of cover that no attempt was made to reoccupy the feature in strength. The Chinese bombarded 227 throughout the day and the Shropshires maintained an observation post to warn of further attacks but none were forthcoming.

During the night of 19th November the Royal Leicesters, to the northeast of Hill 355, were attacked and the Chinese also made a move against 'C' Company of the K.S.L.I. on 355 itself. 'C' Company beat the enemy off and found five dead outside their wire the next morning. Hill 227 was patrolled and searched in the morning of 20th November and some 300 enemy bodies were found but the intensity of the Chinese fire on the hilltop precluded any detailed count. A platoon of the Royal Norfolks reserve company was brought forward as the Shropshires established a new defensive line which excluded the barren top of Hill 227. 'B' Company was sited on the spur between 227 and 355 beside the Machine Gun Platoon and 'D' Company, with the Norfolk platoon, on the Un Dong spur to the South of the derelict hill.

On 21st November, Hill 227 was again patrolled in the early hours of the morning and a search made to recover the Shropshire dead. During the night the Chinese had also been on the hill and had removed the piles of their own dead which had been seen the previous day. Large concentrations of the enemy were observed behind the hills and airstrikes and bombing raids were directed against these targets during the day in addition to artillery interdiction barrages. Even so, the Chinese launched another attack in the evening but this was beaten off with only one casualty sustained by the K.S.L.I. On 22nd November 28 Brigade was relieved in the line by the Canadians and the 3rd U.S. Infantry Division, the latter arriving with turkeys and ice-cream to celebrate Thanksgiving Day on Hill 355.

The battles on Hill 227 cost the Shropshires 21 killed, 64 wounded and 6 men missing. Two of the wounded had been captured but were later released by the Chinese; Private Jones was allowed to walk back and the other man was carried to within 150 yards of the Patricias' position during the night. A large notice was left near him and the Canadians brought him in the next morning. Only one was briefly interrogated and most of the questions were of a political nature.

A captured document, originated by the commander of the 569th Regiment on 8th November 1951, detailed the Chinese plan to take Hill 227:

'In order to annihilate a large number of the enemy's combat strength, create favourable combat opportunities and exploit our gains, the regiment should be prepared at all times and make plans to counter-attack Hill 227 and KOWANG-san simultaneously. The 3rd Battalion will jump off from KUMCH'OK-dong and KOJANGSONG-ni, attack from the North and seize the main heights of KOWANG-san; the 1st Battalion will jump off from Hill 149 and attack the Northwest. If the seizure of Hill 227 is successful, the 1st Battalion will proceed forward and attack KOWANG-san and annihilate the enemy there. The 2nd Battalion will be the second line echelon, remaining at its location and waiting orders to thrust into battle. Before the attack, the following points are to be noted: 1. Conduct 'mind mobilisation', inspire political and military personnel to fight for victory and merit, and establish resolution and confidence to accomplish the mission.
2. Utilise every minute to make preparations before actual combat breaks out. Initiate "military democracy", study tactics and re-iterate manoeuvres. Be familiar with co-ordination between infantry and artillery, the continuous breakthrough in "Four-teams-in-one unit" formation and night combat.
3. Strictly observe battlefield discipline and be of high resolution in carrying out missions. Do not abandon the wounded, the dead or weapons and ammunition.'

The order was counter-signed by Chang Chung-chieh, the political commissar of the regiment.

A persistent, but unsubstantiated, legend circulated amongst the men of the K.S.L.I. that the first wave of attackers on Hill 227 had been led by a 'woman in black'. It has been impossible to verify this claim but several soldiers still maintain that this mysterious woman was in the forefront of the assault on the hilltop. She may have been one of the 'political personnel' mentioned in the regimental order or perhaps a medical orderly but may have been merely a young man with long hair. Another myth of the same period concerns the son of Mao Tse-tung, the Chinese leader. Mao junior incurred his father's wrath and was sent to fight with the Chinese People's Volunteers in Korea where he is supposed to have been killed in action. A completely unfounded rumour claims that the younger Mao may have perished during the attacks on the Royal Australians on Hill 317.

In the event, the Chinese plans were thwarted. After the fight for Hill 227, neither side was able to maintain a permanent position on the desolate hilltop. Standing patrols were mounted in the area at night and observation posts established by day, even so the barren hill was to be the scene of several bitter little squabbles thereafter.

Hill 227 again demonstrated the devastating effect of concentrated artillery fire which accounted for most of the casualties – on both sides. The K.S.L.I. Mortar Platoon fired some 7,000 bombs on 17th November, of which 1,500 were fired in half an hour; on 18th November they fired some 4,000 rounds. One mortarman loaded almost four and a half tons 'down the spout' in one night. The rifle companies were full of praise for the speed and accuracy with which defensive fire was laid during the battle. The physical effort involved was considerable; 11,000 bombs weighing over fifty tons were ferried up the 'Mad Mile' by tracked carriers in under twenty-four hours, always under enemy artillery fire. One carrier driver had the grisly task of evacuating his brother's body after delivering stocks of ammunition to the forward platoons. The gunners also fired a fantastic number of rounds; about 50,000 by the New Zealanders alone who fired their 200,000 round of the war on 7th October and raised this figure to a quarter of a million on 23rd November.

227 was the Shropshires' hill; they had taken it on 4th October and held it against several Chinese onslaughts. Even when forced off the hill, the K.S.L.I. had regained the feature on 18th and 19th November until it was impossible to occupy as a permanent position. The unique battle honour 'Hill 227' was awarded to The King's Shropshire Light Infantry, Major Cottle gained the Distinguished Service Order and Corporal Whitmore the Military Medal for their parts in the action. Nevertheless, the battle involved other units of the brigade who provided support and assistance to the riflemen on the hill, another example of the close teamwork enjoyed within the Commonwealth Brigade.

On 22nd November, the Commonwealth Brigade was relieved in the battered front line positions and retired for a well-deserved rest, withdrawing some four miles behind the front line to the reserve area around Charumul.

# Winter 1951–1952

28 Commonwealth Brigade withdrew from the front line on 22nd November to the divisional reserve area around the old Charumul reservoir, except for the King's Own Scottish Borderers who moved into 29 Brigade reserve to replace the Welch Regiment, another of the new British battalions. Having established the 'Jamestown Line' the 1st Commonwealth Division settled down to a two brigade front with the third brigade in reserve. After Operation 'Commando' and the battles of Kowang-San, Maryang-San and Hill 227, 28 Brigade was fortunate to be the first to enjoy this break from the 'sharp end'.

As with all 28 Brigade moves, it rained inevitably as the weary soldiers set about pitching bivouacs and occupying the valleys in the rear area. Having managed to construct some kind of shelter against the chilling rain, the brigade looked forward to being able to relax and enjoy the luxury of an uninterrupted night. General Hassett recalls: 'The period 3 November to 22 November was a difficult time for the brigade. After the strenuous demands and high spirits of the attacks on 355 and 317, the brigade took quite a battering. It was tired when it went into reserve and, although still full of fight, it had lost its edge.' In fact, the whole brigade was suffering from a delayed form of battle fatigue. After some fifty days and nights of relentless action the symptoms were only too evident. Recent and vivid impressions of comrades killed and injured, coupled with the accumulated stress of danger and constant vigilance, resulted in a sombre and withdrawn attitude interspersed with nervous attempts at forced cheerfulness and sudden displays of temper. The physical and mental weariness was reflected in tired but wary eyes and the phenomenon of men just standing and listening; the nervous tension of being subjected to constant artillery bombardment lingered and most soldiers found themselves unconsciously alert for the shriek of incoming shells. Despite the tiredness, sleep did not come easily and it took some time to adjust to the comparative calm of the reserve area. For the teenage national servicemen of the British battalions it was a traumatic maturing with effects that could never be forgotten. Lieutenant Pembroke, of the 3rd Royal Australian Regiment, looking back after forty years remembers: 'An initial sense of not really being part of the battle; the look on the faces of the men as they stood over their fallen mates; the comradeship and steadfastness of the men of 9 Platoon who uncomplainingly did everything that was asked of them and more. Above all, a frightening but most humbling experience. It taught me about the essential human values of living and dying.' However, the resilience of youth and the need to establish living accommodation in the new area kept the troops occupied and gave them a constructive objective.

Four miles to the North, dominating the local landscape, the bulk of Hill 355, Kowang-San, was clearly visible from the Charumul area. On the night of 23rd November, the troops in reserve were treated to a distant display of 'fireworks' accompanied by the delayed thuds of explosions and the crash of the New Zealand artillery firing in the next valley. Kowang-San was the centrepiece of this noisy show. The following morning it was learnt that two companies of the 7th U.S. Regimental Combat Team ('The Cottonbalers') of the 3rd U.S. Infantry Division had been driven from the top of Hill 355. The Chinese had watched the change of occupation; two large American infantry companies (laden with turkeys and ice-cream for Thanksgiving Day) had moved into the position formerly occupied by 'C' Company of the K.S.L.I. The enemy had timed their attack to catch the new occupants before they had dug sufficient cover for the additional troops. However, 3rd Division mounted an immediate and strong counter-attack and succeeded in retrieving the feature.

That same night the first snow of winter fell and spurred the reserve brigade to consider the construction of adequate winter quarters. During the following days underground accommodation was excavated with pick and spade and a frantic search for roofing materials sent parties scavenging the desolate countryside. Living bunkers took priority and many ingenious 'hoochies' were dug into the hillsides, boasting beds made of old signal cable, NAAFI/E.F.I. beerboxes, straw and anything else that came to hand. American marquee-type tents were provided for cookhouses and even messes for officers and sergeants. These palatial establishments were soon in operation, serving hot meals of British compo rations – a welcome change after months of 'do it yourself' catering with American individual combat rations. The NAAFI provided Japanese beer and other necessities, taking currency vouchers for payment, and a lively night-life took shape. Cinema shows were arranged and, in the Charumul area, the Canadian Brigade's 'A' Echelon boasted a magnificent straw basha with the grandiose title of 'The Royal Canadian Theatre'.

As the temperature dropped and winter began to grip Korea, British soldiers received the first issue of the new type of combat clothing, later to become standard issue throughout the army. The 'Boots, Cold, Wet' were especially welcomed and were to save many toes from frost-bite in the months to come. In addition to the combat clothing, and its attendant winter underwear, the superb outer parka, tested in Antarctica and proof against the bitterest of Manchurian winds, was also issued to all ranks. The old 1937 pattern webbing equipment, religiously 'blancoed' and polished from Chelsea to the New Territories of Hong Kong, was replaced by the 1944 type webbing, which required no cleaning and polishing. The old battle-dress clothing together with the discarded 1937 webbing equipment were snatched by the Korean porters to replace their inadequate clothing and were worn with some pride, indicating that the wearers were part of the Commonwealth Division. Thus, snugly housed, well fed and warmly clothed, 28 Brigade looked forward to a comparatively comfortable winter in reserve.

However, life in reserve was not all Asahi beer and film shows. On 4th December the 3rd Battalion of The Royal Australian Regiment was formally paraded to receive the American Presidential Unit Citation from General Van Fleet, the Army commander, for the action at Kapyong in April 1951. Members of the battalion were thereafter entitled to wear the blue ribbon of the award on their uniforms. On 15th December, the brigade was turned out to participate in Operation 'Skunk Hunt', a sweep of the divisional rear area designed to flush out any guerillas or infiltrators who may have established themselves behind the lines. No recognisable enemy agents or terrorists were discovered in the barren countryside and the porters of the Korean Service Corps. now resplendent in cast off Britain battle-dress, were the only natives in the divisional area. The King's Shropshire Light Infantry were slightly disgruntled when they were sent to relieve the Royal Norfolk Regiment in a fairly quiet sector of the line along the Samichon Valley two weeks before Christmas. However, during the Shropshires' fairly uneventful occupation of the Yong Dong positions, the Chinese left seasonal presents and cards on the forward barbed wire. Chinese propaganda efforts had improved considerably since the introduction of crude posters and pamphlets aimed at the United Nations forces and the K.S.L.I. amongst others, were the recipients of plastic Christmas stockings filled with handkerchieves, brooches, and cards all bearing propaganda messages and decorated with the Picasso dove of peace. One example of such seasonal goodwill bore a little poem: 'Greetings from the Chinese People's Volunteers. Whatever the colour, race or creed, All plain folks are brothers indeed. Both you and we want life and peace, If you go home the war will cease. Demand Peace! Stop the War!' Such mementoes were sought eagerly since they were of great value in the bartering trade with rear area troops, a business which thrived whilst the brigade was in reserve. The King's Own Scottish Borderers spent most of the Christmas period in the line at various places, relieving companies of the 25th Canadian Brigade between 24th and 28th December. The Shropshires heaved a sigh of relief when the Royal Norfolks returned to the line just before Christmas and the K.S.L.I. were able to celebrate Christmas in style; the K.O.S.B., being Scots, were returned to the reserve in time for the traditional Hogmanay celebrations.

Whilst in reserve, the battalions tried to send as many eligible men as possible on their five days rest and recuperation leave in Tokyo and also took the opportunity to introduce the latest reinforcements to the Korean way of life. Drafts to the British battalions were mainly drawn from the parent administrative brigades in Great Britain but it was not uncommon for Highlanders to be sent to the King's Own Scottish Borderers and Home Counties men to the Shropshires. The veteran 3rd Battalion of the Royal Australian Regiment had virtually undergone a complete change of personnel after some fifteen months in Korea, one Korean winter being considered enough for one tour of duty with a front line unit. Whilst serving in Korea the Australians received an extra two shillings a day in pay (four shillings and nine pence in the case of married men) and, if the soldier had served outside Australia for more than two years with at least eight months of such service in Korea, he was eligible for a home posting. Many of the original members of the 3rd Royal Australians had served in the Occupation Forces in Japan and therefore fell into this category. British soldiers, on the other hand, did not receive any extra pay for service in Korea – although this was later changed when a retrospective form of 'bounty' was introduced for each month served in Korea, payable on return to Great Britain. Ironically, those who had come to Korea from Hong Kong were worse off financially, losing their Hong Kong local overseas allowance when they embarked for Korea. Apart from the greatly prized five days R. & R. leave in Tokyo and the purchase of NAAFI/E.F.I. supplies, there was nothing to spend money on in Korea – hence the thriving bartering trade with the Americans.

The integrated character of the Commonwealth Brigade with its representative national battalions and regiments was also reflected in the brigade's supporting services. 10 Company of the Royal New Zealand Army Service Corps rendered sterling service in the provision of supplies and ammunition to the fighting troops and the brigade's repair service, in the form of 16 Infantry Workshops, Royal Electrical and Mechanical Engineers, included one Australian officer and thirteen Australian craftsmen. Brigade headquarters was similarly integrated and included officers from the British, Australian and New Zealand armies whilst divisional headquarters was more cosmopolitan with a strong Canadian element and even South African staff officers. Brigadier MacDonald remarked on this successful mixture: 'The intense but friendly rivalry that existed between units and formations in the 1st British Commonwealth Division produced a remarkable *esprit de corps* and standard of efficiency.'

Although the component battalions of the brigade were necessarily separated during operations in the front line, a period in the reserve provided great opportunities to meet and mix both formally and on a soldier to soldier basis. It was on such occasions that the friendly rivalry between units blossomed, especially that between the Royal Australians and the New Zealand gunners. The Antipodean propensity for adopting unattended vehicles – be they Chinese, American or even Commonwealth – had begun in the early chaotic days of 27 Brigade and, during this period in reserve, the 3rd Royal Australians claimed their fiftieth jeep, much to the chagrin of the Royal New Zealand Artillery. The Shropshires were still running a Russian GAZ truck which they had inherited from the Middlesex Regiment. It was found that American spare parts fitted this former North Korean vehicle and it was used as an additional ammunition carrier by the Mortar Platoon.

The winter of 1951/1952 was not as severe as the preceding winter when the poorly equipped 27 Brigade advanced to the far North of Korea and subsequently fought a retreat back to the South in the face of the Chinese People's Volunteers. Compared to the conditions endured by the original Commonwealth Brigade, 28 Brigade had a reasonable winter in Korea – despite sub-zero temperatures and bitterly cutting winds coming down from the north. One hazard of Korean life, the so-called 'Manchurian Brain Fever' carried by the ubiquitous rats who found shelter in the trenches and dug-out 'hoochies', was soon recognised by the medical authorities. Mass anti-encephalitis inoculations countered this threat but did not get rid of the swarming rats.

Nineteen fifty-two was greeted by the firing of one round from every gun on the divisional front into the Chinese positions at the stroke of midnight. Strangely enough, the Chinese did not retaliate. In retrospect, it seemed to be a rather telling return for all the little propaganda stockings and packets the Chinese had left at Christmas. 28 Brigade enjoyed a further two weeks in the reserve area before moving back into the line to relieve the 25th Canadian Brigade between 18th and 20th January 1952. Although not on the higher hills taken by the brigade the previous autumn, the Canadian positions were near enough to remind their relief of those hectic days spent under Chinese bombardment. As the brigade took over its new positions the Chinese did send harassing fire at selected targets but the 'stonks' were mild compared to those endured in the past. Artillery exchanges were a normal daily routine as winter gripped the bleak hills and frozen padis and actions were limited to vigorous patrolling on both sides. Standing and ambush patrols by night were chilling experiences and the new clothing soon proved its worth. Many ingenious heating devices were introduced into the front line trenches and small stoves, made from old ration tins and fuelled with charcoal produced by the Korean porters, were amongst the safest. Some petrol burning stoves were tried but proved to be extremely dangerous, several casualties resulted from premature explosions or blow-backs caused by the wind. Latterly, an issue of 'derv' was approved and stoves were manufactured from metal ammunition boxes using the drip-feed principle; rubber tubing then became a much sought after asset and those who were lucky enough to obtain a length guarded it jealously; chimneys were knocked together from artillery cartridge tins and, as the countryside lay under a blanket of snow, such chimneys protruding from an underground 'hoochie' were sometimes mistaken for 'desert roses'.

Early in February the brigade received the unexpected news of the death of His Majesty King George the Sixth. The battalion padres conducted memorial services amongst their scattered flocks and the soldiers found it strange to find themselves singing 'God save the Queen' at the conclusion of these services. In later years, many of those who were serving at that time and continued in their respective armies until the Silver Jubilee of Her Majesty Queen Elizabeth the Second, felt slightly disappointed when the Queen's Jubilee Medal was not awarded to those who had served since Her accession in 1952.

The brigade continued its policy of aggressive patrolling to dominate no-man's land. All the battalions took part in this programme, whatever the weather, and the Shropshires' regimental account mentions several such ventures across the Samichon River. On 29th January Second-Lieutenant Whybrow took a patrol out to demolish a Chinese bunker but, as he was laying the demolition charge, a Chinese popped out of an inner chamber of the dug-out and Mr. Whybrow was wounded. An ambush patrol of 'C' Company was rushed by twelve of the enemy who wounded two Shropshiremen but were driven off after one Chinese had been killed. On 7th February Second-Lieutenant St. Clair-Morford led a night patrol which was ambushed by an enemy patrol; the Shropshires were pinned down by enemy fire and split to break out of the ambush. During the subsequent confusion and dispersal of the trapped patrol, St. Clair-Morford became separated from his men and was never seen again.

Meanwhile, the truce talks were dragging on at Panmunjon and, as a possible prelude to a final settlement, it was agreed to call an experimental truce along the front from 10th to 16th February, the experiment to be called Operation 'Snare'. For a week an almost uncanny silence existed although defensive work on wiring and mining continued apace. This strange period of unrealistic peace was, however, marred by minor incidents. During the night of 12 February a Royal Engineer party working on the roads behind the front line had a truck ambushed and one sapper snatched. 'B' Company of the K.S.L.I. caught sight of a small party of men who escaped across no-man's land but failed to catch them. A similar infiltration party ran into a standing patrol of 'C' Company of the K.S.L.I. but, to quote a contemporary report 'the night shooting on both sides had been, as usual, deplorable.' 'B' Company did intercept another party of three North Koreans who had made their way into the defensive minefield during the night. The infiltrators had negotiated the minefield by probing, slowly and patiently, with rice stalks to detect the mines but were discovered at first light by an alert sentry before they had cleared the danger area. The North Koreans panicked and tried to escape but set off two mines in their hurry. One of the enemy was seen to be still alive and efforts were made to extricate him. There had been a dearth of prisoners for interrogation to ascertain the enemy's intentions after the so-called experimental truce. As an incentive, the Corps Commander – General 'Iron Mike' O'Daniel – had offered an extra five days leave in Tokyo for the first man to take a prisoner after Operation 'Snare' and the Divisional Commander – General Cassels – had also offered a bottle of whisky to the first Commonwealth soldier to bring in an enemy for interrogation. The K.S.L.I. succeeded in recovering the wounded North Korean and the body of one of his comrades from the minefield and the platoon commander promptly laid claim to the generals' prizes.

The brief and unreal period of quiet along the front line soon ended and artillery engagements resumed, although the searchlight marking the truce

site at Panmunjon continued to shine up into the night sky. The brigade's
patrolling programme was intensified by night and work to strengthen the
defences of the forward positions with more wire and mines occupied the
daylight hours. The battalions were given one or two days a week, depending on the situation, in which they could call harassing fire from the
American Corps Artillery, using 8 inch or 155 mm howitzers (the
'Persuaders' of the Arkansas National Guard) for precision shoots on
selected targets. The British battalions of the brigade were suffering a
turnover of national servicemen and some of the platoons in rifle companies were down to sixteen or seventeen men. The 1st Royal Australian
Regiment, Lieutenant-Colonel I. Hutchinson, arrived in Korea to
strengthen the brigade but underwent training in the rear before joining.
The infantry also received additional firepower with the introduction of
Browning Machine Gun Platoons to supplement the existing Vickers Medium Machine Gun Platoons. Commonwealth soldiers were given three
days training on these American weapons by the Canadians before manning the guns in the line. Lieutenant-Colonel R. McK. Paterson assumed
command of 16 Field Regiment R.N.Z.A. in March and Lieutenant-Colonel V. W. 'Bill' Barlow of the K.S.L.I. was temporarily loaned to act as
commander of 29 Brigade. As the winter gave way to the spring thaw,
patrol activity increased and all battalions suffered casualties during minor clashes in the Samichon valley.

The 3rd Royal Australians mounted a patrol in force to take Hill 227,
taking with them prefabricated timber to establish a permanent outpost.
Once again the Chinese drenched the hill with artillery fire and the Australians suffered many casualties. General Hassett (then Lieutenant-
Colonel commanding 3rd R.A.R.) remembers: 'I gave it up. Retaking it
was my decision which I later regretted. It wasn't worth the casualties
involved in taking and holding it. I believe it was a mistake to continue
attacking 227 as we continued to do – its capture was no real problem, but
the inevitable heavy defensive fire was certain to come and certain to
cause heavy casualties.'

The K.S.L.I. and the K.O.S.B. were visited by Arthur Helliwell, a
British journalist who wrote rather sensational articles for *The People*, a
Sunday newspaper. Helliwell was one of the very few journalists who
actually visited the front line and shared the troops' trenches for a few
days. 'D' Company of the K.S.L.I. were cited as the men on 'Hungry
Hill', comparing the American combat rations issued to the front line
units with the plethora of fresh food enjoyed by the rear area troops.
Visiting the K.O.S.B. Helliwell composed a very accurate description of

the life of an infantryman in Korea, taking Private Sammy Wilson as a typical sharp-end soldier. These articles, when they eventually came to Korea with the sea mail from Great Britain, were very well received by the men of the infantry battalions concerned who were pleased that someone was able to present an honest picture of their conditions.

Despite the experimental truce period and the apparent lull along the front, the Chinese were determined to demonstrate that they were far from beaten. Captain Richard Hill, temporarily commanding 1 Platoon of 'A' Company, K.O.S.B. remembers:

'A Company 1 K.O.S.B. was out on a limb and could only be supplied at night. The "drill" during the day was that if we spotted a "Chink" on the hillside opposite was to "ring-up" the nearest Centurion tank who promptly fired a 20 pounder shell. I got somewhat bored with this business and, during one of my rare visits to the Q.M., managed to scrounge from him a sniper's rifle complete with telescopic sights (unzeroed!). One bright day I happened to be "attending to nature" on my private "thunder box" dug into the communication trench close to my C.P. I suddenly heard someone running down the trench and a very excited Corporal Pat Devenney (who had won the Military Medal during the Maryang-San battles) said: "Sir, I can see one of them opposite. Can I borrow your sniper's rifle?" "Yes," says I, "but make certain you clean it afterwards." A few seconds later, as I was still "about my business", I heard the familiar "crack-thump" over my head. Seconds later a very white faced Corporal appeared before the "throne" (an Asahi beer box) to inform me that "The b***** had fired at him!" '

On 2nd April 'A' Company of the King's Own Scottish Borderers were subjected to a steady artillery bombardment which increased to a fury between 9.00 p.m. and 9.30 p.m. before dying down. On 4th April the bombardment was repeated to almost exactly the same pattern, dwindling to sporadic shelling by 10.00 p.m. The veterans of Maryang-San recognised the signs and braced themselves for another fierce onslaught. On Saturday 5th April, the Chinese artillery battered the K.O.S.B. positions remorselessly throughout the day. A wireless intercept indicated that the enemy were planning an attack at 11.00 p.m. and the Borderers stood to, ready and waiting. At 9.00 p.m. a single signal shell fell on 'A' Company, Captain A. M. Thorburn, which was on the right of the battalion front, adjacent to the Shropshires. The signal shell heralded an intense thirty-minute artillery barrage. One observer with the Shropshires reported that the enemy's gun flashes extended for over a mile behind the hills West of the Samichon. Defensive fire was c. .ed down in front of the K.O.S.B. and flares were put up to illuminate the area which was soon obscured by whirling smoke and dust. Waves of Chinese infantry came trotting through the artillery fire and were soon in contact with the forward platoons of 'A' Company. After fierce fighting the enemy were beaten off, suffering heavy casualties from the defensive artillery and mortar fire and the supporting machine gun and small arms fire from 'D' Company of the K.O.S.B. and 'A' Company of the K.S.L.I. By midnight the Chinese had been forced to retire and were caught by ranging defensive fire which also prevented reinforcements moving forward to stiffen the attack. This attack on the Borderers became known as the 'MacBeth Attack' since many of the Chinese were carrying foliage as a form of camouflage as they approached their assault line.

This was the last determined enemy operation of any strength in the spring and, between 13th and 14th April, 28 Brigade was relieved in the line by the 25th Canadian Brigade and returned to the Charumul reserve area.

# The Static War

28 Brigade withdrew to the divisional reserve area – in the pouring rain. One of the brigade's battalions occupied an area vacated by a battalion of 29 Brigade to find that the previous occupants had stripped the 'hoochies' and left roofless holes filled with water. A miserable beginning for a rest in reserve. Nevertheless, the brigade settled in and made the best of the bad weather. As the skies cleared, spirits rose and the training programme began. The latest drafts to the battalions were put through their paces. Drill squares were bulldozed over the derelict padi fields and short courses were instigated for those who had attained N.C.O. status during the months in the front line. Repairs and renovations of living bunkers and messes were made and in the Shropshire's area an underground church was excavated and dedicated to St. Chad, after the parent church in Shrewsbury. The altar candlesticks were fashioned from mortar bomb fins and the church boasted a bell, a trophy taken from a Chinese defence position.

Meanwhile, off the South coast of Korea on the island of Koje-do, Communist prisoners-of-war had staged an uprising and had kidnapped the American commandant as a hostage. The situation was serious and on 25th May 'B' Company of the King's Shropshire Light Infantry and 'B' Company of the Royal Canadian Regiment were detached to 'Peterforce' to assist the Americans in reforming the prisoner-of-war camps on Koje-do. The K.S.L.I. regimental account describes the conditions encountered by the Commonwealth troops:

'For some three months no member of the guard force had been inside most of the compounds. The occupants were highly organized and plentifully supplied with spears, knives and other equipment of a kind not normally found in prison camps. Intensive indoctrination was carried out and where this failed in its purpose more violent methods of persuasion were commonplace. The prisoners were quite prepared to accept casualties in the interests of guard baiting. Neither the conditions and facilities in the camps nor the methods of handling prisoners bore much resemblance to those laid down in the Geneva Convention, of which the United States is not a signatory. The steady application of what were to us the normal methods of prisoner control quickly produced excellent results in Compound 66. In an initial show of force the compound was entered and the prisoners' command post demolished. After this there was no real trouble. In due course the compound was cleared of prisoners without difficulty. A mass of weapons, maps and stores was found, also two tunnels and a dead body. The state of the area was such that it had to be cleared by bulldozers before reoccupation. On 25th June,

*Soldiers of B Coy., 1st Bn. King's Shropshire Light Infantry, guarding communist prisoners at the Koje-do P.O.W. Camp, May 1952.*

(IWM KOR 629)

"Peterforce" took over the complete running, including administration, of the new compound. Strict discipline was enforced, the prisoners worked hard on improving amenities and every effort was made to run a normal and peaceful camp. By 10th July, when "Peterforce" left Koje, a great measure of success had been achieved.'

Back in reserve the brigade enjoyed some good weather after the heavy rain of mid-April. ANZAC Day 1952 was celebrated in style. The 1st Battalion of The Royal Australian Regiment, which was undergoing training preparatory to joining the brigade, sent a contingent to join the

*Field Marshal Lord Alexander, British Minister of Defence, visits 28 Commonwealth Brigade, May 1952.*
*From left to right: Maj. Gen. Cassels (Commander 1 Commonwealth Division), Lord Alexander, Maj. Gen. McLaughlin (Commander 1 U.S. Marine Division), Lt. Col. Hassett (C.O. 3 R.A.R.), Lt. Col. Barlow (C.O. 1 K.S.L.I.).*

(AWM HOB 3223)

3rd Battalion and the 16th Field Regiment, R.N.Z.A. Great Britain was represented by the King's Own Scottish Borderers and the occasion was made unique by the presence of the commander of the Turkish Brigade with several of his soldiers. The highlight of the day was a formal parade and wreath-laying ceremony followed by various convivial gatherings well supplied with Asahi and Australian beer.

The 1st Battalion of the Royal Australians, Lieutenant-Colonel Hutchinson, joined the brigade in May, thus bringing it back to its former 'four-square' composition. A Commonwealth Games was held in the reserve area and was attended by Lord Alexander, the British Minister of Defence who was visiting the troops in Korea. The two Australian battalions swept the board with Great Britain (represented by the Shropshires) in second place and New Zealand a close third. One British spectator noted: 'A boxing match under ANZAC auspices is rather a different affair from the English version. Shouting, including a steady flow of encouragement and invective and suitable comments to the referee, is continuous and hearty. Bets are offered and taken freely across the ring and pound notes change hand in considerable numbers. The whole thing is thoroughly uninhibited, most sporting and, unless the spectator has been too heavily indoctrinated in the stricter amateur ethics, great fun.'

This period in reserve, with the fine early summer weather, offered many opportunities for training and sport. Swimming parties were regularly sent back to the Imjin River, a healthy and hygienic practice. During the winter months the soldiers had made infrequent visits to the divisional mobile bath and laundry unit to remove the grime of the line, the summer trips to the river were far more enjoyable and much more frequent. The new arrivals to the brigade were not allowed to enjoy themselves too much and the 1st Royal Australians were put into the line to relieve the Royal Leicesters of 29 Brigade. On 19th June, 1 R.A.R. fired its first shots in anger when one of the machine guns engaged a lone Chinese on a distant hilltop. This initiation was quickly followed by the battalion's first casualty, a soldier killed during an ambush patrol.

With the preponderance of Australians in the brigade it was not surprising when Brigadier T. J. Daly, D.S.O., O.B.E., of the Australian Army, relieved Brigadier 'Long John' MacDonald as commander of the Commonwealth Brigade on 28th June 1952. The growing Antipodean influence was quite evident amongst the British members of the brigade who soon fell into the habit of speaking basic 'Strine'. However, as an Australian officer commented, it was almost impossible for the Australians to assimilate the wide variety of accents which distinguished the speech of their British 'cobbers', ranging from the brogue of the Scots, the sound of Bow bells to the incomprehensible dialects of the North of England.

The halcyon days of reserve in the fine summer weather ended on 29th June when the brigade moved forward to relieve the 25th Canadian Brigade along the comparatively quiet front of the Southern Samichon Valley. The move was a signal for the heavens to open and it rained heavily as the brigade occupied the positions between 29th June and 2nd July. The downpour caused several Canadian-built bunkers to collapse under the weight of the rain-water and many had to be reconstructed by the new occupants.

The 1st Royal Australians had already been in the line with 29 Brigade for more than two weeks and mounted their first operation on 2nd July. Captain P. J. Cook describes Operation 'Blaze':

'It was decided that "A" Company would carry out a company strength daylight raid on 227 on 2 July 1952. The specific aim was

*Mortar pit, 1st Bn. King's Own Scottish Borderers, 1952.*

(IWM KOR 601)

to capture a prisoner. As a participant in the raid I believe a major aim was to demonstrate offensive action, particularly in the centre of the Corps front. In any case we had the Corps Commander, Divisional Commander and Brigade Commander as spectators. The whole divisional artillery was in support. "A" Company was allotted extra riflemen to act as stretcher bearers; Phil Greville with some of his Pioneer Platoon to blow up bunkers and flamethrowers to search into the bunkers. H hour was at 0900 hours and the artillery opened up at 0859 hours. The war diary states, "there were five dropshorts, this was corrected by the fire controller." The cool voice with which the FOO corrected his range won him almost as many marks as those which his guns had just lost. The platoons moving up each side of the front of the hill had been exposed for about twenty minutes and were almost on the top of the hill when the enemy D.F.s, mostly mortar, began. Enemy D.F.s could be slow to come down, probably because of communication difficulties, but they were heavy, sustained and accurate when they did. Platoon Commander Gil Lucas was standing on the roof of one bunker attempting to remove a section of it when it partly collapsed. One of his section commanders, Corporal Patch, was shot in the chest trying to enter the doorway. Corporal Taylor took a section 100 yards beyond the crest to prevent enemy reinforcement of the hill. Casualties were growing, almost all due to enemy mortar D.F.s. Enemy mortar bombs could be seen by those near the top of the hill falling in long black streaks. Due to the slope, a lot of these fell much further down the slope than the uphill observer. Our counter-battery programme was not effective due to the fact that the enemy weapons were well dug in. As an hour went by the enemy fire increased. When we chided the gunners about this later they replied, "It would have been worse if we weren't helping." This became a battalion expression for inconclusive activities that were designed to be helpful. At 1015 hours the Company Commander David Thomson was ordered to withdraw the company, which was just as well. Casualties were being taken over a wide area, many amongst the stretcher parties on the rear slope and around the minefield gaps. If we had remained much longer there would not have been enough fit people to carry the thirty-seven casualties off the hill. The two obvious approaches were well registered and we received a warm exit. The minefield gaps, which were no secret due

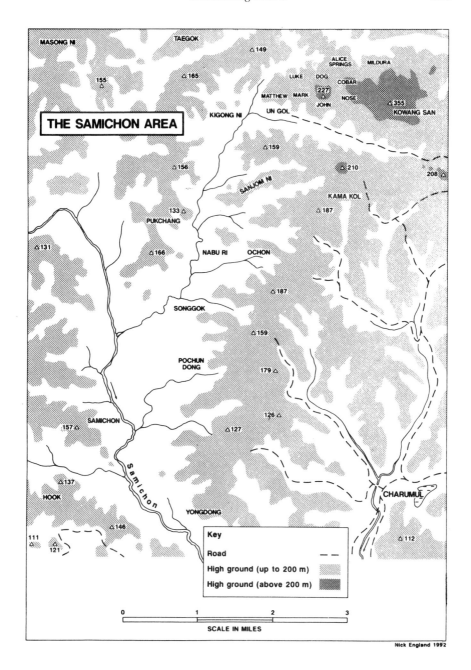

THE SAMICHON AREA

MASONG NI

TAEGOK
△ 149

ALICE
SPRINGS    MILDURA

155
△

△ 165

LUKE   DOG
COBAR
227
MATTHEW  MARK    NOSE
JOHN

△ 355
KOWANG SAN

KIGONG NI

UN GOL

△ 159

△ 156

210

208
△

SANJOM NI

KAMA KOL

133 △
PUKCHANG

△ 187

△ 131

△ 166    NABU RI    OCHON

△ 187

SONGGOK

△ 159

POCHUN
DONG

179 △

126 △

SAMICHON

157 △

△ 127

S
a
m
i
c
h
o
n

△ 137

HOOK

YONGDONG

CHARUMUL

111
△

△ 146

△ 112

△
121

| Key | |
|---|---|
| Road | − − − |
| High ground (up to 200 m) | |
| High ground (above 200 m) | |

0        1        2        3

SCALE IN MILES

Nick England 1992

to months of worn tracks through them, were hot areas. A lesson learnt here was that the walking wounded must walk. The R.M.O. Captain Nordstrom, and Padre Frank Shine worked effectively in the Company Aid Post area with the company stretcher bearers. A priority of need via jeep ambulances to a helicopter pad 2,000 yards back behind a line of hills saved lives. The company medical orderly, Nelligan, received a well-earned M.I.D. and three wounds for his work that morning, which happened to be his twenty-first birthday. It is noteworthy that a stretcher party that went out an hour after the attack to retrieve the only body left beyond the minefields was obviously observed by the enemy and not fired upon. The total casualties were 3 killed and 34 wounded in one and a half hours. The company acted very coolly during its prolonged raid. We did not capture a prisoner. There were no more daylight company size raids in the Commonwealth Division.'

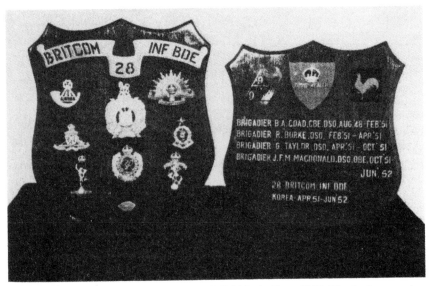

*Shields made by 16 Infantry Workshops R.E.M.E. in June 1952. The badges on the left are: K.S.L.I., R.A.R., K.O.S.B., R.N.Z.A., Indian Field Ambulance, R. Signals, R. Engineers, R.E.M.E. On the right 27 Brigade ("Fire Brigade"), 40 (Bantam) Division and Commonwealth Division.*

This operation confirmed Lieutenant-Colonel Hassett's opinions on the advisability of attempting to retake Hill 227.

The other battalions of the brigade were committed to intensive night patrol activity in an effort to obtain prisoners. Lieutenant Pack, Corporal Axe and Privates Punyer and Luckhurst of the Shropshires were killed when they 'bumped' the enemy in the river valley on 9th July; Corporal Newton succeeded in extricating the patrol after a fierce fire fight and was recommended for the Military Medal.

The King's Own Scottish Borderers spent a very short time in the line and were relieved by the 1st R.A.R. on the Naechon feature on 10th July. The K.O.S.B. retired to work on the reserve defence positions before leaving Korea after some fifteen months and the brigade was temporarily reduced to three battalions pending the arrival of the 1st Battalion of The Royal Fusiliers. On 25th July the K.O.S.B. gave a party to present silver cigarette boxes and salvers to the Royal Australian Regiment, the Royal

*General Lawton Collins, U.S. Army Chief of Staff, with Brigadier Thomas Daly, commander 28 Commonwealth Brigade; Maj. Gen. A. J. Cassels, commander 1 COMWEL. Div., in the rear. 16 July 1952.*

(IWM MH 28036)

New Zealand Artillery and the Indian Army Medical Corps. On Minden Day, 1st August, with roses in their bonnets, the Borderers handed over their reserve position to the Royal 22e Regiment of Canada and left the divisional area for Pusan, there to embark on the 12th. The King's Own Scottish Borderers had gained one Victoria Cross, five Distinguished Service Orders, four Military Crosses, three Distinguished Conduct Medals and twelve Military Medals but left 65 of the battalion in the U.N. Cemetery at Pusan and had 228 men wounded.

Lieutenant-Colonel Hassett, of the 3rd Royal Australians, also left the brigade on 11th July, passing command of the battalion to Lieutenant-Colonel R. L. Hughes. 'B' Company of the K.S.L.I., Major Bancroft, duly returned from Koje-do to relieve a company of the R22eR (The 'Van Doos') which had been borrowed from 25 Brigade to hold the Yong Dong hill. Second-Lieutenant Parry took a patrol of 'A' Company, K.S.L.I. through the Chinese lines to lay an ambush in their rear; although

*A patrol of 2 Platoon, A Company, 1st Bn. King's Shropshire Light Infantry, enjoy a last smoke before going out; 2lt. J. D. Parry, Pte. J. Norris, Pte. G. Hodgson, Sgt. B. Skelton. July 1952.*

(IWM KOR 602)

executed with considerable skill no Chinese fell into their hands and the patrol returned safely after lying up for several hours. During the daylight hours the troops were kept hard at work in the summer heat thickening the brigade's defensive wire and minefields whilst the gunners, of both sides, kept themselves busy by engaging opportunity targets and laying harassing fire. The Chinese gunners seemed to pick on 'A' Company of the K.S.L.I. particularly – although little real damage was done. After the departure of the K.O.S.B. the Shropshires were anticipating their relief but soldiered on patiently. Captain Pennel led a patrol from 'D' Company across the Samichon to search the hills around Point 157 but found no sign of the enemy. Even so, the Shropshires were still taking casualties during brisk little patrol engagements and lost three men on 27th and 28th July. On 9th August the K.S.L.I. took two prisoners who were caught in the minefield but, again, they turned out to be more deserters coming in to surrender.

By this time, 16 Field Regiment, R.N.Z.A., had undergone an almost complete change of personnel but the 'new Kiwi gunners' were as keen and proficient as their predecessors. An artillery regiment has the flesh and blood of an infantry battalion but greatly exceeds it in firepower and mobility. The infantry and the artillery are complementary; neither can assume the role of the other. They are so interdependent that the success of any operation depends on an integrated effort on the part of both. 16 Field Regiment had its forward observation officers deployed with the front line companies of the Australian and British battalions of 28 Brigade. During the 'static war' period it had become a standard 'drill' for the brigade commander to 'take post' in the caravan of his artillery adviser, the commanding officer of 16 Field Regiment. This was because of the relatively sophisticated nature and reliability of the artillery communication and operational control network in instant touch with not only the forward defences (through the forward observation officers and observation posts) but also with the battalion command posts where the affiliated battery commanders were at their posts with the respective battalion commanders. Each had the ability to call up within minutes not only the fire-power of an affiliated battery of eight guns but, when required for 'Mike Targets', the twenty-four guns of 16 Field Regiment. The support could be increased to the seventy-two guns of the Commonwealth Divisional artillery with the additional 5.5 inch medium guns and 4.2 inch mortars of the Royal Artillery. Corps artillery could also be called upon when available with the heavier 155 mm and 8 inch howitzers.

During the night of 13th/14th August, 'B' Company of the 3rd R.A.R. Captain R. P. Richardson, launched a raid on the Chinese position on Hill

75 across the Samichon valley where they met with strong opposition. The enemy called down mortar fire and one Australian was killed, fourteen wounded and one missing after the company had withdrawn. The Assault Platoon commander of the 1st RAR, Lieutenant Phil Greville, was captured on the night of the 22nd/23rd of August when his party was ambushed whilst working on minefield fences in front of the battalion. On 24th August it began to rain heavily! The downpour continued unabated and almost brought operations to a complete halt as well as causing havoc in the rear. Unlike the heavy rains of August 1951, traffic across the Imjin was maintained – although the timber trestle bridge at 'Teal' lost two spans to the flood waters. The bridges at 'Pintail', 'Widgeon' and 'Gloucester Crossing' withstood the spate and remained in use. Even the normally shallow Samichon was transformed into a raging torrent and the 3rd Royal Australians almost lost a patrol on 26th August when they tried to make a crossing.

On 25th August the 1st Battalion of The Royal Fusiliers, Lieutenant-Colonel Stevens, relieved the K.S.L.I. in the front line. The Shropshires retired to the divisional rear area on the first stage of their journey home. The 1st Battalion of The Durham Light Infantry had arrived in Korea and their advance party met the K.S.L.I. in the rest area. Before leaving the brigade the King's Shropshire Light Infantry held a farewell parade and presented miniature silver bugles to the Royal Australians, the New Zealand gunners and the Indian Field Ambulance. The commanding officer of the Shropshires, Lieutenant-Colonel 'Bill' Barlow, unwillingly left another souvenir of his battalion's tour in Korea; the leaping silver fox which had adorned the bonnet of his jeep unaccountably disappeared before the K.S.L.I. withdrew to the rear. The Shropshires moved South to Seaforth Camp at Pusan and there paid tribute to the fifty-three of their comrades buried in the U.N. Cemetery. The battalion had also suffered 161 wounded and three missing in action but had gained eighteen major awards for gallantry during their sixteen months in Korea. Colonel Barlow reminded a press reporter that his battalion had been at war: 'People in England seem to think there is nothing much happening in Korea, whereas there is a full-scale war just as bloody and bitter as anything in World War II.' On 9th September, the King's Shropshire Light Infantry were officially relieved in the brigade by the 1st Battalion of the Durham Light Infantry, Lieutenant-Colonel P. J. Jeffreys, D.S.O., O.B.E., and the K.S.L.I. sailed for England on 18th September.

Major-General 'Gentleman Jim' Cassels, the first commander of the Commonwealth Division, relinquished his command on 7th September to Major-General M. M. Alston-Roberts-West, C.D., D.S.O. General

Cassels was a popular and capable commander and was held in high esteem by all the units of the Commonwealth Division and by those American officers under whom he served. During the month of September the Chinese maintained their artillery 'stonks' and brought their heavier guns into action. On 5th September the 1st Royal Australians were subjected to a fierce bombardment which spread along the brigade front. The same night the 3rd Royal Australians sent a patrol into the Samichon valley which met thirty of the enemy, one Australian was killed and nine wounded during the ensuing fight. 'C' Company of the 1st R.A.R. mounted a patrol on the night of 13th September but ran into a Chinese ambush. The patrol fought back vigorously and put the enemy to flight, wounding at least two and Lance-Corporal McCarthy, the patrol commander, succeeded in taking the battalion's first prisoner. Later that night the Chinese laid heavy artillery fire on the 3rd Royal Australians' positions and brought long-range guns to bear on the brigade's rear area. The New Zealanders' gun lines were hit and 'R' Battery suffered one gunner killed, two wounded and a fourth who was to die of his wounds. The Indian Field Ambulance was also hit, killing one man and wounding seven others, two of whom refused treatment for face and ankle injuries so that they could assist with the wounded coming in from the front. One of the Indian doctors was amazed by one walking wounded soldier who had a serious mortar injury to his neck. 'If I practised for ten years I could not pierce your neck where that blast did without killing you. Son, you are just plain lucky.'

Brigadier Daly recalls:

'I had previously, on a number of occasions, urged the C.O. of the Field Ambulance, Colonel Rangaraj, to move his unit further to the rear since I felt that he was much too exposed where he was. After the shelling I again suggested that he should move. He replied that it was out of the question. I told him that I understood that it was a matter of his unit's pride but what about his patients? However, the Ambulance remained where it was. Although it was, for all practical purposes, a part of 28 Brigade it was actually in support and not under my command. Therefore I couldn't order him back!'

Whilst the 'veteran' battalions of the brigade were probing the enemy across the Samichon, the 'new Boys', the Royal Fusiliers, were discovering what life was like in the front line.

'The King's Shropshire Light Infantry had handed over hilltop positions as a going-concern, the Fusiliers found deep entrenchments and bomb-proof dugouts. Barbed-wire hedgerows discouraged unwelcome callers; minefields further ensured that the locality's tone would not easily be lowered. Westwards the ground sloped off for a quarter-mile to the valley floor where a usually fordable river ran laterally. Beyond, on other scrub-covered, inscrutable hills were the inscrutable Chinese, unseen by day and – initially – unenterprising by night. It was very quiet: 1914-1918 men would have thought it an idyllic spot, with all-round defence in depth and pleasing aspects. The young N.S. men did not pretend to like it. It was inferior to Hackney. This was the drill: six weeks forward, working night shift and sleeping all day; then six weeks in brigade reserve. Forward, a man ate vastly of tinned foods and tasted nothing fresh but he kept remarkably fit. Once a week he had a day off at 'A' Echelon, two miles back where, on a portable screen, he might see a "flick" to remind him that such things as Odeons existed in a better world. And about once a week each platoon furnished a fighting patrol. During that first spell up the enemy refused to co-operate. The patrols came back through the wire at the tail of the night, unblooded and frustrated, to an unreasonable society which insisted that a man clean his weapons and kit and even shave before turning in. Older soldiers accepted the "bull" and seemingly needless chores; until the shooting started they had to be kept busy or life on the wired-in hill-tops would be intolerable. The youngsters did not comprehend the purpose; they groused at being chivvied about, at practically everything except the Chinese, whose inactivity was the chief cause of their discontent. This "phoney" war was bad for them. It lacked the one thing needed to round off their training – enemy fire. True, the area was sometimes mortared and hidden snipers would smarten up chaps who disdained to use communication trenches and sauntered above ground (men walking in pairs drew fire; never the solitary promenader). Generally the young Fusiliers fell into the error of thinking lightly of the invisible Chinese, adopting a couldn't-care-less attitude about the whole thing. Korea was a bore.'

The other 'new boys' to the brigade, the Durhams, occupied a more lively sector of the front line. At the end of September the D.L.I. moved forward to relieve the 1st Royal Australians for ten days. 'Our ten days in the line

were relatively quiet, although we suffered a few casualties, including one
N.C.O. who was killed. Major J. W. Kelley, who was in command of 'D'
Company, was hit by a mortar bomb and was evacuated.' On 29th September the 3rd Royal Australians carried the fight to the enemy when one
of their patrols made contact with some forty to fifty Chinese. The enemy
took heavy casualties in the fight and two Australians were killed and
three wounded. This spell of duty in the front line came to an end early in
October and 28 Brigade was relieved along the Samichon by 29 Brigade.
The brigade returned to the reserve area by 5th October.

Back in reserve again, the new battalions underwent further training but
managed to enjoy several entertaining social functions and visits to other
units of the brigade. After some two years at war in Korea, it was decided
to equip British soldiers with steel helmets. Hitherto, Commonwealth
troops had gone into battle wearing berets, slouch-hats, tam-o'-shanters or
cap comforters; steel helmets were something which only the Americans
wore and as long as each soldier carried his personal weapon and at least
fifty rounds of ammunition – reminiscent of Wellington's attitude in the
Peninsula – he was deemed to be ready for battle. The unwieldy steel
helmet was considered to be a liability in the days of climbing and
assaulting Korean hills and was awkward to wear on patrols; however, the
advent of Chinese heavy artillery and the static, troglodyte existence of
the front-line troops dictated that some adequate measure of personal
protection was necessary. A number of American bullet-proof waistcoats,
or 'flak-jackets', were also made available, mainly for standing patrols.
During this period in reserve, Lieutenant-Colonel Hutchinson handed
over command of the 1st Royal Australians to Lieutenant-Colonel M.
Austin and, on 27th October, the 3rd Royal Australians were brought out
of the reserve to take over from the Welch Regiment of 29 Brigade who
were withdrawn from the line preparatory to their departure from Korea at
the end of their tour of duty. Meanwhile, the New Zealand gunners – as
part of the divisional artillery – remained in action to support the Canadian Brigade who were occupying the northern sector of the divisional
line around Kowang-San. A company of the Royal Fusiliers was detached
from the battalion to serve as an immediate reserve for the Canadians at
the 'sharp-end'.

Between 27th October and 2nd November, 28 Brigade moved up to
relieve the Canadians, returning to 'their' higher hills which the brigade
had taken over one year earlier. However, the relieving troops were not
at all happy with the state of the defences left by 25 Brigade which,
in accordance with the divisional roster, was always relieved by the

Commonwealth Brigade. Not only were many of the weapon pits, mine-fields, wire and bunkers in a poor condition but, more seriously, the Chinese were 'leaning on the wire' every evening at dusk. The Canadians had been under close pressure in the Kowang-San area and their method of operation was different to that of 28 Brigade. Nevertheless, 28 Brigade set to work to make good the defences but it took a good two weeks of backbreaking toil to effect repairs with casualties from unrecorded mine-fields. Of greater urgency was the need to initiate a programme of aggressive patrolling to regain control of no-man's-land.

The Royal Fusiliers received their baptism of fire at the beginning of November. 'A new factor entered into the hitherto boring routine of patrolling when a party returned and reported two killed. The same thing happened the next night and was repeated on the third. War had suddenly become serious; the shaken N.S. men came to realise that a slap-happy Fusilier was likely to become a dead one.' The Fusiliers mounted a raid on Point 133, across the Samichon valley, and killed some fifteen Chinese with a loss of thirteen Fusiliers wounded and three missing.

The divisional front had been extended to the South, across the Samichon River to include a hill known as 'The Hook'. 29 Brigade occupied this sector adjacent to the 1st U.S. Marine Division. The Black Watch held 'The Hook' and were subjected to very heavy Chinese attacks on 18th November. Major Hassett, of the Royal New Zealand Artillery, recalls that the Kiwi gunners were in action to support the Highlanders and on the night of 18th/19th November fired upwards of 400 rounds per gun, mainly V.T. (air-burst) to fall on the attacking masses. This was the heaviest bombardment fired by 16 Field Regiment in 1952 and played a major part in the Black Watch's successful defence of the hill.

The Durham Light Infantry mounted a raid called Operation 'Blaydon'.

'A raid was planned on Point 133 to take place on the night 21st/22nd November with the aim of capturing a prisoner, of killing the enemy and blowing up a tunnel which the Chinese were known to be constructing. 'A' Company were chosen for the task and went about the business of planning and rehearsing in secrecy. The plan was for Company H.Q. and No 3 Platoon under the command of Major C.P. Donoghue, M.C., to occupy a firm base to the Southwest of the feature. No. 1 Platoon, Second-Lieutenant B. D. Perrott, was to move round the left of the objective and assault from an F.U.P. previously reported clear by a patrol commanded by Captain. E. B. Burini. The movement of the assaulting

platoon was to be muffled by fairly continuous M.M.G. fire. Once
in position, and ready to assault, the platoon commander was to
pass a codeword by wireless, which would cause a swift 'crump'
from supporting arms on and about the objective. This was to be
followed by a searchlight lighting up the objective by the light of
which No. 1 Platoon would attack. Five minutes later, the platoon
was to withdraw, its task completed, through the firm base. When
the operation started the assault platoon found themselves behind
schedule on the start line and were forced to call for the postpone-
ment of the supporting fire programme. This was unfortunately
misread and one tank fired six rounds before it could be stopped. It
was felt afterwards that this may have alerted the Chinese on the
objective. In the assault No. 1 Platoon were engaged at the outset
by L.M.G. fire and grenades and a number of casualties were
incurred among the leading men. These enemy posts were quickly
overcome, however, and the platoon made its way on to the crest
of the hill. This was encircled by a deep communication trench
which was difficult to scale, forcing the platoon to split up into
parties which ran right and left down the trench. A number of
Chinese were seen to disappear through trapdoors, but apart from
occasional bursts of firing the hill appeared to be ours. After some
minutes, when no success signal had been received from either the
demolition party or the "snatchers", the platoon was ordered to
withdraw. As they passed through the firm base, heavy fire fell on
the objective once more. The raid was successful in that it captured a steep, strongly held hill; it failed to capture a prisoner
because after the initial fire fight the enemy, as is his normal
custom, went into deep dugouts, preferring the risk of slow evic-
tion action to that of fighting it out above ground. Corporal Moore
was among the first to reach the objective during the assault and
after the signal to withdraw had been given, he returned to the hill
alone to search for a wounded man. By this time the hill was under
heavy fire from the enemy and from our own guns who were
covering the withdrawal. With complete disregard for his own
safety, he found a wounded man and carried him on his back for a
distance of over 800 yards. For his gallant conduct, he received an
immediate award of the Military Medal.'

Further raids were mounted on the Chinese positions. On 25th November
the Royal Fusiliers and the 1st Royal Australians co-ordinated in a two-

prong assault; Operation 'Beat Up' by the Australians and 'Pimlico' by the Fusiliers. The Fusiliers' objective was a Chinese position on Kigong-Ni whilst the Australians launched another raid on Hill 227. 'D' Company of the Royal Fusiliers, Major Michael Chard, fielded two platoons commanded by Second-Lieutenants Christopher Hoare and A. de Roper.

'Pimlico's object was the capture of prisoners. The two platoons went out in steady rain and darkness and moved slowly forward to the chosen objective. A firm base was set up between the lines and the platoons crept forward. Sheer bad luck arranged that the Chinese should have two, and possibly three, companies heading for the British positions at the same time. The opposing parties bumped into each other. Almost every man on both sides carried an automatic weapon and grenades and the Chinese were maybe ten times as numerous. Burp guns, Stens and Brownings answered each other at zero ranges. The platoons which had advanced and reached their objective were heavily shelled and were forced to retire to their base, which was besieged by this time. There was intense hand-to-hand fighting and heavy casualties were suffered by both sides. Second-Lieutenant Christopher Hoare was killed and his half-platoon surrounded. His men occupied a rise and shot back at the flashes of the enemy's weapons. One of them, Fusilier George Hodkinson, a nineteen-year-old wireless operator from Bermondsey, calmly reported the situation to those in the battalion area. Within the ring of fire the Fusiliers' numbers steadily decreased. Hodkinson continued to keep H.Q. informed of events; as unflurried as a man calling numbers at housie-housie, and his reports were interlarded with cheerful Cockney understatement. He learned of preparations for a rescue sortie and coolly commented that there were too many Chinese in between for it to succeed. When he received an order for survivors to break out and get back as best they could he firmly stated that such action was out of the question – the wounded could not be abandoned. It became clear to the listeners that Hodkinson regarded the position as lost. Large numbers of the enemy appeared near at hand. He reported "This is it – out." The "out" meant that there would be no further message but Hodkinson's set was still transmitting and shortly afterwards the officer commanding the Fusiliers' 'D' Company heard his last words: "They're coming!" At 4.30 a.m. it was decided to break off the engagement. After an hour's bitter fighting the Fusiliers were able to force a way through the Chinese cordon and return to their own lines.'

The Royal Fusiliers lost fourteen men killed, twenty wounded and eight missing, including Fusilier Hodkinson who was wounded twice and captured by the Chinese.

Meanwhile, 10 Platoon of the 1st Royal Australians, under Lieutenant E. Boyd, gained its objective on Hill 227. However, true to form, the Chinese brought heavy defensive fire to bear and the platoon was forced to withdraw with four wounded. Sergeant Corcoran was recommended for a Mention in Despatches for his evacuation of the wounded men under enemy artillery fire. The New Zealand gunners replied to the Chinese barrage, firing 5,126 rounds in the twenty-four hour period and, on the morning of 26th November, General West, the divisional commander, fired 16 Field Regiment's 500,000th round at a target selected by Brigadier Daly. The 500,000 rounds represented 30 rounds per gun per day for the 22 months that the regiment had been involved in the Korean campaign. By 25th June 1953, seven months later, when the 750,000th round was fired the average had gone up to 35 rounds per gun per day.

These aggressive actions drove the Chinese back into their side of no-man's-land and Brigadier Daly was able to claim:

'It is worth recording that the Brigade was never attacked during my period of command. Any attempt by the Chinese to form up for an assault – and there were a number – were detected by standing or fighting patrols and dispersed by artillery fire. As a result of all this, General West offered me the alternative of remaining on the 355-159 positions for as long as the Division remained in the line. This was, of course, the vital ground for the sector and we held it thereafter with two battalions forward and arranged our own reliefs. The only drawback was that Brigade H.Q. was never rested!'

The divisional line was adjusted on 29th November. Instead of the former practice of having two complete brigades forward and the third brigade in reserve, it was decided to commit all three brigades to the front with one battalion of each in reserve. 29 Brigade held the Southern part of the Samichon valley, 25 Canadian Brigade the central area and 28 Commonwealth Brigade the Northern end with the higher hills. 28 Brigade, again a 'four-square' formation, had two battalions in the line and two in reserve.

The Durhams withdrew to the brigade reserve area. The weather had already become quite cold and, on the day of the move, it began to snow. 'Thus in early December we found ourselves once again in the reserve area – one of which we had known before – but which was not improved by six inches of snow and a temperature well below zero. A few days spent in pitching tents, digging hoochies and installing stoves soon restored it to its previous state of semi-comfort, however, and we were able to concentrate on a variety of interesting projects.'

In the front line, the 1st Royal Australians occupying the 355 area also undertook an 'interesting project' in the snow and frost.

'On the night 10/11 December 1952, Joe Mann's "B" Company carried out a deep company raid code-named "Fauna" on an enemy spur known as "Flora". Due to our aggressive night fighting patrols over the last month we now controlled no-man's-land. The plan was to move down to the valley floor which, due to the size of 355, was over a kilometre distant; then West along the valley floor for a kilometre; and then swing North for almost a kilometre behind "Flora" spur. The assault was to be through the enemy outpost from the rear. It was estimated that the enemy strength was about fifteen. With skilful navigation the company followed its route successfully. However, partly due to steep, frozen, slippery ground the operation took longer than expected.'

'B' Company penetrated the Chinese defences and succeeded in destroying several bunkers and emplacements. Some ten to twenty of the enemy were killed before the Chinese rallied and offered strong opposition. One officer (Captain John Salmon of the Royal Australian Artillery who was serving with 16 Field Regiment, R.N.Z.A.) and twenty-one soldiers were wounded and two men missing before Major Mann brought his company back across the valley into the Australian lines. 'On their return to our lines Bruce Hearn's "C" Company sent two platoons down the forward slope of 355 to help carry up the casualties as it was now daylight. No prisoner was captured but again we demonstrated our control of no-man's land.' Again, the Kiwi gunners supported the raid but were also called upon to lay defensive fire for the 1st Republic of Korea Division on the brigade's right flank. More than 3,400 rounds were fired on 11th December to help the Koreans resist a very strong enemy attack.

During the month of December, the 60th Indian Field Ambulance bade farewell to its commanding officer, Lieutenant-Colonel Arcot Rangaraj, who returned to India after commanding the unit since its arrival in Korea in December 1950. Colonel Rangaraj was awarded the Indian decoration of the Mahar-Vir Chakra for his outstanding service and took with him the high esteem of the British, Australian and New Zealand members of the brigade and of the whole Commonwealth Division – and many of the United Nations forces as well.

The 3rd Royal Australians relieved the 1st Battalion on 355 in the latter half of December. During their two months on 'Little Gibraltar' (Kowang-San), 1 R.A.R. had suffered 18 killed, 74 wounded and the 2 men missing during Operation 'Fauna'. Instead of withdrawing into the brigade reserve area the 1st Royal Australians were sent well to the rear, back to Corps reserve, to occupy an American 'rest' area called Camp Casey. The 1st R.A.R. were, in effect, the advance party for a complete Commonwealth Divisional withdrawal to the Corps reserve.

'During the Christmas period, the brigade received its first seasonal greetings in card form – from the enemy. From the night of the 16th/17th December until December the 31st 1952, the division was greeted with cards, pamphlets, placards, banners, gifts, innumerable broadcasts and a Christmas tree which was presented to the 1st Battalion, Royal Fusiliers. Many of these pamphlets and cards were dropped by enemy aircraft.' The Chinese again took advantage of the festive season to launch another propaganda offensive and, since the first propaganda exercise of Christmas 1951, their methods and materials had improved considerably. Broadcasting over loudspeaker systems from the front line was a technique which was to be developed during the coming months. An antiquated aircraft – 'Bedcheck Charlie' – had flown over the forward positions occasionally, usually at dusk, and seemed to bear a charmed life although it did drop hand grenades which rarely did any damage. Christmas passed fairly peacefully and the British members of the brigade were the recipients of long-range seasonal cheer, enjoying bottles of beer donated by the *Melbourne Sun* to the men in Korea.

The Durham Light Infantry spent Christmas in the brigade reserve and reported:

'Certainly one of the refreshing aspects of reserve is the Regimental Canteen. All manner of goods from tinned fruit and packets of tea, to cameras, kimonos and crockery sets may be bought there, while the basic requirement of beer is supplied in enormous quantities. Perhaps the person who owes most to the Korean War is the proprietor of the Asahi breweries in Tokyo – his takings must be enormous. One of the chief pastimes of all regiments in Korea (particularly in reserve) is the setting alight of Officers' Messes. The very nature of the materials used to build and warm such places makes ultimate conflagration inevitable, but it is trying to stand and watch one's only hope of comfort being razed to the ground. The plop of exploding brandy bottles is familiar to many of us – it is a sad, melancholy noise which lives long in the memory.'

In contrast, the acting Bishop of Korea, the Right Reverend Arthur E. Chadwell, visited brigade units to conduct seasonal services and also confirmed several soldiers during his tour of the Commonwealth Brigade in the front line.

Nineteeen fifty-three dawned frostily. The first action of any note on the brigade front fell to 'B' Company of the 3rd Royal Australian Regiment. A patrol commanded by Lieutenant D. F. Lloyd was ambushed by the

*B Coy., 1 D.L.I., Christmas Dinner 1952.*

Lt. Col. R. G. Atkinson, O.B.E., M.C.

Chinese but Lieutenant Lloyd, although wounded twice, managed to gather his men and bring them back to the Australian positions. During the second week of the new year, the brigade front was heavily shelled and, on 14th January, a patrol from the 3rd Royal Australians encountered an unknown number of the enemy on the Northern slopes of Hill 227. A brisk fire fight developed and the patrol withdrew. A second patrol was sent out shortly afterwards to recover some wounded men but also came under intense Chinese fire. The New Zealand gunners were quick to support the recovery party by laying smoke and defensive fire to cover the operation. Nevertheless, 3 R.A.R. suffered one killed, five wounded and one missing during this brief but bitter engagement.

On the night of 23rd January another patrol of the 3rd Royal Australians, operating to the Northwest of Hill 355, met five Chinese and promptly killed two and wounded another with no Australian casualties. The following day, 24th January, 'A' Company of the 3rd R.A.R. mounted another 'snatch' raid in the same area. The patrol rehearsed the operation carefully and moved out with a 'snatch' group of a sergeant and four men protected by two cover groups, each of thirteen men, all under the command of Lieutenant Frank Smith. The 'snatch' group penetrated the Chinese lines and encountered two sentries who would not be taken prisoner and had to be killed. The alarm was raised and the patrol received a savage counter-attack. Artillery was called down but, in the confused night fighting, one cover group was surrounded by Chinese whilst the other group surprised a party of twenty Chinese and killed them all. The struggle continued in the darkness and Lieutenant Smith was killed whilst gallantly covering the withdrawal of his patrol; Sergeant E. J. Morrison fought off several attempts by the enemy to cut off his retreat and succeeded in bringing back eighteen members of the patrol by 1.30 a.m. on 25th January. Sergeant Morrison was awarded the Distinguished Conduct Medal for his courage and inspiring leadership – and was later to win a bar to this award in Vietnam. 3 R.A.R. lost thirteen men during this encounter but killed an estimated ninety Chinese – 'mainly owing to the aggressive attitude of the Australians.'

Meanwhile, orders had been issued for the 1st Commonwealth Division to withdraw to the Corps reserve, the first time the division had been relieved in the line since its formation in July 1951. The move back began on 29th January and the division's positions were taken over by the 2nd U.S. Infantry Division – which included the French battalion. By 31st January the Commonwealth Division had occupied rest camps far to the South of the front line, although the divisional artillery was left in the old area to support the newly arrived Americans.

16th Field Regiment, R.N.Z.A., was allocated to support the U.S. 9th
Regimental Combat Team, the 'Manchus', a brigade-sized formation
which had the Thai Battalion attached and occupied the Kowang-San area.
The 'Manchus' had one battalion on 355 and another on Hill 159 with a
third battalion in reserve. The Americans were impressed by the British
system of controlling artillery fire, which differed markedly from their
own in its speed and fluency and the appointment of relatively senior
artillery advisers to the infantry commanders at all levels from division to
battalion and below if necessary. The Kiwi forward observation officers
were thoroughly familiar with the area and their advice was invaluable to
the newcomers. Lieutenant-Colonel J. Burns, M.B.E., assumed command
of 16 Field Regiment in February when Lieutenant-Colonel Paterson
completed his tour of duty and returned to New Zealand. Colonel Burns
remembers Saint Patrick's Day, 1953:

'On the eve of Saint Patrick's Day one of the 'Manchu' reserve
battalions was routinely ordered up to relieve the battalion on 355
during the night. Earlier, on the 16th, Captain Vern Duley with
the battalion H.Q. on 355 reported the sighting of some Chicoms
in their forward trench apparently consulting a map. This advice
prompted the upgrading of the artillery defensive fire tasks round
the perimeter. The battalion relief, however, was well under way
by this time. The anticipated Chinese assault came in the early
hours accompanied by devastating artillery and mortar fire. The
Chinese infantry swarmed over the forward defences facing Hill
227, hurling grenades down the dugout chimneys and high explosive satchel charges into the entrances and trenches. Immediate counter-attack was difficult because of the battalion relief in
progress but the guns were already in action, controlled by the
forward observation posts. Tons of high explosive, both airburst
and groundburst, descended on the assaulting troops and a lethal
curtain of fire was laid across the valley to deny the enemy any
chance of effective reinforcement. During the battle, Captain
Duley reported a flashing light on 227 immediately in front of his
OP. He reacted by calling for an "Uncle Target Scale 5" (i.e. five
rounds gunfire from the whole of the divisional artillery). Subsequently, the intelligence staff reported a radio intercept from the
Chinese that their main body could not proceed with the attack as
they had been heavily hit by artillery fire.'

The 16th Field Regiment fired 4,600 rounds during this action and was credited with many of the casualties inflicted on the enemy, thus breaking the attack on the 9th R.C.T.

> 'During this same night of March 17, Gunner W. L. Clarke won an immediate Military Medal. He drove his jeep up and down a heavily shelled road to evacuate wounded American soldiers. The regiment at the time was firing in support of the Americans on "Little Gibraltar Hill" who were under heavy attack. Gunner Clarke was checking the artillery telephone cables which ran up an open valley next to the hill. The battle was raging fiercely and the area was being shelled continuously when Gunner Clarke approached a partly overrun American platoon. He saw wounded being evacuated to the rear and he helped to take them out with his jeep. From that time on, Gunner Clarke voluntarily drove his jeep from forward to the rear of the platoon position no fewer than ten times in spite of the fact that the enemy were in occupation of the centre of the position. On these trips he evacuated thirty-one casualties and on each return trip he brought forward much-needed supplies and ammunition. Each journey was made under heavy shell and mortar fire and, in the early stages, under enemy machine-gun fire. Before the division was replaced in the line by the returning Commonwealth Division, its commander, Major-General James C. Fry, presented two Divisional Certificates – "The Order of The Indian Head" to members of the regiment. At a special presentation parade, he described its work in support of his division as "Magnificent".'

Colonel Burns 'in recognition of his special place in regimental continuity, tradition and *esprit de corps*' was created a 'Distinguished Member of the 9th Infantry Regiment' and understands that the 9th Infantry Regiment still drink a toast to the Kiwis as a permanent part of their dining-in ritual. Captain Duley was awarded the Military Cross for his actions on Kowang-San and various American and French awards were later made to other members of the Commonwealth Divisional artillery.

Meanwhile, well to the South, the rest of 28 Brigade spent the first half of February winterising the accommodation and equipment in the reserve camps; by the middle of the month a training programme was in full swing. The Durhams were not impressed by Camp Casey: 'At first sight it seemed an unlovely place – unpleasantly situated in a dust bowl at the convergence of all the prevailing winds in Korea – an enormous sprawling shanty town with row upon row of tents, with here and there a corrugated iron hut graced with the lagoon-like name of a "tropical shell". The whole was surrounded with a ragged barbed wire fence reminiscent of the worst type of concentration camp' – although General Daly recalls that 'Camp Casey wasn't as bad as the Durhams suggest!'

During this unreal period of training well behind the front line, the brigade underwent several changes of personalities. Brigadier J. G. N. Wilton, D.S.O., O.B.E., of the Australian Army arrived in March to be the second Australian to command the four-battalion brigade. Brigadier Daly was given a farewell parade on 14th March in which the Durham Light Infantry, and the other battalions, participated: 'During the time we have been in Korea everyone in the battalion had come to know and admire Brigadier Daly, and we were most sorry to see him go. Although there were four battalions on parade, the 68th insisted on performing light

*Presentation of the Birthday Cake to Brigadier Daly, Camp Casey, 19th March 1953, with the Bugles of the D.L.I., Band of the R.A.R. and Drums of the R.R.F.*

Lt. Gen. Sir Thomas Daly.

*Senior Officers of 28 Commonwealth Brigade, March 1953.*
*From Left to Right:*
*Lt. Col. G. F. Larkin, O.B.E., C.O. 2nd R.A.R.*
*Lt. Col. A. L. MacDonald, O.B.E., C.O. 3rd R.A.R.*
*Lt. Col. M. Austin, D.S.O., C.O. 1st R.A.R.*
*Brig. J. G. N. Wilton, D.S.O., O.B.E.*
*Maj. W. J. Morrow, R.A.R., Brigade Major.*
*Brig. T. J. Daly, D.S.O., O.B.E.*
*Lt. Col. G. R. Stevens, O.B.E., C.O. 1st R.F.*
*Maj. R. King-Clark, Manchester Regt., D.A.A. & Q.M.G.*
*Lt. Col. P. J. Jeffreys, D.S.O., O.B.E., C.O. 1st D.L.I.*

(Lt. Gen. Sir Thomas Daly)

infantry drill throughout, culminating in a double past by companies. Despite the muddiness of the ground the manoeuvre went very well, and was well commented on.' Later that week Brigadier Daly 'was disturbed early in the morning by pipe music outside my quarters on the 19th of March, my birthday, and on investigating found a deputation to present me with a superb birthday cake with the phrase "Daly at Dawn" iced on top. This was a double entendre referring, I suspect, to my habit of visiting units at first light before the incoming patrols had retired to their hoochies but it was also a slogan carried on the mast head of a Melbourne

newspaper, *"The Sun* – Daily at Dawn".' Later, when Brigadier Daly was
actually leaving, the Durhams turned out before breakfast to chair him
over the bridge at the entrance to the camp and sang him out to 'He's a
jolly good fellow'.

Lieutenant-General Sir Thomas Daly recalls:

'Commanding 28 British Commonwealth Brigade was a splendid
experience. It was composed of fine units, both British and Australian while the support given by the New Zealand gunners and
the Indian Field Ambulance was magnificent. There was, not
unnaturally, a friendly rivalry between units of different nationalities which kept everyone on their toes but the comradeship
which developed ensured that units from widely varying backgrounds came together as a homogenous whole, close-knit and
mutually supportive. The Divisional Commander expressed his
confidence in the Brigade by entrusting to it the sector's vital
ground – Point 355 – on a permanent basis which from our point
of view not only had the advantage of enabling the Brigade to
carry out continuous improvements to the position but which also
enabled us to have the New Zealand Field Regiment and the
Indian Field Ambulance permanently in support.'

Another parade was held on 21st March. The 2nd Battalion of The Royal
Australian Regiment, Lieutenant-Colonel G. F. Larkin, had arrived to
relieve the 1st Battalion of the regiment who had completed their twelve
months in Korea. The 1st Royal Australians had lost 34 killed, 107 wounded, 3 missing and 2 known to have been taken prisoner but gained 14
major awards for gallantry. The farewell parade for 1 R.A.R. was a unique
occasion for the Australian Army; for the first time all three battalions of
the regiment were on parade together – under the command of an Australian Brigadier. Also on parade was Private Belville who, when posted from
2 R.A.R. in Australia, stowed away on the troopship to Korea; on discovery he was fined five pounds and taken back on the strength of the 2nd
Battalion. At about the same time, Lieutenant-Colonel A. L. MacDonald
assumed the command of the veteran 3rd Battalion of the Royal Australians from Lieutenant-Colonel Hughes and Lieutenant-Colonel M. B. K.
Nair arrived to command the 60th Indian Field Ambulance.

During the month of March the brigade received some more new arrivals – not to Korea but to the Commonwealth Division. Each battalion
received a draft of Korean soldiers. These 'KATCOMs' – Korean

Augmentation Troops Commonwealth – had received basic military training and were to be integrated amongst the allied forces to gain practical experience. About a dozen 'Katcoms' were introduced into each rifle company 'doing the same job as our own men. Language, of course, is a problem and it is unfortunate that their pay is so little but they are keen and most anxious to do well.' One soldier observed: 'Our section is commanded by Sergeant Smith, who has under his command me, Jones, Robinson, "Daisy" Bell, Brown, Ferguson and Wu and Wong.' The system soon proved to be successful and the Koreans became enthusiastic members of their new units, picking up basic, soldierly English fairly quickly and, in most cases, becoming efficient soldiers. In addition to the newly arrived Katcoms, Commonwealth units were still loyally supported by the hard-working and indispensable porters of the 120th Battalion of the Korean Service Corps, the courageous 'Gunga Dins' of the Korean War.

During the stay at Camp Casey, the brigade was involved in 'a whirlwind of exercises and training schemes. On a number of occasions we practised a middle-of-the-night move, spending the following day in pursuit of imaginary enemy, digging or weapon firing. There were a lot of minor training points which required putting right and these were attended to.' A brigade shooting competition was won by the Royal Fusiliers with Brigade Headquarters in second place and the Durhams a good third.

The 'rest' period in reserve came to an end in early April and Operation 'Cotswold' returned the Commonwealth Division to the front line to relieve the 2nd United States Infantry Division.

It is of interest to note that, at the time of writing, the 2nd United States Infantry Division, the 'Indian Head Division', still occupied Camp Casey in the Republic of Korea.

# The Last Battles

On 6th April 1953, Operation 'Cotswold' was put into effect and the 1st Commonwealth Division moved forward from the Corps reserve at Camp Casey to return to the front line – back to its own corner of Korea, North of the River Imjin around Kowang-San and the Samichon. By 8th April 28 Brigade was in occupation of its old positions and Brigadier Wilton was dismayed to find the defences in poor condition. 'During the absence of the Commonwealth Division the Chinese had been allowed to dominate much of the valley, with the result that they were able to carry out detailed reconnaissance of the wire and approaches to our positions, and were thus able to assimilate enough information to allow them to make an attack through the weakest points. The task of regaining ascendancy fell on night patrol teams – the commanders of which were in many cases new to the job. Ambushes and reconnaissances were pushed nightly further out, until we were able to feel that it was we who watched the Chinese rather than the other way about.' Again, the Durhams and the Fusiliers realised that the Australians were not the only 'Diggers' in the brigade and the pick and spade were as essential to the infantryman as his rifle.

Major Atkinson describes the positions occupied by the Durham Light Infantry:

'My company, 'B' Company, occupied three positions on Point 355. The first was on a spur behind and below the main feature which was known by some as Little Gibraltar. Here we relieved the Americans and set about digging and providing patrols to go out in front of the main position. Our second position was the left forward one which faced the enemy held feature called Point 227 or John. Here there was no wide valley floor to separate the opposing sides but just a steep saddle with diggings at the bottom. I suppose it was here and at Point 187, a position to the left and further forward than Point 355, that one could expect not only the most patrol clashes in No-Man's-Land, but also the most shelling and mortaring from the Chinese. In fact only the greatest degree of alertness prevented infiltration into these company positions at night so persistent were the enemy in probing them.'

This was well-remembered and familiar ground to the old hands in the brigade but the newcomers found it rather confusing. The 2nd Royal Australians were split up amongst the 'veteran' battalions to introduce the new boys to the sharp end. Private Ron Kirley of 'B' Company, 2 R.A.R., was one such novice: 'The 1st Battalion Royal Fusiliers were selected to

*A mortar pit of the 1st Bn. Royal Fusiliers, Hill 210, May 1953.*

(Mr. R. L. Kirley.)

*The Sharp End – forward trenches on Hill 210 occupied by the Royal Fusiliers, May 1953.*

(Mr. R. L. Kirley.)

give about one-third of my battalion their first baptism of fire. I was with the first group to go, and arrived a little nervy at Hill 210. After being allocated a trench and keeping my head well down, I asked a young soldier (I was also 19) how far ahead the Chows were, and with that he turned me round 180 degrees and pointed that way about 400 yards. I had been looking backwards towards Australia, very embarrassing.'

The truce talks had been dragging on at Panmunjon but some measure of agreement was reached and it was announced that the more seriously sick and wounded prisoners of war would be exchanged. The first such exchange began on 20th April and amongst the first twelve Commonwealth prisoners released by the Communists at Munsan-Ni was Fusilier George Hodkinson, who had been captured during Operation 'Pimlico' the previous November. On his return to the United Nations lines Hodkinson was informed that he had been awarded the Distinguished Conduct Medal for his gallantry during the fight. Some forty Commonwealth prisoners were returned by 25th April but there were still many more held in camps in North Korea.

'The freed prisoners arrived at Panmunjon in seven battered fawn ambulances, blunt-nosed, Russian-built vehicles which had long seen better days. They waited anxiously inside, peeping furtively through the narrow windows, while a squad of strutting commissars handed out lists. And then they were free – blinking uncertainly in the fitful sunlight, hesitating at the tape marking the edge of the reception zone and stumbling across towards the reception committee. The Britons slept that night in comfort at an emergency hospital at Seoul and were then flown to the British hospital at Kure, Japan – and then home.'

'On a truly glorious day, the 28th British Commonwealth Brigade observed the thirty-eighth ANZAC Day. A parade was held in the morning in which New Zealand gunners, Australian infantry and detachments from two British regiments which had fought at Gallipoli took part. The Durham Light Infantry was privileged to be represented by sixteen buglers who sounded the Last Post and Reveille. A feature of the ceremony was the presence of the commander of the Turkish Contingent in Korea, Brigadier-General Sirri Acar, who had himself fought against the Anzacs and who still remembered the gallantry of his old enemies. A field gun was put to use as a cenotaph and against this wreaths were laid by the senior members of all the units and formations there. At the end of the parade the detachments marched past the cenotaph and four jet aircraft of the Royal Australian Air Force flying wing to wing abreast thundered down to offer their salute. Most of the rest of the proceedings was spent by the Australians telling the British what dreadful rogues all New Zealanders are and by the Kiwis giving similar warnings about the Aussies, not a word of which deceived anyone. This is simply one of their ways of demonstrating their mutual affection and respect. And, of course, as is their custom, they made much of their guests.'

Despite the ceremonial and the tributes to the dead of earlier wars, the enemy was still very active on the brigade front. On 26th April a patrol of 'C' Company of the D.L.I., commanded by Second-Lieutenant J. W. Parker, observed about thirty-five Chinese attempting to cut them off as they returned to their own lines. The Durhams engaged the enemy and killed six; a second patrol, led by Second-Lieutenant Woodbridge, went out to assist and accounted for another three Chinese. The D.L.I. lost one man killed and three wounded – including Lieutenant Woodbridge. The following night Second-Lieutenant D. A. Margetts took a patrol out from Hill 355 and found one dead Chinese and another wounded at the site of the previous night's encounter. Both were brought in and the wounded man provided information of interest to the intelligence staff. The Royal Fusiliers also met strong enemy opposition when one of their patrols was attacked to the north of Hill 159 during the night of 29th/30th April; the Fusiliers lost one officer and one soldier killed, three wounded and two missing. On 4th May the Durhams engaged an enemy patrol in front of Hill 355, killing some twelve Chinese at the cost of seven wounded. Lieutenant E. W. Ratcliffe and Private J. K. Christie, an Australian, were posted as 'missing' after another patrol action in the Hill 355 area.

Fusilier Micklewhite, a national serviceman of 9 Platoon, 'C' Company of the 1st Royal Fusiliers, remembers his experiences of that time:

'I remember the boredom and the bull. I also remember the sheer naked terror of finding that I, a kid from the Elephant and Castle, actually had to go out into a paddy field at night while Chinese soldiers were trying to kill me. It was trench warfare, just like the First World War. There were Chinese troops opposite us; the amazing thing about them was their numbers. There were thousands of them. After an attack you would find their bodies in groups of four. They only had one rifle between them; when one fell, the next one picked it up. The Americans used to fly over and napalm hell out of them and when the smoke cleared you'd see one of them come out of a hole and shovel up some burning napalm and start to cook on it. One night, the only time in my entire life I knew I was about to die, four of us were out on what was laughingly called Observation Patrol. The first inkling we had was when we smelt the Chinese. They ate garlic like apples. For years afterwards I couldn't eat garlic. Then we heard them talking and we knew they had sussed us; it was very eerie in the moonlight in a paddy field knowing that we were about to die.

None of us had the least idea why we were fighting in Korea but the odd thing was we all thought, 'We're going to die expensive. We'll take as many of them with us as we can.' Our officer shouted "run" and, by chance, we ran towards the Chinese. Which is what saved us; in the dark we all lost each other. I grew up that night.'

Maurice Micklewhite is now better known as Michael Caine, the film actor.

During the night of 4th/5th of May, the 2nd Battalion of the Royal Australian Regiment moved up to relieve the Royal Fusiliers in the line. The Chinese observed the preparations for the exchange and one of the regular propaganda broadcasts directed towards the divisional front by loudspeakers featured a charming female voice which announced: 'Welcome, Aussies – here is some Australian music . . .' and a recording of 'The Twelfth Street Rag' blared across the Samichon Valley. The Fusiliers were transferred to the 29 Brigade reserve to replace the Black Watch who had moved forward to re-occupy 'The Hook', on the division's left flank. The 2nd Royal Australians suffered their first casualty on 5th May during heavy shelling of their new positions. To complete the battalion's introduction to the delights of the Korean front line, heavy rain fell throughout the day.

The 3rd Royal Australians also returned to the front line, replacing the D.L.I. in the Hill 355 area. Before the Durhams withdrew from their positions they had

'one very interesting day. Opposite our company positions and some 400 yards away was a very prominent hill overlooking us. It was arranged that the best airstrike ever should be made against it in the hope of destroying the deep caves and tunnels the enemy were known to have dug there. These were reputed to be forty feet below the surface and unsupported by props. It was further said that an almond-eyed maiden broadcast from this fastness, languishing, as she thought, in complete safety. The plot was therefore to drop deep-penetrating heavy bombs, which would burrow down into the ground and blast the tunnels open. How successful the strike was we shall never know, but it afforded a most interesting spectacle from our side. While an American Air Force officer in a yellow and blue chequered cap (like a schoolboy's) talked conversationally to the aircraft from a wireless bunker, we

*The Durham Light Infantry hand over their positions to the 3rd Royal Australians,
May 1953.*
*(Note the different marks of Lee Enfield rifles and the Australian Owen Gun.)*

(AWM HOB 4217)

watched in complete safety while a two hour air raid took place
before our eyes. Soon afterwards we handed the hill over to our
good friends the Australians (whose hill, incidentally, it really
was; with a claim of first ownership going back to 1951).'

The Australian claim was well founded. Hill 355 was first scaled by Major
Jack Gerke's 'C' Company of the 3rd R.A.R. on 4th October 1951, whilst
the King's Own Scottish Borderers battled their way up the Western ridge
of the hill. 'C' Company was also the first to take Maryang-San (Hill 317)
the following day.

Meanwhile, to the left of the divisional front, the Turkish Brigade
received heavy attacks during 15th and 16th May and the Chinese offensive overlapped into the area of 'The Hook' – where the Black Watch had
fought gallantly the previous November. The Duke of Wellington's

Regiment, of 29 Brigade, occupied 'The Hook' on 13th May and the first determined Chinese assault in force was launched on the 18th. The 'Duke's' held the feature but the enemy seemed intent on capturing the hill.

On the Commonwealth Division's right flank, well to the North of 'The Hook', the 3rd Royal Australian Regiment stepped up its offensive patrolling programme in the Hill 355 area. On 24th May a patrol of seventeen men from 'A' Company, under the command of Lieutenants

*'No mate – the Light Infantry.'*

C. P. Yacopetti and A. C. Weaver, encountered a strong Chinese patrol in no-man's-land. A fierce fight ensued and the Australians were surrounded. Lieutenant Yacopetti, although wounded twice, managed to extricate his men from the encircling enemy but, when the patrol returned to their own lines, he was missing and had, in fact, been taken prisoner whilst covering the patrol's withdrawal. Lieutenant Yacopetti was awarded the Military Cross and was also Mentioned in Despatches for his conduct whilst a prisoner of war.

The 2nd Royal Australians also had a brush with the enemy on 26th May when a Chinese force was engaged forward of Hill 159. The Chinese retaliated with a heavy mortar bombardment on the battalion's left-hand company, killing four and wounding fifteen whilst two Australians were listed as missing after the encounter.

The expected attacks on 'The Hook' came on 28th May and the Duke of Wellington's fought a bloody and costly battle to hold the feature. On the

*Chinese shell exploding forward of D Company, 3rd R.A.R., on Hill 355, May 1953.*

(AWM HOB 4248)

29th the remnants of the Dukes were withdrawn after inflicting heavy casualties on the Chinese and the Royal Fusiliers were brought forward from 29 Brigade reserve to occupy the shattered positions. Repairs to the hill's defences were rendered almost impossible by the weight of enemy mortar fire which fell continuously on the battered hilltop. Airstrikes were called down to remedy this inconvenience and some twenty-six sorties were flown on 31st May, one after another throughout the day, to blast the Chinese trenches opposite the hotly contested hill. The New Zealand gunners had, as always, made a vital contribution to the defence of 'The Hook' and fired over 4,500 rounds in support. After a day of concentrated airstrikes and artillery bombardment of the enemy positions, the Royal Fusiliers were able to effect some repairs to the defences but their occupation of 'The Hook' was never very comfortable.

Early in the month of June the 1st British Commonwealth Division made preparations to celebrate the coronation of Her Majesty Queen Elizabeth the Second. Commonwealth representatives had already left Korea to join the Coronation Parade in London, including Captain T. M. Renton and Gunner T. Crapp of the Royal New Zealand Artillery. On the eve of Coronation Day, Lieutenant W. J. Nott-Bower and a patrol of 6 Platoon, 'B' Company of the Durhams, crossed the valley in front of Hill 355 and laid aircraft recognition panels on an enemy hill. At first light on Coronation Day Major Atkinson saw:

'On the slopes of a hill across no-man's-land and facing us on Point 355 was the Royal Cipher – E II R – pegged out boldly in fluorescent twelve-foot-high air recognition panels. This was the work of Lieutenant W. J. Nott-Bower, one of my platoon commanders, whose father, Sir John Nott-Bower, was even more heavily involved in the Coronation as Chief of the Metropolitan Police in London. We gave three cheers from the trenches in the right hand position on Point 355 and the divisional artillery fired salvoes of red, white and blue smoke into the enemy positions. Chinese reaction, for once, was phlegmatic.'

'On Coronation Day, a ceremonial parade was held by the Division in the rear area. Motoring down from the line in one's jeep one noticed the way in which units had made a bold effort to display their feelings. Symbols and banners made with indescribable ingenuity from the most unsuitable materials proclaimed the Commonwealth's loyal greetings, and Americans and other nationals were to be seen on all sides admiring them and taking

*New Zealand gunners, Royal Fusiliers and pipers of the Black Watch, Coronation Day, 1953.*

(IWM BF 11062)

photographs. The parade itself was tremendous. A patch of muddy field had been transformed into a fine drill square hung with regal trappings and peopled with spectators from all the United Nations. Among these were Dr. and Mrs. Rhee (the President of the Republic of Korea), many of the United States general staff, Frenchmen, Turks, Norwegians, Italians, Abyssinians, Belgians and many more – all displaying a wide variety of national and formation patches such as the horse-head insignia and yellow scarves of the U.S. Cavalry. On parade were troops from every component part of the 1st Commonwealth Division, representing the greater part of the Empire. During the first part of the ceremony Major-General M. M. Alston-Roberts-West, C.B., D.S.O., presented honours and awards to men of the Division. The general then spoke briefly on the significance of the day. As the Royal Standard was broken three rousing cheers were given for

Her Majesty. A march-past followed. It was a delight to leave the line for one morning to join in the world-wide celebrations of such a day.'

Back in the line, a patrol of 'C' Company, 2nd Royal Australians, led by Sergeant W. J. Bruce, met the enemy on Hill 227 on 6th June. After a sharp fire fight the Australians put the Chinese to flight, killing six and wounding many others. On 11th June, Major J. A. Tresawna, D.S.O., an officer of the Oxfordshire and Buckinghamshire Light Infantry serving with the Durhams, was killed whilst controlling patrols forward of 'C' Company on Hill 355. A few days later Second-Lieutenant J. Grubb was killed by a mortar bomb which also wounded Second-Lieutenant T. V. S. Gordon; both officers had only been with the Durhams for four days which made the occurrence the more poignant. On the night of 19th/20th June an ambush patrol commanded by Second-Lieutenant Hill of 10 Platoon of the D.L.I. was engaged by some twenty to thirty of the enemy on a small feature known as 'Alice Springs'. After a brief exchange of fire, during which the patrol inflicted several casualties, 10 Platoon withdrew to the main position without loss. On the night of 20th/21st June it again fell to 10 Platoon to mount the 'Alice Springs' ambush. The patrol was commanded by Sergeant McCabe and consisted of fourteen men, split into a control group and two sections. Each section had an N.C.O. and five men armed with three Brens, three Stens and grenades. The patrol reached 'Alice Springs' by 9.00 p.m. and settled down in pairs to watch the approaches to the hill. At 10.15 p.m. the most Northerly pair heard slight movement to their front, Sergeant McCabe happened to be visiting this pit at the time and remained to watch developments. After some five minutes, the silhouettes of five men were seen creeping over the crest of the hill and were immediately fired upon, three were seen to fall. Simultaneously, a larger party was heard moving up the hill through the minefield to cut off the ambush patrol and a shower of stick grenades was hurled amongst the Durhams, wounding two men. Sergeant McCabe regrouped his patrol to face this larger group who were met by concentrated fire as they crested the hill. Although many of the enemy were killed they were numerically superior to 10 Platoon's patrol and Sergeant McCabe ordered a withdrawal. Lance-Corporal MacDonald remained with a Bren to cover the patrol's movement but one Katcom was killed and four Durhams wounded during the withdrawal. The casualties were successfully evacuated and the Chinese laid a mortar barrage on the ambush site. The following night, 11 Platoon provided the ambush patrol under Second-Lieutenant

Cunningham; since the Chinese were aware of the site of the previous two ambushes, the patrol took up position to the rear of 'Alice Springs' but, to ensure that the ambush itself was not surprised, Corporal Lofthouse and four men kept watch from the top of the hill. The ambush was in position by 9.00 p.m. in a steady drizzle of rain. At 10.00 p.m. the lookouts on 'Alice Springs' saw two Chinese approaching the former ambush site and, finding it unoccupied, the enemy waved for the rest of their group to advance and twelve more Chinese appeared. Corporal Lofthouse waited patiently for the enemy to bunch and then opened fire at short range, killing half of the enemy party whilst the remainder fled down the hill. A larger group of Chinese then assaulted the hill and again Corporal Lofthouse coolly engaged them before withdrawing to the main ambush, closely followed by the enemy. Once the corporal's group had rejoined the patrol, Second-Lieutenant Cunningham opened fire on the enemy who dispersed after suffering heavy casualties. Meanwhile, the Chinese were also attacking two of the Durhams' standing patrols; one on the 'Nose' was driven in after a short fire fight in which two men were wounded; the other patrol on 'Cobar', commanded by Lance-Corporal Rosevear, beat off the enemy attack, killing at least two Chinese. Lieutenant Cunningham's patrol was again attacked by about thirty of the enemy and fought them off although half the ambush patrol, including the lieutenant, had been wounded. Lieutenant Cunningham decided to withdraw only to find that yet another enemy group had moved between his patrol and the battalion's forward positions. The patrol regrouped defensively whilst the Chinese attacked the forward trenches, there to be beaten back after wounding three Durhams. Second-Lieutenant Cunningham took advantage of the enemy's retreat to bring his patrol in, carrying their wounded as they fought their way through the retiring Chinese to the security of the battalion's lines. 'D' Company was then subjected to a heavy mortar barrage during which some 1,500 bombs fell amongst the trenches. At 1.00 a.m. the Commanding Officer ordered a fighting patrol from 'A' Company, under Second-Lieutenant Parker, to sweep the 'Alice Springs' area. This was carried out successfully and the patrol was returning when Lieutenant Parker and five men were wounded when a mortar bomb fell amongst them as they neared the friendly lines. After four hours of continuous bombardment the enemy mortaring ceased at 3.00 a.m. and the Durhams were able to reoccupy their shattered forward trenches. For this night's action Second-Lieutenant Cunningham received the Military Cross, Corporal Lofthouse and Private Rawlings the Military Medal and Lance-Corporal Rosevear was mentioned in despatches.

'B' Company of the 3rd Royal Australians also mounted a patrol in the area of Hill 227 on 24th June. The patrol, led by Lieutenant A. W. Gargate and consisting of fifteen men, clashed with a stronger force of the enemy in another bitter night fire-fight. Lieutenant Gargate was wounded and Corporal Cashman assumed command, managing to extricate the patrol successfully. The New Zealand gunners provided support for all these vicious little battles and fired their three-quarter millionth shell of the war on 25th June. The Kiwis were also in action to support the Republic of Korea Division, on the Commonwealth Brigade's right flank, firing some 2,300 rounds when the Koreans were attacked during the month of June.

An official casualty return of the 28th Commonwealth Brigade for the months of May and June 1953, provides sobering evidence of the cost of the 'minor' actions undertaken at that time:-

| May 1953 | Killed | Wounded | Missing | Total |
|---|---|---|---|---|
| 1 Royal Fusiliers | | 9 | | 9 |
| 1 Durham Light Infantry | 2 | 14 | | 16 |
| 2 Royal Australians | 5 | 21 | 1 | 27 |
| 3 Royal Australians | 12 | 62 | 5 | 79 |
| KATCOMs | 1 | 10 | 1 | 12 |
| Totals: | 20 | 116 | 7 | 143 |

| June 1953 | Killed | Wounded | Missing | Total |
|---|---|---|---|---|
| 1 Royal Fusiliers | | 20 | | 20 |
| 1 Durham Light Infantry | 5 | 39 | | 44 |
| 2 Royal Australians | 5 | 36 | 2 | 43 |
| 3 Royal Australians | 10 | 38 | 1 | 49 |
| Totals: | 20 | 133 | 3 | 156 |

At the end of June, the Commonwealth Brigade received orders to leave 'their' hills – for the last time. Operation 'Emperor' was put into effect on 9th July 1953 and reshuffled the divisional front line. 28 Brigade was moved from the Northeastern end of the line, around Kowang-San, to relieve 29 Brigade in the Southwest, around the hotly disputed 'Hook'. The 1st U.S. Marine Division was on the left with the 3rd Marine Regiment immediately alongside the Commonwealth Brigade. The 2nd Royal Australian Regiment took over from The King's Regiment (of 29 Brigade) on 'The Hook' whilst the Durham Light Infantry occupied the hills on the East side of the Samichon, in the Yong Dong area. As with all operational moves in Korea the rain fell and heavy downpours were endured on 14th and 15th July. On 18th July, Lieutenant-Colonel Stevens of the Royal Fusiliers presented a tattered flag, which had flown from the peak of Hill 355, to the Brigade-Major, Major I. H. McBride of the Australian Army. The presentation was made as a token of the alliance which existed between the Royal Fusiliers and the 6th Battalion, Royal Melbourne Regiment (The Royal Victoria Regiment) of the Australian Citizens' Military Force, a bond formed many years earlier and revived in the Commonwealth Brigade.

Major Atkinson's 'B' Company of the D.L.I. had its

*Lt. Col. Stevens presents the flag of the Royal Fusiliers, flown on Hill 355, to Maj. I. H. McBride, Brigade-Major, for the 6th Bn. of the Royal Melbourne Regiment.*

(AWM HOB 4453)

*Pte. G. E. Rose, B Company, 2nd. Bn. Royal Australian Regiment, with a Browning machine gun on The Hook, 18th July 1953.*

(IWM KOR 651)

'last position before the ceasefire on the left of the line at Yong Dong. Even here we were not left in peace. My cookhouse was hit by a shell and my Army Catering Corps cook was killed. On the final night we were moved at short notice to an unoccupied hill to the right and rear of the United States Marine Division which had a massive assault launched against it. Fortunately for us, who were lying out in the open on rocky ground, the attack on the Marines was eventually halted, but not without severe casualties. I visited the scene of the battle a few days later. One of the forward positions was a scene of complete devastation. An enemy trench had been dug forward into the position and there was a Chinese soldier standing facing us at the end of it.'

During the move to support the U.S. Marines Private Savage, of 'A' Company, became a casualty in a minefield, the last Durham to be injured in the Korean war.

The truce talks at Panmunjon were approaching a settlement but the Chinese were determined to gain ground before the armistice was agreed. On 24th July, the enemy mounted a vicious attack on the U.S. Marines to the West of 'The Hook' and subjected the allied positions to heavy artillery and mortar bombardments. The 2nd Royal Australians gave supporting fire to the hard-pressed American marines and one of their positions received over 4,000 mortar bombs during the night. Forward observers of 16 Field Regiment were with the marine companies and directed defensive fire with great accuracy and efficiency. Private Ron Kirley recalls: 'We in "B" Company, 2 R.A.R., were pulled out for a rest on the 24th July and within eight hours were sent back just behind Hill 111, 3rd Marines, which was next to Hill 119, then "The Hook". Therefore we did not have much rest.' During 24th and 25th July there was little rest for any of the front-line units of the U.S. Marines and 28 Brigade.

'C' Company of the 2nd Royal Australians on Hill 121 and 'D' Company on 'The Hook' were attacked during the night of 24th July but the enemy were repulsed after a fierce battle. A company of the Durhams was moved up to come under the command of 2 R.A.R. and, by 10.00 p.m., the Chinese artillery bombardment of the Australian positions was intensified. A second attack on Hill 121 soon followed but petered out as a result of heavy casualties inflicted on the attackers, mainly by the guns of 16 Field Regiment. The weight of the Chinese assault swung upon the U.S. Marines on Hill 111, to the West of the Australian positions, and the machine guns of 2 R.A.R. under the direction of Sergeant B. C. Cooper, were brought to bear on the mass of the attackers. With the help of the Australian machine guns and mortars and the New Zealand artillery the attack was contained but spasmodic and confused fighting continued throughout the night. The Chinese maintained their artillery bombardment of the hills during 25th July and at 9.00 p.m. another attack was launched on 'D' Company on 'The Hook'. This attack was repulsed with Lance-Corporal R. H. Crockford and his section holding their key position successfully although under intense mortar fire. The U.S. Marines were attacked again during the night and another bitter battle ensued; 'C' Company of the 2nd Royal Australians accounted for some 35 Chinese killed and a further 35 wounded during the fight which overlapped 2 R.A.R.'s front, at least 300 Chinese dead were estimated around the Marines' positions on Hill 111. By 1.00 a.m. on 26th July the situation was serious enough for 'D' Company of the 3rd Royal Australians and 'B' Company of the Durhams to be called forward but, in the event, they were not committed to the battle. By 3.00 a.m. activity along the front had decreased and the Chinese artillery fire subsided although exchanges of small arms fire continued until dawn. At daybreak, the Chinese could be seen evacuating their casualties from Hill 111 and one party of some twenty men were engaged by the Anti-Tank Platoon of 2 R.A.R. During the night of 26th July further light attacks were made by the enemy but were fairly easily repulsed. The Chinese artillery fire dwindled from an estimated 43,000 rounds received through 25th and 26th July to only 54 rounds on the 27th. The New Zealand gunners fired their last shells at 5.30 a.m. on 27th July; the last of some 800,000 rounds fired in anger, the highest number for any field regiment in Korea, a record the regiment remembers with pride.

At 10.00 p.m. on 27th July 1953, six buglers of the Durham Light Infantry sounded the ceasefire from the Commonwealth Division's lines and the guns fell silent after 1,301 days of fighting. In the forward trenches there was not a sound nor a flicker of light; in the rear the night sky was ablaze with flares as 'the stalwart warriors manning the "blunt end" positions celebrated to the fullest extent'. For those at the 'sharp end', to know that it was over was enough.

At first light on 28th July the 2nd Royal Australians on 'The Hook' could see that the Chinese had decorated their forward positions with colourful flags and paper and music was broadcast across the valley on the propaganda loudspeakers. 'D' Company occupied the same ridges as the most forward Chinese company with only about 200 yards separation. Heads appeared slowly from the trenches, both sides showing themselves

*Armistice – a New Zealand gunner and an Australian infantryman, 28th July 1953.*

(AWM RANK 273)

very cautiously, neither quite trusting the other but moving instinctively forward to meet. The tension soon eased, both sides shook hands, some gifts were exchanged. Two Chinese officers later appeared, probably political and certainly not front line; both spoke excellent English but 'were only too ready to promote the Peking line and were crashing bores.' As the sun rose the Chinese came out to clear the battlefield of their wounded and dead. It was estimated that there were about 2,000 bodies strewn in front of 'The Hook' and many funeral pyres could be seen burning in the Chinese lines. Colonel Burns, commanding the 16th Field Regiment of the Royal New Zealand Artillery, commented on the scene: 'On the Marine front, leading across from Point 111 to the twin, superbly contoured features known as Betty Grable, the ground was covered with bodies, parachute flares, craters and all the debris of war.' Brigadier Wilton (who was a former gunner) also viewed the evidence of the Kiwis' firepower:

*Soldiers of the 3rd. Bn., Royal Australian Regiment, retire from the demilitarised zone after the armistice, July 1953.*

(IWM BF 11125)

'The floor of the valley between the Hook and the Chinese positions was almost carpeted with dead Chinese who had been caught in our artillery concentrations. On the immediate approach to 2 R.A.R. the bodies literally covered the ground, sometimes two deep, evidently victims of mortar and machine gun fire. Most of the bodies had been there for two to three days and in the hot humid weather had started to putrify and there was a strong nauseous smell of death. It was a terrible sight which I shall never forget.'

For its participation in this last battle of the war, the 2nd Battalion of the Royal Australian Regiment was awarded the battle honour 'The Samichon' and gained one Military Cross and five Military Medals, including those of Sergeant Cooper and Corporal Crockford.

After three years of war, a ceasefire agreement was finally concluded between the Communists and the United Nations delegations at Panmunjon. The agreement was signed at 10.00 a.m. and became effective at 10.00 p.m. on 27th July 1953. Commonwealth servicemen who had served in the war were awarded two medals: the Korean Medal – the first to bear the head of Queen Elizabeth the Second – and the United Nations Medal with the clasp 'Korea'.

Brigadier Wilton issued an order of the day to the 28th Commonwealth Infantry Brigade:

'Now that the cease fire has come I wish to express to you all the admiration and pride I feel for the way in which you have kept up the same high standard and fighting spirit and efficiency right up to the last moment. It has made me realise more than anything else what a fine Brigade I have the honour to command. You will be asked to work hard for the next few days but at least you will have the respite from danger and discomfort you so richly deserve. Well done and good luck to you all.'

# Truce

'An uneasy peace now settled over Korea. Across a narrow no-man's-land which stretched from one coast to the other, two great armies stood face to face. There was a truce; not a complete and satisfactory peace.'

At first there was an almost stunned silence along the front coupled with a somewhat cynical suspicion. During the brigade's last tour of duty in the line, from April to July, the Indian Field Ambulance had treated some 230 casualties and it was almost unbelievable that the fighting would not flare up again. Many of the casualties evacuated by the Indian Field Ambulance were sent to the NORMASH, the Norwegian Mobile Advanced Surgical Hospital, which had been in support of the Commonwealth Divisional sector and enjoyed a close relationship with the division. The Royal Fusiliers, whose time in Korea was almost ended, breathed a great sigh of relief but the other battalions were still wary. Orders for Operation 'Swanlake' were issued on 28th July, the withdrawal of the combatants from the battle line. For the Commonwealth Division this meant a return to the 'Kansas Line' along the River Imjin, a withdrawal to the line occupied in May 1951 before the actions which carried the fight into the North. The Communists were also obliged to retire to the North, leaving a demilitarized zone between the opposing forces.

'In fact, the signing of the Truce Agreement meant more work for everyone. New positions had to be prepared, training was intensified, exercises were frequent; and in addition to all this, the normal routine tasks had to be carried out.' For the New Zealand gunners this meant that

'the first big task was to clear the gun positions and observation posts in the Demilitarized Zone. This had to be completed by September 13 1953. Every piece of equipment that could be

145

salvaged was brought back to be used in a new defensive line. At the same time, the regiment had to move back to a new truce position. This was an area that had never been occupied before and roads, drains, living sites and gun parks had to be constructed. It meant long hours of arduous labour for all ranks, but before the regiment left Korea the result of their efforts was very plain to see.'

Operation 'Swanlake' was implemented between 28th and 31st July with the 2nd Royal Australians beginning the withdrawal at 6.00 a.m. on the 29th. The Durhams also moved: 'With the coming of the truce the battalion was ordered to withdraw over the Imjin River and to assume a number of new roles. 'A' Company was despatched to staff Britannia Camp, where repatriated Commonwealth prisoners will be brought on release, and set about its task with the greatest energy.' Nevertheless, 'Swanlake' required the abandonment of the hills the brigade had taken in the battles of 1951 and held against determined opposition for the last one and three-quarter years – Kowang-San, 210, 159, 189, Yong Dong and The Hook. The only consolation was that they were not abandoned to the enemy.

Colonel Burns of the Royal New Zealand Artillery had reservations about the siting of his regiment on withdrawal:

'Sixteen Field was a regiment of volunteers – a very mixed bag of professions and occupations. Probably over ninety percent of the men were "out for a bit of adventure" and although no-one could seriously fault their conduct and performance in action, I had some misgivings about the possible lapses in control and soldierly discipline following the Armistice, particularly if the post-Armistice stay in Korea became prolonged. So, following representations to the Divisional Commander of Royal Artillery, Brigadier Gregson, it was agreed that the Kiwi Regimental Camp could be established North of the Imjin River – which had proved such a formidable barrier against the foe in wartime and now was to become an equally formidable barrier (policed by M.P.s at Pintail Bridge) separating the troops from the peacetime fleshpots lying to the South.'

The 3rd Battalion of the Royal Australian Regiment also occupied a camp to the North of the Imjin.

The withdrawal to the 'Kansas Line' was completed by 31st July and preparations to receive the repatriated Commonwealth prisoners of war began. The first batch was released from Munsan-Ni on 5th August and exchanged for Chinese and North Korean prisoners at Panmunjon. These exchanges continued until 1st September and amongst those returned was Gunner Garland, the only New Zealander to be taken prisoner during the war. On arrival at Panmunjon on 7th August, Gunner Garland introduced himself to Major-General West, the Commonwealth Division commander, with the cheerful greeting: 'My name is Garland, sir. I'm a Kiwi.' Amongst those waiting to welcome him back was Captain Hector MacLean who had been with Garland on Hill 227 the night he was captured. The gunner looked surprisingly well although he was very thin after twenty-one months in Communist prison camps and related his experiences:

> 'Two days after we were captured we started on a 125-mile march North to a mining camp. We were on the road for about ten days and found it very cold as we were still in light clothing and there was much snow around. At the mining camp, the Chinese issued us with their quilted winter clothing and took us part of the journey in trucks to Camp Five. At Camp Five I was put in a United Kingdom company and lived with these men all the time. For food we generally had two cups of rice a day. In winter this was augmented with a midday snack of "charred barley" brew. Monotony was the worst enemy.'

Another repatriation occurred when the 1st Battalion of The Royal Fusiliers left the brigade at the conclusion of their tour of duty in Korea. The Fusiliers had gained three Military Crosses, one Distinguished Conduct Medal and three Military Medals during their actions. The Royal Fusiliers were relieved by the 1st Battalion of The Essex Regiment, Lieutenant-Colonel P. S. C. Smith, who had arrived just too late to participate in the hostilities and took up residence in Salamanca Camp, South of the Imjin River, there to enter upon a strenuous training programme. The Royal Fusiliers bade a cheerful soldier's farewell to Korea whilst the Durhams waited impatiently for their relief to arrive.

One of the brigade's veteran units, the 60th Indian Field Ambulance, also left the division on 29th August 1953, to join the Indian Custodian Force – the 190th Indian Infantry Brigade – which had arrived to supervise the establishment of the demilitarized zone and the keeping of the truce. The Field Ambulance received a Meritorious Unit Citation from the commander of the United Nations Forces in Korea. The citation read: The

60th Indian Field Ambulance displayed such outstanding devotion and superior performance of exceptionally difficult tasks as to set it apart and above other units with similar missions. The individual and collective professional standards and conscientious achievements of members of this particular organisation reflect the highest credit on themselves, their homeland and the United Nations forces. During their service in Korea the 60th Indian Field Ambulance was awarded one Mahar Vir Chakra (that awarded to Lieutenant-Colonel Rangaraj), four Vir Chakras and twenty-four mentions in despatches. 'Of the political relationship of India to the Commonwealth very few soldiers, I imagine, could tell you much; but of the Indian Field Ambulance they will say: "It is the smartest unit in Korea".'

The following month, the Durham Light Infantry left the brigade after a year in Korea. Lieutenant-Colonel Jeffreys was proud of his battalion: 'They are good lads, they are sensible in the line; they dig like beavers and keep their heads down when shells fall and are not foolhardy. By this means, we have saved many casualties. Their health has been fine and most of them avoided the recent slight "flu" epidemic. I'm very proud of them – particularly the National Service lads.' The Durhams lost 21 soldiers killed, 124 wounded and 3 missing during their year in action and gained nine major awards for gallantry. Before leaving they bade farewell to the brigade. 'We were leaving behind a few hills and camps that had meant much to us. We were leaving behind our friends of the Commonwealth Division who had come to mean much more. In a round of farewells we realised that it would be a long time before we should ever again make such staunch friends as our comrades in the Royal Australian Regiment or the Royal New Zealand Artillery upon whom we depended on many occasions. The day we left Korea it was raining. The day we had arrived it rained.' The Durhams were relieved in their 'Kansas' location, South of the Imjin, by the 1st Battalion of The Royal Warwickshire Regiment, Lieutenant-Colonel R. C. MacDonald, D.S.O., O.B.E. Colonel Jeffereys's little yellow lurcher 'Fiona', who had accompanied him faithfully throughout the battalion's tour in Korea, was handed over reluctantly to Colonel MacDonald. Unfortunately, 'Fiona' later strayed into a minefield and was killed.

On 12th September the brigade participated in Operation 'Finder', a somewhat grisly search to discover missing bodies in the demilitarized zone North of the river. This operation did give the new battalions a chance to cover and appreciate the former battlegrounds over which the brigade had fought for the best part of three years. However, the Essex and the Warwickshires were kept busy constructing defence works and undergoing hard training.

'From August to January, we spent the majority of the working hours constructing defensive positions along our allocated sector of the defence line on some hills which appeared to be made entirely of rock. By Christmas, there was no doubt that, had it been necessary to do so, our defences were sufficiently well developed to enable the battalions to hold their sector against all comers. Training for mobile warfare in mountainous country is the order of the day, and this goes on until the end of April, when training concludes with a three-day Brigade and a five-day Divisional exercise and then back to our defences in the hills for the summer.'

The 2nd Royal Australians had to deal with a mutiny by eighteen of their Katcoms on 19th December. The recalcitrant Koreans were rounded up and marched off to be dealt with by the Korean Army. Christmas 1953 was spent in the luxury of the 'truce camps' on the 'Kansas Line' and much work had gone into establishing these almost idyllic bases. The New Zealand gunners boasted: 'The regimental truce position ranked among the best in the divisional area. Quonset huts were erected for messing and a regimental theatre was built.' Colonel Burns amplifies:

'To compensate in part for our isolation to the North of the Imjin it was decided to construct the biggest and best wet canteen. This was no problem to our built-in team of carpenters, joiners, plumbers, electricians, etc., and soon the job was done, complete with cosy alcoves and heating in the fashion of some of the better English Pubs and certainly not in any way resembling the swill troughs of some Kiwi liquor outlets that I know of. This concentration on vice and alcohol had to be given a proper balance. With the approval of our Padres, Rangiihu, Smith and Father Ned Cashman (dubbed the "Mercenary Monk" by the admiring if rather irreverent soldiery) we made our offering in that direction by commencing the construction of our Ecumenical Chapel of Saint Barbara by the Imjin, which boasted a tower. A rugby field was flattened out and gun and vehicle parks were made by two D2 bulldozers acquired many months before, no-one remembers how. As the site developed, the Regimental-Sergeant-Major,

WO1 J. Dickinson ("Dracula"), hoisted the New Zealand Ensign
in tandem with that of the United Nations on the highest point in
the campsite; on the hillside below the flagpole he drew out the
shape of an enormous white Kiwi (some said with its backside
deliberately facing Fort George, the Commonwealth Divisional
H.Q.) within a black diamond. Over the months, this outline was
filled in with black and whitewashed rock tediously quarried,
carried and laid in position – a special chore for anyone who
happened to be on field punishment. The Regimental Lock-Up
was sited above the quarry at the beginning of the road as a
permanent warning sign to those who thought that the Queen's
Regulations and Regimental Standing Orders were just casual
reading matter.'

Despite these architectural gems 'the emphasis was on training. Many
men had arrived in the theatre since the end of the war and they had to be
prepared for whatever the future might have held. At the same time, the
"veterans" were not allowed to forget what they had learned by hard
experience.'

The Essex Regiment occupied

'Salamanca Camp, as this small piece of "real estate" has become
known, has been developed into a camp of which we are justly
proud, and there is not a man in the battalion who had not con-
tributed something towards its layout, construction or maintenance. The camp is composed of a variety of structures consisting
of American squad tents, British M.U.G.s and 180 lb. tents, together with a number of improvised canvas and timber structures
used as individual living quarters, workshops, ablution shelters
and stores. Each company also has a Quonset hut, which is the
American equivalent of a Nissen, and which is used as a Company canteen. Finally, hidden in the undergrowth may be seen
two caravans, an authorised one for the Commanding Officer and
an unauthorised one occupied by the Second-in-Command.'

The Essex also built a battalion church which was duly dedicated to St
Alban by the Rev. W. G. A. Wright.

'Despite all the "Arctic weather" stories, the winter has apparently been one of the mildest on record. In fact, we did not even

have a white Christmas, for on Christmas Day it poured with rain, most unseasonable. However, the rain did little to dampen our spirits and all enjoyed Christmas dinner in the Company canteen, where it was traditionally served by the officers and sergeants.'

The Essex Regiment renewed a long standing association with another unit in Korea. An officer of the 7th U.S. Infantry Regiment visited the battalion to meet R.S.M. McCeever, with whom he had served in the Parachute Regiment before joining the American Army. As a result of this reunion, an officer of the Essex Regiment was invited to visit the 7th Regiment. During this reciprocal visit it was discovered that the 7th U.S. Infantry Regiment and the 1st Battalion of the 44th (Essex) Regiment had opposed each other at the Battle of New Orleans in 1814. The 7th had received their first battle honour – or 'honor' – for repulsing the British attack from behind their defensive line of cotton bales, this earning their regimental nick-name of 'The Cottonbalers'.

*Vickers machine gun team of the 1st Bn., The Essex Regiment, in winter clothing. 1953.*

(IWM KOR 609)

Nineteen fifty-four began reasonably pleasantly. 'So far, although we have had some cold nights and unpleasant mornings, the Korean winter has not seemed so terrible as it was painted. But the thought persists that we are lucky to be living in winterised tents and to be issued with such a mass of winter clothing. Opinions on the severity of the weather would be very different if we were living in ill-equipped dug-outs.'

Major-General West had relinquished command of the 1st Commonwealth Division to Major-General H. Murray, C.B., D.S.O., on 10th October 1953, and 28 Brigade was to lose its commander early in 1954. Brigadier Wilton was due to return to Australia on completion of his year of command. The Essex Regiment were paraded to bid farewell to the brigadier and he told them:

*Brigadier Wilton inspects the Royal Warwickshire Regiment. February 1954.*

(AWM HOB 4836)

| *Pte. Moody* | *Pte. Harvey* | *Lcpl. Hunter* | *Pte. Kim* | *Pte. Potts* |
|---|---|---|---|---|
| *Essex* | *R.A.R.* | *Essex* | *Katcom* | *R.A.R.* |

*Brigadier J. G. N. Wilton, O.B.E., inspects the Essex Regiment. February 1954.*

(Journal of the Essex Regiment)

'Despite the disappointment the battalion had experienced by arriving just after the ceasefire, you have carried out your duties under the Truce in a highly satisfactory manner. I have watched the battalion and I am convinced that you would have distinguished yourselves admirably if you had been given the opportunity for which you were trained. I have observed the keenness and enthusiasm with which you have served here in Korea and I want to thank you for the hard work you have put in on the new defence positions. And I hope that when your time comes to leave Korea you will look back on this tour of duty as an experience that has been worthwhile.'

Brigadier Wilton was relieved by Brigadier I. T. Murdoch, O.B.E., another Australian, on 19th February.

The 1st Battalion of the Royal Australian Regiment, Lieutenant-Colonel M. Austin, returned to Korea to relieve the 2nd Royal Australians on 6th April 1954. 2 R.A.R. had gained the battle honour 'The Samichon' and seven major awards for gallantry during its service in Korea. Lieutenant-Colonel Burns handed command of the 16th Field Regiment, R.N.Z.A., to Lieutenant-Colonel J. A. Pountney, M.B.E., and the sense of urgency began to disappear as the opposing forces settled to occupy the truce positions.

'Early in 1954, the regiment found itself slipping severely under strength. For some months, recruiting in New Zealand had been slackening off and replacements were just not coming forward to take over from the men whose period of service in Korea was completed. The position became serious and it was decided to augment the New Zealand personnel in the regiment with British National Servicemen who were already posted to the theatre. A number of British artillery officers were already attached to the regiment. At first a trial group of ten British gunners were attached to the regiment to see if the suggested scheme was practicable. They were all volunteers and at the end of their trial period, it was quite apparent that the scheme could be a success. About seventy volunteers were called for among the British units but more than 200 put their names forward. There was no problem in obtaining British officers to serve with the regiment for the remainder of the time it stayed in Korea, there were always about seven or eight on attachment. The British gunners who were attached to the regiment stayed until early October 1954, when the "running down" process started. They served the regiment well and they certainly seemed to enjoy their period of attachment. It was something of a novelty for them to serve with "the Kiwis".'

The 'running down' process heralded the end of the 28th Commonwealth Infantry Brigade in Korea. It was decided to reduce the Commonwealth forces under the United Nations command, leaving only a token force to represent Commonwealth interests. The Commonwealth Division was to be reduced to a third of its strength and to effect such a drastic reduction, 28 Brigade was to disappear. On 31st August 1954, Brigadier Murdoch had the unenviable task of relinquishing his command on the disbandment of the 28th Commonwealth Infantry Brigade.

*ANZAC Day, 25th April 1954; representatives of the 1st and 3rd Battalions of the Royal Australian Regiment, the Royal New Zealand Artillery and the Essex Regiment.*

(AWM MELJ 53 JC)

The brigade units did not disappear immediately from Korea. The 16th Field Regiment of the Royal New Zealand Artillery was declared non-operational on 7th October 1954, and prepared to return to New Zealand. The official historian of the regiment noted: 'The 16th Field Regiment, R.N.Z.A. which had acquitted itself with honour both in war and peace, ceased to exist.' During its three years and ten months in Korea, the regiment had earned four Distinguished Service Orders, eleven Military Crosses, one Distinguished Conduct Medal, seven Military Medals and a Presidential Citation from the Republic of Korea. Thirteen members of

*Brigadier Murdoch, March 1954.*

(AWM HOB 4862)

the regiment had been killed in action, 79 had been wounded and 11 had died in Korea. As gunners, 16 Field Regiment were not awarded any particular battle honours but shared the 'Ubique' of the Royal Artillery, indicating that they had taken part in all the battles of 28 Brigade and given support to other formations of the United Nations forces.

The 3rd Battalion of the Royal Australian Regiment, the 'veteran' battalion and the very core of the Commonwealth Brigade for the last four years, held a farewell parade on 12 October 1954. The 3rd Royal Australians, or 'Old Faithful' as the battalion became known, had rendered superlative service during its stay in Korea. Although the battalion had undergone several changes of personnel, its reputation as a fighting unit was maintained and it returned to Australia with all its battle honours plus a U.S. Presidential Citation. Members of the battalion had gained one George Cross, four Distinguished Service Orders, seventeen Military Crosses, four Distinguished Conduct Medals and one bar to the D.C.M., one George Medal and twenty-nine Military Medals.

The 1st Battalions of the Essex Regiment and the Royal Warwickshire Regiment also left Korea in the latter part of 1954. 'We have made many friends in Korea at all levels, and we were particularly fortunate to have served in the British Commonwealth Brigade which included the Royal Australian Regiment and the New Zealand Gunners.' Only the 1st Battalion of the Royal Australian Regiment, reduced to twenty-one officers and 509 other ranks by November, remained in Gallipoli Camp as the representative Australian element of the British Commonwealth Contingent of the United Nations Forces until they also left Korea on 24th March 1956. The Commonwealth Contingent was latterly commanded by Brigadier Barlow, formerly commanding officer of the King's Shropshire Light Infantry during their tour with 28 Brigade in Korea.

So ended the life of the 28th Commonwealth Infantry Brigade in Korea, a unique formation which inherited all the flair and panache of the original 27th Commonwealth Brigade and added a sound and battle-proven reputation to that foundation. The brigade's greatest achievement was the last successful major attack of the war, pushing the front line deep into North Korea in October 1951, when it established itself as an aggressive and determined fighting force. Thereafter, the component units of the brigade exhibited all the dour stubbornness of the Anglo-Saxon in defence, dominating their sector of the front line for almost two years and, with Celtic dash, carried the fight into the enemy's positions. The brigade was in action right up to the sounding of the cease-fire and its official battle-honours – Kowang-San, Maryang-San, Hill 227 and The Samichon –

reflect the indomitable spirit of this fighting formation. Four British and
three Australian infantry battalions were 'blooded' with the brigade, supported by the ubiquitous gunners of the Royal New Zealand Artillery and
the superlative Indian Field Ambulance.

The last word comes from Australia:

> 'It is instructive to note that respective commanders of the Com-
> monwealth Division, when questioned in later years, had no
> hesitation in describing the 28th Commonwealth Brigade as the
> best of their three brigades. Yet the 28th Brigade was the most
> nationally diverse of the three brigades, with two Australian and
> two British battalions, an Indian Field Ambulance and a New
> Zealand artillery regiment. The necessity for working together
> gave them something extra.'

# Renaissance

After the Korean Armistice of 1953 there was a deterioration in the stability of the countries of Southeast Asia. The French abandoned the whole of Indo-China after the disaster at Dien Bien Phu. The new independent Republic of South Vietnam, suffering from a precarious economy, lived in fear of its Northern neighbour, the People's Republic of North Vietnam. The inexperienced government of the Kingdom of Laos was struggling with Communist insurgents and neutral Cambodia wavered under the unpredictable rule of Prince Sihanouk. The Kingdom of Thailand felt very vulnerable to the actions of these turbulent states. Only in the Federation of Malaya, where some two divisions worth of British, Gurkha, Malay and Fijian troops together with the Malayan Police were slowly but surely gaining the upper hand over the Communist Terrorists (C.T.s), was there any prospect of a settled and secure future.

The Southeast Asia Treaty Organization, comprising the U.S.A., Australia, New Zealand, Great Britain, France, Pakistan and the Philippines and Thailand as an associate member, was formed to counter this threat. Although similar in name, SEATO was quite different to NATO. There was no unified command structure and no commitment by member states to intervene but merely to consult if any of the designated states, including Thailand, were seriously threatened by Communist forces or insurgents.

By 1955 it was evident that there was a need for a Commonwealth force to combat any further encroachment by the Communist bloc, whether by direct attack or infiltration. A SEATO strategic reserve force was envisaged which would consist of earmarked land, sea and air forces to be provided by Australia, New Zealand and Great Britain who would train together in peacetime and form the nucleus of an intervention force. The

159

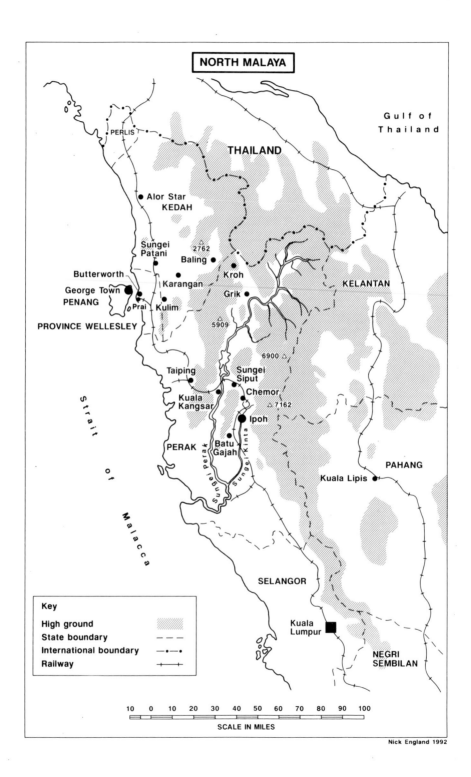

# NORTH MALAYA

Gulf of Thailand

THAILAND

PERLIS

Alor Star
KEDAH

△ 2762

Sungei Patani

Baling

Kroh

Butterworth

Karangan

KELANTAN

George Town
PENANG

Prai

Kulim

Grik

PROVINCE WELLESLEY

△ 5909

6900 △

Taiping

Sungei Siput

Chemor

Kuala Kangsar

△ 7162

Ipoh

PERAK

Batu Gajah

Sungei Perak

Sungei Kinta

PAHANG

Kuala Lipis

Strait

of

Malacca

SELANGOR

**Key**

High ground

State boundary

International boundary

Railway

Kuala Lumpur

NEGRI SEMBILAN

10  0  10  20  30  40  50  60  70  80  90  100

SCALE IN MILES

Nick England 1992

land element of a Commonwealth Far East Strategic Reserve should initially consist of a brigade group. The 28th Commonwealth Infantry Brigade in Korea had demonstrated that such a formation could be effective operationally and viable administratively and, after its disbandment in 1954, it was decided to reform the brigade in Malaya.

The first step on the ground, as distinct from in the planners' offices, was the assembly of a skeleton brigade headquarters on 16th September 1955, in offices kindly lent by Group Captain Baxter, commander of the R.A.F. Station Butterworth in Province Wellesley, North Malaya. The first two staff officers to assume their appointments were Major Peter Oxley of the Royal Australian Regiment as Brigade-Major and Major Ken Davidson of the Royal Artillery as Deputy-Assistant-Adjutant and Quartermaster-General. Within a few days they were joined by Brigadier P. N. M. Moore, the Brigade Commander. Other staff officers joined at the same time: Major Newell, Royal Signals, commanding the brigade's signal squadron; Major Watherham, Royal Warwickshire Regiment, General Staff Officer III; Captain David White, Royal Australian Army Service Corps, Staff Captain Q; Captain John Inglis, 15/19 Hussars, Staff Captain A; Captain John Tattersall, Royal Army Ordnance Corps, Brigade Ordnance Officer and Major P. M. Shanahan commanding the advance party of the 2nd Battalion of the Royal Australian Regiment, the first infantry battalion of the new brigade group. Other units designated to join the brigade were scattered all over Malaya and the Australian infantry battalion and artillery field battery, with families, had to be fitted in to the unfamiliar British administrative system. The brigade came under the command of the 1st Federal Division, Major-General Sinclair, with its headquarters at Taiping in Perak. A suitable camp site in a coconut grove on the seashore, temporarily occupied by part of a field squadron of Royal Engineers, was selected for the brigade headquarters and the Royal Engineers Works Services built a number of additional 'bashas', or straw huts, in a remarkably short time. The 2nd Royal Australians were to be accommodated in Minden Barracks on Penang Island, one of the best barracks in Malaya, and the field battery would occupy bashas on the other side of the road from brigade headquarters.

Brigadier Moore left Malaya on 23rd September to attend the presentation of new colours to the 2nd Royal Australian Regiment in Australia. *En route*, in Singapore, the brigade commander was briefed on the discussions then taking place between the Australian, New Zealand and British governments on the brigade's role. The Australians wanted the brigade to concentrate on training for large scale operations of the kind undertaken by the French in Vietnam and were particularly anxious to avoid the role of the brigade becoming an issue in the forthcoming Australian general election. The politicians in Malaya wanted the brigade group to be used in the anti-terrorist campaign in Malaya and the British government wanted the brigade to be available for both tasks.

On 28th September the 2nd Royal Australians, Lieutenant-Colonel Jim Ochiltree, received their colours from Field Marshal Sir William Slim, the Governor-General of Australia. Brigadier Moore attended and then took the opportunity to visit the battalion and 105 Field Battery, Royal Australian Artillery, Major Bruce Bogle, stationed near Sydney. Other Australian contingents were also visited at Queenscliffe and Puckapanyal in Victoria. Brigadier Moore noted that

> 'The Australian Army had its own jungle training centre at Canungra in Southern Queensland but the terrain lacked the lush tropical secondary jungle encountered in Malaya. It was considered that training at Canungra was a complete substitute for training at Kota Tinggi in Johore, Malaya, and it had the added advantage that there was no risk of a premature involvement of Australian troops in anti-terrorist operations before public opinion was thought to be ready for it. With hindsight, this proved to be a mistake and some of the troubles from which 2 R.A.R. suffered in their early months can be attributed to the decision not to send them to Kota Tinggi. This error was later recognised and subsequent Australian and New Zealand battalions all went through the Jungle Warfare Training Centre in Malaya just like their British and Gurkha counterparts.'

By the time Brigadier Moore got back to Butterworth on 9th October brigade headquarters was getting firmly established. Captain David Mann of the Australian Army joined the H.Q. as intelligence officer and the brigade commander was able to make his formal call on Mr. R. C. Bingham, the Resident Commissioner for Penang and Province Wellesley. The operational organization in North Malaya was to have a considerable impact on the arrangements for training the brigade group. In principle, the army, although operating at full stretch against the terrorists in the jungle and its fringes, was not at war but was deployed in aid of the civil power. Because of the effect of military operations on the daily life of the people and the importance of the fight for their hearts and minds, the Emergency was run by a series of State War Executive

Committees (SWECs) under the general supervision of a Director of Operations in the capital, Kuala Lumpur, at that time General Sir Geoffrey Bourne. These committees comprised the Resident (or British Adviser to the local Sultan), the Mentri Besar (Prime Minister) representing the civil power, the chief police officer and the military commander – usually a brigade commander – together with any necessary advisers such as the Secretary for Chinese Affairs and the head of the information services. In addition, there were co-opted members including representatives of the three communities – Malay, Chinese and Indian – and representatives of the Malayan Rubber Planters Association. The SWEC was an unwieldy body and security of information was a potential problem; it dealt with the longer term aspects of operations such as the establishment of new villages, food control plans, etc. An operational SWEC was established for the control of operations and was limited to the Resident (or more often his deputy), the military commander, the chief of police and, most importantly, the head of the police special branch in the State who was responsible for intelligence. The Ops SWEC met weekly and, if the situation demanded, could meet daily for about half an hour at 'morning prayers'.

The next tier down was the District War Executive Committee headed by the District Officer of the Malayan Civil Service and comprising the military commander, usually a battalion or company commander, the district police officer, a representative of the special branch, the Home Guard commander and, where appropriate, the local assistant protector of aborigines. DWECs met at least once a week and sometimes more frequently with 'morning prayers' sessions. They were concerned with the nuts and bolts of food control, curfew timings and detailed co-operation between the police and the army.

In the State of Kedah, part of 28 Brigade's area, there was a State War Executive Committee at Alor Star and the Kulim War Executive Committee in the Southern part of the State. Penang had a Settlement War Executive Committee which controlled both Penang Island and Province Wellesley on the mainland; Province Wellesley was one of the Straits Settlements and a Crown Colony rather than a protected state and had its own District War Executive Committee. Only one Communist Terrorist was believed to be at large in the jungle of Penang Island and the Penang SWEC was more concerned with police rather than military matters. Province Wellesley was graded as a 'white area' – an area which was considered to be free of C.T.s and where it was possible to travel unescorted on the roads by night and where emergency food controls and other regulations did not apply.

On 20th October the *Georgic* arrived off Penang carrying the 2nd Battalion of the Royal Australian Regiment and 105 Field Battery, R.A.A. Sir Alec Watt, the Australian High Commissioner in Southeast Asia, went aboard to welcome the troops. The *Georgic* berthed under her own power the next morning to be greeted by the band of the 1st Battalion of The Royal Scots Fusiliers, resplendent in white drill tunics, green plaids, kilts and tartan trews. The 2nd Royal Australians, who had previously served in 28 Commonwealth Brigade in Korea from March 1953 to April 1954, were the first infantry battalion to join the new brigade. The Royal Scots Fusiliers were earmarked for the brigade but were not yet under command as was the third infantry battalion, the 1st Battalion of The Royal Lincolnshire Regiment, then operating in the South of Malaya. Brigadier Moore, who had commanded the 28th Engineer Regiment of the 1st Commonwealth Division in Korea, was amongst many other Korea veterans and the brigade's traditions were maintained. The new 28 Brigade boasted its own insignia: the Queen's Crown over the title 'Commonwealth' on a light and dark blue background, obviously derived from the 1st Commonwealth Divisional sign of the Korean War. 'Commonwealth' was abbreviated as 'Comwel' and this abbreviation was often confused with Cromwell and his Commonwealth, despite the symbolism of the Royal Crown.

*Formation Sign*
*28 Commonwealth Infantry Brigade Group*
*Malaya*
*16th September 1955 – 31st October 1971.*

An Australian contingent in Malaya was very much a novelty and attracted a continual stream of visitors and, at that time, much press coverage. The High Commissioner, Sir Donald MacGillivray, paid an informal visit to the 2nd Royal Australians in Minden Barracks on 20th October and on the 25th the Australian Minister for External Affairs, Mr. R. G. Casey, inspected a parade of the battalion, to be followed a few days later by the Commander-in-Chief, Far East Land Forces, General Sir Charles Loewen. These events received extensive publicity which was an embarrassment to the Australians and an annoyance to the British whose units had been fighting in the emergency for a considerable number of years. This unsatisfactory state of affairs was resolved by a conference at Brigade Headquarters attended by the State Information Officer and the Australian Public Relations Officer. The main problem, however, was to complete the Australian troops' jungle training before they could be deployed.

The major difficulty was that the Australian Government was extremely anxious that their soldiers should not be involved in anti-terrorist operations, even by accident, during the period before the Australian general election in December. This, while irksome to the troops themselves and not least to the various formation headquarters, was understandable. Training on the mainland was severely restricted, in spite of the help given by the 1st/6th Gurkha Rifles, Lieutenant-Colonel Bredin, and the Gurkha Depot at Sungei Patani. The 2nd Royal Australians were therefore limited to Penang Island where there was plenty of jungle but no field firing range. The inhabitants of Penang had not heard a shot fired in anger for many months and they were free to wander in the jungle at will. The last thing the civil government wanted was for anything to disturb the peaceful atmosphere of the island. This was exasperating for the troops but there were genuine difficulties in promulgating a prohibited area and keeping the locals out. The field battery was less troubled with such restrictions and 25 Field Regiment, Lieutenant-Colonel James Heard, ran a practice camp on the mainland for the Australians to calibrate their guns.

Several demonstrations and visits were staged in November. 'B' Squadron of the 15th/19th Hussars, under Major George Lewis, put on a superbly stage-managed demonstration for 2 R.A.R. and 105 Field Battery; Lieutenant-Colonel Hart, of Malaya Command, gave a detailed and interesting lecture on the Communist organisation. In Kuala Lumpur, Lieutenant-Colonel Ochiltree, Major Bogle and Brigadier Moore, attended a review of the operational situation by Lieutenant-General Sir

Geoffrey Bourne, the Director of Operations. In the afternoon they 'heard a brilliant and very witty exposition of the origins of the Communist terrorists from the late Mr. Brimmel. This was an outstanding performance. With one ten-minute break, he talked without a note for three and a quarter hours to some twenty or thirty potentially somnolent or restive senior officers on a hot tropical afternoon. He held them spellbound and received an ovation at the end.' Brigadier Moore also visited 16 Field Ambulance, Lieutenant-Colonel Longden, in Kuala Lumpur. The Brigade Ordnance Field Park of forty-five men and twenty vehicles arrived in Butterworth Camp, two of the Malay train guards were found under an ammunition wagon – trying to light a fire to cook their evening meal.

General Bourne visited the Brigade Headquarters at the end of November to give verbal authority for the Australians to be used in counter-terrrorist operations, subject to the agreement of the Kedah SWEC. However, on 28th November, arrangements for the 2nd Royal Australians to go to two company training camps in Central Kedah were cancelled at the last moment. No reason was given but it later became clear that this was because of the proposed peace talks at Baling between Chin Peng, the Communist terrorist leader (who had taken part in the Victory Parade in London in 1945), and Tengku Abdul Rahman, the Prime Minister of Malaya, who had won an overwhelming victory in the July elections. To have established Australian training camps within twenty miles of Baling would have appeared provocative.

At the beginning of December, the Resident Commissioner agreed to use his emergency powers to designate a field firing area in the jungle on the Northwest of Penang Island. The area was remote, one hour's drive from Minden Barracks followed by a two-hour march up a very steep track, but it was an improvement on the existing facilities. Field firing had to be done at either the Gurkha Depot at Sungei Patani or a quarry near Butterworth worked by an Australian Air Force airfield construction squadron. Both sites involved at least an hour's wait and crossing on the Penang ferry with a further one and a half hour's drive – making a round trip of some four or five hours. On 6th December it was announced at the Penang SWEC that the range on Penang had become a political issue in Kuala Lumpur and the Resident Commissioner had been requested not to use his emergency powers!

On 10th December Major-General Pollard, the Quartermaster-General of the Australian Army, visited the 2nd Royal Australians and 105 Field Battery and also inspected the two company camps prepared in Central Kedah. The main aim of his visit was to investigate the arrangements for families' accommodation and amenities. Meanwhile, General Bourne indicated that 2 R.A.R. could move into Kedah but, at 10.45 a.m. on 14th December, the troops – who were due to move on the 15th – had their deployment postponed to 1st January 1956, by higher authority for 'political reasons'.

However, on 19th December, Mr. Menzies, the Australian Prime Minister, announced that Australian troops could be employed in anti-terrorist operations at the end of the month, thus ending a period of great frustration and uncertainty. A particularly trying time for Lieutenant-Colonel Ochiltree and his company commanders who succeeded in maintaining the morale of the 2nd Royal Australians despite all the disappointments and confusion.

At the same time, a truce was declared over 400 square miles of the Malayan-Thai border for the Baling peace talks. Shades of Panmunjon.

# Deployment

The last two weeks of 1955 – apart from the Christmas celebrations – were spent planning Operation 'Deuce', the introduction of the 2nd Royal Australian Regiment and the 105th Field Battery to anti-terrorist operations in the Kulim area.

Kulim is situated near the border between the State of Kedah and Province Wellesley, sufficiently far enough from Baling to avoid any risk of prejudicing the peace talks which were about to begin. Most of this area in North Malaya is covered with tropical rain forest, the trees growing to sixty feet or more and affording an average field of vision of some ten to fifteen yards. The villages, or kampongs, are on the flat valley floors, surrounded by old tin mine workings, cultivated land and rubber estates which allow about 100 yards field of view, depending on the maturity of the trees. Bordering the rubber estates and cultivated areas there is often a 50-100 yard wide belt of secondary jungle which limits visibility to as little as three or four yards. Contacts between the terrorists and sympathisers would often take place in these thick strips of overgrown jungle or three or four armed terrorists would waylay Chinese or Indian rubber tappers in the rubber estates. All the Chinese had been resettled in new villages which were surrounded by wire fences and guarded; from these villages the Chinese had to walk or bicycle to their vegetable or tapioca plots on the jungle fringe. The rubber tappers lived in fenced-off labour lines, close to the estate manager's bungalow, and went out in groups every morning, usually just before dawn. A dusk to dawn curfew was in force throughout the whole area, even for the Malays – who were mostly hostile to the terrorists – and lived in their own kampongs near their farm lands in the valleys.

The security forces' constant problem was to make physical contact with the C.T.s. The classic method was to impose very strict controls on the movement of any food from the new villages and rubber estate labour lines. To obtain food, the C.T.s would then have to risk meeting their contacts and food suppliers in or near the villages or labour lines. The Special Branch of the Royal Malay Police, through their network of informers, would hear of any contacts and this knowledge enabled ambushes to be laid on the C.T.s' return route to the jungle. Very often it was necessary to 'freeze' a wide area around such an ambush site and prohibit any patrolling for several days beforehand to lull the terrorists into a false state of security. Active patrolling, and sometimes harassing fire, would be encouraged in other areas to keep the terrorists on the move and hamper their activities elsewhere.

In the 2nd Royal Australians' new operational area it was estimated that about ten to fifteen C.T.s remained in the jungle around Kulim; they had good contacts with the labour force on some of the larger rubber estates and there was little military supervision of the food searches. The chances of laying ambushes were therefore rather remote. Lieutenant-Colonel Ochiltree proposed to make some areas uncomfortable for the C.T.s by a combination of harassing fire by night and airstrikes by day. Patrols of platoon strength would enter the jungle elsewhere and lay night ambushes on likely escape routes. To cover these movements, it was planned to give the impression that operations were beginning some ten miles further North by ostentatious ground and air reconnaissance.

The Baling talks started on Boxing Day 1955 and concluded on 28th December without result. Where restraint and caution had been urged before the talks, immediate action was now called for.

On 1st January 1956 the 2nd Royal Australians (less two companies) and the 105th Field Battery moved into the operational area. The battalion command post was established at Kulim with two rifle companies in camps on rubber estates. Later that evening one company infiltrated into the jungle whilst the field battery fired harassing tasks. By the following morning the leading company's patrols were in the jungle and had established satisfactory communications with the command post. The R.A.F. at Butterworth had mounted rocket and machine gun airstrikes on likely terrorist camping sites outside 2 R.A.R.'s patrol area during the 1st of January. These airstrikes were designed to distract the C.T.s' attention away from the Australians' area and to encourage movement into it.

On 3rd January a third company of 2 R.A.R. and later a fourth company, entered the jungle to complete the battalion's deployment with the four rifle companies in the Kulim area and Support Company at Karangan. Thereafter, one rifle company at a time was rotated through Minden

Barracks for training and relaxation. At the Penang and Province Wellesley SWEC on 5th January, attended by the GOC, the full meeting was briefed on the progress of the operation. The 2nd Royal Australians made their first contact on 6th January and, on 9th January, got their first terrorist.

Meanwhile, Brigade Headquarters had been making administrative arrangements for the assembly of the supporting arms and services. 11 Field Squadron Royal Engineers and 16 Field Ambulance R.A.M.C., with their families and the families of the Ordnance Field Park, were due to arrive at the end of July. The field squadron would occupy the field battery's lines when 105 Battery was deployed; there was room for 16 Field Ambulance and the vehicles of the Ordnance Field Park in Minden Barracks but there was a very real shortage of housing for the families. The Australian Families Hostel was opened on Penang Island on 21st January. A former hotel had been very well converted by the Australian Government, largely due to the efforts of Colonel F. W. Speed who, since the arrival of the Australian contingent, had been very active visiting North Malaya and ironing out all the difficulties arising from the expenditure of Australian Government funds; his staff was also responsible for all personnel matters and keeping the contingent up to strength with drafts coming through Singapore. The arrival of the first families from Australia on 22nd January was evidence of their success.

General Bourne, Director of Operations, visited the 2nd Royal Australians in their company camps in Kulim on 23rd January and also attended the Kedah SWEC. On 26th January, a platoon of the Police Field Force took two C.T.s, one of whom was captured alive and gave useful information. The Police Field Force, or P.F.F., comprised platoons of Malay constables, fully armed and equipped, under the command of European Police Lieutenants. Apart from manning forts deep in the jungle to prevent the C.T.s dominating the aborigines, the P.F.F. were of great value in patrolling in conjunction with army units. The 2nd Royal Australians suffered a tragic set back on 31st January. A sergeant moved whilst in ambush and was shot and fatally wounded by one of his own patrol. He was evacuated to the Kulim civil hospital but could not be moved and died there some days later. On the same day, the Kedah Home Guard – who were delighted to be working with the army – shot and wounded one of six C.T.s.

February was, on the whole, a quiet month. Support Company of 2 R.A.R. were equipped with 4.2 inch mortars, their upper register shooting was more effective in the jungle than the flatter trajectory 25 pounder guns but had, of course, a much shorter range. In reality, a quiet month for the infantry meant many hours of arduous patrolling with little to show for it in the way of contacts. The Australians killed a Malay curfew breaker whilst in ambush, which was very unfortunate, but missed two C.T.s at a range of sixty yards on 22nd February, which was disappointing. An Auster aircraft on reconnaissance on 21st February saw a party of C.T.s harvesting in a clearing some 1,000 yards inside the Malayan border. Airstrikes in the border area required Thai clearance, in case of cross-border movement by Thai nationals. Such clearance was not given until 4.00 p.m. by which time the weather had closed in. The following morning the party had gone and could not be located. This was particularly frustrating for Group-Captain Baxter, commanding R.A.F. Butterworth, who had been most helpful in laying on airstrikes for the 2nd Royal Australians. A strike against a known target would have been a satisfying reward for the pilots and ground crews.

During the latter part of February, 2 R.A.R. conducted a series of snap-shooting sweepstakes and competitions on the short ranges of their company camps for troops coming back from jungle patrols. The battalion was in high spirits when another C.T. was killed on 4th March. A further contact was made on the 11th and a trail was followed for 1,000 yards but without result. On 17th March, three platoons lay in ambush near the site of a suspected C.T. camp but the elusive enemy did not appear. The 2nd Royal Australians had a very frustrating time towards the end of March. In addition to the lack of contact with the terrorists, the battalion suffered three fatal shooting accidents in one week. In retrospect, it was considered that at least one of those lives might have been saved if 2 R.A.R. had been able to make full use of the field firing range on Penang Island to practise jungle shooting skills.

Meanwhile, the brigade was gathering strength. The remainder of the Ordnance Field Park arrived at the beginning of March; one innocent young national serviceman was persuaded to report to the Brigade Headquarters Sergeant-Major for duty as 'coconut catching orderly'. An impassioned telephone call from Prai Railway Station heralded the arrival of a corporal and four war dogs, requesting that they be collected by the brigade as soon as possible since one dog has already bitten the harassed movement control officer.

On 20th March, General Bourne and the Prime Minister of Malaya, Tengku Abdul Rahman, attended the Kulim Combined War Executive Committee during which the Tengku put his finger on the weak spot of the whole operation – the lack of an organised and effective food control system.

On 23rd March Brigadier Moore visited 'A', 'B' and 'D' Companies of the 1st Battalion of The Royal Lincolnshire Regiment in their camps in South Malaya. It was planned for the Royal Lincolns to replace the 1st Battalion of the Federation Regiment (a mixed Malay/Chinese battalion) in Kuala Kangsar, in Perak, there to come under command of 28 Brigade. However, due to the need for troops elsewhere in Malaya, the move of the Royal Lincolns was delayed.

In April the brigade at last assumed operational command of the 1st Battalion of The Royal Scots Fusiliers, Lieutenant-Colonel J. D. O. Deleno-Osborne. The Fusiliers, who were by then seasoned jungle fighters, operated with the Ulu Kinta D.W.E.C. on the East side of the Ipoh Plain. The battalion occupied a hutted camp in Ipoh except for 'B' Company, which was some miles away in a rubber estate at Tanjong Rambutan. At the same time, the inter-brigade boundary between 28 Brigade and the 2nd Malay Brigade was established at the Ipoh SWEC – of which the brigade commander then became a member.

*Major Peter Oxley (Brigade Major) and Brigadier Moore (Commander 28 Commonwealth Brigade), March 1956.*

(Brigadier Moore)

Operation 'Deuce' concluded at the end of April and the 2nd Royal Australians were relieved in the Kulim area by the Police Field Force. 2 R.A.R. moved South to Perak to occupy the camps vacated by the 1st Federation Regiment with battalion headquarters at Sungei Siput (where the Malayan Emergency started in 1948) and the companies in camps in the Sungei Siput-Kuala Kangsar area. From their new base the Australians were committed to Operation 'Shark', directed against the C.T.s in the Ipoh – Chemor – Sungei Siput area. There were considerably more terrorists operating in this area than at Kulim and they were better organized. Deep in the jungle to the West of Ipoh and South of Sungei Siput was 13/15 Platoon which consisted of about 25 C.T.s who had committed a number of atrocities over the years and formed the local striking force. Supporting this hard core were the Sungei Siput Armed Work Force, the Jalong Tinggi Armed Work Force operating to the East of Sungei Siput and the Lintang Armed Work Force in the jungle surrounding the rubber estates some eight miles North of Sungei Siput. In the Royal Scots Fusiliers' operational area were the Chemor Armed Work Force on the plain to the North of Ipoh and the Tanjong Rambutan Armed Work Force further to the South on the East side of the plain. The task of the Armed Work Forces was to frighten villagers and rubber estate workers into providing food and medicine, spreading propaganda amongst the locals and obtaining intelligence of army and police movements and dispositions. The armed work forces usually operated in parties of six to ten persons and avoided contact with the security forces.

With brigade headquarters at Butterworth and the battalion command posts established at Sungei Siput and Chemor – working with their respective district war executive committees – it became necessary to organize a system to determine boundaries in the jungle between the battalions and co-ordinate the activities of the gunners and sappers without constant reference to the Ops SWEC at Ipoh. This was achieved by setting up a 'supporting arms conference' which met weekly or more frequently if necessary. This arrangement worked well and continued until 1958, advising the Ops SWEC of any changes in the allocation of supporting arms at the daily 'morning prayers' meetings.

Early in May intelligence reports from the Special Branch indicated that the C.T.s intended to lay an ambush on the main road in the Kuala Kangsar area. Check points were established along the road and convoys were escorted by the armoured cars of the 16th/5th Lancers who were stationed at Ipoh. These measures thwarted the C.T.s' plans and no ambushes were attempted. At the same time, the Kuala Kangsar DWEC

suddenly decided to divert the 2nd Royal Australians from their main task
in Operation 'Shark' to mount an operation astride the Kuala Kangsar-
Grik road where a party of C.T.s had been reported. Lieutenant-Colonel
Ochiltree advised against the operation since there was no food control in
this largely Malay area and the deployment would have meant a serious
dispersion of effort. After a long argument, Support Company of 2 R.A.R.
was committed to a short-term operation in the area but no contacts were
made and no further signs of C.T.s were reported.

On 14th May the 2nd Royal Australians made their first kill in the
Operation 'Shark' area. It was the first kill in that particular work force
for over two years and a good start to the operation. By this time the law
of diminishing returns applied in North Malaya; those terrorists who
survived were the most intelligent, alert and skilled in junglecraft. As
their numbers dwindled, they needed to make less frequent contacts with
the local population and thus became progressively harder to discover and
eliminate. The police were given the task of food control duties which,
with the help of 2 R.A.R., were tightened before the end of 1956. This
involved protecting and supervising the check of all labourers leaving
rubber estate compounds and people leaving the new villages.

The Commonwealth soldiers normally did ten days on patrol in the
jungle followed by five days off for refitting and training in the company
base camps. Lieutenant Chinn of the 2nd Royal Australians describes the
supply routine in the jungle:

'On the fourth day after deployment and depending on the duration of the patrol, on successive fourth days, air resupply by
parachute was usually undertaken. As the airdrop clearly indicated the presence of a Security Force patrol, the pattern of activity was to search an area around a patrol base in three days
having identified a suitable D.Z., then completing the clearance of
the D.Z. early on the fourth day with a supply drop between mid-
morning and mid-afternoon. If practicable, the old base camp
would be vacated that day to start the move to a fresh area in
terms of the platoon's orders. Some supplies occasionally fell
outside the D.Z., compass bearings being taken to assist recovery.
Some parachutes hung up on trees, making recovery difficult.
Morale suffered when the hang-up included the rum ration
(overproof S.R.D. rum in baked clay demijohns) especially if the
demijohn smashed, filling the jungle with the enticing odour of its
contents! Nothing built up spirits more – after a heavy day's

movement in steep country, fully laden, in heavy rain, having based and changed into dry greens – than a tot of rum issued by the platoon sergeant from a rubber water bottle cap. The A510 wireless was able to pick up the B.B.C. News during stand-to at night and key features of world news could be passed by platoon commander or sergeant in standing down each hoochie's occupants. B.B.C. news of the Suez crisis in 1956 was sufficient to start a rumour in one platoon patrol base that Battalion Headquarters had called for volunteers for Suez!'

On 23rd May 1956, after three weeks of waiting in ambush, the Royal Scots Fusiliers challenged a civilian who promptly opened fire with a concealed Sten gun and ran away. On the same day, six C.T.s walked into an Australian ambush but the Bren gun jammed and the C.T.s made good their escape. Lieutenant Mack, a platoon commander in 'C' Company of the Royal Scots Fusiliers, remembers that '1956 was rather a quiet year in that the Kinta Valley appeared to have been over-shot and was short on

*1st Battalion Royal Scots Fusiliers, on patrol in a tin mine, June 1956.*

(Soldier Magazine 4686)

bandits; there were a few contacts and only one bandit was killed that year.' However, in an operation near Chemor, Lieutenant D. G. H. Andrews led his platoon of the Fusiliers in an attack on a C.T. camp and killed three terrorists, three others were wounded during the fire fight but managed to escape. For this successful little action, Lieutenant Andrews was later awarded the Military Cross.

Major Bruce Bogle, commanding the 105th Field Battery, controlled the brigade's artillery support: 105 Field Battery and a section of 3.7 inch guns of the Singapore Regiment of the Royal Artillery.

'The task of the artillery in 28 Brigade Group in 1955-1957 is simple to define, if less easy to understand and accept. It was wholly to support infantry operations which were inevitably prolonged, patiently conducted and only occasionally productive in demonstrable terms. This fire support was almost always deep beyond the actual infantry patrol areas, partly because of the natural uncertainty of patrol location and activity in the jungle, partly because of the technical problems of providing accurate fire and partly because of the lack of good target information and the total absence of observed targets. The aim was simply to attempt to harass the C.T.s. There was almost no observed fire, resulting from ground or aerial observation of actual or potential targets. The fire was predicted and the correction of map data to provide for prevailing atmospheric conditions was based upon infrequent and fairly stale meteorological telegrams emanating from somewhere well to the South. Thus it was all a fairly imprecise effort but since it was designed to harass an enemy whose actual location was merely presumed or suspected, there was little point in worrying about the accuracy of the gunnery. Sometime in 1956 it was decided that the guns of 105 Battery should be calibrated. In those days the only available method of calibration was by observation of fall of shot. In view of the nature of anti-terrorist operations, perhaps it is doubtful if calibration was necessary; however, it was another element of the training required and the battery was, after all, a unit of the strategic reserve, liable to be deployed at any time anywhere in the SEATO area. All units in the brigade were required to form and train an infantry patrol, which was to be available at base camps to respond instantly to any call from Brigade H.Q. to cope with sudden local C.T. adventures. Ours was formed and trained most effectively and enthusiastically by our first-rate and thoroughly war-like B.Q.M.S. (a former Royal Marine who years later commanded a rifle company in Vietnam). Its great and enduring value lay in the wonderful opportunity to test gunners and junior N.C.O.s in the tactical element of promotion examinations, which remained an Australian Army requirement. Since patrol training was conducted in "Black Areas", with all that this entailed, it was a most realistic qualifying test. There was never any doubt in anyone's mind (including the gunners in the patrol) as to whether or not a candidate displayed the required leadership qualities.'

11 Field Squadron of the Royal Engineers joined the brigade in early June and occupied part of the field battery's lines in Butterworth. 28 Brigade was beginning to look like a field formation with its own supporting arms and services.

The 1st Federal Division of the Malayan Army moved from its headquarters at Taiping in Perak. 28 Commonwealth Brigade took over, assuming responsibility for the administration of the North Malayan Sub-District which extended from the Thai Border in the North to Ipoh in the South as well as the operational command of units in the area, five infantry battalions and two field batteries of artillery.

# North Malaya

28 Commonwealth Infantry Brigade Group's area of responsibility was established in 1956 and the commander, Brigadier Moore, was given the additional task of commanding the North Malaya Sub-District. This administrative area covered all the military establishments and units in North Malaya and its headquarters was collocated with the brigade headquarters at Taiping. As dual commander of the brigade and the sub-district, Brigadier Moore wore two formation insignia on his uniform – but only one hat. The sub-district included British, Gurkha and Malay units as well as the Commonwealth forces.

The two battalions under the brigade's direct control continued to patrol the jungle territories to the North and East of Taiping. The Royal Scots Fusiliers took part in Operation 'Unity', a joint army and police sweep of the area along the border with Thailand. The 2nd Battalion of the Royal Australian Regiment established itself at Sungei Siput and patrolled the surrounding jungle country. Lieutenant-Colonel Ochiltree was fortunate in having Captain D. M. Ramsay as his adjutant; Captain Ramsay was 'a Brit in the Aust Army' and found that 'it was rather fun being able to "interpret" to both the British and Australian armies'. After the initial administrative problems, however, the Australian component of the brigade soon overcame any minor difficulties and became effectively operational alongside the British elements.

The third battalion of the brigade, the Royal Lincolnshire Regiment, eventually moved North from Negri Sembilan to join the brigade at Taiping in October 1956. 'B' and 'C' Companies of the Lincolns remained with the 26th Gurkha Brigade in Negri Sembilan whilst the other companies and battalion headquarters occupied their new camp at Taiping. The battalion's move was complicated by the sudden sickness of

178

*The Chief of the General Staff meeting officers of 28 Commonwealth Independent Brigade Group at Ipoh, 1957.*
*From left to right:*
*Brigadier P. N. M. Moore, D.S.O., M.C., Commander 28 Comwel Bde.*
*Field Marshal Sir Gerald Templer, G.C.B., G.C.M.G., K.B.E., M.C., C.I.G.S.*
*Major B. L. Bogle, R.A.A., Commanding 105 Fd. Bty. R.A.A.*
*Major P. H. G. Oxley, R.A.R., Brigade Major 28 Comwel Bde.*

(Brigadier Bogle)

the commanding officer, Lieutenant-Colonel Goulson, who went down with amoebic hepatitis and the second-in-command, Major G. J. S. Cotton, had to cope with all the difficulties of a major move. The Lincolns found Perak to be quite different from their previous operational area:

'The operational area is completely different to our last one. A bowl of tin mines and rubber plantations surrounded on all sides by mountains which contain the terrorist hideouts. Living in this lowland were some 30-40,000 inhabitants described as mainly apathetic, terrorised or actively anti-government. These locals

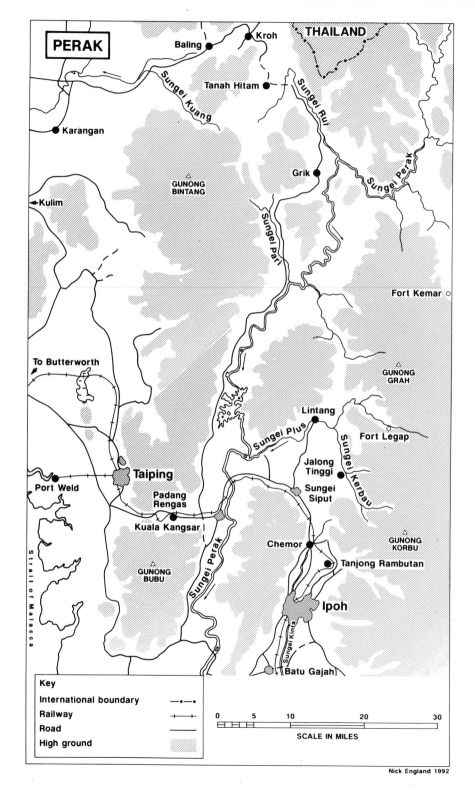

PERAK

THAILAND

Baling

Kroh

Karangan

Tanah Hitam

Sungei Kuang

Sungei Rui

Kulim

GUNONG BINTANG

Grik

Sungei Perak

Sungei Pari

Fort Kemar

To Butterworth

GUNONG GRAH

Sungei Plus

Lintang

Fort Legap

Taiping

Jalong Tinggi

Sungei Kerbau

Port Weld

Padang Rengas

Sungei Siput

Kuala Kangsar

Chemor

GUNONG KORBU

Sungei Perak

Tanjong Rambutan

Strait of Malacca

GUNONG BUBU

Ipoh

Sungei Kinta

Batu Gajah

Key

International boundary     •–•–

Railway     +–+–+

Road     ——

High ground

0     5     10     20     30

SCALE IN MILES

Nick England 1992

provided excellent intelligence, not to mention food, to the C.T. Food control was therefore a serious affair and men on duty at one gate alone, in conjunction with the police, had to search 2,000 tappers going out to work each morning.'

The New Year brought some excitement for the brigade. Major Mack, of the Royal Scots Fusiliers, recalls:

'1957 was more lively, starting with most of the battalion being turned out on New Year's Day, in the midst of our celebrations. "B" Company had already been warned for turnout but my company, "C", got its marching orders at about noon; it was just as well that my platoon was helicoptered in as most of the Jocks were still half-cut. My platoon, 9, went on to lose its hangover and kill the battalion's first two bandits of the year in an ambush where the pipeline crossed the Seni-oi River. They were Sui Tit, a branch committee member, and his wife Ah Go Tsai.'

The Royal Lincolns were also called out and Major Cotton had to cope with further problems.

'Not only had the initial plan to move the entire battalion to Perak before Christmas fallen through, but an internal security situation caused further disruption. This meant that Major Cotton had to try to control military aid to the civil power in Penang together with emergency operations in Sungei Siput, about 120 miles apart. Fortunately, the internal security problem in Georgetown, Penang, fizzled out. It had been caused by centenary celebrations in Georgetown which Higher Authority had decided, at short notice, should not be left to a Malay Battalion. However, a battalion tactical H.Q. and one company on Penang were kept on stand-by from January 4 to January 17, during which there were a number of stabbing and assault incidents but no serious trouble developed. The company involved was first "A" Company then "D" Company.'

After acting as 'policemen' in Penang, the Royal Lincolns returned to their new base and jungle operations.

'It was "D" Company which registered the battalion's first success in Perak. This was on January 17 when Second-Lieutenant M. J. T.

Earl took out two ambush parties in response to information received. Half way through the morning of January 18, Corporal Danby spotted through his binoculars three male C.T. consorting with tin-miners at the mine they were ambushing. The range was 400-500 yards. While trying to stalk the C.T., fire was opened on the patrol by other C.T. in the jungle edge a few hundred yards away. In the fire-fight that ensued, one C.T. was killed and another wounded without loss to the patrol.'

The Royal Scots Fusiliers 'bagged' another terrorist in January and in March 3 Platoon of 'A' Company was particularly commended by the Perak Operations Sub-Committee for a successful action. The platoon had been ambushed some three miles from its base. The company commander, platoon commander and four Fusiliers were wounded but the C.T.s were beaten off. One terrorist was killed and another wounded and captured to provide useful intelligence.

The Royal Scots Fusiliers won another hard-fought battle before leaving the Commonwealth Brigade on completion of their tour of duty in Malaya. The football finals between the 1st Royal Scots Fusiliers and the 2nd Royal Australian Regiment was a close-run match as Lieutenant Chinn reported: '2 R.A.R. was defeated by only 7-0 by 1 R.S.F. at soccer because it appears that nine of the eleven Australian players were nick-named "Jock", the confusion from which evened up to some degree the 1 R.S.F. advantage of being B.A.O.R. "runners-up" and FARELF champions.' The 1st Battalion of The Royal Scots Fusiliers sailed from Penang on the troopship *Dilwara* on 17th May 1957. The 'Jocks' were replaced in the brigade by another English regiment, the 1st Battalion of The Loyal Regiment (North Lancashire), under the command of Lieutenant-Colonel C. L. Thompson, who moved in to occupy Colombo Camp in Ipoh.

The Royal Lincolns completed their move into the brigade area.

'The battalion was now deployed with battalion headquarters in Lincoln Camp, Taiping, and with "D" Company a mile away. The remaining companies were in operational camps in the Ipoh area. "A" Company was at Kroh, only five miles from the Thai border, and other companies subsequently sampled the delights of Kroh. "B" Company were in the Kinta Valley in which are dotted isolated hills, about 700 feet high, steep and rocky and looking like overgrown warts. The eastern half of "B" Company's area was all jungle, rising from 400 feet to an extreme high of 7,160 feet with

Gunong Korbu which "B" Company believed was either the highest, or second highest, in Malaya.'

4 Platoon of 'B' Company soon found a C.T. camp for sixteen which had been evacuated only a few hours earlier. Six hundred yards from the camp was a well-concealed food dump which they ambushed for twelve days but without success. On 13th March a three-storey go-down collapsed in the outskirts of Taiping. The Lincolns provided troops to work four shifts until the last body was recovered and received the deep appreciation of the Directors of the Syn Lee Rubber Company for their labours.

The British battalions of the brigade received the first issue of the new self-loading rifle, the 7.62 mm Belgian F.N., which was to replace the .303 inch Lee-Enfield rifle which had been the British infantryman's personal weapon for over sixty years. The limited number of S.L.R.s available required each battalion to devote training time for every soldier to receive initial instruction on the new weapon. Another factor which was to effect the British battalions was the gradual release of the last of the national servicemen who had given such sterling service in Korea and Malaya over the years. The British Army was about to become an all regular force. In July 1957 the re-organization of the British Army was announced. Many of the famous old infantry regiments were to be merged to form a smaller regular army. One of the regiments so effected was the Royal Lincolnshire Regiment which was to be amalgamated with the Northamptonshire Regiment between 1960 and 1962.

Operations against the C.T. reached battalion proportions between 31st May and 21st June. Major Pawlett, commanding 'C' Company of the Royal Lincolns, was told by the manager of the Jalong Tinggi Estate that a group of twenty C.T.s had distributed propaganda leaflets amongst the Tamil rubber tappers. 'C' Company's 'crash section' and 9 Platoon went to the estate and found a resting place for six C.T.s on 31st May. Another resting place was found the next day and 5 Platoon took up ambush positions on likely routes. A third resting place was discovered on Sunday 2nd June with tracks leading Northwards. A platoon was sent to the North to try and stop any exit whilst Captain Walter, acting on a hunch, searched the area and found the tracks of twelve men in the tall lallang grass, probably made two days earlier. Captain Walter and four men of 'C' Company continued their search and, at about 3.00 p.m., caught a glimpse of a C.T. crouching in the roots of a large tree. Captain Walter fired three shots from his S.L.R., the bullets passed through the tree and hit the C.T. in stomach, knocking him backwards. A second C.T. appeared and opened fire with a Sten gun, a grenade was thrown and a third C.T. with a carbine was spotted. Realising that they had been ambushed, Captain Walter attempted to launch an attack but his party met the fire of two light machine guns and they took cover under the steep river bank. 'C' Company rallied to the scene and mounted an attack but the terrorists had withdrawn, taking their wounded. A search of the hilltop revealed a camp for about thirty C.T.s with well-prepared weapon positions. In retrospect, it was clear that the terrorists had planned a classic 'come-on' by making open contact with the rubber tappers and luring the Lincolns into a prepared ambush. It was believed that the notorious 27 Section of 31 Platoon were responsible for the operation.

On 3rd June Lieutenant-Colonel Goulson took command of the operation and laid an outer ring of ambush positions, using three rifle companies and the Machine Gun Platoon to encircle the area. On 4th June 7 Platoon found a resting place for twenty persons which had been used the previous night. A second resting place was soon found with fourteen abandoned food packs, indicating a hasty evacuation. The Assault Pioneer Platoon laid an ambush on the site of the food store in case the C.T.s returned and Captain Walter led a sweep to the East. At first light on 5th June 3 Platoon, on the East bank of the Sungei Kerbau, sighted and engaged four C.T.s at considerable range in the lallang. Several C.T. tracks were discovered during the day and the Lincolns received further support from the Loyals, 'A' Troop of the 105th Field Battery, two 3.7 inch guns of the Singapore Regiment, Royal Artillery, and a troop of the King's Dragoon Guards in armoured cars. The Royal Air Force and the Army Air Corps provided air cover and resupply with Valettas, Austers and helicopters.

On 6th June Captain Walter with two platoons tracked their quarry towards Hill 1291. On gaining the summit, Second-Lieutenant R. I. Sumpner was sent ahead with a tracking team but fell into another carefully laid ambush. Lieutenant Sumpner mounted an assault in the face of light machine gun and rifle fire and was quickly followed by the main body of the force but the terrorists disappeared, leaving a blood trail through the jungle. A wounded C.T., later identified as Wan Tui Lui, was killed during the pursuit but the other terrorists escaped. Two of the Iban trackers, Private Kayan and Alo, were wounded in the brief fight but returned the enemy's fire. The two trackers and the dead Chinese were evacuated by helicopter.

The operation continued but the scent grew weaker. Lieutenant M. A. Aris picked up the trail of the main party of C.T.s on 19th June: twenty men's tracks, about ten days old, were seen East of Hill 1291 and the tracks of another eight, some four days old, headed Southwards. Major H. E. Smyth, M.C., with two platoons of 'A' Company were helicoptered into the Tanjong Rambutan area but found no signs of the C.T.s, although Iban Letak anak Kusing was shot, mistakenly, by a lone aborigine. For their parts in this operation, Captain Walter was awarded the Military Cross and Private Taylor (who had been with Captain Walter in the first ambush) and Iban Alo anak Empang were Mentioned in Despatches.

Attached to each infantry battalion in Malaya were a number of Iban trackers, natives of Borneo, who were invaluable in jungle operations. The Ibans lived and worked with the regiments and were held in high esteem by their Commonwealth colleagues. The Sarawak Rangers continued to operate in Upper Perak until well after the end of the Malayan Emergency. Each rifle company also had tracking dogs with trained handlers drawn from the ranks of the regiment. Much time was spent in simply picking up and following tracks through the dense vegetation and actual contacts with the terrorists were comparatively few. Patrol activity involved days of picking the way through the jungle, cautiously and slowly, ever alert and conscious of the dangers of ambush, often resulting in no contact or subsequent action.

Towards the end of their tour of duty with 28 Brigade, 105 Battery, R.A.A. decided to hold a celebration which Major Bogle still remembers:

'We (I think the battery captain and I – but it may have been our splendid B.S.M.) decided, with the agreement of the Regimental Funds Committee, to have a battery dinner for all ranks (no wives!) when we re-assembled at Butterworth during a retraining period. Almost the entire battery gathered at the E and O Hotel (the premier hotel in North Malaya) for a carefully arranged dinner in the ball-room. It approximated to a guest night in a Mess but sported a floor show – a strip-tease act! All went reasonably well until towards the end, when the beer had flowed abundantly and the strip show began. Then there were noisy gunners milling round everywhere and mostly near the stage. The hotel staff and the M.P.s (warned beforehand) were tolerant and helpful but it was an unnerving night. The battery captain and I spent much time later patrolling in our private cars, "capturing" and transporting to the last ferries small groups of wandering gunners who had small intention of returning to Butterworth that night. There was no damage and there were no offences but there were some rather anxious officers. I vowed never to do such a thing again!'

In 1957 one word was heard over and over again in Malaya: *Merdeka* – freedom. The British rule of Malaya was to cease on 31st August when the Federation of Malaya would become a completely self-governing nation within the Commonwealth. This promise alone had done much to unite the people of Malaya in rejecting the aims of the Communist terrorists and denying them the practical aid and political support they sought. Nevertheless, in the deep jungles of Perak, the hard core C.T.s continued their fight against the security forces.

It fell to 'B' Company of the Royal Lincolns to make the last kill under British rule. The company had spent a fruitless three weeks trying to catch some C.T.s who were taking food from a tapioca factory and a battalion operation was mounted to ambush the terrorists. At 9.35 p.m. on 31st August, Lance-Corporal Bowler saw nine C.T.s advancing towards him and opened fire with his revolver at a range of six feet, the soldier with Corporal Bowler also tried to fire but suffered a stoppage on his new self-loading rifle, the F.N. The C.T.s made a run for it, two of them straight into an ambush commanded by Corporal Askew. One Chinese was killed but the other escaped. Nine packs containing over half a ton of tapioca were found, a considerable loss to the terrorists' food supplies.

'C' Company of the Royal Lincolns also had a success in August. 8 Platoon were in ambush around an aborigine clearing in the Sungei Siput area and, after a four-day wait, three C.T.s walked into the trap and were engaged by Corporal Walker, Private Kirkiland and Private Kayan, an Iban. Two of the terrorists were killed but the third escaped, taking advantage of the smoke when the lallang grass caught fire.

An old and much respected friend of the 28th Commonwealth Brigade arrived in Malaya in September; Lieutenant-General Sir James Cassels, first commander of the Commonwealth Division in Korea, assumed the appointments of Director of Operations in Malaya. General Cassels, more than anyone else, was a strong proponent of the Commonwealth ideal and was known and admired by the Australian element of 28 Brigade. As if to emphasise this bond, another veteran of the Korean War followed close on General Cassel's heels. The 3rd Battalion of The Royal Australian Regiment, 'Old Faithful' as it came to be known in Korea and one of the original battalions of the Commonwealth Brigade, arrived to relieve the 2nd Battalion of the Regiment. 3rd R.A.R., Lieutenant-Colonel John White, had spent the previous three years in Australia before rejoining 28 Brigade.

'Perhaps the most interesting perspective of the 2 R.A.R. tour was that the battalion had experienced the type of "peacetime-colonial" regimental soldiering typical of the British Army in many parts of the old Empire between the wars and earlier. A British garrison base for the unit, families in "theatre", an oppressive tropical environment, operations against an insurgent enemy with constant threat of ambush in movement was 2 R.A.R.'s then unusual lot – the first Australian battalion to gain such experience.' The 2nd Royal Australians had suffered casualties during their time in Malaya, including Sergeant Charlie Anderson, one of the few Aboriginals serving in the regular army (although Captain Reg Saunders had served with 3 R.A.R. in Korea), who had been killed in an ambush. 105 Field Battery of the Royal Australian Artillery and their Light Aid Detachment of the Royal Australian Electrical and Mechanical Engineers, were relieved at the same time by 'A' (100) Field Battery, Major R. E. Seddon.

> 'After two years in Malaya, 105 Battery returned to Australia having handed over to the successor battery and LAD a complete range of equipment in excellent condition, a good camp also in excellent condition, very healthy mess and regimental funds and, above all, a well-established and acknowledged reputation for operational and administrative efficiency. It must also be said that it was never tested in its primary role as a supporting artillery unit in mobile limited war operations as part of the British Commonwealth Far East Strategic Reserve. For that, it would undoubtedly have required considerable retraining, especially in the gunnery techniques required in command and observation posts.

In addition to the two major Australian units – the infantry battalion and the artillery battery – Australian sub-units were integrated amongst the brigade's support and services; 11 Field Squadron included one troop of Australian engineers and the brigade signal squadron also had an Australian troop – and a sergeant from St. Helena. Australians were introduced into other minor units of the brigade such as the provost staff and brigade headquarters which included Australian and New Zealand staff officers and a pay sergeant who came originally from Sri Lanka (Ceylon).

The Royal Lincolns suffered their first soldier killed in action in Malaya on 10th October. Private Thompson, a dog handler with 'A' Company, was leading a patrol commanded by Lieutenant Aris in an area of the Upper Pari, where the Lincolns had ambushed two C.T.s the previous month. Tracks of five persons, about two days old, were found crossing a stream. Private Thompson crossed the stream and climbed the far bank where he was shot. Lieutenant Aris mounted a hurried attack on a section of C.T.s but, after an exchange of shots, the enemy fled. The patrol found a camp for thirty men on the far side of the stream with rice still cooking and washing hung out to dry. 'B' Company later undertook a follow-up operation in the same area and discovered another camp for twenty men, recently vacated, which contained a rifle, documents, printing equipment and two bottles of Benedictine.

Lieutenant-Colonel A. W. Innes, M.C., assumed command of the 1st Royal Lincolns on 5th October when Lieutenant-Colonel Goulson completed his tour of duty. A second Lincoln was killed in action on 25th October; Private Jack was the leading scout of a patrol near some tin mines when he was shot by a lone C.T. Corporal Robinson returned the fire but the terrorist ran away. Corporal Hopkinson, about 1,000 yards away, was warned by radio and took his patrol towards the scene of the attack where they sighted four C.T.s across the tin tailings. The patrol opened fire and wounded one C.T. but he was carried off by his comrades. Corporal Hopkinson gave pursuit and succeeded in wounding another but the terrorists escaped into the thicker woods, taking their wounded.

The Royal Lincolns made a successful contact with the enemy on 29th November. 'B' Company, Major G. D. Cole, laid several four-man ambushes in the Tanjong Rambutan area. One ambush party, commanded by Corporal Shaftoe, was rewarded when a party of C.T.s came down the track; one was quickly killed but the remainder escaped into the jungle. On Christmas Eve a member of the 'Malayan Races Liberation Army' surrendered and a platoon of the 2nd/6th Gurkha Rifles, under the command of the Royal Lincolns, was sent out to follow up and killed a terrorist on Christmas Day. Another C.T. surrendered on New Year's Day 1958 and guided 'B' Company into the jungle on 3rd January. Two days later, in the deep jungle to the West of Ipoh, 'B' Company was fired upon by about seven C.T.s; fire was returned but the enemy disappeared. A wounded C.T. was found during a search of the area and further ambushes were laid. Three Chinese appeared on 6th January and were engaged but escaped, leaving a distinct blood trail. Major Cole's men remained in ambush until 11th January but no more terrorists were encountered. On 13th January, 5 Platoon discovered a considerable force of C.T.s encamped in the deep jungle. The enemy were engaged and put to flight although no casualties were inflicted. Private Scolley was wounded twice during this encounter and was later evacuated to England. Major Cole was awarded the Military Cross and Corporal Shaftoe received the Military Medal for their gallantry and leadership during this extended action in the jungle.

The Royal Lincolnshire Regiment left 28 Brigade on 17th February 1958, to return to operations in South Malaya before leaving for Great Britain. Brigadier Moore thanked the battalion for its contribution:

'I should like to express my admiration for the way the battalion has contained the C.T.s in the whole of the Kuala Kangsar and Ulu Kinta DWEC areas during the period August 1 to November 30 1957. Previously we had two infantry battalions and a company of a third operating in this area. During this period, you have killed four C.T.s, certainly wounded two, and only one civilian has been murdered. It is true that you have lost two of your men but with the large number of C.T.s arrayed against you, this is not surprising.'

Further evidence of the Lincoln's prowess was a terrorist who surrendered to the police at the end of February. He had been a member of the group pursued by 'B' Company and among his reasons for surrendering was the constant pressure of the security forces after 6th January when the C.T.s were on the run, subjected to relentless harassment, deprived of food and rest and completely exhausted.

The other battalions of 28 Brigade were also maintaining the pressure on the C.T.s by a continual programme of jungle patrols. The 1st Battalion of the Loyals described one of their patrols:

'Usually the platoon stays in the jungle for five days, taking with it rations for this period, though it will stay longer with rations brought in by the Supply Company or dropped by air, if the situation demands it. Continuously it is in touch by wireless with its headquarters, reporting its location, its discoveries and progress so that the Commanding Officer knows exactly what is going on and can dispose his forces accordingly. A patrol consists of never less than five men. It has a leading scout who leads the file of men and carries a pump-action shotgun while watching the jungle with unflagging alertness. Behind him comes the N.C.O. in charge of the patrol, the Iban tracker, the Bren gunner, the riflemen and the wireless operator. The N.C.O. carries a compass for in the jungle there are no direction signs. This is the story of one such patrol. Tracks were found and when this discovery was reported to H.Q. the patrol was told to follow them immediately. They led to a camp where nine terrorists had been living that

morning and had left, the Iban decided, four hours before the
patrol arrived. Another patrol 2,000 yards away was called up and
the two sections joined together. For three days they followed
C.T. tracks, the men starting at first light and only ceasing tracking when it was too dark. There was no question of building
"bashas" in which to sleep and the only hot drink was a cup of tea
with a cold breakfast. On the evening of the third day they
thought they were near to the C.T.s; a chopped-down palm tree
showed where they had eaten some jungle cabbage. Suddenly
they came upon a C.T. sentry who saw them at the same time. The
sentry was shot as he was running into the camp and so quickly
did the patrol hit the camp that another was shot as he dashed for
cover. One of them was the senior Indian C.T. in Perak. With two
tracker dogs, the patrols took up the chase and followed the tracks
for another three days. On the fourth day they caught up with
them and killed a third. Ten days later, after some very skilful
tracking, three more of the same group were killed.'

During the Malayan Emergency, Special Air Service units had been operating deep in the jungles. S.A.S. Squadrons from various Commonwealth nations – including Rhodesia – had played an important part in
locating and destroying the terrorists in their remote hides. New Zealand
had sent its Special Air Service Squadron to Malaya in 1955 and, on 1st
August 1957, the 1st Battalion of the New Zealand Regiment was reacti-
vated for service in Malaya. The battalion reached Malaya in December
1957 and spent three months at the Jungle Warfare School at Kota Tinggi
before moving North to join 28 Brigade. On 4th March 1958, the New
Zealand Battalion, under the command of Lieutenant-Colonel W. R. K.
Morrison, D.S.O., joined the brigade at Taiping to replace the Royal
Lincolnshire Regiment. The Commonwealth Brigade then contained major units from three Commonwealth nations with representatives from all
the nations filling appointments in the brigade headquarters.

The New Zealand Regiment arrived in time to participate in Operation
'Ginger' which had begun in December 1957. This was a fully co-ordinated operation designed to clear what terrorists were left in the remaining 'black' areas. 28 Brigade, with the 2nd/6th Gurkha Rifles under command, was responsible for the Kinta Valley area around Ipoh. The Kiwis
established a command post at Ipoh with the main battalion headquarters
at Taiping, 'A' and 'C' Companies at Sungei Kuang, 'B' Company at
Tanjong Rambutan and 'D' Company at Tanah Hitam. The battalion's

first success came on 29th May when 6 Platoon of 'B' Company met a lone C.T. on a track near Ipoh; the man died of wounds but was identified as Man Ko, who had been in the jungle since 1950. On 2nd June, four men from 'D' Company and three policemen, under the command of the battalion intelligence sergeant, Sergeant Jamieson, laid an ambush outside an aborigine village in the Kinta Valley. Three C.T.s walked into the ambush at 8.00 a.m. the next morning. One terrorist cocked his Sten gun and the patrol promptly opened fire, killing one C.T. and wounding another although the third helped the wounded man to escape. The dead terrorist was later identified as Itan bin Pandak, an aborigine known to be working for the C.T.s.

Operation 'Ginger' showed that the ten-year campaign against the terrorists was successful. In North Malaya it was estimated that there were about 1,000 C.T.s who had been remorselessly pressed Northwards, into the Thai border area, whilst only some fifty remained at large in South Malaya. Of the thousands who, when the emergency began, raided openly among the native kampongs and rubber estates, killing and terrorising those who would not help or join them, only a hard core of fanatical Communists remained. By 1955 the C.T.s had retreated into the jungle as security forces tightened their grip, cutting off sources of food and denying them the opportunity to terrorise native villages. The 'Liberation Army' had become fugitives, retreating ever Northwards as hundreds of square miles of 'black' areas became 'white', their numbers diminishing steadily in sudden bursts of Bren, Sterling and F.N. self-loading rifle fire on remote jungle trails. Malaya had gained its independence and the C.T.s' cause was doomed. Most of the operations in Malaya entailed deep jungle patrolling by platoons, aimed at the location and destruction of terrorist camps, ambushing C.T. trails and eliminating sympathisers and couriers. It was also necessary to release the aborigines from terrorist domination. To this end, intense efforts were made to win the friendship of these small jungle people in co-operation with the Department of Aboriginal Affairs. The aborigines, sometimes mistakenly called the 'Orang Sakai', lived in remote clearings and clung to their traditional way of life, preserving their animist religion and customs. A 'home guard' force of aborigines, the Senoi Pra'ak, operated with the security forces in Upper Perak, providing information and canoes for travel 'ulu' (up-river). Despite their environment, the aborigines were not ignorant savages. One headman in particular, Papan Gila ('Crazy Plank'), was far from being as thick as the proverbial plank and proved to be a very knowing, shrewd and wily negotiator when it came to the hiring of canoes for use on the River Perak.

The New Zealand Regiment encountered a hostile aborigine on 22nd June. Bah Payani walked into an ambush laid by 'D' Company. The following day the patrol saw two C.T.s at a range of about twenty yards and the Kiwis fired first, killing Kwong Ming a courier and Anjang bin Pandak, another aborigine working for the 31st Independent Platoon. A shotgun, a .303 inch carbine and several 36 hand grenades were recovered from the bodies. On 28th June Major A. N. King, commanding 'B' Company, with Lieutenant B. D. Lambert and his 4 Platoon, were deployed to Fort Slim by helicopter where a surrendered aborigine terrorist had offered information on a C.T. camp. The next morning the aborigine guided the platoon into the jungle. At 2.00 p.m. a shot was heard and the patrol deployed in case of an ambush. At 5.00 p.m. they found fresh footprints and traces of a slaughtered pig. The tracks led towards a hill and it was decided to camp for the night before ascending this suspected C.T. site. Early the following morning, stop groups were positioned to cut off likely escape routes and a group assaulted the hilltop. As the assault group climbed towards the objective, a lone C.T. walked into one of the stop groups. To avoid warning the enemy of the assault, the stop group allowed the C.T. to pass through but he spotted one of the aborigines and fired a shot. Fire was returned but the terrorist escaped. The alarm was raised and the C.T.s fled from the hilltop camp, one running into Corporal Carrol's stop group who shot him. The camp was deserted but the C.T.s left considerable quantities of food and fresh pork. The fleeing C.T.s were followed by a pursuit party but they ran into an ambush some 1,600 yards from the camp; Private B. J. Tuxworth, the dog-handler leading the party, was killed instantly. Lance-Corporal Dillon led his section in an instant counter-attack but the C.T.s escaped into the jungle. The camp was designed to accommodate twenty people and several documents were recovered, one of which, when translated by the police, was an appreciation of the state of the terrorists in Perak, obviously composed by a senior member of the organization. The C.T. shot by Corporal Carrol was later identified as Ah Yoong, personal bodyguard to Chan Hong, the senior committee member of the Perak Communist Party. It appeared that the Kiwis had narrowly missed a major prize and the ambush which killed Private Tuxworth had been laid to permit the V.I.P.s to get away. Lance-Corporal Dillon was later awarded the Military Medal for his prompt response during this encounter.

The other battalions of the brigade also suffered frustrations. The Loyals maintained an ambush on a river-crossing site for twenty-nine days before withdrawing. The very night after the Loyals had abandoned the ambush, the C.T.s crossed the river. On the other hand, the terrorists were becoming more frustrated. One C.T. who surrendered weighed only four and a half stones and declared that the life of a terrorist was increasingly hard and uncomfortable; constantly harassed by foot patrols, bombed from the air and scattered by mortar fire, they lived on the edge of fear. The sound of an Auster flying over the jungle was enough to make them break camp. Attacks on their camps resulted in the loss of valuable food and equipment, ambushes blocked their lines of communication and made them afraid to collect from their food dumps and 'letter-boxes'.

In July 1958 Brigadier Moore relinquished command of 28 Brigade to Brigadier H. J. Mogg, C.B.E., D.S.O., a former light infantryman. From the early days at Butterworth, three years before, Brigadier Moore had the satisfaction of seeing his command grow from one battalion to a tri-national Commonwealth Brigade Group with all the necessary supporting arms and services, a force which was proving itself to be very effective in the slow, patient jungle campaign against the dwindling number of terrorists in North Malaya. The brigade was sorry to lose its commander who had done so much to re-establish the Commonwealth Brigade as a viable fighting formation. The brigade-major, Colin East of the Royal Australian Regiment, pays tribute to his former commander:

'Peter Moore had a combat record which was the envy of most serving officers. A Royal Engineer who, in World War 2, had collected a D.S.O. and a Military Cross in the Western Desert, a bar to the D.S.O. in Yugoslavia and a third D.S.O. as commander of the Commonwealth Division Field Engineer Regiment in Korea. He brought to 28 Brigade an absolute dedication to the job of eliminating the C.T.s, almost bordering on fanaticism. His was the Rommel type of leadership – from the front – and if the type of campaign fought in Malaya largely precluded this, he was always to be found with the infantry patrols, questioning, enquiring and ordering. His eagerness was not always appreciated by commanding officers or sub-unit commanders, who felt that they should be allowed to get on with their own war. As one Australian company commander commented, "The Brigadier wants to site the Bren gun!" His commitment and enthusiasm undoubtedly provided the drive and maintained the momentum of Operation "Ginger". From C.O. to private soldiers his experience, skill and dedication to the job in hand won him the respect, if at times, grudging, admiration of all. He was not at his best at social gatherings and it became well known that the brigadier was more often than not "in the jungle", particularly when a V.I.P. was visiting the brigade – and the number of visitors to the brigade were huge; cabinet ministers, chiefs of various national armed forces, politicians, heads of philanthropic organizations from the U.K., N.Z. and Australia, arrived at Taiping throughout the year. Peter Moore was ably supported in this demanding area by his deputy, Colonel Walter Scott, King's Own, a former column commander of Wingate in Burma, who deputized at Taiping for his commander when absent "on operations".'

Brigadier Mogg inherited a splendid formation and took command in the middle of Operation 'Ginger', intended to drive the terrorists out of the area to the North of Ipoh. The new commander, recently appointed to the rank of brigadier, won his first D.S.O. in Normandy as the commanding officer of the 9th Durham Light Infantry in 1944 and gained a second D.S.O. in Holland. Colin East recalls:

'As distinct from his predecessor the new commander was an extrovert who was quickly accepted by all ranks throughout the brigade. John Mogg's approach to the operations of the brigade was to make the plan, delegate the tasks to unit commanders and then let them get on with it until he considered it necessary to step in. This worked very well and permitted a greater freedom of initiative and manoeuvre by the C.O.s within the framework of the brigade plan. John Mogg's greatest strength lay in his ability to communicate with all nationalities involved in the Malayan scene, and at all levels. This was demonstrated at the State War Executive Committee in Ipoh, chaired by the Mentri Besar, the chief minister of Perak, his handling of very senior and important government leaders from the U.K., Australia, New Zealand and the Malayan Government, as well as other national Common- wealth visitors of relatively lesser degree.'

The Loyals continued to patrol the Pari Valley but there were breaks from 'jungle bashing'. Major M. B. H. Collins of the Loyals remembers:

'It was customary for those officers not in the jungle on opera- tions to foregather for a drink at noon on Saturdays in the Offic- ers' Mess. Such a gathering often went on for some time and the married officer who was the first to be rung up by his wife to be told his lunch was going cold or was burnt was awarded the "Dragon Cup". However, on occasions on a Saturday officers went to the Ipoh Club, where hospitality from the civilian members was lavish and where there was always the excuse that one was "changing the library books". One Saturday a larger number of officers than usual were "in" from the jungle and somehow gravitated to the club. A very convivial noontide resulted which involved the rendition of a number of well chosen ditties, in the course of which the conductor fell through a table and the descent of the steep grassy slope to the padang on the waiters' tin trays – a sort of oriental Cresta run, which was received with loud acclamation by the Chinese "boys". The next week there was a Club Committee meeting, the military being represented by Lieutenant-Colonel Charles Thompson, the C.O. of 1 Loyals. The Chairman of the Committee at the end of the meeting announced that there had been some complaints about the behaviour of some officers in the Club the previous Saturday and asked Colonel Thompson to speak to the C.O. of the New Zealand Battalion whose officers had obviously been responsible to ensure that such behaviour did not occur again. Afterwards, over a drink, a committee member who had served with 2 Loyals in Singapore in the war, drew Colonel Thompson aside and said, "Charles, I thought it was only the Loyals who wore black lanyards in uniform." Charles Thompson replied, "Yes, of course" and then realised who had been responsible for the previous Saturday's "party". The adjutant was duly told to let it be known that such behaviour would not be tolerated again. What a pity! It was such fun sliding down the bank on a tin tray!'

It is not recorded how the Kiwis reacted to this incident but on 28th July, 8 Platoon of 'C' Company, commanded by Lieutenant Anaru, came across four C.T.s on a hillside. Fire was exchanged and three terrorists were wounded but managed to get away. 'Pim', a Labrador tracker dog, followed the blood trail and after a four-hour chase cornered one of the wounded C.T.s behind a log. The patrol deployed and the terrorist was shot, later to be identified as Yeung Cheong, the political commissar of the East Manong Armed Work Cell. The New Zealanders scored another success on 20th August. A patrol of 'D' Company were in ambush near Tanah Hitam when four people set off a trip flare laid at the site. They

*C Coy., 1 Loyals, in the Pari Valley, Malaya, June 1958.*

*Tracker Team, 1 Loyals, North of Sungei Siput, Malaya, December 1958.*

(Brig. M. H. H. Collins, M.B.E.)

were seen to be uniformed terrorists and three were killed immediately, the fourth threw a grenade which did not explode and ran off. Two members of the patrol gave chase and captured the fourth man when he dived into a pool. Corporal Brown dragged the terrorist from the water and sat on him until the rest of the patrol, under Sergeant-Major Carrington, secured their captive. The three dead were Ah Chok, a branch committee member, Pun Tung Kwai and Lau Choo, the wife of the captured terrorist.

Meanwhile the Loyals were searching an area to the North of Sungei Siput together with the 2nd/6th Gurkha Rifles and the Sherwood Foresters, both under the command of the Commonwealth Brigade. On Sunday 17th August, a patrol of the Machine Gun Platoon, under Captain M. Smith, found tracks of six people. The battalion's tracker teams of Ibans and dogs, commanded by Captain D. L. Bruce-Merrie, was brought up to follow the spoor. The following day, the 18th, a patrol led by Corporal

*Lt. Gen. Sir James Cassels with Pte. Sigai Anak Jugam, Sarawak Rangers, and Lt. Jim Barlow, 1 Loyals, at Ipoh, 9th September 1958.*

(Gen. Sir John Mogg)

*Gen. Sir Cecil Sugden, Quartermaster-General, inspects the Commonwealth Provost Coy. with Brig. Mogg at Taiping, 8th February 1959.*

(Gen. Sir John Mogg)

John Riley found a recently abandoned camp for fifteen persons. The trackers soon picked up a faint scent leading from this camp site and, on the 20th, Anau anak Genasi, the leading Iban tracker, caught sight of a C.T. sentry hiding in a tree. Corporal Riley and Anau promptly killed the guard and Captain Bruce-Merrie mounted an immediate attack which accounted for another three terrorists. The dead C.T.s were identified as Lau Fong, the local district committee member, Wong Sau, Kong Siew and Hing Tak. It was deduced that Lau Fong had held a conference at the camp site found by Corporal Riley which had been attended by Ah Chok, who had been killed by the New Zealanders the same day. Captain Bruce-Merrie was later awarded the Military Cross for this successful action.

General Cassels visited his favourite brigade in September and congratulated the Loyals and the New Zealand Regiment for their actions which had accounted for two of the leading terrorists in the Operation 'Ginger' area. The brigade's tally of terrorists killed since 27th July was then fourteen, valid evidence of the success of the operation which was wearing down the terrorists, driving them ever deeper into the inhospitable jungle and depriving them of contact with the outside world.

These successful actions emphasised the valuable skills of the Sarawak Rangers attached to the brigade's battalions and the Loyals recorded:

'To track the Communist terrorists in the jungle the regiment employed no fewer then twenty-nine Ibans, trackers whose skill in reading signs is a constant source of joy to the soldiers who accompany them. They are friendly people with a ready smile which shows a mouth full of gold teeth and are firm favourites with the boys. Against the Communists they match jungle skills and little escapes their notice. Though the C.T. may try to hide his track by covering it with a leaf, the Iban, with the long stick he invariably carries, disdainfully flicks it aside to reveal the footprint to his company commander. One of the handiest weapons in the jungle is the "gollock". It is used to hack a way through the vines and creepers, it clears the undergrowth when base camp is being established, it cuts the poles which form the framework of the bashas, digs the level spots for food and cooking and even opens tins. The Ibans use their own gollocks, elaborately scabbarded, decorated with gay patterns, lighter than the army issue but as sharp as a razor. The scabbards and hafts they carve from a jungle branch; the blade is a piece of discarded car spring, retempered and sharpened by a local blacksmith and then ground down to a razor edge. One of the distinguishing features of these Ibans is their tribal tattooing. Not a few of the Loyals give evidence of their attachment to them by adopting tattoos of a similar pattern though on by no means as extensive a scale. From them they learn a great deal of jungle lore – between them there is a very good understanding.'

One of the Sarawak Rangers attached to the Loyals, Private Sigai anak Jugam, was Mentioned in Despatches for his skill and courage on jungle operations.

The New Zealand Regiment also appreciated the Ibans' skills and formed a battalion tracker team commanded by Lieutenant F. H. Woods. The team consisted of 25 New Zealanders, 23 Ibans of the Sarawak Rangers, 3 surrendered terrorists, a civilian liaison officer and 16 dogs – Golden Labradors, Black Labradors and Alsatians – trained as tracking and patrol dogs. Lieutenant Woods had five years jungle experience with the Special Air Service in Malaya and had a legendary reputation for his tracking ability. One of Wood's surrendered terrorists, Suppiah, had survived for ten months on jungle foods alone and he taught the lieutenant the tricks of living off the forest. The team was the 'eye' of the battalion and always had a group ready to leave camp for operational tasks at thirty minutes notice.

The 3rd Royal Australians had a similar battalion tracking team which included dogs and Sarawak Rangers. 'The team was held in reserve until fresh C.T. tracks were discovered and was then guided to the tracks by the relevant platoon and a follow up operation was launched.' The 3rd R.A.R., like all the other battalions engaged in jungle operations, usually operated at platoon level.

*3rd Royal Australian Regiment; left to right: Pte. F. K. O'Brien who shot a terrorist – the third 'kill' by 3 R.A.R., Pte. A. Clauson and Sergeant R. Moyle, with shotgun.*

(AWM 1957 ELL 201 MC)

'As a rule of thumb, one platoon could search one map grid
square in one day and it took approximately one hour for a platoon to move through 1,000 yards of undulating jungle territory.
In rugged country, swamp or secondary jungle, the figure could
be reduced to about 200 to 400 yards in one hour. Platoon patrolling tactics were generally based on the fan patrol system. From
the platoon base or a selected RV (rendezvous), about six patrols
each of three men, were sent out to search on selected diverging
bearings about ten degrees apart. Each patrol was briefed according to ground and the area to be searched was related to
natural boundaries. On encountering C.T. ground evidence, the
patrol would collect all relevant information and return to base.
Subsequent action depended on successive appreciations by the
platoon commander and higher commanders effected. As very
few targets were available at this stage of the Emergency, maximum troops were deployed to take advantage of any likely C.T.
target presented. Tracks normally led to or from a camp, therefore
plans had to be formulated quickly to close in on the C.T. camp as
soon as its location had been established.'

The brigade-major, Colin East, emphasises the vital part played in these
operations by the local police.

'The Officer Commanding the Sungei Siput Police District, a
Tamil Malayan named Sockalingam, is worthy of special mention. Responsible for a district with a particularly hostile and
large Chinese population, he worked tirelessly with the Security
Forces against the C.T. As a member of the DWEC, which co-
ordinated and planned all operations in the district, he was involved fully in the campaign. The imposition of central cooking
for Sungei Siput village with a population of 8,000 people was a
major achievement on his part. He was fully accepted and respected by all officers and men of 28 Brigade and his worth was
recognised when he was promoted to Officer Superintending
Police Circle, Kuala Kangsar, in 1959. For a Tamil to be given
this appointment in such a strongly Malay Royal Family area
emphasised his ability. The Special Branch operated under a
cloak of secrecy and one little publicised facet of their work was
the task of inducing surrenders by the covert use of SEP (Surrendered Enemy Personnel). The skill and efficiency of the Chinese

officers of the Ipoh Special Branch, as well as their persuasive powers, were most impressive. Equally of interest was the apparent ease with which the previously dedicated hardcore Chinese troops who had abandoned their ideology and loyalty to their erstwhile comrades in the jungle, and were prepared to eliminate them if necessary.'

The Australians were equipped with the 510 wireless set at platoon level and this set produced an outstanding performance in Malaya. Although 3rd R.A.R. operated in an area of some 300 square miles, wireless communications were of a high standard and contact was maintained with every patrol in the jungle. The Australians also received the F.N. self-loading rifle which they found to be excellent. The Bren light machine gun was the main fire power of a patrol and the C.T.s feared it. The 9 mm Australian Owen submachine gun was the favoured weapon for forward scouts and ambushes and it was claimed that the Owen had produced the most kills in Malaya. Mobility in the jungle was in direct proportion to the weight carried by the soldier and the number of days rations he could carry. The C.T.s could normally carry up to thirty days food supplies, composed mainly of rice. Commonwealth troops carried seven days rations and consideration was given to reducing the bulk. The Australians found the British twenty-four hour ration pack to be satisfactory but were concerned as its weight; it was suggested that an individual, lightweight, ten-day ration pack might be better, using rice and, of course, vegemite! The soldiers' health was of the greatest importance in jungle operations. Each man carried Paludrine tablets to ward off malarial infection, salt tablets to compensate for excessive perspiration and prevent heat exhaustion, mite repellent to deter the swarms of tiny insects, water sterilisation tablets and foot powder. In addition to the mosquitoes and mites, soldiers also had to contend with all the other varieties of local wildlife – such as leeches, snakes and hornets. Field dressings and basic first-aid kits were always carried to cope with any wounds or injuries sustained. Emergency evacuation by helicopter ensured that most casualties were brought out to receive medical treatment in good time. Communications, weapons, ammunition, rations, water, medical supplies – all carried by the foot soldier on patrol. Disposable canvas and rubber jungle boots were worn but feet softened in the heat and dampness of the jungle. On returning from patrol, troops were usually excused boots for several days and wore the local 'flip-flop' slippers to allow the air to harden their feet.

Major R. S. Garland, M.C., of the 3rd Royal Australians, describes one of the operations mounted by his company:

'C.T. forces operating in my company area included the Jalong Armed Work Force led by Lam Poh and 27 Independent Section led by Chan Fei. Both leaders were experienced and tough opponents. Chan Fei was wanted for ten murders. Amongst the litter that always gathered on my table was the following Special Branch report:-

'"Jalong Area. The following report is graded C3. On 9 July 1958 information was received by a rubber tapper that C.T. Lam Poh still wanted to move to the area of Jalong New Village to contact communist supporters and collect supplies. Instructions were also given for the retention of all tappers employed on Yoong Fan Estate and caution was to be exercised in the selection of new tappers. On 11 July 1958 it was arranged for a quantity of tobacco to be delivered to the mangling shed on the Hock Lian Estate. Comment: Lam Poh has been unable to make direct contact with supporters in the Jalong New Village since December 1957 owing to the activities of 3 R.A.R. On several occasions he has said that he was going to see them but, as yet, has failed to do so. This last letter may be an attempt to boost morale of communist supporters in that area."

'It was 22 July 1958, and no doubt the tobacco would have been collected. However, the report was worth checking, so I decided to do so. I waited until 4.30 p.m., when curfew is effective in rubber estates, and then proceeded by scout car to the mangling shed on the Hock Lian Estate. It was raining very heavily and the tracks of the scout car were washed away as they were made on the road in the rubber estate. My search did not locate the tobacco, but I found a large drum of sweet potatoes carefully hidden in the mangling shed. It was obvious that the potatoes were hidden for use by the C.T.s and that the C.T.s were expected in this area in the next week or so. Resultant discussions between the C.O. and the Special Branch led to the decision to maintain a small ambush by night on the potatoes. "B" Company was heavily committed covering other possibilities at the time and the Assault Pioneer Platoon, under the command of "B" Company, was given the task of maintaining a three-man ambush on the potatoes during the subsequent nights. On the following evening I took Lieutenant John McGhee on a foot reconnaissance into the area and indicated the task to him. Care was taken to conceal tracks and leave things undisturbed in the mangling shed.

If the local rubber tappers were made suspicious of our presence, the C.T.s would be warned to keep away.

'It was decided to place the ambush in the mangling shed as it afforded excellent fire positions and good concealment. The moon was approaching the full and ensured good shooting light. Consequently torch attachments and flares were not used. There were four entrances to the shed and dispositions were selected to cover each of these. The shed was of timber construction enclosed by "chicken wire". This placed the ambush group in darkness whilst permitting all round vision into the surrounding estate. To avoid leaving tracks that might alert the rubber tappers or C.T.s, local hockey boots were worn. Also, calico overshoes were worn to help conceal boot prints. (This is a trick we have learned from the C.T.s.) A covered approach from the rear of the shed to a nearby road was used as the route in and out. The ambush party lived about five miles away from the mangling shed and it was necessary to drop them by vehicle to ensure that the ambush was manned at dusk each evening. A scout car was used and the ambush party debussed on the move. (C.T.s always listen for the movement, slowing down and stopping of troop carrying vehicles.) The scout car also conducted dummy patrols on main roads in the area to assist deception. The ambush group was collected at 5.00 a.m. each morning. Ambush personnel were changed on alternate nights so that the ambush could be maintained for a long period. (Some ambushes in this theatre are maintained for months.)

'The ambush group on 27 July 1958 consisted of Lance-Corporal Hanley, F.N. rifle, Private Ramsay, Owen machine carbine, and Private Mullings, F.N. rifle. At 9.15 p.m. the barking of a dog was heard from the North. It seemed like an imitation and the ambush was alerted. All was quiet for the next half hour. At 9.45 p.m. the ambush saw and heard movement coming from the direction of a nearby footbridge. Four C.T.s were seen approaching the mangling shed. The C.T.s left the darkness of a tree and doubled towards the footbridge, twenty-five yards from the ambush. The ambush commander held his fire. When the first C.T. placed his foot inside the mangling shed (five yards range) Lance-Corporal Hanley sprang the ambush by killing him with his F.N. Fire was opened immediately and two more C.T.s were killed by the ambush. The first two C.T.s died with their eyes open, the third fell into a rather smelly drain and died there. The fourth C.T., obviously wounded, ran away into the night, followed by bursts of fire. The C.T.s did not return the fire. During the rest of the night, the bodies, together with weapons, equipment and documents, were recovered and passed to Sungei Siput for identification by Special Branch. A follow up operation was launched to capture the wounded C.T. The following morning he surrendered, together with a female C.T., to a scout car patrol. He was later identified as Lam Poh, a Branch Committee member and leader of the Jalong Armed Work Force. He was suffering from a hole in the neck made by an Owen bullet. The three killed C.T.s were identified as members of the notorious 27 Section. They were all hard core terrorists and were all wanted for murder. Exploitation of this success led to the further elimination of eight more C.T.s, totalling thirteen C.T.s eliminated and being the end of the Jalong Armed Work Force and 27 Section. And it was all because of a tin of sweet potatoes. Three days later I revisited the mangling shed on a further scout car patrol. The sweet potatoes had gone!'

The 1st New Zealand Regiment took the surrender of thirteen terrorists during October 1958. On 10th October a patrol from 4 Platoon of 'B' Company was told by a village penghulu (headman) that a terrorist wanted to surrender. Sergeant Len Hepi took his sub-machine gun and walked down a jungle track where he was met by a barefoot Chinese, wearing a faded uniform and holding a Japanese rifle above his head. Suspecting, rightly, that the remainder of the terrorist gang were watching from ambush positions, Sergeant Hepi took the man's rifle and escorted him back to the patrol's camp where he was given food. Two days later the same penghulu told Sergeant Hepi that a further seven C.T.s wished to surrender. Again he went down the track, the first man he encountered was an Indian and behind him were two Chinese men and two Chinese women to be followed by a male and a female Temiar aborigine. The terrorists surrendered gladly and some of them had been living in the jungle since the Emergency began in 1948. They told the patrol they were starving and that no recruits were joining their organization, their communications and courier routes were worthless as a result of constant ambushing by security forces. They had had enough. On 12th October another New Zealand patrol, also acting on information received from a village penghulu, captured a further five disgruntled terrorists. All these terrorists had been members of a group under the command of Tsei Ko Yin, a District Committee member.

The Loyals reported similar success:

> 'Since the present operation began in the brigade area of approximately 1,000 square miles, 94 communist terrorists have been "eliminated" leaving approximately 70, although the exact figure is not known, still at large. Nearly all of them are Chinese. They are controlled by the Communist party secretary and various areas have their own district committees from which directives to their supporters are issued. Altogether during the time they have been in operation the Loyals have killed 17 and captured 2. Surrenders do not count as captures. The Loyals, with some notable successes behind them in the eighteen months they have been in action, will probably see the Communist threat in Malaya ended. It will be for them a job well done.'

Lieutenant-Colonel C. V. Thompson handed over command of the battalion to Lieutenant-Colonel J. C. Johnson. Colonel Thompson was awarded the O.B.E. for his battalion's work in Malaya and was justifiably proud of his North Country lads, many of whom were National Servicemen: 'They are the finest set of men I have ever served with. They are well-behaved; they became mature overnight and they have a wonderful spirit and sense of humour.'

Despite the Loyals' optimism, the Malayan Emergency was to continue for a further nineteen months although the numbers of active terrorists were diminishing drastically with a corresponding diminution of incidents and contacts. In December 1958 Lieutenant-General Cassels made a farewell tour on relinquishing his appointment as Director of Operations for Malaya. His visits to units of 28 Brigade were particularly poignant since the General had the Commonwealth Brigade under his command both in Korea and Malaya and many of the members of the brigade – such as Colin East, the brigade-major, and Jim Stewart, the brigade intelligence officer (who had won the Military Cross during Operation 'Commando' in 1951) – were known to General Cassels from their service in Korea and, of course, the 3rd Royal Australians were a stalwart component of the General's Commonwealth Division. Nevertheless, operations continued and, on 23rd December, Brigadier Mogg fired the 50,000th shell delivered by 100 Field Battery against a jungle target – although there few terrorists left to shoot at.

One of the highlights of 1958, for brigade headquarters at least, is recalled by Colin East:

'The D.A.Q.M.G. (Deputy-Assistant-Quarter-Master-General) of H.Q. 28 Brigade in 1957-1958 was a diminutive, energetic, caustic-witted R.A.S.C. major named Tony Chadwick. Highly efficient, he never lost an opportunity to "score" points against the General Staff. His absolute moment of triumph occurred in 1958 when on a liaison visit to Jalong on the road East of Sungei Siput village where 3 R.A.R. had a detachment, he was signalled from the roadside by a C.T. who wished to surrender. Tony Chadwick, travelling in his scout car, accepted the SEP and brought him back to H.Q. in Taiping and delivered him to the General Staff. None of us on the "G" side were ever allowed to forget that the only C.T. who was ever "captured" by Brigade Headquarters, was taken by the 'Q' staff!'

The New Year, 1959, brought operational changes for the Commonwealth Brigade. The Operation 'Ginger' area was almost cleared of the terrorist

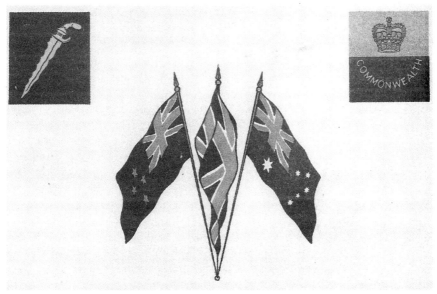

*HQ 28 Commonwealth Infantry Brigade Group and North Malaya sub-district.*

*C Coy. patrol, 1 Loyals, Perak River, Malaya, January 1959.*

(Brig. M. H. H. Collins, M.B.E.)

threat and only a residual pocket of some fourteen terrorists remained in the Bruas area, to the West of Ipoh. To clear this remnant, Operation 'Jaya' was launched on 9th January whilst the rest of the 'Ginger' area was declared officially 'White' by the Malayan Government on 14th January. 28 Brigade's main area of responsibility was switched to the Northern jungles of Upper Perak where the C.T.s sought sanctuary after the success of 'Ginger'. Operation 'Bamboo' was to be a campaign waged far from any roads and built-up areas amongst the remote and undeveloped forests around the headwaters of the Sungei Perak and its many tributaries. Troop movement in river craft was to become a normal mode of transportation coupled with air support, in the form of resupply, insertion and extraction. The aboriginal inhabitants of these distant forests became the main target for both the Commonwealth forces and the C.T.s as sources of intelligence and food. Operation 'Bamboo' was integrated with the Royal Malay Police, particularly the P.F.F. (Police Field Force) who constructed and manned strategic jungle forts throughout the area.

*Brig. Mogg at a Bde. T.E.W.T. at Sungei Kuang, Malaya, 5th August 1959.*

(Brig. M. H. H. Collins, M.B.E.)

These forts provided sanctuary for the aborigines who wished to avoid the C.T.s and also firm bases from which troops could deploy for deeper patrols. A Brigade Tactical Headquarters was established at Grik, up the Perak River, to control operations in Upper Perak and along the Malay-Thai border.

Operation 'Bamboo' claimed an early casualty in February 1959. Private F. Burdett, of the 1st New Zealand Regiment's Pipes and Drums, was asleep in his hammock whilst on a jungle patrol – when he was attacked by a tiger. The tiger, rarely seen in the Malayan forests, dragged Private Burdett several yards from the overnight basha. Roused by the victim's cries, Corporal Donnelly fired a burst from his sub-machine gun and scared the tiger, who dropped its prey and disappeared into the jungle. Private Burdett had been severely mauled and was evacuated by helicopter early the following morning. After surgery and five weeks in hospital, Private Burdett recovered and returned to duty, the only member of the Commonwealth Brigade to be savaged by a tiger.

*Lt. Col. J. C. Johnson, 1 Loyals, with the Loyals' tiger cub at Grik, 28th November 1959.*

(Gen. Sir John Mogg)

Almost coincidentally, the Loyals also had an encounter with a tiger in jungle near the Thai border. A tigress threatened a patrol and was shot but the reason for her belligerence was soon apparent, her only cub. The tiger cub was taken back to the base at Grik and thrived on the soldiers' attention, sleeping under the bed of Captain Ian MacLean, an Australian attached to the Loyals. The cub disappeared on 'walkabout' one day but returned to its new home the next morning. It was decided that the Loyals would take the cub back to England and arrangements were made with the Bellevue Zoo at Manchester to receive the battalion's pet.

During the latter part of 1959 the brigade underwent a complete change of battalions and supporting units. The 3rd Battalion of the Royal Australian Regiment returned to Australia in September and were credited with 14 C.T.s killed and 32 captured at the cost of 1 Australian killed and 2 wounded. The 1st Battalion of the Royal Australian Regiment, Lieutenant-Colonel W. J. Morrow, replaced the 3rd Battalion in the brigade. The 1st Battalion of the New Zealand Regiment held a farewell parade at

*Brig. Mogg fires the 75,000th shell delivered against the terrorists by 100 'A' Field Battery, Royal Australian Artillery, 5th September 1959.*

(AWM ELL 57 512 MC)

Taiping on 9th November 1959, at which Tun Abdul Razak, the Prime Minister of Malaya, presented the battalion with a kris, a ceremonial Malay dagger, in appreciation of their successes against the terrorists. The 2nd Battalion of the New Zealand Regiment, Lieutenant-Colonel D. J. Aitken, arrived in Malaya on 26th November to replace the 1st Battalion. The 1st Battalion of the Loyals were relieved in December by the 1st Battalion of the 3rd East Anglian Regiment, Lieutenant-Colonel D. J. Barrow. The 3rd East Anglians, 'The Pompadours', was one of the newly formed British infantry regiments resulting from the reductions announced in 1957. The regiment was an amalgamation of the Bedfordshire and Hertfordshire Regiment and the Essex Regiment, the latter having served in 28 Brigade from 1953 to 1954. The advent of this amalgamated regiment gave the members of the Royal Australian Regiment reason to prophesy gleefully: 'It won't be long before you're down to the Royal English Regiment!' 'A' Field Battery of the Royal Australian Artillery completed its tour of duty with the brigade after firing its 75,000th shell on 5th September and was relieved by 101 Field Battery, Major P. J. Norton, on 1st October. 1 Field Troop of the Royal Australian Engineers also returned to Australia at the same time and was replaced by 2 Field Troop.

The new arrivals were soon committed to operations. Operation 'Jaya' was a slow and unrewarding search of the forested limestone crags where the terrorists were believed to be hiding in caves. Two C.T.s had been eliminated by 5th August but the enemy was very elusive. Major East remembers

> 'attending a "safe house" in Kuala Kangsar during Operation Jaya where four surrendered C.T.s had been held incommunicado by the Special Branch (under Peter Coster) for some weeks; they had been briefed and indoctrinated to return to their area of operations in the jungle SW of Kuala Kangsar and West of Ipoh. Their surrender had not been made public and the aim was to insert them into their old area with the task of contacting other C.T. elements in the area, and either convincing them of the advantages of surrender, including the financial rewards, pardons, etc., or killing them. Looking at the four ex-C.T.s in the "safe house" at Kuala Kangsar in their worn green uniforms, cap with red star and weapons, it was hard to believe that we were planning a joint operation. It was this type of operation in the late months of 1959 and early 1960 which led to numerous surrenders and a number of kills among the remaining C.T. members in Perak.'

*B Company, 1/3 East Anglian Regiment, on jungle patrol, Perak, Malaya.*

(Soldier Magazine 5661/27/5)

The East Anglians, from their base at Ipoh, were operating in the hilly country to the West of the town. Two platoons of 'C' Company were sent into the area on Christmas Eve and spent the festive season in very uncomfortable ambush positions which they maintained for a week. The rest of the battalion soon followed. 'Companies have been going in for ten days and out for six. The Battalion has been mainly working in the South of Operation "Jaya", which is an area of about 15 miles by 20. It is very hilly, rising to about 5,400 feet in the centre. 'B' Company ascended Gunong Bubu to establish a base and received an air supply drop once the cloud cleared sufficiently for the aircraft to see the dropping zone.' Four C.T.s surrendered voluntarily on Christmas Eve as a result of the campaign by the 'turned C.T.s' but the troops on the ground made very few contacts.

Lieutenant-Colonel M. W. Holme assumed command of the 1st/3rd East Anglians in January 1960 when Lieutenant-Colonel Barrow left to take up an appointment in Hong Kong. The battalion (often miscalled the East 'Anglicans') slogged away at 'Jaya' but 'few tangible results have been achieved, although a great deal of valuable ground information has been found. Seven terrorists were reported to be in the area and all available troops were rushed in. All the companies are now staying in permanently, and a platoon of each is coming out in rotation for a few days' rest. A fleeting glimpse of a C.T. was had by "A" Company on April 16 and this, after months of searching, has put our tails up and we hope for better luck soon.' 101 Field Battery supported the troops in the jungle and fired 8,064 rounds of 25 pounder shells and 1,231 4.2 inch mortar bombs during Operation 'Jaya'.

In February 1960, Brigadier and Mrs. Mogg were hosts to a very welcome visitor, the Countess Mountbatten. Lady Mountbatten was making a grand tour of the Far East in her Red Cross capacity and was greeted with genuine warmth wherever she went, renewing old acquaintanceships, opening hospitals and visiting local welfare agencies. Brigadier Mogg noted: 'She had a very strenuous and exacting itinerary and insisted on talking to everybody but she hardly ate a thing whilst she stayed with us.' After her visit to Taiping on 8th February, the Countess continued her tour to Singapore and thence to Borneo, where, on February 21st, she collapsed and died suddenly, a tragic loss mourned by all those who had known her personally and by many more who had heard of her splendid work. Amongst the many V.I.P. visits to the Commonwealth Brigade, that of the Countess Mountbatten was particularly memorable.

In March, Major Colin East concluded his tour of duty as Brigade-

*Lady Mountbatten and Brig. Mogg at the new hospital at Kamunting, 8th February 1960.*

(Gen. Sir John Mogg)

Major and paid tribute to his commander: 'John Mogg had a sense of humour, was a good raconteur and enjoyed a party. He was fond of sport, cricket especially, and these qualities endeared him to rank and file, particularly with the Maori soldiers of the New Zealand Regiment. Like Peter Moore, a few years earlier, he was the right man at the time and his command of 28 Brigade saw the end of the C.T.O. in North Malaya. John Mogg was an excellent example of the soldier/diplomat, which was recognised later in his distinguished career.' The new Brigade-Major was Major R. D. P. Hassett, of the Royal New Zealand Artillery, a former second-in-command of the 16th Field Regiment in Korea. Major Hassett describes his new environment:

'The Commonwealth was truly represented on the staff of Brigade Headquarters. British, Australian and New Zealand officers and other ranks were fully integrated and mixed. The appointment of Brigade Commander and Brigade Major rotated between the three Commonwealth countries but at no stage did any one country hold both appointments; the D.A.A. & Q.M.G., however, was always a British officer because the administrative system above Brigade was fundamentally British. Among the staff nationalities became quickly irrelevant and an intense feeling of Commonwealth became the predominant motivation with a pride in 28 Brigade. Perhaps the greatest concern of Brigade staff was to be seen to be even handed and not to be dispensing favour to their own national units. As a consequence there was always a feeling of relief among the battalions when the senior appointments at Brigade were held by officers from Commonwealth countries other than their own. In those circumstances if there were any perks going they had a better than even chance of being the recipient. It was a unique experience serving commanders who came from different ends of the earth but who had exactly parallel methods of working – whose philosophies were basically the same and whose fundamental characteristics were identical – they were good soldiers; excellent commanders and trainers of men and long time students of the military art. At the other end of the scale commanding a staff of Brits, Aussies and Kiwis was a unique experience – unique in the sense that nationalities became irrelevant (except, of course, when there was an International rugby or cricket test being played).'

On 26th March 1960, the oldest soldier in the brigade celebrated his sixty-first birthday. Sergeant F. J. W. Bennett, B.E.M., of the 3rd East Anglians, joined the British Army in 1917 and had served through both World Wars, a unique record of continuous service. Sergeant Bennett's anniversary was followed by the death of the Paramount King of Malaya, the Yang di-Pertuan Agong, on 4th April 1960. The Federation of Malaya enjoyed an unusual monarchial system; those states which were ruled by royal families elected one of their kings, or sultans, to serve as the head of state of the whole Federation. The reigning head of state was then the Yang di-Pertuan Besar of the State of Negri Sembilan. The Yang di-Pertuan Agong was given a state funeral on 4th April which was attended by representatives of the national units of the Commonwealth Brigade and the other military forces then serving in Malaya. The Sultan of Selangor was selected to replace the late King as Yang di-Pertuan Agong of Malaya.

Meanwhile, the brigade was still operating in the jungles of Perak and the 2nd Battalion of the New Zealand Regiment, based at Taiping, were sending patrols deep into the Operation 'Bamboo' area. During their tour of duty in the jungles of Upper Perak, the Kiwis did succeed in capturing four disillusioned terrorists, evidence of the success of the Security Forces in wearing down the few C.T.s still at large.

From 11th to 14th April 1960, 17 Gurkha Division staged Exercise 'Maiden Flight' involving elements of the headquarters of 63 and 99 Gurkha Infantry Brigades and 28 Commonwealth Infantry Brigade. The previous April it had been announced that a 'Fire Brigade' force would be made available to support the Southeast Asia Treaty Organization and 'Maiden Flight' was the first of a series of exercises to consider the implications of such a drastic change in operational roles. 28 Commonwealth Brigade was to form a 'Task Force' to operate with other 'Task Forces' drawn from SEATO nations to counter the effect of the so-called 'domino theory' – should the Republic of South Vietnam fall to the North Vietnamese communists then Cambodia, Laos and even Thailand could also fall in their turn. Plans were made for the deployment and role of 28 Brigade should such intervention be called for. Brigadier Mogg held several TEWTs (Tactical Exercises Without Troops) for the senior members of his command and liaised with military representatives of other SEATO nations, including Lieutenant-General Manuel Cabal, Chief of Staff of the Philippine Army, who visited Taiping to learn how the Commonwealth Brigade and the Malayan Army were conducting anti-terrorist operations, a campaign which had much in common with operations then underway in the Philippine Islands.

*Lieutenant-General Manuel F. Cabal, Chief of Staff of the Philippine Army, visiting 28 Commonwealth Brigade at Taiping with Brigadier Mogg and Major East, Brigade Major.*

(AWM CUN 17 MC)

Lieutenant-Colonel S. P. Weir succeeded Lieutenant-Colonel Morrow as commanding officer of the 1st Royal Australian Regiment at Kuala Kangsar but the jungle campaign was drawing to a close and advance parties from the battalions were beginning to move South, to Terendak in Malacca, where a new brigade base had been prepared. 'A' Company of the 1st/3rd East Anglians moved to Terendak in May to get the barracks ready for occupation by the rest of the battalion later in the year. At about the same time, the brigade lost its faithful Sarawak Rangers and the New Zealand battalion undertook the training of battalion trackers to take the Ibans' place in the regiments.

On 31st July 1960 the state of emergency in the Federation of Malaya was declared to be over and a grand Victory Parade was held in Kuala Lumpur to mark the occasion. All the armed forces in Malaya participated, including the major units of 28 Brigade. Those who had served prior to 31st July received the General Service Medal with the clasp 'Malaya'. New arrivals, who joined the brigade after 1st August, even although they may have served in the last 'black' area – the Operation 'Bamboo' zone along the Malay/Thai border – were not eligible for the medal. With the end of the emergency the Commonwealth Brigade began to train for its major strategic role in support of SEATO. Studies of likely areas of deployment and the Vietminh campaigns against the French in Indo-China were initiated and studied in detail. Brigade exercises reflecting this new role were held, including an almost pleasant 'outing' to the heights of the Cameron Highlands where Brigadier Mogg ran an exercise set in an imaginary part of the Indo-China peninsula.

On 1st September, the recently appointed Yang di-Pertuan Agong, the Sultan of Selangor, died and another full-scale state funeral was staged in Kuala Lumpur on 4th September, again attended by detachments from the

*The Victory Parade, Kuala Lumpur, 2nd August 1960. The New Zealand Regiment.*

(Gen. Sir John Mogg)

Commonwealth Brigade. The Sultan of Trengganu acceded to the national throne for, it was hoped, a longer reign.

The New Zealand Regiment had the satisfaction of being the last brigade unit to capture a terrorist in Upper Perak. In November 1960 Lieutenant A. R. Fraser, commanding 12 Platoon of 'D' Company, was sitting in his jungle base basha when a bearded, unkempt and hollow-cheeked Sakai aboriginal appeared. When challenged the man stated, 'I am Kerinching', and surrendered quietly. For the last two years, Kerinching, who was considered to be the most influential of all the aborigine terrorists, had been hunted by the 1st and 2nd Battalions of the New Zealand Regiment. He had been a foreman in a tin mine but was recruited by the Communists early in the emergency. The police had captured him in 1955 but Kerinching escaped to join his family in the remote depths of the Upper Perak jungle. Kerinching's brother, Rejek, had already surrendered and Lieutenant Fraser had persuaded him to return to the jungle to contact Kerinching. Rejek came back to report that his brother would surrender for 600 dollars and immunity from prosecution. Kerinching's sudden appearance at the base brought Lieutenant-Colonel Aitken, the Commanding Officer, and his Intelligence Officer, Captain MacLeod, to the platoon base by helicopter to accept Kerinching's surrender. Colonel Aitken pledged that the New Zealanders would stay to help Kerinching as long as he relinquished his contacts with the terrorists. This was agreed by Kerinching and he was duly presented with his 'surrender fee' of 600 dollars which was divided amongst the members of the tribe. Under the New Zealanders' protection the aborigines cleared an area near the post and put it to cultivation. Thus, 'Kerinching's Ladang' came into existence as an aboriginal settlement. Kerinching himself was friendly and always wore a pleasant but thoughtful-looking smile. With his brother Rejek and his small son he was a frequent visitor to the neighbouring post and, as Captain MacLeod observed: 'While we continued to watch Kerinching, to all intents and purposes he became a useful citizen.'

Since its reformation in Malaya, 28 Brigade had enjoyed the status of being an 'accompanied posting' for most of its members and wives and families from all three nations lived in the brigade's stations. Much emphasis was placed on family welfare, health and junior education whilst boarding school facilities were available for older children in the Cameron Highlands. The various unit wives' clubs played an important part in everyday life and did much to maintain morale and interest amongst the womenfolk. An added advantage was the opportunity to meet and mix with families from the other Commonwealth nations on neutral ground and, like their husbands, the wives found that the inter-regimental and international composition of the brigade gave that extra impetus to their activities. British wives were particularly fascinated by the Australian wives' pay parade at which the wives received the family allowance directly from the pay office, ensuring that the housekeeping money ended up in the right hands. Each family was officially provided with an essential amah, a local woman who undertook the heavier household tasks which could be trying to ladies from more temperate climes; many of the amahs also became very devoted to the children and often spoilt them outrageously. Although the NAAFI provided most of the familiar everyday necessities in their garrison shops, the wives discovered the pleasures and fascination of local shopping and soon became adept at haggling and bargaining with Chinese and Indian shopkeepers. Some of the wives volunteered for part-time service with the Soldiers', Sailors' and Airmen's Families' Association (SSAFA) and accompanied the local SSAFA Sister on her visits to the families of Malay soldiers serving with the British Army; such visits to nearby kampongs provided insights to the local customs and the Malay way of life. Mrs. Mogg, the Commander's wife, was unobtrusively active amongst the families and many wives welcomed her friendly and helpfully informal calls on new arrivals and those in need of advice and guidance. Mrs. Mogg's genuine approach struck the right chord amongst the Commonwealth families and dispelled any resentment at being visited by the 'Mem' on an official duty visit. Such a background added considerably to the 'family atmosphere' that existed in the brigade as a whole.

The 'single men in barracks' also enjoyed off duty amenities – including the Army Kinema Corporation's chain of cinemas, often merely a screen rigged in the open air. A myth popular in North Malaya at that time was that the A.K.C. had only film on circulation in Perak: *The Red Beret* starring Alan Ladd, and it is a fact that this epic was screened more than once in most stations. In the integrated cookhouses, where British and Australians fed together, there was some 'Pommy' resentment at the Australians' receipt of ration allowance for enduring British scales of messing – which did not extend to steak and eggs for breakfast. Far from being 'plaster saints', the single men of the brigade's units were readily susceptible to the many tawdry 'night clubs', 'bars' and 'dance halls' which sprang up to cater for the military presence in North Malaya. Such establishments were, inevitably, the venue for several minor brawls and displays of 'high spirits'. The incidence of venereal disease contracted in such establishments was subject to severe disciplinary measures but, as the Deputy-Assistant-Adjutant and Quartermaster-General of the brigade at that time, Major Richard Jerram, commented 'it could not be completely eradicated'.

Despite such transitory 'liaisons' the presence of the Commonwealth Brigade was generally welcomed by the local population of Taiping and district – and not just the commercial element. The part played by the Commonwealth soldiers during the State of Emergency was appreciated by most of the people of Perak who gave their whole-hearted support to the security forces. Malayan and Commonwealth units enjoyed good relationships and often worked together in the fight against the terrorists. 28 Brigade was particularly fortunate in its locally employed staff who gave loyal and dedicated service. Mr. Beh Cheng-Chuah, the brigade commander's personal assistant for civilian affairs, remembers that 'they were very happy times and we made many good friends.' Mr Beh had

*Sgt. Harris, East Anglian Regiment, instructs Sgt. Pullen, Royal Australian Regiment, on the 7.62mm Self Loading Rifle.*

(AWM CUN 198 MC)

previously worked for the 1st Federal Division in Taiping and served under Brigadiers Moore, Mogg and Hassett; his knowledge of the North Malayan Sub-District – which included the Gurkha Training Centre at Sungei Patani, the units on Penang Island, Ipoh, Tapah and Taiping – was invaluable to the succession of brigade commanders. These efficient and reliable working contacts resulted in several long-lasting friendships. Many of the former civilian staff of 28 Brigade Headquarters at Taiping still gather for reunion parties – 'just like the Christmas parties we used to have when everybody was very relaxed' as Mr. Beh recalls. Amongst such loyal local veterans are Mr. Yeoh Siew-Lye of the D.A.A. & Q.M.G.'s branch, Mr. Roy Muniandy the headquarters' peon and messenger, Mr. Boon who ran the headquarters coffee shop and is now a Taiping town councillor, Mr. Wong and Mr. Anthony of the North Malaya Sub-District administration office and, until her death in 1985, Miss Martha Cheong who was secretary to the 'G' (Operations) Branch. After his retirement, Mr. Beh visited Australia to meet General Hassett and Colonel East (formerly Brigade-Major) and Mr. Corcoran who had been the Brigade Headquarters Sergeant-Major. Sergeant-Major Corcoran was Mentioned in Despatches whilst serving with the 1st Battalion of the Royal Australian Regiment in Korea and after leaving the army he entered politics to become the Labour Premier for the State of South Australia; he later visited Penang in this capacity and took the opportunity to meet Mr. Beh and his friends in Taiping. The indefatigable Mr. Beh also visited Great Britain to contact Generals Mogg and Jerram and the author, who enjoyed a very pleasant lunch remembering 'the good old days' at Taiping.

In November 1960 Brigadier Mogg relinquished command of his brigade. During the two years of his command the brigade had controlled the rivers and forests of Upper Perak and gained the ascendancy over the few terrorists still surviving along the Northern border. The ending of the emergency had given the opportunity for the Brigadier to lay the foundations for the brigade's future role as a strategic reserve force. The brigade-major, Major R. D. P. Hassett, remembers the Brigadier's departure:

> 'Brigadier John Mogg had placed his personal mark on the Brigade and everybody was sorry to see him go. Some, however, may have breathed a sigh of relief as he drove away from Commonwealth House in Falaise Road. The hectic whirlwind of his farewell functions extending over a period of three weeks starting daily with Corporals' Clubs then Sergeants' Messes followed

by formal dinners in the Officers' Messes was physically and mentally demanding, particularly for those who had to accompany him and still be in their offices before he arrived the following morning.'

The new commander of the 28th Commonwealth Brigade Group was no stranger to the formation; as a battalion commander he had served in the brigade during the bitter battles of Kowang-San and Maryang-San in the autumn of 1951 and had been awarded the Distinguished Service Order for his leadership of the 3rd Battalion of the Royal Australian Regiment in the Korean War. Brigadier F. G. Hassett – 'Frank' – was the first Australian to command the brigade since its disbandment in Korea in 1954. On his arrival, Brigadier Hassett was pleased to observe that 'General Mogg left me an efficient and happy Brigade H.Q. and a well-run formation. He had the same capacity for creating good relationships between the various nationalities as did F. M. Cassels, who was admirable as the first G.O.C. of 1 Comwel Div.' The new commander's brigade-major, another Hassett, notes:

'The new commander, Brigadier Frank Hassett, very quickly made his presence felt. Those who served close to him in Korea during the time he commanded 3 R.A.R. were aware of the formidable reputation he had established as a battalion commander during that particularly trying period of the Korean War. It was soon clear that little was going to change. Like his predecessor his communication skills were excellent, not only with the many visiting dignitaries but also with the humblest soldier in the brigade. His was a hands-off approach, clear directions to all concerned, delegation of responsibility to subordinates and then absolutely no interference with his commanders or his staff while they were carrying out the tasks allotted to them.'

The presence of two Hassetts in the Brigade Headquarters was slightly confusing in the early days of the new brigadier's command. Shortly after the new commander's arrival, one of the 'humblest soldiers' in the brigade, a newly arrived Australian member of the intelligence staff, received a telephone call in the operations room and, innocently, wandered around brigade headquarters until he found an occupied office. 'Is your name Hassett?' he asked the officer behind the desk. 'Yes,' was the surprised reply. 'Well, there's a call for you in the ops room,' said the young soldier – only to learn that he had found the wrong Hassett.

*Brigadier Hassett serves Private Schneider's Christmas Dinner, Taiping, Christmas Day, 1960.*

(Captain H. B. Eaton)

To Brigadier Hassett fell the task of preparing the brigade for air-portable operations in the Far East whilst maintaining operations in the remaining 'black' area of North Perak. The jungle patrols and manning of remote posts continued and the 2nd New Zealand Regiment lost Private Solia on 10th December, drowned whilst on river patrol on the Sungei Perak.

Nineteen sixty-one was to be a year of hard and practical training interspersed with unit detachments to the border area. Brigadier Hassett announced his policy very succinctly: 'There is one standard of training in this brigade,' he declared, 'mine.' The Commonwealth Brigade had been designated 'Task Force Blue' of the SEATO Strategic Reserve and was intended for deployment to South Vietnam and the South-Central area of Laos, like Korea another unheard-of country but one to be studied in detail by the staff and units of 28 Brigade in the months to come. To achieve deployment to South Vietnam or Laos the brigade was to be flown

*Brigadier F. G. Hassett, Brigade Commander, and Major R. D. P. Hassett, Royal New Zealand Artillery, Brigade Major.*

(AWM CUN 521 MC)

from the Royal Air Force base at Changi, in Singapore. Malaya was not a member of SEATO and the political climate required that such a move had to be made from the State of Singapore, operational planning therefore had to allow for movement to Singapore before emplanement. In addition to preparing for war in a strange land, the brigade also had to learn all the arts and skills of air travel and 'air portability' became a major factor in training. The brigade's transport would be limited to light vehicles, mainly stripped-down Land Rovers, and most equipment would have to be man-packed. Load planning was the essence of air portability and it was envisaged that resupply and logistical support would also be delivered by air.

Early in the New Year, Brigadier Hassett held a brigade study group and TEWT in the old Residency at Taiping where battalion and unit commanders considered all the factors of operating in Indo-China and the problems of moving the brigade by air. The training policy of the brigade was defined and planned. There were many obvious differences to be solved should 28 Brigade be required to operate in Indo-China: unlike Malaya, where the local population resisted Communist terrorism, it was likely that local nationalism and intimidation by Communist force of arms would isolate intervention by SEATO forces; the difficulties of maintaining air supply after the force had been deployed and the extended lines of communication and logistical support; the probability of facing a Communist army – as opposed to terrorist gangs; the terrain, ethnic and linguistic varieties likely to be encountered and the political and economic state of the countries in which the brigade might be committed. Much attention was given to the experience of the French forces in Indo-China prior to 1954 and it was hoped that study groups would produce valuable lessons which could be incorporated into the training programme.

In March 1961 28 Commonwealth Brigade Group participated in Exercise 'Rajata', a SEATO exercise held in Thailand. A skeleton brigade headquarters and representatives of brigade units were flown to Ubon in East Thailand and assumed the role of 'Task Force Blue' with other task forces fielded by the United States and the Royal Thai Army. Although only one Beverley and one Hastings transport aircraft were available to ferry the token force from Changi to Ubon, the flights did provide an opportunity to practise loading and lashing vehicles. In comparison, the American task force thundered into Ubon on a fleet of C-130s (The Mighty Hercules) and disgorged men and vehicles with the minimum of fuss. Eastern Thailand was a surprise to 28 Brigade. Ubon sat in the middle of a vast, open and dusty plain which stretched Eastwards to the

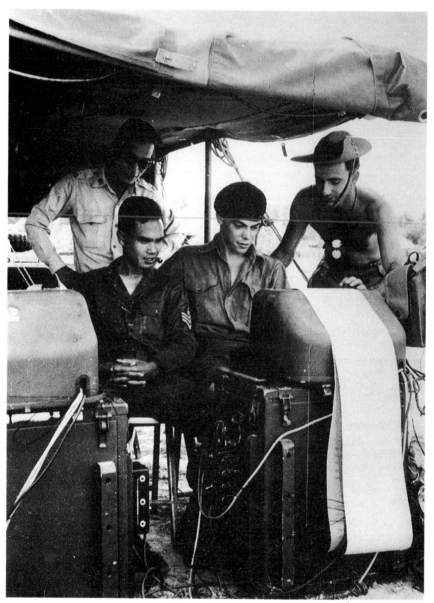

*Commonwealth and Thai signallers, Exercise Rajata, Ubon, Thailand, March 1961.*
*(Sig. Allen, R. Sigs, and Sgt. Rickus, R. Aust. Sigs.)*

(Capt. H. B. Eaton)

River Mekong and the Laotian border, a considerable change from the dense rain forests of the North Malayan highlands.

'Rajata' was a command and communications exercise but offered opportunities to meet representatives of the other SEATO forces and learn something of their methods and procedures. Members of the Commonwealth Brigade were flattered to receive gifts of small lead figures of the Buddha from Thai soldiers. When worn, these charms conferred immunity from bullets; this claim was guaranteed since the charms had been hung on targets on the rifle ranges and emerged unscathed! The small Commonwealth contingent distinguished itself during its stay at Ubon. A fire broke out amongst the wooden houses of the township and the brigade headquarters staff, with their Royal Air Force colleagues, were first on the scene with firefighting equipment and prevented the spread of the conflagration. For this prompt action the brigade was commended by the local Provincial Governor. At that time, Ubon was a comparatively unspoilt

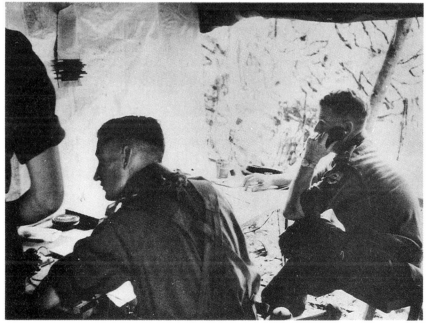

*Brigade Command Post on exercise, Malaya, 1961. Captain Sims (GS03 Ops.) and Major Hassett (Brigade-Major).*

(Capt. H. B. Eaton)

Thai town distinguished only by a large earthen airstrip and its proximity to Laos. In later years the strip was to be developed into a huge airbase by the United States Air Force to support the war in Vietnam.

In April the brigade made an emergency move. Events in the Republic of South Vietnam had assumed a critical state when the reigning president and his government were in imminent danger of being ousted by a coup. SEATO forces were alerted to support the South Vietnamese government and the alert state was suddenly upgraded to an order for intervention. The 28th Commonwealth Infantry Brigade Group was 'scrambled', vehicles were stripped down, essential supplies loaded and readied to move. The married soldiers bade solemn farewells to their families, drew ammunition and boarded the transport. The brigade was soon on the road to Singapore – only to be halted and returned to barracks. The crisis in Vietnam had been resolved but at least the brigade had proved that it could muster and move off at short notice. After the emotional farewells of the previous evening, many of the soldiers returned to their families in a somewhat embarrassed state.

However, the brigade commander and some of his senior officers did make a journey to South Vietnam to visit the Army of the Republic of Vietnam (A.R.V.N.). The Commonwealth officers were particularly interested in the Rangers School where the A.R.V.N. received their jungle training and exchanged ideas and advice as well as gaining first-hand experience of the terrain and operations in that country. Back in Malaya, the brigade began a series of testing exercises in its strategic role. Since 'Task Force Blue' would have to fly to its area of operations, the exercises were all code-named 'Angel', commencing with 'Blue Angel' in April. Although it was not possible to load and move in actual aircraft, an ingenious system of simulating air travel was devised. Full-scale outlines of aircraft were laid in white tape on sports fields; the stripped-down vehicles – or requisite number of passengers – were driven into the taped 'aircraft' and loading and lashing drills were performed. Once completed to the satisfaction of the Unit Emplanement Officer, the load (or 'chalk') then travelled by road to the designated 'landing field' where another taped outline had been prepared. The arriving vehicles drew into the taped 'aircraft' and the time of 'landing' was noted; the vehicles were unlashed, unloaded and driven away. Thereafter the exercises assumed a more realistic form of deployment against an Asian Communist force.

Communications were of the greatest importance in such exercises since the brigade would be working with allied forces in the event of an actual deployment. 28 Brigade enjoyed good communications. The cheerful Kiwi telephonic greeting 'Are ye there?' always ensured a friendly response whereas one keen subaltern's constant checking of the radio net: 'How do you hear me? How do you hear me? Over,' received a laconic reply from an Australian outstation: 'Too loud, too clear, too often. Out.' The continuity of the Commonwealth Brigade spirit was evident in these exercises; many of the code-names of terrain features were echoes of the Korean War. On learning that his unit was to occupy the 'Jamestown Line', one sergeant was heard to say: 'Jamestown Line? I dug the flaming thing ten years ago!'

'Blue Angel' was followed by 'Trinity Angel' in July and August when the Commonwealth Brigade was 'flown' to 'Southland' to counter aggression by the 'Vandals'. 'Faith Angel' continued the series in November and the battalions became proficient in this new form of training for war. The 1st Battalion of The Royal Australian Regiment was relieved by the 2nd Battalion, Lieutenant-Colonel A. B. Stratton, in October and 101 Battery by 103 Battery under Major J. R. Salmon – who had served in the 16th Field Regiment, R.N.Z.A., in Korea. 2 R.A.R. were introduced to the brigade's role:

> 'Only two weeks after the unit's arrival, it took part in a strenuous brigade exercise "Arunta Pack I" in some really hot, hilly country. All ranks were made aware of the requirements of additional salt and water, and the necessity for this was illustrated on the exercise where water resupply took priority over rations. This first exercise, as with all the others to come, was "air-portable" and was the unit's first taste of this very important aspect of training. The unit was fortunate in having comprehensive standing orders for air-portable operations prepared by the advance party, but was lacking in trained and experienced personnel such as unit emplaning officers, loading and lashing teams, together with a general lack of unit "air-mindedness". Many lessons were learnt from this exercise. Perhaps the greatest was the value of mock-up aircraft for training. They are essential for the training and practice of unit loading and lashing teams and for all drivers in reversing drills. They are a "must" for any unit which is likely to be engaged in air-portable operations. Because of the limited weight factor, the battalion must be able to operate on a light scale of vehicles, weapons and equipment. This involves twelve trucks ¼ ton and twenty-four trailers, no cooks or cooking equipment and a reduced scale of heavy weapons. The balance of

twelve trucks ¼ ton, making a total of twenty-four, would
normally be transported to the theatre of operations by sea.
Twelve vehicles to a battalion must sound very meagre, especially as vehicle loads are severely restricted to comply with
maximum permissible all-up weight for air movement. However,
it must be said that 2 R.A.R. has conducted all but one of its
exercises to date on this scale and has not been found lacking.'

Although 28 Brigade still had a vestigial role along the Malay-Thai border, the small detachments in the jungle were withdrawn gradually as
troops of the Federal Malay Army took over this last 'black area'. Brigade
units began to move South to the new camp at Terendak as 1961 drew to a
close. 4 Field Troop of the Royal Australian Engineers joined 11 Field
Squadron in the new location and other units arriving to join the brigade
went directly to Terendak.

The 1st Battalion of the 3rd East Anglian Regiment was coming to the
end of its tour of duty with the brigade and the Anglians appear to have
enjoyed their time in Malaya:

'Being part of the Commonwealth Brigade has, in many ways,
broadened our outlook. No longer do we wince when an Australian friend asks if " Blighty" is a town or county in England. Our
vocabulary has changed considerably: "Digger" is NOT a
roadworker; "Creek" is something to go up WITH a paddle, and
so on. We have entertained and been entertained by many Brigade
units. We would like to mention specially the Battery of Royal
Australian Artillery, who we hope have not yet finished the rum
(come back for more if you dare), and the Royal Australian
Regiment, who thought Op Bamboo rather more of a holiday than
Op Jaya.'

As in Korea, it was noticeable how quickly the British (or U.K.) members
of the brigade soon employed the rather descriptive and laconic Australian manner of speech. At about this time, the first of the Australian 'pop'
songs began to be heard – Slim Dusty and Rolf Harris with 'The Pub with
no Beer' and 'Tie me Kangaroo Down'. This exposure to Australian
culture left an abiding impression on those from Great Britain and many
returned to 'Blighty' speaking passable 'Strine'. Another remembered
tune returned to haunt the Korean veterans: 'Moon above Malaya', a
Westernized version of 'China Nights' – a popular Japanese song of the

Korean War era heard *ad nauseum* by soldiers on R. & R. leave in Tokyo which described the delights of a 'cushy' posting in China during the Second World War.

# Terendak

A permanent home for the Commonwealth Brigade had been planned and construction of a 'made to measure' cantonment began in June 1957. The site of the new base was at Bukit Terendak, some fourteen miles North of the City of Malacca on the West coast of Malaya. The Royal Engineers started work on the site and the construction was taken over by the War Office in 1959. Responsibility for the cantonment was passed to the British Ministry of Works and Public Buildings in 1964. General Sir Richard Hull, Commander-in-Chief of the Far East Land Forces, named the new base 'Fort George' to commemorate the headquarters of the Commonwealth Division in the Korean War. After some criticism by the Government of Malaya it was later agreed that the cantonment should be known as 'Camp Terendak'.

The original estimate of the cost of the camp was £7.5 million but, by the time of the Melbourne Conference in June 1958, the figure had risen to £11 million. Protests by the Australian and New Zealand Governments reduced the cost to £8.25 million but, inevitably, by March 1960 the revised estimates had crept up to some £8.9 million. At a conference in Canberra in November 1960 it was agreed to review the cost of the new base and effect economies. By January 1961 the estimate had been cut by some £2 million but there were still many contentious items to settle. A third meeting, the Singapore Conference of February 1962, accepted a revised estimate of £7.77 million. The Commonwealth Governments agreed to share the cost in proportion to the number of troops of each nation in the brigade; Great Britain would pay 54.1%, Australia 27.7% and New Zealand 18.2%. The maintenance of the camp would also be shared at the same rates but, since the cantonment also contained a garrison serving units other than the Commonwealth Brigade, the British contribution towards maintenance was increased accordingly.

*Terendak Camp, Malacca.*

(Soldier Magazine 5661/29/1)

*Corporal Ray Folbigg, Royal Australian Signals, and family in their quarters, Terendak Camp.*

(Soldier Magazine)

Terendak Garrison consisted of a military hospital, a transport unit, a supply depot, an education centre, a civil labour unit, a hygiene and malaria control unit, a detachment of army depot police and the barracks services. These garrison units were housed in Baldwin Lines.

The Commonwealth Brigade was accommodated in distinct barrack areas:

| | |
|---|---|
| Brigade Headquarters | Maryang-San Lines |
| British Infantry Battalion | Imjin Lines |
| Australian Infantry Battalion | Canberra Lines |
| New Zealand Infantry Battalion | Wellington Lines |
| Artillery Regiment | Solma-Ri Lines |
| Field Engineer Squadron | Kohima Lines |
| Ordnance and Workshops | Arakan Lines |
| Field Ambulance and Hospital | Mandalay Lines |

The camp contained two estates of married quarters, one for officers' families and another for other ranks. However, the number of families exceeded the accommodation available and many were housed in hirings in Malacca and Bukit Bahru. This overspill was of great benefit to local property owners and tradesmen. In the middle of the cantonment was a community centre which featured a large NAAFI shop, several local traders' shops, a cinema, the 'Crown Inn', a children's school (which also served as the garrison church) and a kindergarten. All the usual sports amenities were provided, including a golf course. On the seaward side of the garrison were three beach clubs: officers, warrant-officers and sergeants and junior ranks. A sailing club was open to all ranks. Although Terendak boasted a scenic tropical beach, the water was infested with jelly fish which restricted sea bathing and water sports. The garrison covered an area of 1,500 acres of former rubber plantations and included a small Chinese temple which was left intact. An adjacent site of 3,500 acres was converted into a jungle training area which featured a 600-yard landing strip for light aircraft, a 600-yard range, a 400-metre range and a grenade range. A realistic mock-up of a defended village for anti-terrorist training was later built by the 1st New Zealand Regiment.

One of the first occupants of the new camp was the brigade's own artillery regiment. Since the brigade's main role was that of the Commonwealth Strategic Reserve for the Southeast Asia Treaty Organization, it required more artillery support than was necessary for anti-terrorist operations in North Malaya. The Regimental Headquarters and two batteries of 26 Regiment, Royal Artillery, came under the command of 28

Commonwealth Infantry Brigade Group in October 1961. 103 Field Battery of the Royal Australian Artillery was converted and took its place with the two British batteries: 16 (Sandham's Company) Light Battery and 17 (Corunna) Light Battery. The regiment was equipped with the new Italian 105 mm Pack Howitzer which was the ideal weapon for airportable operations in the Far East. The three batteries were normally allocated so that the Australian battery supported the British battalion whilst the two British batteries supported the Australian and New Zealand battalions.

When the 1st Battalion of the New Zealand Regiment, Lieutenant-Colonel L. A. Pearce, replaced the 2nd Battalion in November 1961, the new arrivals (many of whom had served in Malaya between 1958 and 1959) moved into Wellington Lines at Terendak.

'During its second tour in Malaya the battalion carried out intensive training and adjusting to a South Asia role which involved a complete change from our deep jungle patrolling experience in

*The New Zealand Regiment on the Sungei Perak, April 1962.*

(Soldier Magazine 5661/22/8)

the Perak mountains. The battalion took part in periodic operations along the Malaya-Thailand border and numerous exercises all over Malaya.'

The 1st Battalion of The King's Own Yorkshire Light Infantry, Lieutenant-Colonel H. C. I. Rome, arrived to occupy Imjin Lines in January 1962, taking the place of the 3rd East Anglians. The K.O.Y.L.I. were soon plunged into the brigade's training programme. 'Training out here, under the Brigade Commander's rugged training direction, is hard work in a tiring climate. B.A.O.R. veterans will agree that Germany was a piece of cake. There, Colour used to come up regularly in his "fwee tunner" with the grub. Now, lads, you carry your rations on your backs, or starve.'

The order of battle of the 28th Commonwealth Infantry Brigade Group in 1962 was:-

26 Regiment, Royal Artillery (Air Portable); 16 (Sandham's Company) Light Battery, 17 (Corunna) Light Battery, 103 Field Battery R.A.A.

1st Battalion, The King's Own Yorkshire Light Infantry.

2nd Battalion, The Royal Australian Regiment.

1st Battalion, The New Zealand Regiment.

11 Independent Field Squadron, Royal Engineers, including 4 Field Troop R.A.E.

208 (Commonwealth) Signal Squadron, Royal Corps of Signals, including a troop of the Royal Australian Corps of Signals.

7 Reconnaissance Flight, Army Air Corps.

3 Company, Royal Army Service Corps.

16 Commonwealth Field Ambulance, Royal Army Medical Corps and R.A.A.M.C.

28 Ordnance Field Park, Royal Army Ordnance Corps, including an Australian detachment.

2 Infantry Workshops, Royal Electrical and Mechanical Engineers and R.A.E.M.E.

28 Commonwealth Provost Unit, Royal Military Police and Australian and New Zealand Provost Staff.

368 Postal Unit, Royal Engineers.

32 Army Dental Unit, Royal Australian Army Dental Corps.

22 Intelligence Platoon (Brigade), Intelligence Corps.

Headquarters Company and Light Aid Detachment.

The Brigade Headquarters Staff, Headquarters Company and the Light Aid Detachment were completely integrated with officers and other ranks from all three nations filling the various appointments and posts. The brigade also had 'X' Squadron of the Royal Dragoons, then an armoured car regiment, stationed at Ipoh in Perak under operational command but not an integral part of 28 Brigade. The Commonwealth Brigade Group was subordinate to the 17th Gurkha Infantry Division at Seremban which also included 63 Gurkha Infantry Brigade in Malaya and 99 Gurkha Infantry Brigade in Singapore.

Nineteen sixty-two began with a four-day study exercise at the new brigade headquarters, Exercise 'Red Angel', which concentrated on the Savannakhet area of Central Laos. During the course of the exercise, Brigadier Hassett defined the new tactical doctrine which would employed should the brigade be deployed to that part of Indo-China. A special 'Commonwealth Edition' of a well-known weekly American news magazine was produced and issued to all participants as a contemporary form of briefing on the background to 'Red Angel' and the ensuing practical exercises in the field. The thespians of the 'Commonwealth Players' were pressed into service to present well-produced and informative 'playlets' illustrating some of the experiences of French Union Forces during their operations in Indo-China. These novel presentations set the scene very effectively and inspired considerable interest and further study.

After 'Red Angel' the brigade took to the field in two strenuous exercises to practise the doctrines established during the indoor exercise. 'Charity Angel' followed hot on the heels of 'Hope Angel' and most of the month of February was spent under field conditions. For 'Charity Angel', Royal Navy helicopters were obtained to lend realism to the airlifting of troops in the Gemas and Segamat areas. Even when not out in the field, each brigade unit held itself in readiness.

'Because of the Brigade's strategic reserve role, it must be in constant readiness to mobilise at all times and many exercises have been held to test this system – to have the unit ready to move in five hours. During this busy five hour period, sub-units of the battalion follow a pre-planned timetable to complete the following tasks:- pack personal gear, prepare and load vehicles, draw and test signals equipment, bring inoculations up to date, replace worn clothing and equipment, distribute ammunition, collect pay, arrange for disposal of personal property, notification of families,

handing over the administration of the barracks to the rear party
and the despatch of the administrative advance party to the staging area. On completion of these tasks, the unit stands by to be
called forward to a staging area, where any deficiencies of equipment are made up and where final preparations are made for the
air move. The final stage is the movement to the airfield and
emplaning.'

In addition to the hard training for the brigade's major war role, the battalions also gained realistic and valuable experience of actual operations in the
Far East. The New Zealand Regiment returned to the Thai border area:

'Our first three month tour saw battalion headquarters established
with a very hospitable 7 Royal Malay Regiment at Alor Star in
Kedah. The Kiwi companies carried out day after day of close
searching through this rather flat jungle which contained a wealth
of bamboo. We had considerable success in locating camps,
dumps, tracks and other C.T. sign and we began to call ourselves
"high powered rubbish collectors". However, our only live contacts were with one leopard, several tigers, elephants, many snake
varieties and, of course, the inevitable mosquitoes. The Australians warned us about a particularly nasty strain of mosquito
which penetrated our rigid adherence to anti-malarial practices to
give us a number of malaria cases.'

The King's Own Yorkshire Light Infantry sent two companies to Singapore to participate in Exercise 'Rabbit Punch', an internal security exercise with the Queen's Own Highlanders of 99 Brigade in May. During the
same month, members of 26 Regiment, Royal Artillery, tackled a fire in a
kampong near Terendak. Battery-Sergeant-Major Cross and Battery-
Quartermaster-Sergeant Austin received the Queen's Commendation for
Bravery for their actions and Lance-Bombardier Tasker was commended
for rescuing an old woman from her blazing house – but failed to recover
her life's savings which were lost in the fire.

The Queen's Official Birthday was celebrated with a parade on 2nd
June to be followed on Whit Sunday by another brigade 'scramble' –
Exercise 'Trumpeter'. The brigade was soon off the mark and drove South
to Nee Soon, in Singapore, to 'emplane' at the exercise 'airfield'. 'Trumpeter' was a divisional exercise with a 'live' enemy and covered a large
area of Malaya. 1 K.O.Y.L.I. recorded their impressions of the exercise:

'Exercise Trumpeter saw us dashing to Nee Soon followed by an air trip to Triang (in trucks). Here we set up protective cordons before actually flying, by Pioneer, from Kerayong Airstrip to Kuala Krau for an eight-day march to attack a defended village. The exercise simulated a realistic operation in Southeast Asia and consisted of first hunting for the enemy position and then finally attacking and destroying it. The battalion spent most of the time moving from place to place in the jungle, rarely seeing the enemy – the most obvious enemy was the jungle itself. Little was known about the defended village we were attacking. We had rather expected to find a conventional Asian village with, perhaps, a stockade around it. For, rather than a village, we found a system of camouflaged trenches, almost impossible to see in the undergrowth until suddenly the blast of a rifle would indicate the position of a gleeful little Gurkha of the 2nd 10th Gurkha Rifles. The exercise finished on 27th June.'

The New Zealanders 'found that the Kiwi soldiers were too big, only five Kiwis could fit into a Twin Pioneer aircraft scheduled to carry seven or eight passengers. Another unusual technique involved using individual cookers to light up night time D.Z.s and L.Z.s.'

The 2nd Royal Australians reported:

'In the first eight months of 2 R.A.R.'s present tour in Malaya, it has taken part in two divisional exercises, two major brigade exercises and three minor ones, together with the normal run of battalion and company exercises. Most of these have involved going through the mobilisation procedures, all but one have been on air-portable scales, and six of them have involved the use of "live" aircraft. Most exercises have lasted from ten to twenty days and have been held in areas throughout Malaya and Singapore. The Army of the Federation of Malaya has been most co-operative in providing troops and services in double-sided exercises and as host units at camps on the battalion's travels. Some Federation officers and N.C.O.s were trained by 2 R.A.R. in air-portability before their departure for the Congo (to join the United Nations Force). This particular course confronted the instructor with a class of six officers and ten N.C.O.s, of which only the officers spoke or understood English. The problem was soon resolved when the officers stuck to the theory and documentation and the N.C.O.s to the practical loading and lashing. The high standard achieved conclusively proved that demonstration and practice are far more important than wordy explanations. Some officers and N.C.O.s have been fortunate enough to be attached to Gurkha units for certain exercises, and have gained much from their association with these tough but merry people, every inch professional soldiers. The Maoris in the N.Z. battalion fascinate them, whom they call with considerable awe "big Gurkhas".'

By August 1962 the brigade had completed the move from North Malaya and was concentrated in the barracks at Terendak. There were, inevitably, initial problems to be resolved as the cantonment became fully occupied. Malacca was drier than Perak and water supplies were difficult; when the tide was in, domestic water supplies produced sea water which entered via the drainage system. During rainless periods fresh water had to be brought to Terendak by water trucks but this was later remedied. The Australians complained of the insufficient number of showers in the barracks, the sports fields were found to be inadequate for the numbers of players in the garrison and the numbers of families far exceeded the quarters and official hirings available. With all the battalions in the same camp there were minor infractions of the peace and the Commonwealth Provost Unit, supported by regimental police picquets, were fully employed at communal focal points such as the 'Crown Inn'. Such disturbances were relatively minor and only to be expected when large numbers of soldiers occupied the same garrison. On the other hand, the proximity of the three national contingents did engender some genuine harmony and good-natured inter-Commonwealth competition. Sports contests were keen and energetic and even cultural pursuits, such as the rivalry between the predominantly New Zealand Methodist Church choir and the Church of England choir, brought an extra zest to their performances. The New Zealand Regiment's band included 'a number of specially recruited N.Z. champion instrumentalists who brought a new dimension to the quality of the band's music. The Maori Meeting House complex built near the 1 N.Z. Regiment Officers' Mess became the focal point for a number of stirring cultural performances by the Maori Concert Party formed by battalion members and wives. This group were also greatly appreciated at local civic and village functions. The N.Z. Ceremonial Parade included many Maori elements which delighted guests at parade and retreat ceremonies.' Each battalion took regular turns to mount retreat ceremonies on the main garrison parade ground. The New Zealand and Australian battalions 'beat' the retreat whereas the King's Own Yorkshire Light Infantry 'sounded' the retreat with gleaming silver bugles and their jaunty light infantry marching pace. The Royal Australian Regiment's band paraded in number one dress, complete with solar topees. This stirring display gave rise to the popular 'Pommy' belief that the Royal Australian Marine Corps had joined the brigade.

As a 'break' from Brigadier Hassett's rigorous training schedule, the battalions continued to take their turn in supplying sub-units for operations along the Northern border. The 2nd Royal Australians moved up to Kedah and Perlis at the end of July to come under the command of the 2nd Federal Brigade of the Malay Army. The battalion entered the 'black area' by night and the four rifle companies were dispersed in the jungle along a sixty-mile stretch of the border by 1st August. Surprise had been maintained and the platoons began to patrol their areas almost immediately. On the morning of 3rd August, 3 Platoon of 'A' Company discovered a recently occupied terrorist camp for about forty people. The camp was left undisturbed and ambushes were laid on the approaches.

'By 1500 hours on 4th August 3 Platoon had maintained an ambush on the C.T. camp for a period of thirty hours. The ambush was of section strength with the rest of the platoon about 400 yards away in a rest area from where regular relief of the ambush section was carried out. At 1515 hours the ambush party saw a C.T. approaching the camp through the thick bamboo on the flank of the ambush position. He was dressed in shorts, shirt and hockey boots, with black webbing and carrying a carbine. The L.M.G. number actually had the C.T. in his sights but held his fire when he saw the C.T. beckon to someone in his rear. A second C.T. then came into view, again from the flank of the position. As the second C.T. approached, the first C.T. spotted the flank man of the ambush, shouted and jumped into the thick bamboo. Both C.T.s and the ambushers opened fire simultaneously at a range of about forty yards through bad visibility. The C.T.s disappeared into the thick undergrowth.'

The ambush gave chase and found a blood trail; a police tracker dog was brought up but a heavy downpour washed away all traces. Several days after the contact, cross-border police liaison reported that a group of C.T.s had purchased medical supplies in Southern Thailand and were returning to Malaya. A study of recent aerial photography of the area towards which the C.T.s were probably heading indicated three sites with fresh water where camps could be located and 2 R.A.R. moved in. The most likely site was cordoned whilst patrols investigated the other locations. At last light on 11th August, the patrol to the second site caught a strong smell of curry. 'A' and 'B' Companies surrounded this site and 'C' Company moved into the jungle on the 12th. Despite a detailed search, nothing was found apart from some old surrender pamphlets. The companies returned to the original site and, on 15th August, a resting place for two people and a trail was found leading to a camp which had been in recent use. Footprints and other evidence showed that the camp had been evacuated two days before. A blood trail was picked up, probably that of the C.T. wounded by 3 Platoon on the 14th, and was followed northwards towards the border but a heavy fall of rain obliterated the spoor and no further contact was made. But for the misleading smell of curry, the C.T.s might have been caught in the jungle near the first site. It was later discovered that a certain jungle tree does emit an odour similar to that of curry. 2 R.A.R. moved on to the third site but nothing was found and, on 15th August, Operation 'Hot Trail' was called off.

Such forays into the jungle gave valuable experience of operational conditions and introduced newcomers to the brigade to the patient and painstaking attention to detail so necessary in anti-terrorist warfare. These minor operations were of great value, not only as training experience but also to demonstrate to the Malay authorities that the Commonwealth Brigade was still available to assist in the suppression of the Communist terrorists.

Major W. S. Slocombe relieved Major Salmon as commander of 103 Field Battery, R.A.A., and found himself commanding a water-borne airportable battery! The gunners were experimenting with a variety of methods of moving their guns; the 105 mm Pack Howitzer was normally towed by a stripped-down Land-Rover but, in the rugged terrain of Southeast Asia, alternative forms of transport might be required at short notice. One experimental method involved breaking the guns down into their component parts and loading them on water buffaloes. However, no sooner were the buffaloes loaded than they rolled over in the muddy padi fields and refused to move. Another, more successful, attempt placed the 105s on rafts and they were floated on the river; only the gunners got wet and they welcomed the cooling off after their strenuous labours. All the brigade units experimented and tested ideas to lighten their equipment loads for air movement and deployment into hostile territory. The New Zealanders tried dispensing with the issue ration packs and sent platoons into the jungle with the barest necessities – a bag of rice, some salt and tea. Anything else they found in the jungle and lived off the land much as an Asian guerilla might. The unfortunate Kiwis survived for several days but retained the issue ration packs for future operations.

In October 1962 Brigadier Hassett relinquished his command at the end of his tour of duty with the Commonwealth Brigade. His training policy had been hard and realistic and the brigade was fit and pared down to the essentials for operations in the Far East. Brigadier Hassett had the satisfaction of knowing that 28 Brigade was completely prepared for its task and served as an example of what could be attained by sensible training and the right sort of motivation. By the same token, Brigadier Hassett had the confidence of all under his command and many others in Malaya. His well-founded reputation for being a firm and decisive commander was confirmed and enhanced by his leadership and direction of the Commonwealth Brigade's activities and its readiness for deployment. In Brigadier Hassett's place came the first New Zealand commander of the brigade, Brigadier R. B. Dawson. His assumption of command confirmed the trinational character of this unique formation and emphasised the integration of the Commonwealth contingents. Under Brigadier Dawson's command the brigade continued to train hard and kept itself in instant readiness for operations in support of SEATO.

A brigade unit undertook another sort of task in another part of the Far East in October 1962. 11 Field Squadron, Royal Engineers, under Major Campbell, was detached from the brigade to undertake a construction task in North Borneo. The sappers, including 4 Field Troop of the Royal Australian Engineers, constructed a forty-ton bridge over the River Tempasuk at Kota Belud, near Jesselton, in response to a request from the local authorities. Although not in the brigade's area of responsibility, the task proved to be excellent training in the type of engineering work which might be expected in similar tropical territories.

Plans for the creation of the Federation of Malaysia had been laid and a committee was working on the practicalities of establishing this larger state which would embrace the existing Federation of Malaya, the State of Singapore, Sarawak, Sabah (North Borneo) and the Sultanate of Brunei. Referendums were held in these former British territories and the majority were in favour of the new concept. However, this enlarged state was seen as a potential threat by its southern neighbour, the Republic of Indonesia, which included the greater part of Borneo, or Kalimantan. On 8th December 1962, Azahari, one of the leaders of the Partai Ra'ayat (the leftwing People's Party), staged a revolt against the merging of the North Borneo territories into the proposed new Federation of Malaysia. The aim of the revolution was to establish a new state called Kalimantan Utara (North Borneo) to include Sabah, oil-rich Brunei and Sarawak. Indonesian support was offered to Azahari and there can be little doubt that this was an attempt by Indonesia to establish a footing in the North Borneo states to expand the frontiers of a new Indonesian 'Empire'. The initial attacks on the Sultan of Brunei's Palace and the Brunei police station were contained, mainly due to the efforts of the Commissioner of Police who received twenty-four hours warning of the uprising. The Sultan of Brunei appealed for British help and two companies of Gurkhas from 99 Brigade in Singapore were flown out to support the local police.

General Sir Walter Walker, former commander of 17 Gurkha Division, was appointed Commander British Forces Borneo on 19th December 1962 and the British military presence was increased to combat the activities of the Tentara Nasional Kalimantan Utara (North Borneo National Army). Borneo was considered to be a British responsibility and 28 Commonwealth Brigade were not involved initially but, as troops from other brigades in Malaya and Singapore were flown to Borneo, it became necessary to call upon the United Kingdom element of 28 Brigade to relieve the pressure. 'B' and 'D' Companies of the King's Own Yorkshire Light Infantry were 'borrowed' from 28 Brigade and sailed from Singapore on the aircraft carrier H.M.S. *Albion* in the third week of January 1963. The K.O.Y.L.I. reached Brunei on 8th February and relieved elements of the Queen's Own Highlanders (of 99 Brigade) at Seria, where they were accommodated by the Brunei Shell Petroleum Company. The new arrivals were made responsible for the Belait District and platoons were deployed to seek out the rebel Tentara Nasional Kalimantan Utara led by Yassin Affendi. Such operations were very reminiscent of the Malayan emergency and involved cordons, searches, river patrols, visits to remote Iban longhouses and the establishment of good relations with the locals, including medical treatment of children and the gaining of confidence to obtain information.

The K.O.Y.L.I. were spread over a wide area with platoons scattered over Brunei, Sarawak and North Borneo (Sabah). The Assault Pioneer Platoon ran the Belait River Fleet which consisted of the *Tiger* and the *Anchor* (two storm boats named after local beers), the *Sri Blalang* and the *Raja Menua* (two Iban longboats), three assault boats and the *Gamecock*, an abandoned aluminium boat which was patched up and made riverworthy. This motley little fleet cruised up and down some ninety miles of river delivering supplies and keeping contact with the local inhabitants with the help of four attached Iban policemen: Tien, Ahtieu, Enteba and

Charlie. In March the platoons were redeployed and 'B' Company was sent upriver to Long Akah, a journey of over 100 miles into Sarawak. 'D' Company was detached under the command of the 2nd Battalion of the 7th Gurkha Rifles and 16 Platoon of 'D' Company, under the command of Lieutenant Mike Deedes, spent fifty-seven continuous days in the jungle without a break and found a camp recently occupied by Yassin Affendi's guerillas.

On 12th April 1963 an Indonesian force crossed the border and attacked the police station at Tebedu, in the far West of Sarawak. 'A' Company of the K.O.Y.L.I. was given four hours to move to Brunei airfield and flew to join 40 Commando of the Royal Marines at Kuching. Operation 'Parrot' was launched in an endeavour to seek the invaders. Another brigade unit joined the forces in Borneo when 3 Troop of the 11th Field Squadron, Royal Engineers, came under the command of 3 Commando Brigade at Kuching on 3rd April 1963. Yassin Affendi was captured and the Brunei Revolt ended on 18th May. The K.O.Y.L.I. handed over to the Queen's Own Highlanders and returned to Terendak – just in time to participate in another exercise.

*Corporal Noel Freeman, 1st Battalion The New Zealand Regiment. August 1963.*

(Soldier Magazine 6269/38)

Exercise 'Dhanarajata' was again held at Ubon in Eastern Thailand and the Commonwealth Brigade was represented by a headquarters element and company size detachments from the battalions, including a hastily organised composite 'H' Company from the K.O.Y.L.I. The 1st New Zealand Regiment fielded

> 'a small battalion headquarters under Colonel Pearce and a composite company participated in Exercise "Dhanarajata" in which we were located at Ubon and points North. A recce flight for a number of our officers over a goodly length of the nearby Mekong River proved a futile exercise when unpleasant fumes from a freight carried oil container filled the plane's cabin. It was "eyes down and looking wretchedly into paper airsick bags" with no time for looking out plane windows. We were delighted to be visited North of Ubon by our ambassador to Thailand, Major-General Sir Steve Weir, a former C.G.S. and very popular C.R.A. of 2 N.Z. Division and later commander of 46 U.K. Division in Europe.'

In comparison with the normal run of 28 Brigade exercises, 'Dhanarajata' was considered to be very mild and concluded with a SEATO parade at Bangkok.

26 Regiment, Royal Artillery, held a farewell parade before Brigadier Dawson at Terendak on 10th July 1963 and were commended for their pioneering work with the 105 mm Pack Howitzer in the Far Eastern airportability role. 26 Regiment was relieved by 45 Regiment, Lieutenant-Colonel R. N. W. Lydekker. 45 Field Regiment had served in Korea in support of 29 Brigade during 1950 and 1951 and still had several Korean veterans in its ranks, such as Major J. B. Keenan commanding 70 Light Battery and Major G. D. S. Truell commanding 176 (Abu Klea) Light Battery. The third battery of the regiment was 170 (Imjin) Battery which had been awarded an American Presidential Citation for the action in 1951 when it had been a mortar battery. 170 Battery was equipped with 5.5 inch medium guns and was stationed with the divisional headquarters at Seremban. The regiment inherited 103 Field Battery, R.A.A., from 26 Regiment as its third 105 mm Pack Howitzer battery.

Another unit which had served in Korea returned to the brigade in August when the 3rd Battalion, Royal Australian Regiment, 'Old Faithful', under Lieutenant-Colonel W. F. White, relieved the 2nd Battalion at Terendak. 3 R.A.R., also awarded the American Presidential Citation for the Kapyong Battle, joined for its third tour of duty. Other brigade units were replaced during the following months: 102 Field Battery, R.A.A., Major Brian Forward, relieved 103 Battery in 45 Regiment and 2 Field Troop, Royal Australian Engineers, relieved 4 Field Troop in 11 Field Squadron.

In November, the commanding officers of the three infantry battalions were all relieved within weeks of each other. Lieutenant-Colonel R. G. Saltonstall took command of the King's Own Yorkshire Light Infantry in place of Major Elcomb who had commanded the battalion since July; Lieutenant-Colonel R. M. Gurr relieved Lieutenant-Colonel Pearce as commander of the 1st New Zealand Regiment and Lieutenant-Colonel B. A. MacDonald took the place of Lieutenant-Colonel White as commanding officer of the 3rd Royal Australians.

Brigade training continued apace with 3 R.A.R. receiving its introduction to air-portability during Exercise 'Kangaroo Hop' and 70 Battery practising slinging their 105s under Whirlwind helicopters. Exercise 'Zigzag II' gave the gunners further practice in floating and flying their guns in and out of the jungle. In September the brigade organised and mounted a week's firepower demonstration on the Asahan ranges. In December 11 Field Squadron moved to Thailand to participate in Operation 'Crown', a construction project which also involved a detachment of 2 Infantry Workshops, R.E.M.E., and other sapper units from Malaya. Crown Camp was constructed some ten miles North of Ubon to be a base for the Commonwealth task force should it be deployed to Eastern Thailand. The three field troops of 11 Squadron began to lay out the camp and an airfield at Loeng Nok Tha, together with roads connecting the site to Korat and Ubon.

The creation of the new Federation of Malaysia had been proceeding according to plan, despite the Brunei Revolt, and was due to be formed on 16th September 1963. The Indonesians regarded the enlarged Federation with hostile eyes and mounted a raid across the border into Sarawak in August, attacking the village of Song on the Rajang River. It took a battalion-size force a month to eliminate the sixty-strong raiding force. On 28th September, a larger force armed with mortars and machine guns launched an attack on a Gurkha outpost at Long Jawi, in Central Sarawak. Thirty of the raiders were killed during the ensuing month-long operation which strained the available air support resources. In October three parties of raiders, totalling about 140 men, crossed the border near Selepong with the intent of capturing Simanggang, in the West of Sarawak, but were dispersed fairly quickly. Eighty raiders attempted an attack on

Pensiangan and Sepulot in Sabah in November but were scared off before they could fire a shot. These raiding parties were composed mainly of locally recruited natives of Kalimantan with some Javanese and Chinese from the Celebes under the command of regular Indonesian Army officers. The raiding forces were equipped and trained by the Indonesian Army and their task was to 'liberate' the inhabitants of North Borneo and encourage them to rise against the government of the new Federation of Malaysia – in which they failed miserably.

The Malaysian and British forces were spread thinly over a large area. The land border between the North Borneo states and Indonesian Kalimantan was almost 1,000 miles long and the Indonesian raiders could make an incursion anywhere along this line. The confrontation between Indonesia and Malaysia was to be settled on this wild frontier.

# Confrontation

28 Commonwealth Infantry Brigade was never committed to operations in Borneo as a complete formation. However, most of the subordinate units of the brigade did serve on that island, albeit under the command of other brigades, and their individual contributions are worth recording in this account of 28 Brigade and its operations in the Far East. Throughout the period of confrontation with Indonesia in Northern Borneo, the Commonwealth Brigade retained its role as the strategic reserve for SEATO although it was hard-pressed to maintain its readiness state with at least one of the battalions detached for service in Borneo.

170 Medium Battery of 45 Field Regiment R.A. was warned for operations in Borneo and was given two months intensive training in jungle warfare and conversion from their 5.5 inch guns to 4.2 inch mortars. Colonel Lydekker remembers the reaction of the battery when he told them of their new role: 'Half the men looked pleased, half looked startled and one, a bombardier, fainted.' By the end of October, 170 Battery joined 99 Gurkha Infantry Brigade, Brigadier A. G. Patterson, O.B.E., M.C., in Sarawak. In the event, Major Latham's gunners did not use their mortars. Their first operational task was at Bau, in the First Division of Sarawak, where a patrol of 'B' Company of 40 Commando, Royal Marines, had been ambushed by about forty terrorists and had withdrawn, leaving the body of their patrol commander at the scene. Second-Lieutenant E. C. D. Carter led a patrol from 170 Battery to the ambush site where they recovered the remains of the Marine N.C.O. The gunners picked up the enemy's trail and gave close chase for thirty hours as the Indonesians headed back to the border. So close were the pursuing gunners that the enemy had to abandon the bodies of two men, presumably killed in the first engagement, together with a mortar, ammunition and many pieces of equipment.

251

The King's Own Yorkshire Light Infantry had performed a four-month tour of duty in Borneo from January to April 1963 and returned on 10th December 1963 to relieve the 1st Royal Greenjackets in Brunei. The rifle companies were later dispersed along the border in Sarawak and Sabah. The K.O.Y.L.I. described their area:

'Borneo is the third largest, second wettest and first roughest island in the world. Any form of road or track good enough to take even a bicycle is a rarity and only then likely to be found along the coast. Inland travel is by long-boat, a hollowed out tree trunk often fitted with an outboard engine, or by causeways over the swamps and rivers. The rivers themselves have their own hazards with rapids falling several feet, whirlpools, rocks and submerged trees. Only long-boats will stand up to these dangers. For those in a position to fly there are a number of airstrips, but most of these are exceedingly small with difficult approaches.

*'A' Company, 1 K.O.Y.L.I., February 1964. Bareo Airstrip, Sarawak, with an R.A.F. Whirlwind helicopter and a Beaver.*

(Light Infantry Office (Yorkshire))

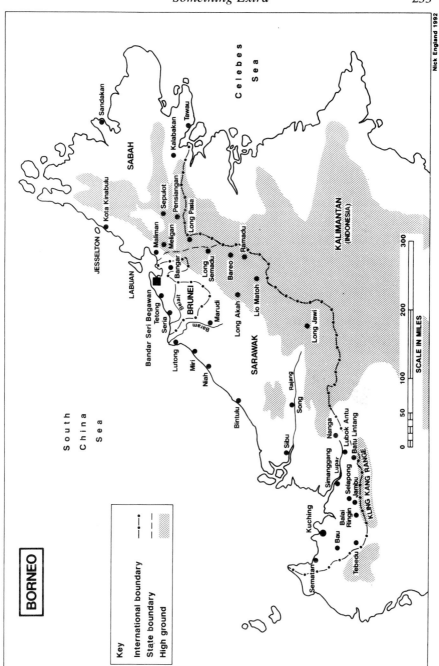

BORNEO

Key

International boundary
State boundary
High ground

Nick England 1992

South
China
Sea

Celebes
Sea

SABAH

Sandakan
Tawau
Kalabakan
Kota Kinabalu
JESSELTON
Sepulot
Pensiangan
Long Pasia
Maliman
Mengan
Ramadu
Bangar
Long Semadu
Bareo
LABUAN
Bandar Seri Begawan
Tetong
BRUNEI
Lio Matoh
Seria
Marudi
Long Akah
Lutong
Baram
Long Jawi
Miri
Niah
SARAWAK
KALIMANTAN
(INDONESIA)
Bintulu
Rajang
Song
Sibu
Nanga
Lubok Antu
Simanggang
Lupar
Batu Lintang
Selapong
Jambu
KLING KANG RANGE
Kuching
Balai
Ringin
Bau
Tebedu
Sematan

SCALE IN MILES

0    50    100    200    300

*Mortar Team, 1 K.O.Y.L.I., July 1964.*

(Light Infantry Office (Yorkshire))

They are only suitable for very small aircraft and the airstrips are out of action for several hours every day by low cloud and rain. The indigenous population, the only inhabitants of the interior, is exceedingly cheerful and friendly. They live a communal life in their longhouses. As the name implies they are long, sometimes up to 400 yards, and are villages under one roof. Many of the people are Christians and hospitality is one of their great characteristics. It may be taken as an insult if travellers do not accept the local wines, tuak and burak, and enjoy evening revelries. Although headhunting has now been given up, heads may still be seen in some of the longhouses as relics, in some cases of the not so distant past. All longhouses are sited on or near a river which provides the highway as well as water for drinking and washing. The staple food is rice, supplemented by game, fish, chicken, fruit and vegetables. Rice is grown on hillsides where a new area of jungle is burnt down each year before the planting season. After the harvest some of these areas are planted with fruit and rubber trees but most of it reverts to a tangled mess of secondary jungle, adding further to the problems of movement.'

For much of its length, the border with Indonesia runs along a steep mountain range rising to 6,000 feet in the centre but sloping down to sea-level on the East and West coasts. There are many recognised border crossing places but many more which could be used by intruders. In the coastal areas and along the main rivers there is a Chinese population, trading in merchandise and timber and cultivating market gardens; some of these were known to have Communist sympathies and were active members of a clandestine Communist organisation. The main threat, however, lay along the Indonesian border. The Indonesians, under President Soerkano, were jealous of the stability and prosperity of the new Malaysia. They saw the new Federation as a threat to their security since it revealed the weakness, poverty and hunger of the Indonesian totalitarian regime. From the outset, Soerkano was determined to destroy the Malaysian concept; having failed to do so by threat and intrigue he tried a course of military aggression, mounting a number of cross-border incursions in varying strengths. The British and Malaysian troops in Borneo had three main tasks: first, to destroy any invading forces within a unit's area of responsibility; second, to be ready to reinforce their own or any other friendly forces in the country; third, to prevent any Communist-inspired disturbances in the coastal regions. To accomplish these tasks battalions were dispersed over large areas with companies and platoons often 200 miles from battalion headquarters. For those in the remote forward areas life could often be very lonely; much of the time was spent patrolling the jungle and even in their base camps supplies and mail could only be delivered by air. The appearance of the weekly supply dropping plane was a major event in the lives of the soldiers.

In January and February, 'A' Company of the K.O.Y.L.I. was sent to patrol the area between Pa Lungan and Batu Patong from a firm base at Bareo, in Central Sarawak, and to report any Indonesian activity in the area. A subsidiary task was to produce a 'going' map to record details of tracks, rivers and hills in the locality to bring the inadequate maps of the area up to date. In the latter half of February, 'A' Company's role changed after the burning of the longhouse at Pa Bangia and the ambush of a patrol led by Sergeant-Major Reynolds on 19th February in which Privates Cunningham and Chandler were wounded. The company was detailed to hold firm bases at Pa Lungan, Pa Umor and Pa Main – in addition to Bareo – and to patrol the area to the South of Pa Main, Ramadu Dan and Pa Dali. From these advanced firm bases the K.O.Y.L.I. were to patrol to within 1,000 yards of the border; it had been established that the Indonesians were probably using the border zone itself as a training area and that unnecessary contact should be avoided. Additional platoons were sent to Bareo, particularly the Reconnaissance Platoon from Lio Matoh and 'D' Company headquarters with 13 and 14 Platoons. Two R.A.F. helicopters, Whirlwind 10s, were based at Bareo for some weeks but were later shared with the Gurkhas at Long Semado, about twenty minutes flying time to the North. On 5th March the K.O.Y.L.I. were rewarded with a contact with a party of approximately ten Indonesians at Pa Lungan. Fortunately, the inhabitants of the local longhouse had warned Sergeant Ashcroft of 1 Platoon of the approach of the enemy. At about 4.15 p.m., in heavy and dense rain, the Indonesians appeared, five were killed and one wounded in the ensuing short action. Sergeant Ashcroft claimed that two more Indonesians were hit but no other bodies were recovered in the area. Prolonged ambushes by day were instigated early in April to regain the initiative after a prolonged period of attrition. On 17th April Sergeant Kemp of 13 Platoon of 'D' Company, who had relieved 1 Platoon at Pa Lungan, ambushed a small Indonesian party of two men, killing one and wounding the other. Ambushes were maintained in the areas between Pa Lungan, Pa Umor and Pa Bangia until the K.O.Y.L.I. were relieved by the 1st Battalion of the Argyll and Sutherland Highlanders.

170 Battery of 45 Field Regiment was given an area of some 300 square miles of Sarawak to dominate in January 1964. The battery was given a

local longboat with an outboard motor to cover the numerous waterways in their 'parish' and the craft was skippered by a bombardier, chosen for the command because of his ability to swim. During the following two months the gunners were involved in incessant patrolling and ambushing under miserable monsoon conditions until their relief in March by 70 Light Battery from Terendak. On its return to rejoin 45 Regiment, 170 Battery received a message from General Sir Walter Walker, Director of Borneo Operations, saying that the battery 'had conducted itself with the skill of the professional infantryman'.

70 Light Battery, under Major J. B. Keenan, had battery headquarters and 'B' Troop in brigade reserve at Kuching and 'A' Troop some 100 miles to the East at Lintang, both troops had three 105 mm Pack Howitzers each. Their arrival coincided with an increase in enemy activity as regular Indonesian Army units began to be mixed with the terrorist bands. West Brigade's counter to numerous widespread, but lightweight, enemy incursions was to set up company bases near the border from which to patrol and ambush. These forward bases also protected the longhouses from which Border Scouts were recruited, a major source of valuable intelligence. Tasks for the guns of 70 Battery were to follow once the infantry were convinced of their usefulness in the jungle.

A patrol of the 2nd 10th Gurkha Rifles ran into an Indonesian Army unit high up in the Kling Kang range, the Gurkhas attacked and dislodged the enemy but not before suffering casualties. The same enemy unit reappeared on the Kling Kang but the Gurkhas were more wary and requested gunner support. 'B' Troop, 70 Light Battery, responded and were ranged and controlled by an Auster aerial observation post, hitting the target successfully. The Gurkhas threw the enemy back into Indonesia and suffered no casualties. Thereafter, the 2nd 10th and 'B' Troop co-operated closely:

'A Border Scout had been captured by the Indonesians and taken to a cave high up on the mountainside towards the frontier and then across to a regular camp. He had escaped and reported that the cave was a large stores dump. Watch was kept and regular activity noted. The C.O. of 2/10 G.R., whose manor included this cave, thereupon decided to deal with it. The cave area, 9,000 yards away, could be seen from the road and from the gun position, and the whole thing resembled nothing so much as an All Arms' Firepower demonstration. H Hour was supposed to be at 0700 hours but mist and an argument over the grid references held things up for ninety minutes. The first act was by two Wessex helicopters, who fired missiles with accuracy and impressive effect. The Air O.P. then took over, Sergeant Steele's gun firing the first round at 0840 hours. Fire was tight and accurate and the O.P. soon went to fire for effect, varying three and five round gun-fire serials with the odd half-dozen rounds with fuse delay. Shell bursts could be clearly seen amongst the trees in the target area. One hundred and sixty-six rounds at Charge Seven were fired whereupon 'A' Company, who had meanwhile been staggering through the jungle up to the foot of the mountain and its steep slopes, went into the assault which included a stiff climb up to the actual target. Rifle and automatic fire could be clearly heard. The final score turned out to be two definitely dead and two wounded, with traces of an undetermined number of dead who had been removed across the border. Food, ammunition and clothing by the ton was found in the cave. There were no Gurkha casualties.'

Shortly afterwards, on 13th June, the new commander of 'A' Troop of 70 Light Battery, Captain Don Quinn, an Australian detached from 102 Battery, R.A.A., received information from the local Border Scouts that Batu Lintang was about to be attacked. Captain Quinn borrowed a platoon from the 2/2nd Gurkhas and placed them in ambush on the most likely approach route, he registered defensive fire around the site and back towards the frontier. The enemy attacked as expected. The ambush was sprung and the following counter-attack broken up by gun-fire. The troop then engaged the enemy as they fled homewards towards the border. Don Quinn's next hunch was that Lubok Antu, twelve miles to the east, would be the next to be attacked. A precedent was created by splitting the troop and moving one gun by helicopter to Lubok Antu. Lieutenant A. J. Pinion, the gun position officer, registered the gun quickly and fired a number of harassing tasks on border tracks. Although the enemy was not seen, Border Scouts reported finding evidence of an incursion which had turned back on reaching one of the gun's targets. As a result of these successful shoots the cry went up for guns everywhere and at once; 'B' Troop was kept busy moving two sub-sections by R.A.F. helicopter along a seventy mile front.

The King's Own Yorkshire Light Infantry prepared to return to Terendak in April and recorded some of their activities in Borneo:

'As a complement to the military operations we were heavily involved in a campaign to "win the hearts and minds" of the

Borneo people, who for the most part, were confused by the
political changes which had overtaken their country in the last
twenty years. The form of this campaign varied in different areas
but the most important aspect was perhaps our ability to provide
medical assistance which, until the emergency, had been beyond
all expectation. The courage and skill with which the young
medical orderlies handled their large sick parades was most
gratifying and our ability to fly the seriously ill to the hospitals at
the coast was a great comfort to the local population. Of equal
importance was the assistance we and the R.A.F. helicopter crews
gave to move isolated longhouses to places of greater security.
Known as "Operation Pork Chopper" this movement consumed
all available helicopter flying hours lifting pigs, chickens, rice
and household goods and chattels over the jungle-covered hills to
the newly developing community centre at Bareo. In our last
week in Borneo the Police Special Branch succeeded in breaking
into a communist cell in the Miri area and arresting its leading
members, some of whom were our near neighbours at Lutong.
This brought home to us the need for constant vigilance and the
importance of the second half of our mission, which was to prevent the spread of militant communism.'

The K.O.Y.L.I. received a surprise reinforcement in Borneo. Faiz Akbar
Khan had been a little boy in Peshawar in 1929 and worked for his uncle
who held the appointment of charwallah to the 2nd Battalion of the King's
Own Yorkshire Light Infantry. On hearing that the K.O.Y.L.I. were in
Brunei, Faiz Akbar Khan left Hong Kong, where he was a contractor to
H.M. Forces, and made his way to Borneo to join 'my old regiment'. The
K.O.Y.L.I. returned to Terendak at the end of April after four and a half
months in Borneo.

The depleted Commonwealth Brigade continued to train at Terendak
for its SEATO role. The New Zealand Regiment returned to Kedah and
Perlis for a tour of border operations but, despite finding several camp
sites, made no contact with the C.T.s. 11 Field Squadron and elements of
the brigade workshops were still employed on the Operation 'Crown'
construction project in Thailand and one battery of 45 Field Regiment was
detached for operations in Borneo. A further temporary loss occurred
when 170 (Imjin) Battery returned after their first tour in Borneo; a
section of two 5.5 inch guns was sent to Aden on the aircraft carrier
H.M.S. *Centaur* in May and spent some weeks in action in the Radfan.

Hardly had Captain Tofield's command returned from the desert than another section was flown to Sabah in Beverly aircraft of the R.A.F., the only occasion in which complete 5.5 inch medium guns were moved by air. Their task was to engage a suspected Indonesian gun but it never materialized and the section joined 176 Battery in Sarawak.

The New Zealand Army had been planning the creation of a unified regular infantry regiment and Her Majesty the Queen had been pleased to grant the prefix 'Royal' in recognition of the loyal service rendered by New Zealand Infantry regiments since the Boer War. The 1st Battalion of the Royal New Zealand Infantry Regiment was officially formed on 1st April 1964, by the amalgamation of the 1st and 2nd Battalions of the New Zealand Regiment. Lieutenant-Colonel R. M. Gurr, M.B.E., assumed command of the new battalion but the ceremonial inauguration of the regiment was deferred since the Kiwis were then deployed on border operations in North Malaya.

In May the brigade participated in the annual SEATO exercise in Thailand. Each battalion and brigade unit was represented by the usual company-strength detachments on Exercise 'Air Boon Choo 1964'. With all three of his infantry battalions back in Terendak Brigadier Dawson was able to implement a full training programme; Exercise 'May Bug' was staged for two weeks in June at Bukit Tapah and was followed by Exercise 'Raven', a full scale air-portable deployment in the Rompin area in July. The Borneo 'veterans' found the return to brigade exercises rather trying. The K.O.Y.L.I. expressed this opinion:

'This strong and splendidly equipped brigade is based in Malaya as an earnest of the firm intention of the British, Australian and New Zealand Government's intention to honour their military commitments to SEATO. Malaysia is not a member of SEATO. Indonesia's "confrontation" of Malaysia is not, therefore a matter of direct concern to SEATO. On the other hand, Britain is allowed to base SEATO committed troops in Malaysia only on the understanding that Britain will aid Malaysia in her external defence. Different political factors affect the employment of Australian and New Zealand troops. Sort that lot out if you can, for I cannot. But the practical effect, until very recently, has been that only British and the British Gurkha troops have been sent on active service in Borneo and within Malaya proper, whilst 28 Brigade as a whole has continued to expect and train for a possible war on the Thailand border or in Laos or South Vietnam. Furthermore, there has been a tendency to regard the periodic departure of the British battalion to Borneo as a "foul" against the SEATO concept and to "grip" it firmly on its return and re-train it without delay in its SEATO role.'

The political influences of the three nations concerned did play a major part in the employment and deployment of the Commonwealth Brigade. A Labour Government was elected in Great Britain in October 1964 and was to make far-reaching decisions on British policy East of Suez. The Australians regarded events in Asia with a more concerned eye. In May 1962 a small Australian Army Training Team had been sent to assist the Army of the Republic of South Vietnam as evidence of Australia's support to the non-Communist nations of the Southeast Asia. In November 1964 the Australians introduced selective national service for twenty-year-olds as a precaution against the need to support Malaysia and SEATO – and for the defence of Australia itself which could be threatened by any major war in Southeast Asia. New Zealand had introduced national service training in 1962 to maintain the Territorial Army at operational strength but, like Great Britain, relied on volunteer soldiers to fill the ranks of the Regular Army.

The 1st Battalion of the Royal New Zealand Infantry Regiment was formally inaugurated at a parade held at Terendak on 5th August 1964, before the New Zealand High Commissioner in Malaysia, His Excellency Mr. R. Hunter Wade. Lieutenant-Colonel R. M. Gurr, M.B.E., commanded the battalion on parade and the New Zealand commander of the Commonwealth Brigade, Brigadier R. B. Dawson, D.S.O., took the salute at this rather special 'Kiwi' occasion. Another ceremonial parade was also held in August at Ipoh, in Perak, to mark the affiliation between the 3rd Battalion of the Royal Australian Regiment and the Queen's Royal Irish Hussars (successors to the 8th King's Royal Irish Hussars). The parade commemorated the two regiments' service in Korea when the Centurion tanks of the Hussars rendered close support to the 3rd R.A.R. and the other battalions of the Commonwealth Brigade.

During the night of 17th/18th August 1964, the 'confrontation' between Malaysia and Indonesia entered a new phase which was to change some of the policies restricting the use of Commonwealth troops. A force of Indonesian 'commandoes' crossed the Malacca Straits from Sumatra and landed on the coast of South Johore to the North of Pontian Kechil. Following this invasion of Malaya, two Indonesian Hercules aircraft dropped ninety-six paratroopers into the jungle near Labis in North

MALAYA

THAILAND

South
China
Sea

PERLIS

KEDAH

PENANG

PROVINCE
WELLESLEY

PERAK          KELANTAN

● Taiping                              Marang ●

Ipoh ●                                TRENGGANU

CAMERON
HIGHLANDS

PAHANG

● Kuala Krau

SELANGOR

■
Kuala Lumpur

NEGRI          ● Triang
SEMBILAN

● Seremban

Segamat
●          ● Ayer Panas
MALACCA   Asahan ●  ● Labis

Terendak ●

Strait of Malacca

JOHORE

Muar ●

Kota Tinggi ●

Johore Bahru ●

Pontian Kechil ●

Key
International boundary   ●—•—●
State boundary           – – –

0         50        100
SCALE IN MILES

SINGAPORE

Nick England 1992

Johore on 2nd September 1964. The Malaysian forces were already stretched with operations in Borneo and along the border with Thailand and, in 28 Brigade, the only British battalion (the K.O.Y.L.I.) was preparing to return to Borneo. There remained the battalions of the other two Commonwealth nations and Brigadier Dawson selected the new Royal New Zealand Infantry Regiment to cope with this new threat. The New Zealanders moved to Majeedi Barracks in South Johore on 4th September but were obliged to wait there for two days whilst permission to engage the enemy was sought from the New Zealand government. The necessary political approval was received and the R.N.Z.I.R. was placed at the disposal of the Malaysian Chief of General Staff. The battalion was despatched to the Labis area to assist the 1st Battalion of the 10th Gurkha Rifles who were rounding up the paratroopers dropped on 2nd September. Colonel Gurr established his battalion headquarters in the

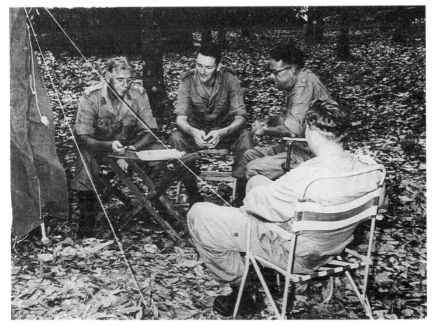

*Brigadier R. B. Dawson, Major J. M. Church (Brigade Major), Major L. A. Eyles (D.A.A.&Q.M.G.) and Lt. Col. R. N. W. Lydekker, R.A., Exercise 'Raven', Bahau, Malaya, 16th July 1964.*

(Brig. Lydekker)

*Sgt. Borley, Queen's Royal Irish Hussars, and Sgt. Keith Payne, 3rd Royal Australian Regiment, at a ceremonial parade to commemorate the affiliation of the two regiments during the Korean War. Ipoh, August 1964.*

(AWM DUN 64 509 MC)

Segamat Police Station and the New Zealanders were deployed as a screen around Labis and Ayer Panas. Royal Naval helicopters were employed to deliver the troops into the jungle and for the next three weeks the Kiwis operated with the Gurkhas in winkling out the Indonesians. The Gurkhas claimed the majority of invaders but three were captured by the R.N.Z.I.R. and they drove many more before them into the hands of Malaysian soldiers and police. All ninety-six were accounted for, either killed or captured, including their commander Lieutenant Soetikno.

After the successful conclusion of the Labis operation, the 1st Royal New Zealand Infantry Regiment moved to the coast to tackle the remnants of the Indonesian commando force which had landed in August. A battalion of the Royal Malay Regiment had accounted for all but thirty of the enemy and the New Zealanders moved in to hunt the Indonesians in the jungle and swamps where they had sought refuge. 'B' Company, Major I. H. Burrows, and the Reconnaissance Platoon, commanded by the aptly named Lieutenant Albert Kiwi (who had served as Intelligence Corporal of the 2nd Battalion in Perak), were especially successful during the week-long operation, killing two of the enemy and capturing another twelve in the swamps. Warrant Officer Suparmin, leader of the force and by no means a 'superman', was killed and his men surrendered although it was believed that they may have coerced some of the local inhabitants to have survived for so long.

Early in October, the 1st Battalion of The Scots Guards, Lieutenant-Colonel A. I. D. Fletcher, arrived to take over from the King's Own Yorkshire Light Infantry who had then completed three tours of duty in Borneo. The Scots Guards were understrength and were reinforced by 9 Company of the Irish Guards – which also included a platoon of the Coldstream Guards! The new arrivals were plunged into a programme of training for their new role in the Far East and were soon introduced to the brigade's way of life. Brigadier Lydekker remembers that

'Colonel Archie Fletcher had obviously taken great pains to instil into the minds of his officers that they must show no "side" to the "Colonials" and the other British in Terendak Garrison. Shortly after they arrived, Archie ordained that there should be a cocktail party in his mess to which all officers in the garrison should be asked. We all turned up neatly dressed, as was our wont, in linen suits with jackets and ties – only to find the officers of 1 S.G. in open-necked shirts and slacks. Afterwards, Bruce MacDonald (C.O. 3 R.A.R.) and Bob Gurr got hold of me, as senior British officer then in the garrison, and told me to tell Fletcher that we did NOT do that kind of thing in the Commonwealth Brigade and that we all tried to keep up a high standard – I laughed myself silly!'

Thus, the Scots Guards discovered that 28 Brigade was not entirely a bunch of 'ockers' in the mythical pub at Ettamoggah!

Brigadier Dawson completed his tour of duty as commander of the Commonwealth Brigade in October and was relieved by Brigadier T. D. H. McMeekin, O.B.E., of the British Army, thus continuing the policy of rotating the command between the three nations. Brigadier Dawson had inherited a well-trained brigade and had maintained that standard during his command although he had to contend with the periodic losses of his British units for service in Borneo. Latterly, with the approval of the New Zealand government, he had the satisfaction of being able to use his own troops in decisive actions against the Indonesian invaders. During his stay with the brigade, Brigadier Dawson had seen a change of national policies which gave the Commonwealth Brigade wider scope and was to give all the battalions a chance to engage in active service.

The new brigade commander soon had the opportunity to deploy his command on active service against an enemy. On 29th October 1964 another force of some fifty-two Indonesians landed at the mouth of the Kesang River on the border of Johore and Malacca. The Commonwealth Brigade was committed to counter this latest invasion. The 3rd Royal Australians, Lieutenant-Colonel A. B. MacDonald, had returned from the Thai border area and were alerted together with 102 Field Battery, R.A.A., of 45 Field Regiment. 'B' Company of the Royal New Zealand Infantry Regiment had just returned to Terendak from South Johore and joined the force. The 1st Battalion of the 10th Gurkha Rifles were placed under the brigade's command and the force moved to the coast, there to contain the invaders within a tight cordon. The remainder of the New Zealand battalion moved up to rejoin the brigade and, on 1st November 1964, 28 Brigade closed on the Indonesians who were driven into the jungle close to the coast. The gunners flushed the enemy out of their deep cover and within thirty hours six of the invaders had been killed and the remainder taken prisoner. So ended 28 Commonwealth Brigade's only action during the confrontation. It had been a swift and efficient engagement which had removed the threat within three days with no casualties to the brigade. Thereafter, the brigade was given the additional responsibility for watching and guarding the West coast of Malaya against any further

*Brigadier T. D. H. McMeekin, Lieutenant-Colonel R. N. W. Lydekker and Mr. T. C. Critchley, Australian High Commissioner to Malaysia. Terendak, 12th November 1964.*

(Brig. Lydekker)

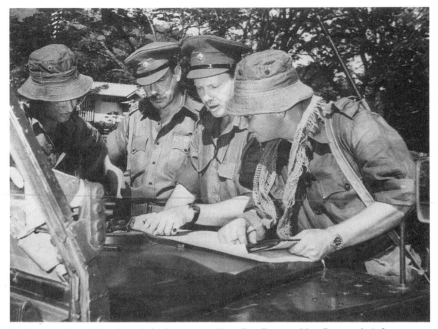

*Lt. Col. A. I. D. Fletcher (left) listens as Maj. Sir Gregor MacGregor briefs two patrol commanders on the Malay-Thai Border.*

(R.H.Q. The Scots Guards)

Indonesian incursions, although none were mounted after the October landing.

Meanwhile, the Scots Guards had relieved the 3rd Royal Australians on the Malay-Thai border and spent a month in the jungles of Kedah. Although no contact was made with the elusive terrorists the battalion gained useful and practical experience of jungle operations. Back at Terendak, after the action near the Kesang River, the 3rd Foot Guards and the 3rd Royal Australian Regiment cemented an inter-regimental alliance which had been formed in 1952. To mark this bond, the Officers' and Sergeants' Messes of the two battalions exchanged silver in December. Over the years, the alliance has been further strengthened and the pipes and drums of the 3rd Royal Australians have adopted the full dress uniforms of the Scots Guards – bearskin caps, scarlet jackets, *et al*. However, the Scots Guards have yet to parade in Australian uniform clothing!

Operations in Borneo continued and 176 Light Battery, under Major G. D. S. Truell, relieved 70 Battery in August. The six 105 mm howitzers were deployed along a frontage of 173 miles, from Biawak to Jambu, and operated as single guns in support of the troops in the jungle. Two of 170 Battery's 5.5 inch guns were still active in Borneo, also operating individually and engaging major targets as required. 176 Battery duly returned to Terendak in December and 70 Light Battery took its place in Borneo. By Christmas 1964 the Indonesians were reported to have increased their forces along the Kalimantan border, mostly regular troops with supporting artillery, especially opposite Western Sarawak. To counter this threat, extra artillery was sent out and the 19th Infantry Brigade flew to Borneo from Great Britain. 176 Battery was allowed to enjoy a few days Christmas leave in Terendak before returning to Borneo, together with the Tactical Headquarters of 45 Field Regiment, under Lieutenant-Colonel Lydekker, which was established at Kuching in Sarawak.

*105mm Pack Howitzer of 176 (Abu Klea) Light Battery, Sarawak, December 1964.*

(Brig. Lydekker)

*5.5 inch Medium Gun of 170 (Imjin) Medium Battery being winched up a 1:2 hill at Batu Lintang, Sarawak.*

(Brig. Lydekker)

Captain John Masters, a gunner serving in the 1st Royal New Zealand Infantry Regiment, was 'loaned' to 45 Field Regiment and served with 170 Battery in Borneo; another Kiwi, Lieutenant 'Wally' Steward of the New Zealand Army Air Corps, flew with the air observation post and played a vital part in detecting targets and registering gun fire.

After celebrating Hogmanay, the Scots Guards left Terendak on New Year's Day 1965 for their first tour of operations in Borneo where they were based in Semengo Camp near Kuching. Whilst in Sarawak the Scots Guards were visited by General Sir James Cassels (formerly commander of the Commonwealth Division in Korea and Director of Operations in Malaya) who was about to assume the appointment of Chief of the General Staff of the British Army.

The Commonwealth Brigade was honoured by its first Royal Visit on the 17th of February 1965 when His Royal Highness The Prince Philip

*Guardsman J. Singler, 1st Scots Guards, meets the headman of a longhouse in Sarawak.*

(R.H.Q. The Scots Guards)

came to Terendak. The Prince arrived in the late afternoon and was accommodated in 'Commonwealth House', the brigade commander's residence. Brigadier and Mrs. McMeekin gave a dinner party to honour their guest which was attended by all available officers commanding brigade units. The dinner was laid on a patio overlooking the Malacca Straits and gaily illuminated by coloured fairy lights; many of those attending were rather apprehensive, the brightly lit assembly was clearly visible from offshore and there was still a danger of another seaborne landing by the Indonesians. As coffee was being served, the lights dimmed and fearsome figures sprang from the surrounding trees with hideous yells. Unfortunately, Brigadier McMeekin had not warned his guests of this surprise appearance of the Maori Concert Party from the 1st Royal New Zealand Infantry Regiment and two battalion commanders and a regimental commander dived for cover – leaving His Royal Highness, the Brigade Commander and the wives still sitting at table. The next morning the rear party of the Scots Guards paraded a Royal Guard of

*102 Field Battery, Royal Australian Artillery, in action in Sarawak.*

(Brig. Lydekker)

Honour on the main square at Terendak and the families were given a brief opportunity to see Prince Philip as he was given a guided tour of the garrison. After lunch in the Brigade Mess, His Royal Highness left for Singapore in the early afternoon.

The brigade's action against the Indonesian invaders in Johore and Malacca resulted in making the other Commonwealth units available for the defence of Malaysia against the Indonesian intrusions. 102 Field Battery, R.A.A., was able to take its turn with the other batteries of 45 Field Regiment in Borneo and, in March 1965, the 3rd Battalion of the Royal Australian Regiment took over from the 1st Battalion of the 7th Gurkha Rifles in Sarawak. 1 Field Troop of the Royal Australian Engineers was also sent to Borneo. By this time, General Walker was able to extend his forces into four brigades stretched along the Kalimantan-North Borneo border with fronts of 181, 442, 267 and 81 miles per brigade, vast distances covering large areas which emphasised the need for helicopter mobility to deliver troops – and guns – to danger spots.

The 1st Scots Guards was the first infantry battalion to receive its own air platoon on 17th March 1965: two Augusta Bell 'Sioux' helicopters were taken on battalion strength together with their pilots and maintenance staff. Captain S. L. Gordon Duff assumed command of the new platoon, henceforth to be known as 'Duffair'. The two helicopters were christened 'Bella' and 'Bertha' to commemorate two milch cows which had accompanied the battalion in Flanders during the 1914-1918 war, the helicopters' main role being very similar in providing sustenance for the guardsmen in the jungle, although reconnaissance and observation tasks were also undertaken. Whilst in Sarawak, a patrol of the Scots Guards claimed they were inadvertently harassed by one of 45 Field Regiment's 5.5 inch guns, this incident coincided with a journalist's visit to write a story about the gunners in Borneo. The report duly appeared in a newspaper under the headline 'Gunners Fire at Random'. The Scots Guards promptly sent an urgent signal to 170 Battery requesting 'Check Grid Reference Random'. On another occasion Sergeant Alexander's 105 mm Pack Howitzer of 176 Battery was airlifted from an infantry base in the jungle to deal with an anticipated attack in another location – which did not materialize. However, in the gun's absence, the original base was attacked and defended successfully without artillery support. The following day Sergeant Alexander received a signal which read: 'Quite safe now. You can come back.'

The 3rd Royal Australians soon settled in to dominate the Bau District of Western Sarawak. In one incident, Lieutenant Patrick Beale laid a river ambush and was rewarded by two boatloads of Indonesians sailing into the trap but, as the ambush was sprung, two more boats were sighted upstream. Private Jackson engaged the second pair of boats quickly and the ambush was completely successful, all four boats and fifteen Indonesians were accounted for in the sharp little action. Whilst the 3rd R.A.R. were engaging the enemy in Borneo, the Australian government made a fateful decision. The 1st Battalion of the Royal Australian Regiment, which had served in the Commonwealth Brigade in Korea and Malaya, was flown to South Vietnam in June 1965 to join the American 173rd Airborne Brigade. 1 R.A.R. was increased to a battalion group with the addition of 105 Field Battery, R.A.A., and later augmented with additional supporting elements in August and September. The creation of this Australian force in Vietnam was rather similar to the reformation of 28 Brigade in North Malaya some ten years earlier and the Australian contingent in Vietnam was to be increased to a task force size formation in the years to come.

The Commonwealth Brigade was hard-pressed to maintain its readiness state for SEATO operations in 1965 with all three of the infantry battalions available for duty in Borneo as well as the artillery batteries and engineers deployed on active service. 'A' Field Battery of the Royal Australian Artillery, Major A. W. Reynolds, joined 45 Field Regiment to relieve 102 Field Battery which had given an excellent account of itself in Borneo. The 1st Battalion of the Royal New Zealand Infantry Regiment took its turn in Borneo, relieving the 1st 10th Gurkha Rifles of 19 Brigade in Sarawak in May. The Scots Guards returned to Terendak from Sarawak in March after killing two Indonesians and wounding one during their tour of duty.

The 3rd Royal Australians engaged a strong enemy force in Sarawak in July when Second-Lieutenant Byers's platoon laid an ambush on a track known to be used by Indonesians crossing the border. After a wait of four days, a large party of the enemy came down the track on 15th June; seventeen Indonesians were killed and eight wounded during the initial ambush but the main body rallied and mounted a counter-attack, wounding two Australians. Artillery fire was called down and the ubiquitous gunners responded immediately. The combination of artillery shelling and small arms fire from the Australian platoon forced the invaders to retire in confusion. Lieutenant Byers withdrew his platoon from the site and the wounded were evacuated by helicopter.

3 Platoon of the Royal New Zealand Infantry Regiment encountered the enemy on 30th June. Lieutenant B. J. Marshall with two of his men were making a reconnaissance of the border area near Lubok Antu when they

found three Indonesians setting up a mortar. Private Ashby killed one and wounded another but the third escaped. The rest of the platoon swept the area but came under small arms, machine gun and mortar fire. The Royal Malaysian Artillery laid defensive fire and the enemy retired, leaving two wounded – both of whom attempted to resist and were killed. An ambush was laid on the site the following day but was itself attacked by about fifty Indonesians. An artillery barrage was laid quickly and the enemy fled, leaving blood trails across the border into Kalimantan.

Private Ashby distinguished himself again in action on 28th July. 'A' Company of the R.N.Z.I.R. were seeking an enemy force when 1 Platoon was pinned down by heavy fire. Second-Lieutenant Brown attacked the Indonesians with hand grenades whilst 3 Platoon gave covering fire for the leading platoon's withdrawal from contact. As 3 Platoon fired, Private Ashby located a machine gun which was engaging 1 Platoon. Ashby moved forward and silenced the gun with his Bren, enabling Lieutenant Brown to extricate his platoon with only one casualty, Private J. Negeri who was shot in the arm. For this action, Second-Lieutenant Brown was awarded the Military Cross and Private Ashby the Military Medal.

Two batteries and Colonel Lydekker's tactical headquarters of 45 Regiment returned to Terendak in May 1965 after being relieved in Borneo by 4 Light Regiment, R.A., who arrived from Great Britain. The 5.5 inch gun troops of 170 Battery continued to serve in turn in Sarawak until the following year. The brigade's engineers were still absent from Terendak, in addition to the troop in Borneo the Field Squadron was still fully employed on construction tasks in Thailand. Loeng Nok Tha airfield was completed on 17th June 1965 and presented to the Thai government. The 5,000-foot runway had been built by the Commonwealth forces as a contribution towards the SEATO defence effort. A guard of honour of the Scots Guards was flown up from Terendak and Field-Marshal Thanom Kittikachon, the Thai Minister of Defence, accepted the airfield during a ceremonial parade. After the completion of the Loeng Nok Tha airfield, 1 Troop of 11 Field Squadron remained in Thailand to continue the construction of Crown Camp, to the North of Ubon. Back at Terendak, the Scots Guards were hosts to a piping spectacular on 26th and 27th July which drew pipers from all the units in Malaysia including the Argyll and Sutherland Highlanders and the Gordon Highlanders from Borneo, pipers from the Gurkha regiments and various other local pipe bands, civilian and military. Fortunately, the 'Sassenach' battalions were away from Terendak at that time! In August 1965 Singapore withdrew from the Malaysian Federation to become an independent state within the

Commonwealth, thus preserving the British military bases and remaining as a staging post for the air-portable Commonwealth Brigade.

The 3rd Royal Australians were relieved by the 2nd 10th Gurkha Rifles in Sarawak and returned to Terendak in August, there to hand over to the 4th Battalion of the R.A.R. commanded by Lieutenant-Colonel Thomson (who had won the Military Cross whilst serving with 1 R.A.R. in Korea) on 3rd September. The 4th Royal Australians was one of the new battalions which contained a number of national servicemen. The Scots Guards duly left Terendak for another tour in Borneo in September, this time to relieve the Gordon Highlanders at Kalabakan in Sabah. The battalion's air platoon became an integrated Commonwealth sub-unit when Captain W. Steward of the New Zealand Army Air Corps joined 'Duffair' as a pilot, thus making the platoon's air crew fifty per cent Kiwi! Major B. A. Stewart-Wilson of the Scots Guards found himself commanding not only an integrated unit but also a joint-service and multi-national force when he became 'SOTAG' – Senior Officer of the Tawau Assault Group. 'TAG' was an amphibious force manned by members of the Malaysian Army, Navy and Police together with representatives of the Royal Navy, Royal Australian Navy, Royal New Zealand Navy and soldiers from Commonwealth units. The flagship of this unusual force was the *Petrel* which had been the Governor of Sabah's yacht before the confrontation; the group comprised various launches, assault boats and other vessels to patrol the coastal waters off Tawau as well as larger vessels such as H.M.N.Z.S. *Taranaki* which provided offshore support.

The Malaysian Rangers relieved the 1st Royal New Zealand Infantry Regiment in Sarawak in October and the battalion returned to Terendak. The following month Lieutenant-Colonel Gurr handed over command of the battalion to a familiar personality – Lieutenant-Colonel Brian Poananga, M.B.E., who had been Mentioned in Despatches whilst serving on attachment to the 3rd R.A.R. in Korea and had served with the 2nd Battalion of the New Zealand Regiment in Perak; he had been detached to brigade headquarters during that latter period to take a leading part in the operational planning, training and exercising of the brigade in its strategical role. In December 1965 28 Brigade lost its title as a brigade group as a result of a British Army re-organisation and reverted to being called 28 Commonwealth Infantry Brigade of 17 Gurkha Infantry Division at Seremban – although this did not detract from the brigade's primary role in support of SEATO.

During 1965 the troops in Borneo had been introduced to several new weapons which lightened the infantryman's load and increased his firepower. The new American Armalite rifle, the A.R.15, proved to be an excellent weapon for jungle warfare and was complemented by the General Purpose Machine Gun (G.P.M.G.) and the 88 mm mortar. Grenade launchers and the 'Carl Gustav' rocket launcher added to the effectiveness of the infantryman's immediate support and were proved in action against the Indonesians. The value of mobile, helicopter-borne artillery was quickly appreciated and the importance of helicopters to sustain widely dispersed troops was a vital factor in the success of the campaign. Such lessons were to be of great benefit to the expanding Australian task force in South Vietnam, which included many veterans of the Malayan and Borneo jungle campaigns.

45 Light Regiment, Royal Artillery, came to the end of its tour of duty with the brigade after firing over 30,000 rounds during its detachments in Borneo. 6 Light Regiment, Lieutenant-Colonel G. C. K. Rowe, replaced 45 Regiment in January 1966 with 'V' Light Battery, 'H' (Ramsay's Troop) Light Battery commanded by Major David Counsell who had served in Korea, 132 (The Bengal Rocket Troop) Medium Battery which was located at Seremban with one troop in Borneo and 'A' Field Battery of the Royal Australian Artillery which 6 Regiment inherited from 45 Regiment, together with its guns and equipment. The gunners were soon introduced to the brigade's air-portable role and were involved in Exercise 'Thunderbolt', a firepower demonstration on the Asahan ranges.

After a visit by Their Royal Highnesses The Duke and Duchess of Gloucester on 13th January, the Scots Guards were relieved in Sabah by the 2nd Royal Greenjackets on 24th January 1966. The relief was notable for its speed and efficiency; a fleet of Royal Navy 'Wessex' helicopters effected the exchange of troops in the forward positions within a mere four hours, a record even under confrontation conditions carried out an aerial equivalent of the Light Division pace. Back at Terendak, Lieutenant-Colonel Sir Gregor MacGregor of MacGregor, formerly second-in-command of the battalion, assumed command of the 1st Battalion of the Scots Guards, just in time to lead the battalion in a series of testing exercises: Exercise 'Lion Roar', a major scheme conducted by 17 Gurkha Division in the Marang area on the East coast with a live 'enemy' provided by a Malaysian brigade, followed by Exercise 'Highland Fling' in May and several battalion exercises and training sessions.

The 4th Battalion of the Royal Australian Regiment managed to escape from this strenuous programme by going operational in Sarawak in April. 4 R.A.R. was deployed in the Bau District and, except for two significant contacts, the battalion had a fairly quiet five months in Borneo. The 4th

*Lt. Col. A. I. D. Fletcher, R.S.M. J. Grant, H.R.H. The Duke of Gloucester, 1st Bn.
Scots Guards, Kalabakan, Sabah, 13th January 1966.*

(R.H.Q. The Scots Guards)

Royal Australians conducted a very successful 'Hearts and Minds' campaign and received maximum co-operation from the local Dyaks who appreciated the presence of the Commonwealth troops in their homeland. The 1st Royal New Zealand Infantry Regiment left Terendak in May for a second tour with 99 Gurkha Brigade in Sarawak where they took over from the Durham Light Infantry, who had served in 28 Brigade during the Korean War. The Light Infantry and the 2nd Territorial Battalion of the New Zealand Regiment (Canterbury, Nelson Marlborough West Coast) had an inter-regimental alliance and this association was briefly observed during the handing over. The Kiwis were impressed by the Durham's stable belt which featured the regimental colours of the R.N.Z.I.R. The two adjutants met at Balai Ringin and the New Zealander persuaded the Light Infantryman to part with his belt. It is said that the Commanding Officer and the Regimental-Sergeant-Major of the R.N.Z.I.R. also obtained Durham belts; as a consequence of this exchange, the Royal New Zealand Infantry Regiment is now officially authorised to wear the Durham pattern stable belt. The Geordies and the Maoris also discovered a common means of communication and the jungles of Sarawak echoed to hearty cries of 'Ho-Way!' The New Zealanders operated in the Kuching area but

> 'it was disappointing for the battalion that immediately after it had assumed responsibility, negotiations commenced to end confrontation so, subsequently, activity died right away. It was mainly engaged in patrolling to ensure that no incursions did occur and in hearts and mind·activities amongst the indigenous people. A few short operations directed at the elements of the underground Clandestine Communist Organisation in the battalion area of operations also met with no success. A few suspects were detained but inevitably they were proved to be innocent.'

The Peace Agreement between Indonesia and Malaysia was concluded on 11th August 1966, effectively bringing 'confrontation' to a close. Those members of 28 Brigade who had served in Borneo were awarded the General Service Medal 1962 with the clasp 'Borneo' and those who had served on the mainland of Malaysia between 24th December 1964 and 11th August 1966 received the clasp 'Malay Peninsula'.

# Peace

The end of 'confrontation' in Borneo brought a period of uneasy peace to the Malaysian territories although war was still being waged in Southeast Asia, particularly in Vietnam. Other minor conflicts continued in the area, even along Malaysia's northern border with Thailand where the remnants of the Communist terrorists still lurked in the remote jungles.

The 4th Battalion of the Royal Australian Regiment withdrew from Sarawak in September 1966 and the 1st Royal New Zealand Infantry Regiment returned to Terendak on 1st September. With all the battalions of his command back in the fold, Brigadier McMeekin was able to concentrate the brigade's efforts in training for its major role, the commitment to SEATO. Exercise 'Quick Step', held in the Batu Arang area in late October, practised the Commonwealth Brigade in its conventional war tasks. The Australian participation in the Vietnam War brought a sense of realistic urgency to such training, particularly amongst the Australian members of the brigade who were destined to serve in that country. Lieutenant-Colonel C. H. A. East, who had served with the 1st Royal Australians in Korea and was Brigade-Major at Taiping, arrived to take command of the 4th Royal Australians in November 1966. 4 R.A.R. noted at that time: 'This year was peacetime soldiering at its best, interesting exercises, plenty of sport coupled with excellent entertainment facilities provided by the Garrison and Malacca district.'

The British and Australian units of 28 Brigade relieved their battalions every two years but the New Zealand battalion relied on the practice of internal replacements, the so-called 'trickle system' which exchanged some thirty men every month, rather similar to the American method of rotation. This had many obvious disadvantages, especially in regard to the battalion's standard of training and readiness for war. Brigadier

McMeekin reported: 'The New Zealand habit of replacing half of its battalion each year instead of a complete battalion every other year, as the other two nations do, gives the brigade a bit of a hiccup and would not be acceptable if the battalion or brigade was on a war footing.' Nevertheless, many of the replacements joining the New Zealand battalion had previous service in Malaya and required only a short period of refresher training to bring them up to standard and, of course, New Zealand had only one regular infantry battalion which necessitated such a relief system.

The Chief of the British General Staff, General Sir James Cassels, paid another visit to 'his' Commonwealth Brigade in January 1967 and was pleased to note that it still enjoyed the reputation it had established in Korea, Malaya and the recent operations in Borneo and mainland Malaysia. On 31st January 1967 Brigadier P. L. Tancred of the Australian Army arrived to relieve Brigadier McMeekin as brigade commander. Brigadier McMeekin had the satisfaction of commanding the brigade during its brief operation against the Indonesian invaders in 1964 but also had to cope with a very turbulent period of the brigade's existence – as had his predecessor, Brigadier Dawson – when he rarely had the complete complement of units under his command at Terendak. Nevertheless, the brigade maintained its high standard of readiness and performed its tasks efficiently, gaining valuable and practical experience during the detachments to Borneo. It was hoped that Brigadier Tancred might enjoy a more stable tenure of command during the years to come.

Even so, brigade units were again deployed out of Malaysia early in the New Year. In response to an appeal from the British Embassy and the Laotian Government, 11 Field Squadron, Royal Engineers, and a detachment of the 16th Commonwealth Field Ambulance were rushed to Vientiane, capital of Laos, to undertake Operation 'Blowpipe'. Severe storms had caused the Mekong River to flood, resulting in considerable damage and disruption of public utilities. The Commonwealth sappers and medics were called upon to provide fresh water supplies and initiate a programme of measures to avert the spread of disease. The task was tackled successfully and the Commonwealth contribution played a major part in relieving the effects of the disaster on the population of Vientiane and district. In effect, this emergency disaster relief deployment was the only occasion upon which elements of 'Task Force Blue' actually served in Laos.

Colonel East remembers the post-confrontation atmosphere:

'The return of 4 R.A.R. to Terendak Garrison following the end of Indonesian Confrontation was inevitably followed by a feeling of anticlimax. After its initial entry into operations, the resumption of unit and formation exercises in peninsular Malaysia, ceremonial parades and training programmes, even though it brought reunion with families and the pleasures of local leave, resulted in a let down feeling among all ranks. There was only one answer, and that was a judicious mixture of concentrated training at all levels, maximum competitive sporting events and an adequate leave and recreation programme.'

On its third birthday, 1st February 1967, the 4th Battalion of the Royal Australian Regiment trooped its regimental colour at Terendak Camp. The parade, and ensuing celebrations, were specially noteworthy because the reviewing officer was General Tunku Osman bin Tunku Mohd Jewa, P.M.N., Chief of the Malaysian Armed Forces Staff, the first time that a senior Malaysian officer had been so honoured by Commonwealth forces.

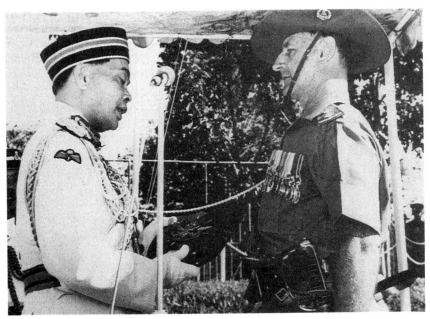

*General Tunku Osman bin Tunku Mohd Jewa and Lt. Col. East, C.O. 4 R.A.R. Terendak, 1st February 1967.*

(Col. East)

*Lt. Col. East with the villagers of Kampong Pantai Merah.*

(Col. East)

The initiative for this occasion had been taken by Colonel East; as brigade-major at Taiping in 1958 he had known the Tunku when he commanded the 1st Royal Malay Regiment. Colonel East had contacted the General but recalls,

> 'The informal approach got somewhat out of hand before a formal request could be lodged with the appropriate Australian and British higher authorities, and I was made to feel a certain amount of official, diplomatic and military displeasure! As the informal approach had, in fact, become *fait accompli*, officialdom put on the best face possible and in the event the occasion was generally accepted as a resounding success on both military and diplomatic grounds.'

In February the 1st Battalion of the Scots Guards came to the end of its tour of duty with the brigade. During their period of residence at

*Air Platoon, 1st King's Shropshire Light Infantry, Terendak, 1967.*

(3 LI)

Terendak, the Scots Guards had exercised the unique privilege of flying the Royal Standard of Scotland over the battalion headquarters. The 'Rampant Lion' was hauled down when the Guards handed over to the 1st Battalion of The King's Shropshire Light Infantry, Lieutenant-Colonel B. N. C. Fletcher. The K.S.L.I. had left the Commonwealth Brigade some fifteen years earlier and had been one of the original battalions – with the 3rd R.A.R. and the K.O.S.B. – during the Korean War. The Shropshires inherited 'Bella' and 'Bertha' (with their crews) from the Scots Guards and older soldiers in the two battalions remembered that the K.S.L.I. had relieved the Scots Guards at Chelsea in 1948 when the Guards were sent to Malaya in the early days of the emergency. 9 Company of the Irish Guards struck up an unofficial alliance with 'D' Company of the 1st Royal New Zealand Infantry Regiment before leaving Terendak, the Irishmen finding the Maoris to be of their liking – a feeling which was obviously reciprocated.

Despite this era of 'peacetime soldiering at its best', thoughts of war were never far from the minds of members of 28 Brigade. New Zealand had sent 161 Field Battery of the Royal New Zealand Artillery to support the Australian contingent in Vietnam and, on 8th May 1967, a composite company from the 1st Royal New Zealand Infantry Regiment was sent to Vietnam. 'V' Company ('V' for Vietnam) was reinforced with a mortar section and an assault pioneer section and came under the command of the Australian battalion, later to be known as the 'ANZAC Battalion'. The loss of a rifle company and support elements, coupled with the New Zealand relief system, was to deplete the R.N.Z.I.R. at Terendak. Another grim reminder of the war was evident in the military cemetery at Terendak, the nearest to the war zone of Vietnam. Some of those killed in the Vietnam conflict are interred in the cemetery and it was the sombre duty of the resident Australian battalion and a gun from the field battery to conduct the funeral ceremonies. Amongst the Australians buried at Terendak is Major Peter Badcoe who was posthumously awarded one of the four Victoria Crosses earned in Vietnam. Major Badcoe had served as battery captain of 103 Field Battery, R.A.A., whilst it was with the brigade from 1961 to 1963 and was killed on 7th April 1967 when serving as an adviser to the South Vietnamese Army.

The Commonwealth Brigade again sent representatives of brigade units to the annual SEATO exercise in Thailand. Exercise 'Aurora', in May, was a fairly genteel affair – unlike most brigade exercises – and took the form of an indoor 'war game' held at Bangkok. The exercise offered the opportunity for a certain amount of tourism and liaison with members of allied forces attending; the usual sightseeing flight along the Mekong did allow a few glimpses of the Laotian side of the river for those privileged to fly. In June, 107 Field Battery, R.A.A., relieved 'A' Field Battery in 6 Light Regiment; 107 Battery had recently returned from a tour of duty with the Australian Field Force in Vietnam and brought experience of that war with them which was of interest and value to the brigade as a whole.

The 4th Royal Australians undertook another type of venture; Operation 'Gotong Royong' (Mutual Assistance) was part of 17 Gurkha Division's 'hearts and minds' programme to promote goodwill between the Malaysians and the Commonwealth Nations. After consultation with the District Officer and local authorities, the Australians obtained the approval of the Governor of Malacca, Tun Haji Abdul Malek, to adopt Kampong Pantai Tanah Merah, a fishing village some five miles from Terendak. The object of the operation was to foster goodwill and to improve the standard of living for the villagers; to this end, all ideas for projects to be undertaken would come from the villagers, technical advice and supervision from the Australians and most of the labour and materials from local resources. Tasks undertaken included the provision of financial aid to buy fishing nets, engines for sampans, buffaloes, poultry and grain; practical aid in the form of improving the water supply by sinking a new well, the establishment of a weekly dental clinic by the Australian Dental Corps, the maintenance, repair and construction of new roads, bridges and culverts and general support by providing sports facilities, school books, desks and blackboards. Colonel East was proud to report that,

'The operation was a great success, and included exchange visits between the people of Kampong Pantai Merah and the soldiers of 4 R.A.R. at Terendak Camp. A real spirit of goodwill was achieved and no minor incident marred relations at any stage. This project perhaps more than any other activity during the battalion's tour of duty was instrumental in my receiving an invitation as C.O. to attend the State Parliament on the eve of 4 R.A.R.'s departure to Australia, to receive the thanks of the State Government. I was accorded the privilege of replying and spoke in the national language which was broadcast over Radio Malaysia.'

In August 1967 Lieutenant-Colonel J. P. St. C. Ballenden took command of the King's Shropshire Light Infantry from Lieutenant-Colonel Fletcher. As a lieutenant in 'A' Company of the K.S.L.I., Colonel Ballenden had won the Military Cross during the taking of Hill 227 in

October 1951. Shorty after his assumption of command the Shropshires were detached for Exercise 'Piping Shrike' – in Australia.

'Originally only two companies were scheduled to go but by dint of begging, borrowing and stealing transport, the bulk of the battalion and the band and bugles were able to go. The purpose of the exercise was to train with the Australian Army in the Rockhampton training area and to act as "enemy" to battalions who had almost completed their training for Vietnam. The battalion travelled in a variety of aircraft and the bulk on the *Sir Galahad*. The main exercise was right up the soldiers' street – they were to act as Vietnamese civilians and Vietcong soldiery. The "Vietnamese civilians" really entered into the spirit of things and spent the exercise disguised as peasants, women and in the case of one of our splendid Fijian soldiers, Corporal Kunadoma, as a Buddha sitting on an altar which concealed the entrance to a tunnel. It was an interesting exercise and showed how easily an irregular and fast-moving force could outwit and out-manoeuvre even well-trained troops and gave an insight into how guerilla forces can tie down regular forces with not too much effort. After the exercise the Lord Mayor of Brisbane very kindly invited the battalion to march through his City and we managed to cover the whole at full light infantry pace to the astonishment of the on-lookers. The battalion was completely overwhelmed by hospitality in Brisbane. The battalion took a few days R. & R. at Surfers Paradise where a camp area was made available to us. In the interests of good neighbourliness, we offered to provide the Surfers Paradise police with some regimental policemen in case of any trouble but were informed that the Surfers Paradise police were well used to dealing with hundreds of burly Australians and the addition of a few hundred Brits would cause them no problems. One highlight was the party given by the battalion for the three Australian battalions taking part in the exercises on the training area. We laid on two 3-tonners full of canned beer which we would thought would be ample but by ten o'clock lorries were being despatched to the local town for reinforcements! It was perhaps a mark of the liking of the Aussies for us and ourselves for the Aussies that despite the consumption of incredible amounts of beer by some 2,000 odd soldiers there was not a single fight or row.'

*The advance party of the 1st K.S.L.I. arrive at Connor Park Aerodrome, Australia,*
*by Argosy aircraft, 15th September 1967, for Exercise 'Piping Shrike'.*

(3 LI)

*Lt. Col. Ballenden at Shoalwater Bay, Australia, 1967.*

(3 LI)

For Colonel Ballenden the exercise renewed an old acquaintanceship. One of the Australian battalions was the 3rd Royal Australians, commanded by Lieutenant-Colonel Jim Shelton. The two officers had occupied adjacent beds in the Military Hospital at Kure, in Japan, after Operation 'Commando' in 1951 and both had served as instructors at the Staff College at Camberley. After some three months, the Shropshires returned reluctantly to Terendak which one Shropshireman described as 'a concentration camp run by NAAFI'.

The brigade's engineers, 11 Field Squadron, left Terendak on 11th August to relieve 59 Squadron of the Royal Engineers in Thailand. The construction of the Post Crown project was continuing and 11 Squadron also laid a new road from Loeng Nok Tha to Bang Nong Phok.

The 4th Battalion of the Royal Australians were undergoing rigorous training at Terendak and sent detachments to the Jungle Warfare School at Kota Tinggi in Johore. Colonel East reported:

'All training was designed to produce a combat ready unit to enter into a theatre of war on a scale which the Australian Army had not experienced since Korea, seventeen years earlier. Following sub-unit and unit training, the battalion embarked on a number of exercises as part of the Far East Strategic Reserve under H.Q. 28 Comwel Bde and H.Q. 17 Gurkha Div direction, and was rewarded in late October by the news that 4 R.A.R., on its return to Australia at the end of the year, would re-organise into an ANZAC battalion for service in Vietnam. Morale amongst all ranks was at a peak – of course it was not so high among the families, whose worries over separation, accommodation, schooling in Australia and fears for the safety of husbands and fathers would begin again. But all this was in the future, while the battalion packed up for a return to Australia for Christmas, with the satisfaction of a job extremely well done in peninsula Malaysia and Borneo. Before leaving Terendak, the second-in-command of 4 R.A.R., Major John McGhee, had cause to investigate the laundry accounts of the battalion's local contractor, Mohammed Rafiq. Mohammed Rafiq had served successive Australian battalions since the mid-fifties and conducted all the tailoring and laundry work from his premises in Terendak. Rafiq probably ran the best intelligence network in Malacca and beyond. He somehow appeared in Sarawak when the battalion joined West Brigade and set up his usual services. He returned to Terendak when

4 R.A.R. concluded its operational term, resumed his trade with the soldiers and their families and continued to appear at crucial moments during unit and formation exercises all over Malaysia. At one stage of the laundry investigation when things looked very bad for Rafiq, he appeared at my house in a highly agitated, emotional and almost tearful state to protest his innocence of any wrong doing. After delivering an impassioned appeal he made his final statement to me, and I quote: "Many men say that Mohammed Rafiq is a rogue, but Colonel Sahib, let me say that Rafiq is an honest rogue." Needless to say, Rafiq stayed as 4 R.A.R.'s purveyor of services until departure for Australia.'

*Senior Officers*
*28 Commonwealth Brigade*
*November 1967*

*Brig. P. Tancred (Rear)*

| *Lt. Col. J. Langtry* | *Lt. Col. J. Brooke* | *Lt. Col. C. East* | *Lt. Col. B. Poananga* |
|---|---|---|---|
| *8 R.A.R.* | *1 R.N.Z.I.R.* | *4 R.A.R.* | *1 R.N.Z.I.R.* |

(Colonel East)

The 4th Battalion of the Royal Australian Regiment was relieved by the 8th Battalion, Lieutenant-Colonel J. C. Langtry, D.C.M. – a Korean veteran – and inherited the 'honest rogue' and his various dhobi and charwallahs. The New Zealand battalion underwent a change of command in November when Lieutenant-Colonel J. Brooke took over from Lieutenant-Colonel Brian Poananga. On 17th December, a second rifle company was detached from the Royal New Zealand Infantry Regiment to serve with the ANZAC Battalion in Vietnam. The increased New Zealand contribution to the Vietnam War reduced the effectiveness of the battalion at Terendak; in addition to the New Zealand system of replacing personnel within the battalion, the R.N.Z.I.R. also had to rotate its soldiers between the regimental depot in New Zealand, the battalion at Terendak and the companies in Vietnam. Colonel Brooke had to plan his manpower requirements and deployments very carefully and was left with only two rifle companies effectively under his command in the brigade. The second New Zealand company in the ANZAC Battalion was designated 'W' Company to follow the existing 'V' Company. Although most members of the 1st Royal New Zealand Infantry Regiment did serve at least one tour in Vietnam, the battalion was not committed in its entirety and was thus not awarded the campaign honour 'Vietnam'.

Meanwhile, Brigadier Tancred commanded the brigade in the largest counter-revolutionary exercise staged in Malaysia, Exercise 'Gedgeley' which involved most of the 17th Gurkha Infantry Division. The exercise provided realistic training for the brigade's role in SEATO and gained much from the experience of the Vietnam veterans serving in the Commonwealth Brigade as well as preparing the Australian and New Zealand contingents for their future tours of duty after leaving Malaysia.

Early in 1968 the brigade was further diminished by yet another call for operations outside Malaysia. Lieutenant-Colonel Ballenden of the King's Shropshire Light Infantry recalls the sudden order to move:

'The Colonel of the Regiment was visiting when suddenly out of the blue, not even being stand-by battalion, we got orders to send a company to Mauritius where trouble had erupted between the Muslim and Creole inhabitants. I do not think I have seen such jockeying for position as took place between company commanders to be the first to be sent. Major Brian Lowe set off with 'B' Company within four hours of the notice to move being given from a state of nil preparation. The journey involved motor coaches from Malacca to Singapore and then an eleven-hour flight with a break of one hour at Gan. This very rapid deployment was somewhat spoilt by the Royal Air Force having been put on stand-by which apparently counted as flying hours and although they had done nothing by the time the company arrived at Changi the aircrews were entitled to another rest period! The company took with them not only all their equipment but a number of the battalion helicopters.'

The British colony of Mauritius, in the Indian Ocean, was due to become independent in March 1968 and Her Royal Highness the Princess Alexandra was scheduled to attend the independence celebrations. However, during the pre-independence period, violent rioting broke out between the Muslim and Creole factions which threatened the handover of power in the colony. 'B' Company of the K.S.L.I. flew to Port Louis, Mauritius, on 23rd January 1968 and were immediately committed to internal security duties. The Shropshires succeeded in keeping intercommunity strife in check and performed their task cheerfully and efficiently. 'There is no doubt that their hard work, good humour and impartiality helped enormously to keep the situation under control as Independence Day, 12 March, approached.' Colonel Ballenden: 'After a few weeks it became apparent that the task was beyond that of a single company and battalion H.Q. with further companies moved to Mauritius. There then followed a period of almost traditional internal security operations, cordons, searches, curfews and so forth. Gradually the situation was brought back under control.' On Independence Day itself, the light infantrymen were plucked from their duties on the streets, changed quickly from battle order into tropical white Number One uniforms and paraded on the Champ du Mars with the band and bugles and the battalion's air platoon. After the ceremony, the troops marched off, changed back into greens and returned to patrol the streets. 'At the request of the Prime Minister, Doctor The Honourable Sir Seewoosagur Rangulan, the battalion stayed for some nine or ten months. It was sad that during this period our Deputy Colonel, The Princess Alexandra, should have visited the colony for its independence but in the light of the internal security situation we had, sadly, to recommend that she did not visit.' For their service in Mauritius, the K.S.L.I. were awarded the Wilkinson Sword of Peace and the Silver Medal of the City of Port Louis.

Another parade was held at Terendak on 15th March to establish the official alliance between the Royal New Zealand Infantry Regiment and the Royal Australian Regiment, represented by the 8th Battalion. The alliance had been formed in Vietnam by the integrated ANZAC Battalion which was then composed of the 2nd Battalion of the Royal Australian Regiment and 'V' and 'W' Companies of the Royal New Zealand Infantry Regiment.

11 Field Squadron, Royal Engineers, rejoined the brigade at Terendak after their labours in Thailand. The new Post Crown road was officially opened on 18th April and brought to a close the brigade's construction project in that country.

On completion of its tour of duty with the Commonwealth Brigade, 6 Light Regiment of the Royal Artillery was disbanded on 10th May 1968. Before the disbandment, Lieutenant-Colonel Rowe opened the Ramsay Pavilion at St David's High School in Malacca. The pavilion was named for 'H' Battery of the regiment and the battery commander, Major David Counsell, was responsible for the planning, construction and completion of this excellent example of community service. 14 Light Regiment, Royal Artillery, Lieutenant-Colonel J. Parham, arrived to take over from 6 Regiment at Terendak. 14 Regiment consisted of 1 ('The Blazers') Light Battery, 5 (Gibraltar 1779-1783) Light Battery, 13 (Martinique 1809) Medium Battery – which relieved 132 Battery at Seremban – and 107 Field Battery, R.A.A., under Major Don Quinn. 14 Regiment had served in the Far East before; originally as 28 Jungle Field Regiment in 1943 to 1944 but was renumbered after the war and, as 14 Field Regiment (which then included The Blazers Battery), it served in the Commonwealth Division in Korea. 14 Regiment also undertook several local community projects including the construction of a nursery school for the Chinese Christian Church at Senai and a Boys Brigade hut at Kulai.

The 8th Battalion of the Royal Australian Regiment held two ceremonial parades at Terendak in June. The first to greet the Prime Minister of Australia, Mr. John Gorton, who was making a tour of the Australian forces in Southeast Asia and the second, on 14th June, to receive new colours. The Colonel Commandant of the Regiment, Lieutenant-General Sir Richard Pollard, K.B.E., C.B., D.S.O., presented the colours to the battalion. The 2nd Battalion of the Parachute Regiment, which is allied to the 8th Battalion of the R.A.R., was on a periodic training visit to Malaysia from Great Britain and was invited to hold the ground for their partners whilst the 8th Royal Australians received their colours with all due pomp and circumstance.

The King's Shropshire Light Infantry lost their proud regimental title on 10th July 1968. As part of the British Army's reduction and amalgamation of many of the well known old infantry regiments, a new Light

Infantry Regiment was formed from the remaining four light infantry battalions; the Shropshires became the 3rd Battalion of the Light Infantry Regiment, the King's Own Yorkshire Light Infantry became the 2nd Battalion whilst the Durhams, who had fought in Korea and Borneo, were reduced and absorbed into the other three battalions. However, old habits and traditions die hard and many still thought of the 3rd Light Infantry as the Shropshires for some time thereafter.

The 8th Battalion of the Royal Australian Regiment was warned for duty in Vietnam in 1969 and, in close co-operation with 14 Light Regiment, underwent a course of rigorous training for their next tour which culminated in Exercise 'Darling Point' in November 1968. During February and March 1969, Headquarters Malaya Command under its G.O.C., Major-General D. Horsford, C.B., C.B.E., D.S.O., spent a great deal of effort and time in preparing and organising an air-portable brigade exercise for the 28th Commonwealth Brigade. Most of the helicopter resources in the Malay Peninsula, including three heavy lift 'Chinooks', were made available to support the brigade in this venture. Exercise 'Crowning Glory' was held in March 1969 and was the last occasion upon which 28 Commonwealth Brigade would be deployed as an operational brigade group. Colonel Ballenden remembers: 'After the return to Malaya and re-joining the brigade, the battalion prepared to move home but fate had one last kick for us. After the advance party and most of the company commanders had gone home, the brigade commander decided to have one last exercise where again we were pitted against the Australians and New Zealanders. The exercise went well not least of all because of the enthusiasm of the "second eleven" who were running the battalion.' Two Gurkha battalions were deployed as exercise enemy which gave a further sense of realism to a memorable ten-day exercise.

Early in 1969 the British Government began to implement its decision to withdraw British forces 'East of Suez'. After Exercise 'Crowning Glory' – aptly named in view of the circumstances – British elements of the brigade began to withdraw in April 1969. The first units to leave were 5 (Gibraltar) Light Battery and the 3rd Battalion of the Light Infantry. It appeared that the 3rd Light Infantry might well be the last British infantry battalion to serve in the 28th Commonwealth Brigade; as the King's Shropshire Light Infantry it had been one of the original battalions in 1951. 'Our final leaving was tinged with sadness as we were to be the last British battalion serving there and the Australians and New Zealanders were shortly to depart also.' Brigadier Tancred was the first Australian to leave. In March he handed command of the brigade to 'the second New

Zealander to hold the post, Brigadier R. M. Gurr. Brigadier Tancred's tenure of command had been difficult; his infantry battalions had dwindled to one and a half with the absences of two New Zealand companies in Vietnam and the Shropshires deployment to Mauritius. Nevertheless, Brigadier Tancred strove to maintain the brigade's high standards of training and readiness for operations. The prospect of service in Vietnam spurred the Australian and New Zealand units but the British disengagement from the Far East gave rise to uncertainty and some doubts about the brigade's future. The new brigade commander had previous service in the Commonwealth Brigade; he had commanded the 1st Battalion of the New Zealand Regiment and was the first commanding officer of the 1st Battalion of the Royal New Zealand Infantry Regiment on its formation in April 1964 and had commanded the battalion during the Confrontation operations in Malaysia and Borneo.

The 1st Battalion of the Royal Australian Regiment arrived in April for its fourth tour of duty in the brigade and relieved the 8th Battalion, which was bound for Vietnam later in 1969. The 1st R.A.R., Lieutenant-Colonel J. B. Trenerry, had served in the brigade in Korea and Malaya and had also completed two tours in Vietnam. 106 Field Battery of the Royal Australian Artillery took over from 107 Battery although 14 Light Regiment had been reduced to just the 1st (The Blazers) Light Battery. 11 Field Squadron of the Royal Engineers, under Major R. F. H. Cole, held a farewell parade at Terendak on 24th September, taken by Brigadier Gurr, and departed for duty elsewhere leaving 2 Field Troop of the Royal Australian Engineers as the brigade's remaining engineer support. By November the brigade had shrunk to one and a half infantry battalions and a field battery of artillery. The 1st Royal Australians trained hard, mounting Exercises 'Jumping Wallaby' and 'Sheer Hell' to test their airportability role. The 1st Royal New Zealand Infantry Regiment also participated in unit exercises whilst still providing two rifle companies to the conflict in Vietnam. Lieutenant-Colonel R. G. Williams took over from Lieutenant-Colonel Brooke as commanding officer of 1 R.N.Z.I.R. in November and, the following month, was faced with the task of moving his battalion from Terendak to Nee Soon in Singapore.

The withdrawal of the British contingent from the Commonwealth Brigade at Terendak meant that the future costs for the maintenance of the cantonment would impose an additional financial strain on the governments of Australia and New Zealand. Negotiations between the State of Singapore and Australian, British and New Zealand representatives resulted in an agreement for the Australian and New Zealand forces to move into accommodation vacated by the departing British services. The 1st Battalion of the Royal Australian Regiment and the 1st Battalion of the Royal New Zealand Infantry Regiment moved from Terendak to Selarang and Nee Soon respectively in December 1969. 2 Field Troop R.A.E. and an Australian motor transport platoon of the Royal Australian Army Service Corps also moved to Nee Soon. The final handover of Terendak Camp to the 1st Malaysian Brigade was effected by Colonel W. C. Currie, Argyll and Sutherland Highlanders, who had been Deputy Brigade Commander for the previous two years. During this time, Colonel Currie had borne the brunt of the detailed and complicated staff work involved in transferring Terendak from a Commonwealth base to a Malaysian brigade garrison. By 22nd March 1970, after eight years in residence, the Commonwealth Brigade had vacated Terendak and handed it over to the Malaysian Army.

*Drum Major Holland, 1st Royal Australian Regiment, and Brigadier R. M. Gurr, commander 28th Commonwealth Infantry Brigade. Selarang, Singapore, 1971.*

(AWM GAR 71 119 MC)

The British political pendulum swung during the elections of 1970 and the new Conservative Government decided to maintain a token force to honour its SEATO and Commonwealth commitments. Meanwhile, the depleted Commonwealth Brigade participated in Exercise 'Bersatu Padu' with the Malaysian Forces in August 1970 as an earnest of Commonwealth co-operation and as evidence of the brigade's capabilities. The brigade gained a rifle company when 'W' Company of the Royal New Zealand Infantry Regiment withdrew from Vietnam to rejoin the battalion at Nee Soon, taking the vacant place of 'D' Company; this addition did ease the relief system slightly although 'V' Company in Vietnam still required the rotation of replacements.

Brigadier Gurr was relieved when the first British unit rejoined his brigade. The 1st (The Blazers) Light Battery of the Royal Artillery returned to 28 Brigade to double its artillery strength at the end of 1970. 9 Field Squadron of the Royal Engineers soon followed to absorb the Australian Field Troop and, in March 1971, Brigadier Gurr welcomed his British successor. Brigadier M. J. H. Walsh had been on an exercise in Germany when he received three weeks notice to take command of 28 Commonwealth Infantry Brigade in Singapore. After two days with the retiring Brigade Commander, Brigadier Walsh found himself ensconced as the new commander. The appointment of a British commander confirmed the reprieve of the brigade and a return to its tri-national composition. The new Brigadier, a former Greenjacket and Paratrooper, was a graduate of the Australian Staff College and proved to be a good choice for this unusual command. Brigadier Gurr, in common with many of the previous commanders of 28 Brigade, had weathered another difficult and politically fraught period of the brigade's existence. Nevertheless, he handed over a keen, well-trained and efficient formation to his successor.

As the brigade began to enlarge to its former size, the New Zealand battalion was moved from Nee Soon to occupy the former Royal Marine Commando base in Dieppe Barracks at Sembawang. The 6th Royal Australian Regiment, Lieutenant-Colonel D. A. Drabsch, arrived in July to relieve the 1st Battalion in Kangaw Barracks. The 6th Battalion had completed two tours in Vietnam where its 'D' Company had been awarded the United States Presidential Citation for the action at Long Tan in August 1966. The third infantry battalion of the brigade's complement arrived in September 1977 and occupied Meerut Barracks at Nee Soon. The 1st Battalion of The Royal Highland Fusiliers, Lieutenant-Colonel D. N. Anderson, M.B.E., had been formed by the amalgamation of the Royal Scots Fusiliers and the Highland Light Infantry in 1959 – after the return of the 1st Battalion of The Royal Scots Fusiliers from the Commonwealth Brigade in Malaya in 1957. With the arrival of the British infantry battalion the brigade was up to strength except for one New Zealand rifle company in Vietnam.

Ironically, one of the first parades performed by the Royal Highland Fusiliers was a farewell to the British Commander-in-Chief of the Far East Land Forces on 29th October 1971. This marked the official end of the British military presence in Singapore and Malaysia, the Malaysian Government assuming responsibility for the defence of its territories whilst the British retained a garrison in Hong Kong. This change also brought to an end the existence of the 28th Commonwealth Infantry Brigade, which had been a part of the 17th Gurkha Infantry Division of the Far East Land Forces in Malaysia.

After some twenty years of active life in Korea and Malaya – with detachments to Borneo, Vietnam, Mauritius, the Radfan, Thailand and even Laos – 28 Commonwealth Infantry Brigade ceased to exist as such on 31st October 1971. However, its demise was painless and involved a mere change of title and superior command; the brigade was to live on as 28 ANZUK Brigade of the ANZUK (Australian, New Zealand and United Kingdom) Force in Singapore.

# Anzuk

The Australian, New Zealand and United Kingdom (ANZUK) Force was formed on 1st November 1971 as the Commonwealth contribution to the Southeast Asia Treaty Organization. The new Force was joint service and joint nation in every respect. The Force was commanded by Rear-Admiral David Wells, an Australian, with its headquarters in the former British Naval Base at Sembawang in Singapore with staff officers representing the naval, air and land elements of the three participating nations. Commodore S. W. Clayden, Royal Navy, commanded the Naval Component based at Sembawang Naval Base; Air Commodore D. D. Hurditch, Royal Australian Air Force, commanded the Air Component which remained at Butterworth in Province Wellesley; Brigadier F. T. Whitelaw, Australian Army, commanded the Force's Logistical Group and Brigadier M. J. H. Walsh commanded the 28th ANZUK Brigade.

28 Brigade was dispersed in the Northern part of Singapore Island with Brigade Headquarters and the Australian battalion in Kangaw Barracks (on the old Sembawang airfield); the New Zealand battalion in Dieppe Barracks (the former Royal Marine Commando Brigade barracks at Sembawang); the British battalion, the field regiment of artillery and the field squadron of engineers in Meerut Barracks at Nee Soon. An inauguration parade was held on 1st November 1971. The pipers of the Royal Highland Fusiliers and the 6th Battalion of the Royal Australian Regiment gave the occasion a stirring musical accompaniment as they paraded with the 1st Battalion of the Royal New Zealand Infantry Regiment and other brigade units which then included the 28 ANZUK Field Regiment, 28 ANZUK Field Squadron, 28 Aviation Squadron and 28 Signal Squadron – all composed of British and Australian sub-units. 28 ANZUK Field Regiment, commanded by Lieutenant-Colonel Noel F. de L. Hunty, M.C.,

Royal Australian Artillery, consisted of 1 (The Blazers) Light Battery, Royal Artillery, and 106 Field Battery, Royal Australian Artillery, both equipped with 105 mm Pack Howitzers.

The 'Blazers' recorded their impressions in response to the frequent question,

> '"What-is-it-like-to-serve-with-British-Gunners-in-an-inte-grated-regiment-commanded-by-an-Australian-in-Singapore?" "Go to Blazers" is one of the more polite terms used by Australians amongst Australians to signify that a particular presence is no longer required in the immediate vicinity. In Singapore the same phrase becomes a set of instructions to sundry bill collectors, barracks repairmen, bus drivers, staff officers and all who

*From left to right: Rear Admiral D. Wells, R.A.N., Commander ANZUK Force, Air Commodore C. L. Siegert R.N.Z.A.F. Chief of Staff ANZUK Force, Commodore S. W. Clayden, R.N., Commander Naval Component, Brigadier M. J. H. Walsh, British Army Commander 28 ANZUK Bde., Air Commodore D. D. Hurditch, R.A.A.F. Commander Air Component, Brigadier F. T. Whitelaw, Australian Army Commander Support Group.*

*Senior Officers – ANZUK Force – Singapore 1971.*

(Maj. Gen. Walsh)

*Something Extra*

## 'THE BLAZERS'

*'My dear chap, we can hit a matchbox at 5,000 yds.'*

*'You've got defensive fire – it's simulated!'*

('Gunner' Magazine)

*Brig. M. J. H. Walsh with Cpl. Harris and Pte. Klein, 6 R.A.R., on exercise at Mersing.*

(AWM GAR/71/497/MC)

wander into 106 Fd. Bty. R.A.A.'s area with queries pertaining to the British contingent of 28 ANZUK Field Regiment. Put them together and what have you got? A battery second to one (One-O-Six Field Battery RAA that is), although that particular claim is a moot point governed by the particular national bigotry one entertains.'

Although Singapore had good facilities for individual training all tactical training had to be conducted in Malaysia since there were only limited training areas available on the island. Major Ray Andrews, Royal New Zealand Artillery, was the brigade-major and had served in the brigade as an Auster pilot of 7 Reconnaissance Flight at Taiping and had commanded a battery of the Royal New Zealand Artillery in Vietnam. As the brigade's chief staff officer Major Andrews found that his job was rather difficult. 28 ANZUK Brigade was, in effect, an independent brigade group with a very foreshortened chain of command. Unlike Terendak, where

28 Brigade was subordinate to 17 Gurkha Division and Land Force Headquarters, the ANZUK Brigade staff were left to make their own arrangements directly with the air and support components of Force Headquarters. The search for training areas presented a particular problem. Considerable deforestration in Johore provided few suitable areas for military training and only Mersing, on the East coast, offered the type of jungle terrain necessary for brigade exercises. The Malaysian Federation Army were, at first, rather suspicious of approaches by this new brigade but Brigadier Walsh and his staff soon established a friendly and sound working relationship with their Malaysian counterparts and obtained the use of suitable training areas. Another new factor which had to be considered was that of internal security. In the mainly urban environment of Singapore there was always a danger of local political reaction and Brigadier Walsh had to draw up a comprehensive protective security plan. This also required diplomatic liaison with the Singaporean authorities and the exercising of brigade troops in internal security duties to cope with the possibility of riots and support to the local police and armed forces. Unlike Terendak, the brigade's families were spread amongst several housing estates in Singapore, the Australians being mainly concentrated in the Serangoon area. In the event of unrest and possible street riots, the families were to be evacuated and brought to the brigade's barracks, a considerable undertaking which required meticulous planning.

*Formation Sign*
*28 ANZUK Infantry Brigade*
*1st November 1971 – 31st January 1974*
*Singapore.*

The Australian and New Zealand disengagement from Vietnam continued gradually and 'V' Company of the New Zealand battalion returned to the 1st Battalion of the Royal New Zealand Infantry Regiment in November 1971. 'V' Company replaced 'C' Company in the full strength battalion and, to commemorate their gallant service in Vietnam, the rifle companies of 1 R.N.Z.I.R. were titled 'A', 'B', 'V' and 'W' Companies. Dieppe Barracks at Sembawang was renamed 'Wellington Lines' and remained as such until the latter part of 1989 when the New Zealanders withdrew from Singapore.

The Australian and New Zealand veterans of Vietnam were somewhat wary of the brigade's training programme when they arrived in Singapore. Nevertheless, Brigadier Walsh's enthusiastic approach to what was described as a 'fierce' training schedule soon proved to be both realistic and even interesting. The introduction and instruction on adventurous training projects was a novelty to the Australians and New Zealanders and they found such schemes to be enjoyable, with opportunities for expeditions to Sabah, Brunei and even Australia. However, Major Andrews did receive complaints from the battalion commanders that the very full brigade training programme left little time to conduct exercises at battalion level, especially since the new arrivals had to be instructed and practised in airportability procedures. After Exercise 'Jalan Ulu' in February 1972, the brigade-major was sent to Great Britain to explore the possibilities of effecting international exchanges, at platoon strength, to foster Commonwealth relations and to afford experience of the other nations' methods and equipment. This pilot scheme was welcomed by the British services, particularly the Royal Air Force.

Meanwhile, 28 ANZUK Brigade was also spending some time on the parade ground, polishing up its ceremonial drill. After some nine rehearsals during which the minor differences in the drill of the three armies and the conveying of words of command over long distances were resolved – the first by dint of hard practice and the latter by equipping detachment commanders with small radios – the brigade was deemed to be fit for inspection. The ANZUK Force was ready to be visited by Her Majesty the Queen, the highlight of 28 ANZUK Brigade's existence. On 5th March 1972 Her Majesty Queen Elizabeth the Second, accompanied by His Royal Highness the Prince Philip, Duke of Edinburgh, arrived at the Sembawang Naval Base on The Royal Yacht *Britannia* and were whisked through a tour of the ANZUK Force which included a wreath-laying ceremony at the Kranji Commonwealth War Cemetery, a combined church service at which the chaplains of three nations and three denominations

*W.O. Pipe Major Alec MacLeod-Lee, 6th Battalion, Royal Australian Regiment, with pipers and musicians of the Royal Highland Fusiliers and the 6th R.A.R., Singapore.*

(AWM GAR 71 524 MC)

officiated, a meeting with the senior personalities and families and, finally, a Royal Review of the brigade on the Kangaw airfield in the heat of the Singapore noon. The parade, commanded by Lieutenant-Colonel John Mace of the Royal New Zealand Infantry Regiment, consisted of three guards of 100 men each backed by the guns and vehicles of the brigade. The occasion was a high compliment to this unique formation. As Queen not only of the United Kingdom of Great Britain but also of Australia and New Zealand, Her Majesty had awarded the Vietnam Medal of 1964 to Her Australian and New Zealand soldiers who had served in that country and many such medals were in evidence on the parade – as was the distinctive brigade insignia featuring Her Majesty's Crown. This memorable review proceeded exactly to schedule to the enthusiastic delight of the many spectators from Great Britain, Australia and New Zealand who were able to see Her Majesty as she drove past. The Royal Visitors departed from the Sembawang Naval Base after lunch to the singing of the Maori Concert Party of the Royal New Zealand Infantry Regiment.

*Royal Review 28 ANZUK Bde. Kangaw, Singapore 5th March 1972.*

(Maj. Gen. Walsh)

The brigade had another Royal Visit on 18th October 1972 when Her Royal Highness The Princess Margaret, Countess of Snowdon, visited her regiment – The Royal Highland Fusiliers (Princess Margaret's Own Glasgow and Ayrshire Regiment) at Meerut Barracks, Nee Soon. The occasion was treated as a 'family' event and Her Royal Highness was shown the many aspects of the battalion's activities and met most of the members of the battalion.

*Royal Review 28 ANZUK Bde. Kangaw, Singapore 5th March 1972.*

(Maj. Gen. Walsh)

Life in Singapore was not all ceremonial parades and Royal occasions. During 1972 28 ANZUK Brigade conducted two major brigade exercises, seven unit exercises and eighty-one minor exercises. These exercises were usually performed as joint service ventures; for example, the Royal Highland Fusiliers were disembarked from New Zealand frigates on the East coast of Malaysia and the Australian fighter squadron supported the land forces during the attack phase of Exercise 'Full Swing'. Although the scope for inter-service misunderstanding and error was wide, any such mistakes were identified quickly and remedied by constant readjustment of procedures and communications, in this way the whole Force learnt from such initial errors. The composition of the ANZUK Force and the personalities of all services and nations made it a remarkably efficient joint organization. As Major Andrews, the brigade-major, commented:

*H.R.H. The Princess Margaret visits The 1st Bn. Royal Highland Fusiliers (Lt. Col. I. MacKay, M.B.E., M.C.), Nee Soon, Singapore 18th October 1972.*

(Maj. Gen. Walsh)

*The Marae (Maori Meeting House) 1st Bn. Royal New Zealand Infantry Regiment Dieppe Barracks, Singapore.*

*Brig. M. J. H. Walsh receives a Maori greeting during the dedication of the Marae; 2nd November 1972.*

(Maj. Gen. Walsh)

'Only these three nations in the world were capable of such successful operational integration from the headquarters down to unit level.
This integration was mainly due to a common history, a common
stock and the ties of the Commonwealth. Even so, all had to make
compromises and learn from their partners. New Zealand also had a
bicultural factor to add to the problem but the Maori element integrated as well, if not better, as the other contingents.'

Brigadier Walsh appears to have been appreciated by the Maori members
of the Royal New Zealand Infantry Regiment. On 2nd November 1972 he
was invited to officiate at the dedication of the battalion's 'Marae', the
Maori meeting house built in traditional style, and was presented with a
carved 'Taiaha' head as a memento of the occasion. Later, on his departure from the brigade, Brigadier Walsh received a five-foot-high carved
totem made by Staff-Sergeant J. H. Tetuhi on behalf of the Maori people
of the battalion. This impressive sculpture now occupies pride of place in
General Walsh's Wiltshire country garden.

Not all the members of the brigade were descended from a common
British stock as Major Andrews suggests. From the earliest days in Korea
many of the soldiers serving in the brigade were the sons or grandsons of
emigrants who settled in Australia, New Zealand and even Great Britain.
Several former Polish Army soldiers, who had joined the British Army
after 1945, served in Korea and Malaya – including a squadron-sergeant-
major who was a Count in his own right. The British Army had also
recruited many Fijians during the 1960s and soldiers from Caribbean and
Asian families also served in British regiments. Amongst the families
were wives who hailed from many lands; a strong proportion of German
wives with the British battalions but also Austrians, Italians, Cypriots,
Gibraltarians and several local Chinese and Malay wives. Nevertheless, as
Major Andrews observed, the ties of Commonwealth superseded ethnic or
national origins and made for a harmonious whole.

In addition to Brigadier Walsh's continuous military training programme, including inter-unit skill-at-arms competitions, the spirit of
friendly international and inter-regimental rivalry was fostered by a lively
sports programme which culminated in an annual Commonwealth Sports
Day, a custom preserved since the brigade's early days in Korea. Further
opportunities for greater understanding and exchanges between the nations came with the visit of General Sir John Mogg, the British Adjutant-
General and former commander of the Commonwealth Brigade, on 30th
January 1973. General Mogg was delighted to recognise and meet several

warrant-officers and senior sergeants who had served under his command in Malaya and had returned for further tours of duty with the brigade. The General was particularly interested in the suggested inter-Commonwealth exchange visits by sub-units and, at his instigation, Exercise 'Long Look' was launched as an annual event. Since then, regular exchanges between the armies of Great Britain, Australia and New Zealand have continued with some ninety Australian and thirty New Zealand soldiers being sent to British units, particularly in Germany, on a reciprocal basis.

On 14th March 1973 Brigadier M. R. Kennedy, M.B.E., of the New Zealand Army continued the rotation of command between the contributing nations by relieving Brigadier Walsh. Brigadier Walsh left the revived brigade as a confirmed devotee of Australian Rules Football. After his retirement, Major-General Walsh was appointed Chief Scout of the United Kingdom and Dependent Territories in 1982 and, on relinquishing the appointment in 1988, was offered a particular honour. At the request of His Royal Highness The Duke of Kent, General Walsh was invited to take the salute at the St. George's Day parade of Queen's Scouts at Windsor Castle. Nineteen eighty-eight was the bicentennial anniversary of Australia and the Royal Australian Regiment was providing the Queen's Guard at the Royal Residences. General Walsh was surprised to be greeted at Windsor by a guard furnished by one of the regiments of his old brigade.

Brigadier Kennedy had served previously as second-in-command of the 1st New Zealand Regiment and had been amongst the first to occupy Terendak Camp in May 1961. After a tour of duty with the brigade he had been a senior planning officer at the Defence Headquarters in Wellington and was well versed in the complexities of the ANZUK Force, its political background and tasks. The new brigadier was soon immersed in the job.

'There had barely been time to settle in before we launched into Exercise "King Cobra", a brigade counter-revolutionary warfare exercise staged in the jungles of Johore. A few days previously I had flown in by helicopter accompanied by a small party to confirm the location of Brigade H.Q. in a small clearing by a logging track. I watched somewhat amusedly as a young signaller, fresh from the streets of Glasgow, idly kicked a heap of matter on the track and enquired what it was – to be informed by a hard-bitten sergeant: "You had better look sharp, soldier, that's fresh wild elephant droppings." The sudden realisation of where we were dawned with shattering effect on the poor chap. The orders for the exercise included one paragraph headed "Snakes" and stated that snakes were prevalent in the area so instruction on the treatment of snakebites was to be carried out by all units. How valid this requirement proved to be. 6 R.A.R. on their long approach march had several soldiers bitten. One rather nasty case involved a soldier believed to have been bitten by a cobra and he had to be carried some miles through jungle at night before a rather dodgy helicopter evacuation could be mounted.'

A ceremonial parade was held early in 1973 by the 6th Royal Australians to celebrate their regimental birthday. Brigadier Kennedy took the parade and noted 'in the United States Army a wartime feat of considerable valour sometimes, but rarely, earns the President's Citation, a very great honour. 6 R.A.R., under the command of Lieutenant-Colonel John Healey, is one of the few foreign units to have earned this citation, the occasion being the battle of Long Tan in Vietnam.' The Brigadier attended another ceremonial parade later in the year:

'Alliances between units from different countries are long-standing arrangements which denote a special relationship or friendship between units which have usually served together to form such bonds. One such alliance, consummated on 9th June 1973, was between the Royal Highland Fusiliers, commanded by Lieutenant-Colonel Ian MacKay, and the Royal New Zealand Infantry Regiment, commanded by Lieutenant-Colonel John Mace (later Lieutenant-General, Chief of the New Zealand Defence Staff in 1987). The parade, which was reviewed by the two respective High Commissioners, was elegantly conceived and well executed. The two sets of regimental colours were first trooped through their own battalion's ranks and then through the ranks of the allied battalion. On this occasion, the Royal Highland Fusiliers carried their third colour, the Assaye Colour, earned in 1803 when the 74th Regiment fought under General Wellesley (later the Duke of Wellington) against some 40,000 Mahrattas in India, an honour greatly appreciated by the Royal New Zealand Infantry Regiment.'

'King Cobra' was to be the last brigade exercise, mainly because of the difficulty of supporting the brigade in the field with an *ad hoc* maintenance organisation gathered from other elements of the ANZUK Force.

Nevertheless, training continued apace at unit level. With the assistance of the Royal Air Force's 'Whirlwind' helicopters, 6 R.A.R. staged a display of the air assault techniques used in Vietnam. The remainder of the brigade, plus military guests from the Malaysian and Singaporean Armed Forces, watched the realistic demonstration with considerable interest. The Brigade Skill-at-Arms competition engendered a fierce rivalry and enhanced leadership at junior level as sections vied with each other over a testing course. Private Koia of 1 R.N.Z.I.R. did not reveal that he was seriously ill and, as a result of his exertions on the course, later died in hospital. The traditional Commonwealth Sports Week provided the usual interest and entertainment for all concerned. Every sub-unit in the brigade competed in every sport; some were knockout competitions, others – like golf – were judged on points. The tug-of-war final between 'The Blazers' and the 1st Royal New Zealand Infantry Regiment was somewhat of a 'David and Goliath' contest with 'David' (the British gunners) winning the first and last of three pulls against 'Goliath', the heavier Kiwi team.

In 1973 the Australian Government decided to withdraw its troops from Southeast Asia. A conference at Canberra in August considered the implications of establishing separate British and New Zealand national forces in Singapore after the Australian withdrawal. Certain administrative functions would be shared between the two nations; for example, it was proposed that New Zealand should provide dental and ration supply facilities whilst the British should handle civil labour and postal services. Brigadier Kennedy was 'double hatted', his second task being to head the New Zealand planning team in Singapore to decide on the composition and role of the future New Zealand Force Southeast Asia – which he would command on its formation.

During the period leading to the disbandment of the brigade, outstanding sporting contests were decided. The New Zealand battalion had dominated rugby in the Far East for some two decades, sending a team to Hong Kong to claim the Far East Championship. Since the Kiwi team was too strong for any unit team in the brigade, Lieutenant-Colonel Mace challenged the brigade commander to pick an allcomers team to play the R.N.Z.I.R. Singapore was scoured to secure the best possible players from the Navy, Army, Airforce and civilian organisations; two very useful forwards were found from teachers at the International School and the coach of Singapore's national rugby team was pressed into service. The match was played during a visit to Singapore by Major-General Sir Frank Hassett, the Deputy Chief of the Australian Army General Staff, a former commander of 28 Brigade, who watched the game with considerable interest – as did all the commanding officers of brigade units who supported the brigadier's team in the hope of seeing the New Zealanders humbled. However, the Kiwis were indomitable to the last, soundly trouncing the opposition to the joy of Colonel Mace.

As the life of 28 ANZUK Brigade drew towards its close, it was decided to mark the event with a formal parade. Brigadier Kennedy recalls the preparations:

'A formal parade for a brigade takes some organizing; nonetheless before our Aussie cobbers left it seemed appropriate that one should be held. Kangaw Airfield was the site, this stretched

*Final Parade of 28 ANZUK Brigade, Kangaw Airfield, Singapore October 1973.*
*Colour Parties of: 1st Bn. Royal New Zealand Infantry Regiment.*
*6th Bn. Royal Australian Regiment.*
*1st Bn. Royal Highland Fusiliers.*

(AWM BUC 73 295 MC)

between the Australian lines and Dieppe Barracks occupied by
1 R.N.Z.I.R. The Brigade Commander was the reviewing officer,
while the senior C.O., John Mace, commanded the parade. The
British R.S.M. from the Field Regiment, being the senior in the
brigade, was parade R.S.M. Giving orders to some 2,000 plus
troops requires either a stentorian voice or some technical assistance – we borrowed the throat microphones from the Singapore
Armed Forces which were used by them for the huge National
Day parades in the central city on the padang. With all those
soldiers, plus the regimental colours and guns of the Field Regiment on parade, it was a brave though rather sad sight and the
mood at the cocktail party that evening for all brigade officers,
wives and guests could only be described as sombre.'

This last parade was held on 8th October 1973 and was attended by the
ANZUK Force commander, Admiral Wells, together with the High Com-
missioners for Australia, Great Britain and New Zealand. Brigadier
Kennedy addressed the brigade during the parade:

'I would like to say "Well Done" to the units on parade; it is you
who make the brigade both a unique and a very fine formation
which I am privileged and very proud to command.

'It is nearly seventy-five years ago that Australia and New
Zealand sent contingents to South Africa where their soldiers
served with the British during the Boer War. Since that time men
of our three countries have soldiered together in many places and
in many different circumstances, some of them legendary like
Gallipoli, others less well known; for example, I saw earlier this
year a photograph of part of the Imperial Camel Corps Brigade
which was formed in December 1916 and served in the desert. It
was made up in the proportions of five-eighths Australian, one-
quarter British, and one-eighth New Zealand. (Think of the cost
sharing problems that that must have caused!) It has now therefore been for some three or four generations that whenever the
need has arisen – as it did in World War I and World War II and
again afterwards – that British, Australian and New Zealand soldiers have served alongside each other.

'But what is remarkable with our brigade is that it was formed
just on twenty-three years ago in 1951 and at that time contained
British, Australian and New Zealand units, just as it does today.

After the Korean War, the brigade moved to North Malaya (as the country was then called) and was rejoined by an Australian battalion in 1955 and a New Zealand battalion in 1957 and battalions from our three countries have served with the brigade ever since. It is also of note that for a large part of its history our brigade, or elements of it, have been on active operations – first in Korea, then the Malayan Emergency, followed by Confrontation, then rifle companies from the New Zealand battalion were detached from the brigade for service in Vietnam.

'Since the time of Oliver Cromwell it had been the lot of the soldier to do the bidding of his government and to do this without question. The departure of the Australian contingent from the brigade marks the end of an era which stretches back almost a quarter of a century during which the brigade has suffered many casualties in action, fluctuations in fortune and changes in name. Now we must say farewell to our Australian colleagues who have worked with us and for us as friends, striven with us as rivals, proud of the units to which they have belonged and keen that these should not be found wanting. To those who are to remain, I say "Close Ranks"; we are now moving into a new era with different challenges ahead.

'Nevertheless, this is the last formal parade planned for our brigade and we are sad to see it so; as also must be, I am sure, our many friends and former members who are spread around the world, and these include four officers who have served with the brigade and each has since reached the highest post in his national army. There are also many of us who have served more than once in this brigade and so have known it well for a long part of our military careers. But history never stands still, and as the times change, so must we.

'Within two months the Royal Highland Fusiliers will have gone but their place will be taken by another good battalion, the Gordons, and grouped with the Gordons will be elements from the gunners, the engineers and the aviation and signals squadrons, so that in them the traditions of 28 Commonwealth Brigade and 28 ANZUK Brigade will continue. The First Battalion Royal New Zealand Infantry Regiment has served in this theatre continuously since 1961 and is to remain, but with some changeover in personnel and under different command. But all the Australians are to leave us, though, we hope, in fact we expect to see Australian

units visiting us here in the future to train with us and so renew
those bonds that we have made over the years.

'Finally, may I say to the Australians of my own headquarters
and the signal squadron, to the gunners of the field regiment, to
the engineers in the field squadron, to the Australians in the
aviation squadron and finally to the major Australian unit, 6th
Battalion Royal Australian Regiment, that Australia has been
worthily represented in the calibre of the soldier, sub-unit and
major unit that has served your country and 28 Brigade so well
these past twenty years. We are sad that you, our comrades-in-
arms, are leaving us. It will not be the same without you. We are
glad to have had the privilege of serving with you and may we
wish you God speed and good fortune in your future endeavours.
Thank you.'

The final parade was a solemn and almost emotional occasion but, like all
28 Brigade operations, was performed efficiently with a minimum of fuss.
As Colonel Dudley Thornton, senior British infantry officer in the
ANZUK Force at that time, said to Brigadier Kennedy:

'It was a most impressive parade and its simplicity emphasized
the sad occasion it marked. The brigade commander's address so
rightly reminded us of the very close ties which have bound us
together as military men; the regard and respect we have for each
others' qualities, matters which are so intangible that the politi-
cian ignores them completely and is ready to destroy them without further thought. It is a sad day to see the ANZUK Brigade
cease to be an integrated formation. As was so rightly said, we
must "close our ranks" and look forward to the future making
certain that we do everything possible to maintain contact with
each other.'

The 1st Battalion of The Royal Highland Fusiliers bade farewell to Sin-
gapore in December on being relieved by the 1st Battalion of The Gordon
Highlanders, Lieutenant-Colonel D. G. B. Saunders. The Gordons had
spent a year in Borneo, during 1965 and 1966, and soon made themselves
at home in Nee Soon. The 1st Battalion of The Royal New Zealand
Infantry Regiment, which was to remain in Singapore as the New Zealand
National Force, was visited by the Prime Minister of New Zealand in
December but, as Brigadier Kennedy noted: 'He was obviously a sick

man, besides looking tired and jaded; sadly within six months he had died.' 28 ANZUK Field Regiment was disbanded with the withdrawal of the Australian Field Battery and its supporting elements leaving 1 (The Blazers) Light Battery, which was retitled as an independent battery on 14th December. The 6th Battalion of The Royal Australian Regiment left the brigade during the same month together with the other Australian sub-units and personnel who had been integrated into the brigade structure.

28 ANZUK Brigade ceased to exist on 31st January 1974 and Brigadier Kennedy relinquished his command to Brigadier G. D. J. R. Russell, C.B.E., who assumed command of 28 Infantry Brigade on 1st February 1974. After some twenty-three years as an integrated Commonwealth formation, the brigade reverted to a British national command consisting of one infantry battalion, one artillery battery and supporting sub-units.

*Brigadier Kennedy (left) presents a plaque bearing the badges of the units of 28 ANZUK Brigade to Brigadier Russell (right) on the formation of 28 Infantry Brigade, Singapore, February 1974.*

(Brigadier Kennedy)

Brigadier Russell was also the Senior British Officer Singapore for joint service matters.

Despite this national fragmentation, the Commonwealth spirit and links engendered over such a long period were too strong to be broken at a stroke. Integrated training involving the three services of the three nations continued. Brigadier Russell recalls:

> 'As an example of this, the last brigade exercise deployment, which took place in the State of Johore in April 1975 involved two British battalions, the 1st Gordon Highlanders and the 3rd Battalion of The Parachute Regiment (which had visited Malaysia on a previous training tour in 1973), the 1st Battalion of The Royal New Zealand Infantry Regiment from Singapore, two infantry companies flown up from Australia, three S.A.S. Squadrons from Australia, New Zealand and the United Kingdom and integrated supporting arms and logistics based on 28 Brigade units. Regrettably by the time of that exercise the decision had been taken to withdraw all British standing forces from the Far East. The final demise of 28 Brigade was painful but quick with all field forces departing by November that year. Perhaps the spirit and economic limitations of 28 Brigade in its closing days can best be illustrated by the Commanding Officer of the 1st Royal New Zealand Infantry Regiment reporting to the Brigade Commander:
>
> "I regret to say I have a tiger in my deep freeze shot by one of my soldiers."
>
> "That is a national affair. You go and explain to the Sultan!"
>
> "Can we make it a Commonwealth affair?"
>
> "All right – but you will pay the fine."'

There is no doubt that the ANZUK Force, although never involved in operations during the short period of its life, continued to demonstrate the commitment of the Commonwealth nations to the stability and defence of Southeast Asia. This was particularly important at a time when the United States forces were withdrawing from Vietnam. The continued presence of the national commanded contingents – the Royal Australian Air Force at Butterworth in Province Wellesley, Northern Malaysia, the New Zealand battalion in Singapore and the miniscule British 28 Brigade in Singapore – was evidence of Commonwealth concern. However, the change of British government in 1974 decided the fate of what was left of 28 Brigade and it was disbanded in November 1975. The barracks at Nee Soon were handed over to the Singapore Armed Forces and the British departed, leaving the New Zealand national force, the 1st R.N.Z.I.R., as the sole survivors of the Commonwealth Brigade in the Far East until its departure in 1989.

# In Retrospect

The Commonwealth Infantry Brigade was formed originally as a combined contribution to the United Nations by the land forces of five independent Commonwealth Nations – Australia, Great Britain, Canada, the Republic of India and New Zealand. Great Britain and Canada increased the size of their forces within the First Commonwealth Division although the Commonwealth Brigade more or less retained its original composition throughout the Korean War. After the Armistice, the Indian element withdrew to join the Indian Force placed at the disposal of the United Nations and the Commonwealth Division was diminished, dispersed and disbanded.

The reformation of the Commonwealth Brigade in Malaya was another example of co-operation between Commonwealth Nations, including the Federation of Malaysia, although the brigade also had a commitment to a military alliance outside the Commonwealth. In addition to their Southeast Asia Treaty Organization role, Australia and New Zealand were also members of the Australia, New Zealand and United States Pact (ANZUS) and their participation in the Vietnam War was a divisive factor which, when combined with Britain's abandonment of an 'East of Suez' presence, presaged the demise of an effective combined Commonwealth military force.

Even so, five years after the disbandment of 28 ANZUK Brigade in Singapore, Commonwealth land forces were to operate together as the Rhodesian Monitoring Force in another Commonwealth territory. The deputy commander of the Monitoring Force noted that one of the lessons from that operation was the ease with which the Commonwealth armies involved could merge together and work as one – a commentary on the years of combined training and standardization experienced in the

Commonwealth Brigade and the continued exchanges between the armies concerned.

Since the creation of Zimbabwe, there have been other Commonwealth crises in which Commonwealth military forces have operated efficiently together, in Namibia particularly. During the Falklands War, the Royal New Zealand Navy offered a warship to relieve the Royal Naval patrol off the coast of Belize, another Commonwealth country. There have been other occasions when a combined military force might have been employed within Commonwealth Nations; for example, Cyprus, Uganda and Fiji. In a turbulent world where demands for United Nations troops to act as peace-keepers or observers increase from year to year, there may still be a place for a combined Commonwealth contribution. Members of Commonwealth land forces have been deployed to supervise the delicate settlements in what was Yugoslavia and Cambodia and, almost certainly, there will be further calls for military forces to undertake such operations in an ever-changing world of disintegration and reformation.

Despite their various political differences, the member nations of the Commonwealth still have much in common and share many military procedures and methods. This shared and recognized military expertise could be put to use by the ear-marking of national units which could be embodied to form an emergency 'fire-brigade' in response to United Nations request for forces, either within the Commonwealth itself or elsewhere in the world. The concept of a lightly equipped, air-portable brigade-size formation – as proved in Malaya and Singapore – would be an ideal force for immediate deployment; the despatch of individual companies from Terendak to Mauritius in 1968 illustrated the effectiveness of units trained and ready for quick deployment.

Obviously, national political attitudes dictate the use of member nations' forces but there have been occasions when some, if not all, of the Commonwealth Nations have acted in concert. It is quite possible that such an occasion could arise in the future and, once again, a combined Commonwealth military force might take to the field, whatever its role. The lessons of Korea, Malaya, Borneo and even Rhodesia could still be of some use.

The Commonwealth Brigade had several significant advantages over other international organizations: a common language, a shared loyalty, similar cultural backgrounds and history and almost identical military procedures and organizations. Despite, or possibly because of, these advantages the national components of the brigade gained an added pride and awareness of their identities. Far from being a divisive factor, this healthy national rivalry ensured that the units of the brigade gave of their best and worked together as an efficient team. The *esprit de corps* of the brigade had far more edge than comparative national formations – or even British brigades composed of English, Scots and Irish units. Evidence of the pride and enthusiasm engendered by membership of the brigade was demonstrated by the many officers and soldiers who returned voluntarily for a second and even third tour of duty. Another important factor was that in its early days the brigade and its component units were commanded by officers who had learned their trade on the battlefields of the Second World War; many of the warrant-officers and senior sergeants also had such practical experience of war-time soldiering. Their knowledge and skill was passed to their successors who added the experiences of Korea, Malaya, Borneo and even Vietnam to this fund of expertise.

In many ways the Commonwealth Brigade resembled the family atmosphere of a good regiment. Several brigade commanders had commanded battalions in the brigade; battalion commanders had often served as company commanders in the brigade's battalions; many of the staff officers had similar previous service in the brigade and this continuity extended to the sergeants' messes and the junior ranks clubs. Of great importance was the fact that such service had been in a formation which had been on active service for most of its existence.

The Commonwealth Brigade proved that a multi-national force was effective during the Korean War, the Malayan Emergency and Confrontation Operations. Service in the brigade provided valuable practical experience of the craft of soldiering for Australian, British and New Zealand soldiers. As Brigadier Kennedy remarked during the final parade of the ANZUK Brigade, four of the brigade's former senior officers subsequently achieved the highest posts in their national armies and many others rose to senior national appointments. Junior officers, non-commissioned officers and soldiers also gained from their service in this operational brigade and, for the Australian and New Zealand elements of the brigade, the practical experience stood them in good stead during the Vietnam conflict.

Above all, service in the Commonwealth Brigade engendered a comradeship that transcended national differences. In the comparatively small world of professional soldiering, many of the friendships first struck in the Commonwealth Brigade have lasted and flourished, revived by military exchanges, shared training and exercises, meetings and conferences and ex-servicemens' associations. A genuine bond still exists between all those who served together in this unique formation. It is no exaggeration to claim that service in the Commonwealth Brigade gave its members something extra.

# Commanders
# of
# 28 Commonwealth Brigade

## Korea

| | |
|---|---|
| Brig. G. Taylor, C.B.E., D.S.O.x, K.H.S. | April 1951 - October 1951 |
| Lt. Col. (A/Brig.) J. F. M. MacDonald, D.S.O., O.B.E. | October 1951 - June 1952 |
| Brig T. J. Daly, C.B.E. D.S.O. (Australia) | June 1952 - March 1953 |
| Brig J. G. N. Wilton, D.S.O., O.B.E. (Australia) | March 1953 - February 1954 |
| Brig. I. T. Murdoch, O.B.E. (Australia) | February 1954 - August 1954 |

## Malaya

| | |
|---|---|
| Brig. P. N. M. Moore, D.S.O.xx, M.C., B.A. | September 1955 - July 1958 |
| Brig. H. J. Mogg, C.B.E., D.S.O.x | July 1958 - November 1960 |
| Brig. F. G. Hassett, D.S.O., M.V.O., O.B.E. (Australia) | November 1960 - October 1962 |
| Brig. R. B. Dawson, C.B., D.S.O. (New Zealand) | October 1962 - October 1964 |
| Brig. T. D. R. McMeekin, O.B.E. | October 1964 - January 1967 |
| Brig. P. L. Tancred (Australia) | January 1967 - March 1969 |
| Brig. R. M. Gurr, O.B.E. (New Zealand) | March 1969 - March 1971 |

Brig. M. J. H. Walsh, C.B., D.S.O.        March 1971 - November 1971

## 28 ANZUK Brigade

Brig. M. J. H. Walsh, C.B., D.S.O.        November 1971 - March 1973
Brig. M. R. Kennedy, M.B.E.              March 1973 - January 1974
(New Zealand)

# Units of 28 Commonwealth Brigade

*Artillery*

Great Britain   6 Light Regiment, R.A.
'H' (Ramsay's Troop) Light Battery
'V' Light Battery
132 (The Bengal Rocket Troop) Medium Battery

14 Light Regiment, R.A.
1 (The Blazers) Light Battery
5 (Gibraltar 1779-1783) Light Battery
13 (Martinique 1809) Medium Battery

26 Light Regiment, R.A.
16 (Sandham's Company) Light Battery
17 (Corunna) Light Battery

28 Light Regiment, R.A.
1 (The Blazers) Light Battery

45 Light Regiment, R.A.
70 Light Battery
170 (Imjin) Medium Battery
176 (Abu Klea) Light Battery

Australia   'A' Field Battery, R.A.A.
101 Field Battery, R.A.A.
102 Field Battery, R.A.A.

103 Field Battery, R.A.A.
105 Field Battery, R.A.A.
106 Field Battery, R.A.A.
107 Field Battery, R.A.A.
108 Field Battery, R.A.A.

New Zealand    16 Field Regiment, R.N.Z.A.
161 Battery ('P')
162 Battery ('Q')
163 Battery ('R')

*Engineers*

Great Britain    9 Field Squadron, R.E.
11 Independent Field Squadron, R.E.
12 Field Squadron, R.E.
28 Field Squadron, R.E. and R.A.E.
368 Postal Unit, R.E.

Australia    1 Field Troop, R.A.E.
2 Field Troop, R.A.E.
4 Field Troop, R.A.E.
24 Support Troop, R.A.E.

New Zealand    Engr Section, R.N.Z.E.

*Signals*    28 Signal Squadron, R Signals and R Aust. Signals
208 Commonwealth Signal Squadron, R Signals and
    R Aust. Signals

*Infantry*

Great Britain    1st Bn. Scots Guards
9 Company Irish Guards
1st Bn. The Royal Warwickshire Regiment (6th)
1st Bn. The Royal Fusiliers (7th)
1st Bn. The Royal Lincolnshire Regiment (10th)
1st Bn. The 3rd East Anglian Regiment (16th, 44th &
    56th)
1st Bn. The Royal Scots Fusiliers (21st)

1st Bn. The Royal Highland Fusiliers (21st, 71st & 74th)
1st Bn. The King's Own Scottish Borderers (25th)
1st Bn. The Essex Regiment (44th & 56th)
1st Bn. The Loyal Regiment (47th & 81st)
1st Bn. The King's Own Yorkshire Light Infantry (51st & 105th)
1st Bn. The King's Shropshire Light Infantry (53rd & 85th)
1st Bn. The Middlesex Regiment (57th & 77th)
1st Bn. The Durham Light Infantry (68th & 106th)
1st Bn. The Gordon Highlanders (75th & 92nd)

| | |
|---|---|
| Canada | 2nd Bn. Princess Patricia's Canadian Light Infantry |
| Australia | 1st Bn. The Royal Australian Regiment |
| | 2nd Bn. The Royal Australian Regiment |
| | 3rd Bn. The Royal Australian Regiment |
| | 4th Bn. The Royal Australian Regiment |
| | 6th Bn. The Royal Australian Regiment |
| | 8th Bn. The Royal Australian Regiment |
| New Zealand | 1st Bn. The New Zealand Regiment |
| | 2nd Bn. The New Zealand Regiment |
| | 1st Bn. The Royal New Zealand Infantry Regiment |

*Air*

7 Reconnaissance Flight, A.A.C.
28 Aviation Squadron

*Transport*

| | |
|---|---|
| Great Britain | 3 Company, R.A.S.C. |
| Australia | Transport Platoon, R.A.A.S.C. |
| New Zealand | 10 Transport Company, R.N.Z.A.S.C. |

*Medical*

| | |
|---|---|
| Great Britain | 16 Commonwealth Field Ambulance, R.A.M.C. & R.A.A.M.C. |
| India | 60 Indian Parachute Field Ambulance, I.A.M.C. |

*Ordnance*          28 Ordnance Field Park, R.A.O.C. & R.A.A.O.C.

*Electrical &*
*Mechanical*       2 Infantry Workshops, R.E.M.E. & R.A.E.M.E.
                   16 Infantry Workshops, R.E.M.E.

*Provost*          28 Commonwealth Provost Unit, R.M.P. & R.A.M.P.C.

*Dental*

Australia          32 Army Dental Unit, R.A.A.D.C.

*Intelligence*

Great Britain      22 Intelligence Platoon (Brigade), Int Corps

# Contributors

| | |
|---|---|
| Brigadier R. J. Andrews, C.B.E. | New Zealand |
| Lieutenant-Colonel R. G. Atkinson, O.B.E., M.C. | Great Britain |
| Mr. J. E. Baker | Australia |
| Colonel J. P. St. C. Ballenden, O.B.E., M.C. | Great Britain |
| Mr. Beh Cheng Chuah | Malaysia |
| Brigadier B. L. Bogle | Australia |
| Brigadier J. Burns, D.S.O., O.B.E. | New Zealand |
| Mr. H. Chamberlain | Great Britain |
| Major P. M. Chambers | Great Britain |
| Colonel D. A. Chinn, M.B.E. | Australia |
| Brigadier M. H. H. Collins, M.B.E. | Great Britain |
| Major D. J. R. Counsell | Great Britain |
| Lieutenant-General Sir Thomas J. Daly, K.B.E., C.B., D.S.O. | Australia |
| Brigadier M. J. Dudman, L.V.O., O.B.E. | New Zealand |
| Colonel C. A. East, O.B.E. | Australia |
| Captain H. B. Eaton | Great Britain |
| Major J. Grant | Great Britain |
| Brigadier R. M. Gurr, O.B.E. | New Zealand |
| General Sir Francis Hassett, A.C., K.B.E., C.B., D.S.O., M.V.O. | Australia |
| Major-General R. D. P. Hassett, C.B., C.B.E. | New Zealand |
| Lieutenant-Colonel J. B. Henderson | Great Britain |
| Major Sir Richard Hill, M.B.E. | Great Britain |
| Major-General R. M. Jerram, C.B., M.B.E. | Great Britain |
| Brigadier M. R. Kennedy, M.B.E. | New Zealand |
| Mr. R. L. Kirley | Australia |

| | |
|---|---|
| Mr. P. Knowles | Australia |
| Mr. R. Larby | Great Britain |
| Brigadier R. N. N. Lydekker, C.B.E. | Great Britain |
| Major D. I. A. Mack | Great Britain |
| Major W. Meldrum | New Zealand |
| General Sir H. John Mogg, G.C.B., C.B.E., D.S.O.x, D.L. | Great Britain |
| Brigadier P. N. M. Moore, D.S.O.xx, M.C., B.A. | Great Britain |
| Brigadier W. R. K. Morrison | New Zealand |
| Major-General I. T. Murdoch, C.B.E. | Australia |
| Lieutenant-Colonel A. J. Pembroke, M.C. | Australia |
| Colonel D. M. Ramsey | Australia |
| Brigadier G. D. J. R. Russell, C.B.E. | Great Britain |
| Mr. G. Scott | Canada |
| Colonel J. R. Stone, D.S.O., M.C., C.D. | Canada |
| Brigadier P. L. Tancred, C.B.E. | Australia |
| Brigadier G. Taylor, C.B.E., D.S.O.x, K.H.S. | Great Britain |
| Mr. D. J. Troedel | Australia |
| Major-General M. J. H. Walsh, C.B., D.S.O. | Great Britain |

# Bibliography

*Publications*

*Our Men in Korea* by Eric Linklater, Her Majesty's Stationery Office, London, 1952

*The First Commonwealth Division* by Brig. C. N. Barclay, C.B.E., D.S.O., Gale & Polden Ltd., Aldershot, 1954

*With The Australians in Korea* by Norman Bartlett, Australian War Memorial, Canberra, A.C.T., 1954

*Korea, The Commonwealth at War* by Tim Carew, Cassell & Company Ltd., London, 1967

*The Undeclared War* by Harold James and Denis Sheil-Small, Leo Cooper Ltd., London, 1971

*Australia in the Korean War 1950-53*, Volume II, *Combat Operations* by Robert O'Neill, The Australian War Memorial and the Australian Government Publishing Service, Canberra, 1985

*Send Port & Pyjamas* by Dan Raschen, Buckland Publications Ltd., London, 1987

*British Forces in the Korean War*, edited by Ashley Cunningham-Boothe and Peter Farrar, The British Korean Veterans Association, 1988

*Marks of Courage*, edited by Ashley Cunningham-Boothe, Korvet Publishing & Distribution, Leamington Spa, 1991

*Regimental Histories and Official Accounts*

*28 British Commonwealth Brigade in Korea*, Lt. C. W. Crossland, The West Yorkshire Regiment (P.W.O.), 1951

*Campaign Korea 1950-1953 Schedule of Battles, Actions, and Engagements,* War Office Battles Nomenclature Committee, 1957

*The History of the United Nations Forces in the Korean War,* Volume II, The Ministry of National Defence, The Republic of Korea, 10 December 1973

*16th Field Regiment 1950-1953,* Lt. Col. J. A. Pountney, Royal New Zealand Artillery

*The Borderers in Korea,* Maj. Gen. J. F. M. MacDonald, C.B., D.S.O., O.B.E., Martin's Printing Works Ltd, Berwick-upon-Tweed

*Regimental Standing Orders,* The Royal Australian Regiment, Directorate of Infantry, Department of Defence, Canberra A.C.T. 2600

*The History of 66 Australian Infantry Battalion and 2nd Battalion The Royal Australian Regiment,* Lieutenant O. J. O'Brien, 2nd Battalion The Royal Australian Regiment, September 1960

*Army Operations in Malaya, 1947-1960,* Riley Sunderland, The Rand Corporation, Santa Monica, California, September 1964

*The Royal Scots Fusiliers History, 1919-1959,* R.H.Q. Royal Highland Fusiliers

*The Last Decade, The Tenth Foot, Royal Lincolnshire Regiment 1950-1960,* Geoffrey Moore, Buckden, Huntingdon, 1981

*101st Field Battery, Royal Australian Artillery, A Short History* by Maj. J. H. Phillips and Lt. D. M. Forster

'Peacetime Soldiering in Malaya' by Captain J. Fletcher, G.M., Royal Australian Infantry, *Australian Army Journal,* No 163, December, 1962

'On Active Service in Malaya 1962' by Lt. Col. A. B. Stretton, M.B.E., 2 R.A.R., *Australian Army Journal,* Melbourne, Victoria, 1963

'Operations in Borneo' by Major C. M. A. R. Roberts, 1/10 G.R., *Australian Army Journal,* No. 194, July, 1965

'Artillery Operations in Borneo' by Major D. Quinn, Royal Australian Artillery, *Australian Army Journal,* No 243, August, 1969

*A Short History of the 1st Battalion Royal New Zealand Infantry Regiment,* Capt. C. E. Brock, R.N.Z.I.R., Singapore, 31 July 1971

*The New Zealand Army, A History from the 1840s to the 1980s,* compiled by Major M. R. Wicksteed, R.N.Z.A., Army General Staff, Wellington, September 1982

'Interoperability: A.B.C.A. Operations Since World War II', Major-General P. C. Gration, O.B.E., *Army Research, Development & Acquisition Magazine,* U.S.A., January-February 1982

*Regimental Journals*

*The Gunner*, Artillery House, 58 Woolwich Common, Woolwich, London
SE18
*Sapper*, Regimental Journal of the Corps of Royal Engineers
*Scots Guards Magazine*, R.H.Q., Scots Guards, Birdcage Walk, London
SW1
*The Wasp and the Eagle*, Regimental Journal of The 3rd East Anglian
Regiment (16th/44th Foot)
*The Journal of The Royal Highland Fusiliers* (Princess Margaret's Own
Glasgow and Ayrshire Regiment), R.H.Q., 518 Sauchiehall Street,
Glasgow G2 3LT
*The Eagle*, The Journal of The Essex Regiment
*The Bugle*, Regimental Journal of The King's Own Yorkshire Light Infan-
try
*The King's Shropshire Light Infantry Regimental Journal*, Sir John Moore
Barracks, Copthorne, Shrewsbury
*The Durham Light Infantry Regimental Journal*
*The Tiger and Sphinx*, The Regimental Journal of The Gordon Highland-
ers
*Duty First*, Royal Australian Regiment Association
*The Minden Post*, The Brunei Press for 1st Bn. K.O.Y.L.I., 1963-1964
*The Bukit Bulletin*, 19 Army Education Centre, Terendak Camp, Malaya
*The Morning Calm*, Journal of the British Korean Veterans Association
*Chopsticks*, The Official Journal of the Korea and South East Asia Forces
Association of Australia

*Press Reports*

*The Japan News*, 26th June 1951 – 'Commonwealth Brigade Had Busy
Two Months'
*The Daily Telegraph*, 26th November 1952 – 'London Troops Break
Through Chinese Ring'
*The Evening News*, 24th March 1953 – 'Then Came Pimlico'
*Daily Express*, 21st April 1953 – 'Hero Hodkinson, D.C.M.'
*Singapore Standard*, 23rd August 1958 – 'Seven Reds Wiped Out'
*The Straits Times* (Singapore), 23rd August 1958 – 'Forces Bag Eight
Bandits; Three Quit'
*The Times of Malaya and Straits Echo*, 23rd August 1958 – '11 More
Reds Are Eliminated In Op Ginger Area'

*Singapore Standard*, 17th October 1958 – 'Eight Terrorists Cry "Surrender"'
*The Times of Malaya and Straits Echo*, 17th October 1958 – 'Biggest Success In Op "Ginger"'
*The Bolton Guardian & News*, December 1958 – 'The Loyals in Malaya'
*The Yorkshire Post*, 1964 – 'In Brunei With The K.O.Y.L.I.' by Alfred M. Lee
*Daily Mirror* (Australia), 16th September 1968 – 'Korean Battle Studded Mount With Enemy Dead'
*The Daily Mail*, 7th November 1987 – 'What Poppy Day Means to a Virgin Soldier Like Me'

*Other Sources*

The Ministry of Defence Library, London
The Imperial War Museum, London
The Australian War Memorial, Canberra A.C.T.
*Soldier Magazine*, Aldershot
Directorate of Infantry, Department of Defence, Canberra A.C.T.
Defence Headquarters, Wellington
R.H.Q. Princess Patricia's Canadian Light Infantry, Calgary

# Index

(P indicates photograph)

| | | | |
|---|---|---|---|
| A.A.C. | 184, 238 | Antarctica | 87 |
| Abdul Malek | 286 | Anthony, Mr. | 223 |
| Abdul Rahman | 166, 171 | ANZUK Force | 299, 300, 301, 305, |
| Abdul Razak | 212 | | 312, 313, 320, P |
| Abyssinia | 3 | ANZUS Pact | 322 |
| Acar Sirri, Gen. | 127 | Applin A. G., Cpl. | 72 |
| Adams, 21t. | 63, 79 | Arakan Lines | 236 |
| Aden | 260 | Arezzo | 4 |
| Ah Chok | 197, 198 | Aris M. A., Lt. | 184, 187 |
| Ah Go Tsai | 181 | Arkansas | 92 |
| Ahtieu | 246 | Armies: | |
| Ah Yoong | 192 | Chinese People's | 7, 88 |
| Aitken D. J., Lt. Col. | 212, 220 | Indonesian | 250, 257, 269 |
| A.K.C. | 221 | Malaysian Fed. | 232, 241 |
| *Albion* H.M.S. | 246 | Malay Races | 188 |
| Alexander, Lord | 97–8, P | Polish | 311 |
| Alexander, Sgt. | 273 | Vietnamese | 230, 261, 285 |
| Alexandra, Princess | 293 | Asahan | 249, 277 |
| Alice Springs | 135, 136 | Asahi | 87, 93, 98, 115 |
| Allen, Sig. | 228 P | Ashby, Pte. | 275 |
| Alo anak Empang | 184, 185 | Ashcroft, Sgt. | 256 |
| Alor Star | 163, 240 | Askew, Cpl. | 186 |
| Alston-Roberts-West | 106, 113, 134, | Assaye | 313 |
| | 147, 152, 197 | Atkinson, Maj. | 124, 133, 138 |
| Anaru, Lt. | 195 | Austin M., Lt. Col. | 105, 121, 154, P |
| Anau anak Genosi | 197 | Austin, B. Q. M. S. | 240 |
| *Anchor* | 246 | Austrian | 311 |
| Anderson C. Sgt. | 187 | Axe, Cpl. | 103 |
| Anderson D. N., Lt. Col. | 298 | Ayer Panas | 265 |
| Andrews D. G. H., Lt. | 176 | Ayrshire | 308 |
| Andrews R., Maj. | 303, 305, 309, 311 | Azarhari | 245, 246 |
| Anjang bin Pandak | 192 | | |

Badcoe P., Maj. 285
Bahau 263
Bah Payani 192
Balai Ringin 279
Baldwin Lines 236
Baldy 61, 64, 65
Baling 166–9
Ballenden J. P., Lt. Col. 47, 48, 286, 289, 290, 292, 295, P
Bancroft Maj. 104
Bangkok 245, 285
Bang Nong Phok 290
Bareo 252, 256, 259
Barlow Jim, Lt. 197, P
Barlow W., Lt. Col. 27, 40, 45, 92, 97, 106, 157, P
Barrow, D. J., Lt Col. 212, 214
Batteries
  1 Blazers 294, 296, 298, 301, 302, 314, 319
  5 Gibraltar 294, 295
  13 Martinique 294
  16 Sandhams 237, 238
  17 Corunna 237, 238
  70 Light 248, 249, 257, 258, 269, 277, 286
  A 100 R.A.A. 187, 206, 211, 212, 274, P
  101 R.A.A. 212, 214, 231
  102 R.A.A. 249, 257, 266, 272, 273, P
  103 R.A.A. 231, 237, 238, 244, 248, 249, 285
  105 R.A.A. 162, 164, 166, 168–70, 176, 184, 185, 187, 274
  106 R.A.A. 296, 301, 303
  107 R.A.A. 286, 294, 296
  132 Bengal Rocket 277, 294
  161 R.N.Z.A 33, 285
  162 R.N.Z.A. 33
  163 R.N.Z.A. 33
  170 Imjin 248, 251, 257, 258, 270, 273, 275
  176 Abu Klea 248, 260, 269
  H Ramsays 277, 294
  V Light 277
Batu Arang 280
Batu Lintang 270
Batu Potong 256
Bau 251, 273, 277
Baxter, Gp. Capt. 161, 171
Beale, P. Lt. 273
Beds & Herts 212
Beh Cheng-Chuah Mr. 222–3
Belait 246
Belize 323
Bella 273, 285
Bellevue Zoo 211
Belville Pte 122
Bennett F. S. W., Sgt. 217
Bertha 273, 285
Betty Grable 143
Biawak 269
Bingham R. C., Mr. 162
Black, Cpl. 51
Blyth, 2lt. 70
Boer War 260, 316
Bogle B., Maj. 162, 165, 176, 179, 185, P
Boon, Mr. 223
Bordon Camp 3
Borley, Sgt. 264, P
Borneo 184, 214, 245, 250, 252, 255, 258–61, 263, 265, 266, 269, 270, 273–77, 279–81, 290, 296, 299, 318, 323
Borrow D. J., Lt. Col. 212, 214
Borwick, Lt. 45, 81
Bourne G., Gen. 163, 166, 170, 171
Bowler, Lcpl. 186
Boyd E., Lt. 113
Bredin, Lt. Col. 165
Bridgford, Gen. 75, P
Brimmel, Mr. 166
Brisbane 287
Britannia Camp 146
*Britannia* R.Y. 305
Brodie, Brig. 12
Brooke J., Lt. Col. 291, 292, 296, P
Brooks, Lt. 69
Brown, 2lt. 275
Brown, Cpl. 197
Brown Knoll 51, 70, 72

| | | | |
|---|---|---|---|
| Bruas | 208 | Celebes | 250 |
| Bruce-Merrie D. L., Capt. | 197–8 | *Centaur* H.M.S. | 260 |
| Bruce W. J., Sgt. | 135 | Ceylon | 187 |
| Brunei | 245–7, 249, 252, | Chadwell A. E., Rev. | 116 |
| | 259, 305 | Chadwick T., Maj. | 207 |
| Bryan Blackshear, Gen. | 12, 21 | Chambers, Lt. | 77, 79, 80 |
| Buchanan, Lcpl. | 69 | Chandler, Pte. | 256 |
| Buddha | 229, 287 | Chan Fei | 203 |
| Bukit Bahru | 236 | Chang Chung-Chieh | 83 |
| Bukit Tapah | 260 | Changi | 227, 293 |
| Burdett F., Pte. | 209 | Chan Hong | 192 |
| Burini E. B., Capt. | 110 | Chard M., Maj. | 112 |
| Burke, Brig. | 7, 8, 10, 11 | Charlie | 247 |
| Burnett, Pte. | 46 | Charumul | 84–7, 94 |
| Burns J., Lt. Col. | 118, 119, 143, | Chelsea | 87, 285 |
| | 146, 149, 154 | Chemor | 173, 176 |
| Burrows I. H., Maj. | 265 | Cheong Martha | 223 |
| Butler, Lt. | 45 | Cherbourg | 3 |
| Butterworth | 161, 162, 166, 169, | Chidwick, Lt. | 37 |
| | 171, 173, 177, 185, | China | 233 |
| | 193, 300, 320 | Chinn, Lt. | 174, 182 |
| Byers, Lt. | 274 | Chin Peng | 166 |
| | | Chojong Chon | 11–13 |
| Cabal Manuel, Lt. Gen. | 217–18, P | Chongchon | 6 |
| Caine Michael | 129 | Chongju | 6 |
| Camberley | 290 | Chonma-San | 18–19 |
| Cambodia | 159, 217, 323 | Chuam-Ni | 6 |
| Cameron Highlands | 219–20 | C. of E. | 242 |
| Campbell, Maj. | 245 | Church J. M., Maj. | 263, P |
| Camp Casey | 115, 119, 120, | Christie J. K. Pte. | 128 |
| | 123, 124, P | Clark, Lt. | 50–1 |
| Camp Five | 147 | Clark, Pte. | 47 |
| Canada | 322 | Clarke W. L., Gnr. | 119 |
| Canberra | 234, 236, 314 | Clauson A., Pte. | 200 |
| Canungra | 162 | Clayden S. W., Comm. | 300, 301, P |
| Canterbury | 279 | Cleaver, Lt. | 80, 81 |
| Caribbean | 311 | Clifton, Pte. | 22 |
| Carrington, S. M. | 197 | Clough, 2lt. | 80 |
| Carrol, Cpl. | 192 | Coad B. C., Brig. | 6 |
| Carter E. C. D., 2lt. | 251 | Cobar | 136 |
| Casey R. G., Mr. | 165 | Coldstream Gds. | 265 |
| Cashman, Father | 149 | Cole G. D., Maj. | 188 |
| Cashman, Cpl. | 137 | Cole R. F. H., Maj. | 296 |
| Cassels J., Gen. | 29, 55, 60, 75, 91, | Collins M. B. H., Maj. | 194 |
| | 97, 103, 106, 107, | Collins, Gen. | 103, P |
| | 186, 197, 198, 206, | Colombo Camp | 182 |
| | 224, 270, 280, P | Congo | 291 |
| Cassino | 4 | Cook P. J., Capt. | 99 |

| | |
|---|---|
| Cooper B. C., Sgt. | 140, 144 |
| Corcoran J. H., Sgt. | 113, 223 |
| Coster Peter | 212 |
| Cottle, Maj. | 18, 41, 45, 81–4 |
| Cotton G. J. S., Maj. | 179, 181 |
| Cottonbalers | 86, 151 |
| Counsell D., Maj. | 277, 294 |
| Crapp T., Gnr. | 133 |
| Crete | 50, 52 |
| Critchley T. C., Mr. | 267, P |
| Crockford R. M., Lcpl. | 141, 144 |
| Cromwell Oliver | 164, 317 |
| Cross B. S. M. | 240 |
| Crown Camp | 275 |
| Crown Inn | 236, 242 |
| Cunningham, 2lt. | 136 |
| Cunningham, Pte. | 256 |
| Currie, W. C., Lt. Col. | 297 |
| Cypriots | 311 |
| Cyprus | 323 |
| | |
| Daly T. J., Brig. | 98, 103, 107, 113, 120, 121, P |
| Danby, Cpl. | 181 |
| Davey, Pte. | 22 |
| Davidson, K., Maj. | 161 |
| Dawson R. B., Brig. | 245, 248, 260, 261, 263, 266, 281, P |
| Deedes M., Lt. | 247 |
| Deleno-Osborne, Lt. Col. | 172 |
| Devenney P., Cpl. | 93 |
| Dickinson J., R.S.M. | 150 |
| Dien Bien Phu | 159 |
| Dieppe Barracks | 298, 300, 304, 310, 316 |
| Dillon, Lcpl. | 192 |
| *Dilwara* H. M. T.     . | 182 |
| Docker, R., Maj. | 73 |
| Donelly, Cpl. | 209 |
| Donoghue C. P., Maj. | 110 |
| Drabsch D. A., Lt. Col. | 298 |
| Dracula | 150 |
| Duffair | 273, 276 |
| Duley V., Capt.     . | 118, 119 |
| Duncan, Maj. | 19, 43, 61 |
| Dyaks | 279 |

| | |
|---|---|
| Eadsforth, Pte. | 78 |
| Earl M. J. T., 2lt. | 182 |
| East C., Lt. Col. | 193, 194, 201, 206, 207, 212, 214, 218, 223, 280–4, 286, 290, 291, P |
| East Manong Cell | 195 |
| Egypt | 4 |
| Elcomb, Maj. | 249 |
| Elephant & Castle | 128 |
| Enteba | 246 |
| E. & O. Hotel | 185 |
| Ettamoggah | 266 |
| Evans, Maj. | 22 |
| Evans G., Gen. | 4 |
| Evison J., Capt. | 70 |
| Exercises: | |
|   Air Boon Choo | 260 |
|   Arunta Pack I | 231 |
|   Aurora | 285 |
|   Bersatu Padu | 298 |
|   Blue Angel | 230–1 |
|   Charity Angel | 239 |
|   Crowning Glory | 295 |
|   Darling Point | 295 |
|   Dhanarajata | 248 |
|   Faith Angel | 231 |
|   Full Swing | 309 |
|   Gedgeley | 292 |
|   Highland Fling | 277 |
|   Hope Angel | 239 |
|   Jalan Ulu | 305 |
|   Jumping Wallaby | 296 |
|   Kangaroo Hop | 249 |
|   King Cobra | 312, 313 |
|   Lion's Roar | 272 |
|   Long Look | 312 |
|   Maiden Flight | 217 |
|   May Bug | 260 |
|   Piping Shrike | 287, 288 |
|   Quick Step | 280 |
|   Rabbit Punch | 240 |
|   Rajata | 227–9 |
|   Raven | 260, 263 |
|   Red Angel | 239 |
|   Sheer Hell | 296 |
|   Thunderbolt | 277 |
|   Trinity Angel | 231 |

Trumpeter 240, 241
Zigzag II 249
Eyles L. A., Maj. 263, P

Faiz Akhbar Khan 259
Falklands 58, 323
FARELF 165, 182, 234, 299
Farthing W., Maj. 15, P
Fellows, Cpl. 35
Ferguson I. B., Lt. Col. 11, 27
Fiji 323
Fijian 159, 287, 311
Finger 42–3, 45–6
Fiona 148
Flanders 273
Fletcher A .I .D., Lt. Col. 265, 266, 268, 278, P
Fletcher B. N. C., Lt. Col. 285, 286
Flora 114
Florence 4
Flying Cheetahs 58
Folbigg R., Cpl. 235, P
Ford, Pte. 45
Formations:
American
8 Army 11
I Corps 12, 21, 38, 60
IX Corps 7, 13, 15, 17, 21
1 Marine Div. 137, 140
1 Cavalry Div. 21, 22, 34, 38
2 Inf Div. 17, 117, 123
3 Inf Div. 34, 38, 82, 86
24 Inf Div. 8, 11–14, 16, 17, 21
25 Inf Div. 18
173 Airborne Bde. 274
British
1 Comwel Div 29, 34, 35, 59, 60, 75, 85, 89, 97, 102, 103, 107, 115, 117, 119, 123, 124, 133, 134, 141, 145, 148, 155, 164, 186, 206, 224, 234, 270, 294, 322
1 African Div. 3
2 African Div. 3
4 Inf Div. 4

9 Scottish Div. 3
17 Gurkha Div. 217, 239, 246, 276, 277, 286, 290, 292, 299, 303
35 Inf Div. 4
40 Inf Div. 4, 11
46 Inf Div. 248
51 Highland Div. 3
2 Gibraltar Bde. 4
3 Commando Bde. 247
19 Inf Bde. 269, 274
26 Gurkha Bde. 178
27 Comwel Bde. 6, 7, 16, 21, 83, 102, 157
28 East African Bde. 3
29 Inf. Bde 7, 12, 22, 25, 27, 29, 37, 40, 58, 64, 72, 85, 92, 95, 98, 99, 109, 110, 113, 123, 130, 137, 138, 248
49 Inf. Bde. 64
63 Gurkha Bde. 239
99 Gurkha Bde. 239, 240, 246, 251, 279
154 Inf. Bde. 3
Camel Corps Bde. 16
South African Bde. 3
Canadian
25 Cdn. Bde. 20, 22, 25, 29, 36–8, 49, 58, 82, 87, 88, 90, 94, 99, 109, 110, 113
Chinese
190 Div 70
191 Div 38, 58, 59
192 Div 38
Indian
190 Bde. 147
Korean
1 ROK Div. 114
6 ROK Div. 7, 19
7 ROK Div. 17
Malaysian
1 Fed. Div. 161, 177, 223
1 Fed. Bde. 297
2 Fed. Bde. 172, 243

New Zealand
2 N.Z. Div.                       248
Turkey
Turkish Bde.                    38, 130
Fort George               29, 150, 234
Fort Slim                         192
Forward B., Maj.                  143
Foulis, 2lt.                       17
France                            159
Fraser, A. R., Lt.                220
Freeman N., Cpl.               247, P
French Bn.                        117
Fry J. C., Gen.                   119

*Galahad, Sir*                    187
Gallipoli Camp                    157
*Gamecock*                        246
Gan                               293
Gargate A. W., Lt.                137
Garland, Gnr.                  80, 147
Garland R. S., Maj.               202
Gemas                             239
George Checkpoint                  90
Georgetown                        181
*Georgic* H.M.T.                  164
Geneva Convention                  36
Gerke J., Maj.               43, 46, 47,
                             52, 54, 130
Germany                      3, 298, 311
Gibraltarian                      311
Glasgow                      308, 312
Gloucester, Duke of          277, 278, P
Gloucester Crossing           36, 106
Gordon T. V. S., 2lt.              35
Gordon-Duff S. L., Capt.          273
Gorton, J.                        294
Goulson, Lt. Col.         179, 184, 185
Grant, J., R.S.M.              278, P
Greece                              4
Green C., Lt. Col.                  6
Gregson, Brig.                    146
Greville P., Lt.              100, 106
Grik                      174, 209, 211
Grubb J., 2lt.                    135
Grundy, Lt.                  19, 80, 81
Gunong Bubu                       214
Gunong Korbu                      182

Gurr R. M., Brig.        249, 260, 261,
                         265, 266, 276,
                             296–8, P

Hampshire                           3
Han River                       10, 14
Hanley, Lcpl.                     204
Hanlon, Lcpl.                      18
Hantan River                       23
Hardiman, Maj.                     50
Harris, Sgt.                   222, P
Harris, Cpl.                      303
Harris, Rolf                      232
Harrison, Maj.               42, 61, 69
Hart, Lt. Col.                    165
Harvey, Pte.                   153, P
Hassett F., Gen.        27, 31, 37, 40, 51,
                        52, 55, 58, 60, 75,
                          76, 85, 92, 97,
                        103, 104, 223–7,
                          239, 243, 245,
                               314, P
Hassett R., Maj.       32, 110, 216, 223,
                           226, 229, P
Healey J., Lt. Col.               312
Heard, K. A. Maj.         18, 47, 79, 80
Heard J., Lt. Col.                169
Hearn B., Maj.                    114
Helliwell A.                       92
Henderson J. B., Lt.       61, 64–6, 69
Hepi L., Sgt.                     205
Hill R., Capt.                     93
Hill, 2lt.                        135
Hills:
75                                106
111                      140, 141, 143
119                               140
121                               140
127                                29
133                               110
149                      63, 76, 79, 83
157                               105
159                     71, 79, 113, 118,
                          128, 132, 146
187                           37, 125
189                               146
194                                23

| | | | |
|---|---|---|---|
| 199 | 40, 41, 45, 47, 50, 58, 72 | Hong Kong | 4, 10, 14, 16, 40, 77, 87, 88, 214, 259, 299, 314 |
| 208 | 41, 43, 45 | | |
| 210 | 40, 45, 47, 53, 125, 126, 146 | Hook | 110, 129, 130, 131–3, 137, 139– 41, 143, 144, 146 |
| 217 | 40, 50, 52–6, 58, 61, 65, 67, 68, 72–4 | Hopkinson, Cpl. | 188 |
| | | Horsford D., Gen. | 295 |
| 222 | 27, 34–6, 38, 49 | Houghton-Berry, Capt. | 43 |
| 227 | 40, 47, 55, 58, 63, 64, 70, 77–85, 92, 99, 103, 110, 113, 117, 118, 124, 135, 137, 147, 157 | Hughes R. L., Lt. Col. | 104, 122 |
| | | Hull, Gen. | 234 |
| | | Hungry Hill | 92 |
| | | Hunter, Pte. | 153, P |
| 238 | 41, 43, 73 | Hunter-Wade R., H. E. | 261 |
| 277 | 12 | Hunty N. F. de C., Lt. Col. | 300 |
| 280 | 61 | Hurditch, Air Comm. | 300, 301, P |
| 282 | 6 | Hutchinson I., Lt. Col | 92, 98, 109 |
| 317 | 40, 51, 52, 54–6, 61, 66, 69, 72–4, 76, 84, 85, 130 | Hyon-Ni | 20 |
| | | Iban | 189, 193 |
| 355 | 38, 40, 41, 43, 45– 7, 49, 50, 52, 58, 74, 80–2, 85, 86, 113–15, 118, 122, 124, 125, 128–31, 135, 138, P | Imjin River | 22, 23, 28, 29, 34–6, 38, 58, 60, 61, 106, 124, 145–9, 236, 238 |
| | | Inchon | 8, 10, 16, P |
| | | India | 3, 148, 313 |
| | | Indian Ocean | 293 |
| 432 | 18, 19 | Indo-China | 219, 227, 239 |
| 462 | 12 | Indonesia | 245, 246, 250, 251, 255, 261, 279 |
| 486 | 17, 18 | | |
| 504 | 7 | Inglis J., Capt. | 161 |
| 534 | 14 | Innes, Lt. | 17 |
| 590 | 17 | Innes A. W., Lt. Col. | 188 |
| 672 | 18, 19 | Ipoh | 172, 173, 177, 179, 182, 188, 191, 194, 195, 197, 202, 208, 212, 214, 223, 239, 261 |
| 677 | 7 | | |
| 1291 | 184 | | |
| Hing Tak | 198 | | |
| Hinge | 54–7, 61, 65, 66 | | |
| H.L.I. | 298 | | |
| Hoare C., 2lt. | 112 | Irish Guards | 265, 285 |
| Hock Lian Estate | 103 | Isaacs, 2lt. | 63 |
| Hodgson, Pte. | 104, P | Italians | 14, 311 |
| Hodkinson G., Fus. | 112, 113, 126, 127 | Italy | 4, 69, 72 |
| Hoge, Gen. | 15 | Itan bin Pandak | 191 |
| Holder, Pte. | 70 | | |
| Holland, D. M. | 296 | Jack, Pte. | 188 |
| Holme M. W., Lt. Col. | 214 | Jackson, Pte. | 178 |
| | | Jalong | 203, 205, 207 |

| | | | |
|---|---|---|---|
| Jalong Tinggi | 173, 183 | K. Force | 32 |
| Jambu | 269 | Kidney | 42, 43, 45, 64 |
| Jamestown Line | 61, 85, 231 | Kigong-Ni | 112 |
| Jamieson, Sgt. | 131 | Kim, Pte. | 153, P |
| Japan | 48, 88, 127, 290 | King A. W., Maj. | 192 |
| Japanese Survey | 34 | King George VI | 90 |
| Javanese | 250 | King P. F., Maj. | 67 |
| Jeffreys P. J., Lt. Col. | 106, 121, 48, P | King-Clark R., Maj. | 121, P |
| Jerram R., Maj. | 222, 223 | K.D.G. | 184 |
| Jesselton | 245 | Kinta | 175, 182, 189–91 |
| Johnson J. C., Lt. Col. | 206, 210 | Kirkiland, Pte. | 186 |
| Johnstone, Pte. | 17 | Kirley R., Pte. | 125, 140 |
| Johore | 162, 261, 263, | Kitchener Lord | 3 |
| | 266, 273, 290, | Kittikachon T., F. M. | 275 |
| | 304, 312, 320 | Kiwi A., Lt. | 265 |
| Jones, Pte. | 70, 83 | Klein, Pte. | 303 |
| | | Kling Kang | 257 |
| Kaesong | 26 | Knight, R. S. M. | 80 |
| Kalabakan | 276, 278 | Knoll | 54–6, 61, 62, 64–6, 69 |
| Kalimantan | 245, 246, 256, | Knowles P., Pte. | 23, 51 |
| | 269, 273, 275 | Koch, Lt. | 13 |
| Kamunting | 149 | Kohima | 236 |
| Kangaw | 298, 300, 307, | Koia, Pte. | 314 |
| | 315 | Kojangsong-Ni | 83 |
| Kansas Line | 22, 23, 25, 26, | Koje-Do | 95–7, 104, P |
| | 29, 36, 145, | Kong Siew | 198 |
| | 146, 148 | Korat | 240 |
| Kapyong | 6, 8, 11–13, 20, | Korean Service Corps | 37, 87 |
| | 87, 249 | Kota Belud | 245 |
| Kapyongchong | 6 | Kota Tinggi | 162, 190, 290 |
| Karangan | 169 | Kowang-San | 40, 45–7, 59, 60, 70, |
| KATCOMS | 122, 123, 137, | | 83, 85, 86, 109, 110, |
| | 149 | | 115, 119, 124, 137, |
| Kayan, Pte. | 184, 186 | | 146, 157, 224, P |
| Kedah | 163, 166–8, | Kranji | 305 |
| | 170, 240, 249, | Kroh | 182 |
| | 258, 268 | Kuala Kangsar | 172–4, 189, 201, 212, |
| Keenan J. B., Maj. | 248, 257 | | 218 |
| Kelley J. W., Maj. | 109 | Kuala Krau | 241 |
| Kemp, Sgt. | 256 | Kuala Lumpur | 163, 165, 166, 218, |
| Kennedy M. R., Brig. | 312–16, 318, | | 219 |
| | 319, 324, P | Kuching | 247, 257, 269, 270, |
| Kent, H.R.H. Duke | 312 | | 279 |
| Kenya | 64 | Kulai | 294 |
| Kerayong | 241 | Kulim | 163, 168–70, 171, |
| Keren | 14 | | 173 |
| Kerinching | 220 | Kumch'ok-Dong | 83 |
| Kesang River | 266 | Kunadoma, Cpl. | 287 |

| | | | |
|---|---|---|---|
| Kure | 127, 290 | MacBeth | 94 |
| Kuun-Chon | 12 | MacDonald A. L., Lt. Col. | 121, 122, P |
| Kwong Ming | 192 | MacDonald B. A., Lt. Col. | 249, 265, 266 |
| Labis | 263, 265 | MacDonald J. F., Lt. Col. | 11, 12, 43, 64, 74, 75, 89, 98, P |
| Ladd Alan | 221 | | |
| Lam Poh | 203–5 | | |
| Lambert B. D., Lt. | 192 | MacDonald R. C., Lt. Col. | 148 |
| Land, Pte. | 63 | MacDonald, Lcpl. | 135 |
| Langtry J. C., Lt. Col. | 291, 292, P | Mace J., Lt. Col. | 307, 313–16 |
| Laos | 153, 217, 226, 230, 233, 261, 281, 299 | MacGillivray, Sir D. | 165 |
| | | MacGregor G. M., Maj. Sir | 268, 277, P |
| | | Mack, Lt. | 175, 181 |
| Larkin G. F., Lt. Col. | 121, 122, P | MacKay Ian, Lt. Col. | 309, 313, P |
| Latham, Maj. | 251 | MacKenzie, Maj. | 19 |
| Lau Choo | 197 | MacLean H., Capt. | 79, 80, 147 |
| Lau Fong | 198 | MacLean I., Capt. | 211 |
| Leary, Lt. | 50 | MacLeod, Capt. | 220 |
| Leggett, Pte. | 49 | MacLeod-Lee A., P.M. | 306, P |
| Letok anak Kusing | 185 | Mad Mile | 47, 63, 80, 84 |
| Lewis G., Maj. | 165 | Maharattas | 313 |
| Lincoln Camp | 182 | Majeedi Barracks | 263 |
| Lintang | 173, 257 | Maktae-Dong | 51, 61, 72 |
| Lio Matoh | 256 | Malacca | 218, 234, 236, 242, 266, 272, 273, 280, 286, 292, 294 |
| Little, Maj. | 42, 61 | | |
| Little Gibraltar | 47, 115, 119, 124 | | |
| Lloyd D. F., Lt. | 116, 117 | | |
| Lock | 61, 68 | Malaya Command | 295 |
| Loeng Nok Tha | 249, 275, 290 | Malaysian Rangers | 276 |
| Loewen C., Gen. | 165 | Man A., Lt. Col. | 12 |
| Lofthouse, Cpl. | 136 | Manchester | 211 |
| London | 133, 166 | Manchuria | 87 |
| Long | 42, 43, 45 | Manchus | 118 |
| Long Akah | 247 | Mandalay | 236 |
| Long Jawi | 249 | Man Ko | 191 |
| Long Semado | 256 | Mann D., Capt. | 114, 162 |
| Long Tan | 298 | Mann J., Maj. | 114 |
| Longden, Lt. Col. | 166 | Mao Tse-tung | 84 |
| Loos | 3 | Maori | 216, 242, 272, 285, 307, 310, 311, P |
| Lowe B., Maj. | 292 | | |
| Lubok Antu | 258, 274 | Marae | 242, 310, 311, P |
| Lucas G. | 100 | Marang | 277 |
| Luckhurst, Pte. | 103 | Margaret, Princess | 308, 309, P |
| Lutong | 259 | Margetts D. A., 2lt. | 28 |
| Lyal, 2lt. | 71 | Marshall B. J., Lt. | 274 |
| Lydekker R. M. W., Lt. Col. | 248, 251, 253, 265, 267, 269, P | Maryang-San | 40, 51–3, 55, 56, 58, 59, 61, 70–3, 76, 77, 85, 93, 130, 157, 224, 236 |

| | |
|---|---|
| Masters J., Capt. | 270 |
| Mau Mau | 64 |
| Mauritius | 292, 296, 299, 323 |
| McArthy, Lcpl. | 107 |
| McBride I. M., Maj. | 138 |
| McCabe, Sgt. | 135 |
| McCabe, Lcpl. | 36 |
| McCeever, R. S. M. | 151 |
| McGhee J., Lt./Maj. | 203, 290 |
| McLaughlin, Gen. | 97, P |
| McMeekin T. D. M., Brig. | 226, 267, 272, 280, 281, P |
| McMillan Scott, Lt. | 19 |
| Meerut Barracks | 298, 300, 308 |
| Mekong River | 229, 248, 281, 286 |
| Melbourne | 234 |
| *Melbourne Sun* | 115, 122 |
| Menzies, Mr. | 167 |
| Mersing | 304 |
| Methodist Church | 242 |
| Micklewhite, Fus. | 128, 129 |
| Miller, Capt. | 63 |
| Miller, Pte. | 22 |
| Millhouse, Sgt. | 73 |
| Minden Barracks | 161, 166, 169, 170 |
| Minden Day | 104 |
| Miri | 259 |
| Mogg H. J., Brig. | 193, 194, 198, 206, 209, 211, 214–19, 223, 224, 311, P |
| Mogg Mrs. | 214, 221 |
| Mohammed Rafiq | 290, 291 |
| *Montrose* U.S.S. | 10, 16 |
| Moodie J. W., Lt. Col. | 6, 32 |
| Moody, Pte. | 153, P |
| Moore, 2lt. | 43 |
| Moore, Cpl. | 111 |
| Moore P. N. M., Brig. | 161, 162, 164–6, 172, 178, 179, 189, 193, 194, 216, P |
| Morgan D. R., Brig. | 4, 7 |
| Morrison E. J., Sgt. | 117 |
| Morrison W. R. K., Lt. Col. | 190 |
| Morrow W. J., Lt. Col. | 121, 212, 218, P |
| Mountbatten, Countess | 214, 215, P |
| Moyle R., Sgt. | 206 |
| Muir K., Maj. | 6 |
| Mullings, Pte. | 204 |
| Muniandy R. | 229 |
| Munsan-Ni | 126, 147 |
| Murdoch, C. S. M. | 69 |
| Murdoch L. J., Brig. | 154–6, P |
| Murray H., Maj. Gen. | 152 |
| NAAFI | 32, 86, 88, 221, 236, 290 |
| Naechon | 103 |
| Nair M. B. K., Lt. Col. | 122 |
| Naktong | 6 |
| Namibia | 323 |
| Nee Soon | 240, 241, 296–8, 300, 308, 309, 318, 321 |
| Negeri J., Pte. . | 275 |
| Negri Sembilan | 178, 217 |
| Nelligan, Pte. | 102 |
| Newell, Maj. | 161 |
| Newcastle | 29 |
| Newmarket | 29 |
| New Orleans | 151 |
| Newton, Cpl. | 103 |
| Nicholls, Capt. | 41, 50 |
| Nordstrom, Capt. | 102 |
| Norris, Pte. | 104, P |
| Northamptonshire | 183 |
| Northland | 29 |
| North Korea | 4, 58, 127, 157 |
| North Malaya Sub D | 177, 178, 207 |
| Norton, Pte. | 45 |
| Norton P. J., Maj. | 212 |
| Norwegian MASH | 21, 145 |
| Nose | 135 |
| Nott-Bower J. Sir | 139 |
| Nott-Bower W. J., Lt. | 138 |
| N.Z.A.A.C. | 270, 276 |
| N.Z. Div. | 19 |
| O.B.L.I. | 135 |
| O'Brien F. K., Pte | 200 |
| O'Daniel J. W. Gen. | 38, 59, 75, 91 |
| Ochiltree J., Lt. Col. | 162, 165, 167, 169, 174, 178 |
| Operations: | |
| Bamboo | 208–9, 217, 219, 232 |

Beat Up 112
Boomerang 35
Blaydon 110
Blaze 99
Blowpipe 281
Commando 38, 42, 43, 46, 48, 49, 56–61, 85
Cotswold 123
Crown 249, 259
Deuce 168, 173
Emperor 137
Fauna 114, 115
Finder 148
Ginger 190–1, 193, 194, 198, 207–8
Gotong Rogong 286
Hot Trail 244
Jaya 208, 212, 214, 232
Minden 36
Parrot 247
Pimlico 112, 126
Pork Chopper 259
Shark 173, 174
Skunk Hunt 87
Snare 91
Swanlake 145, 146
Unity 178
Orang Sakai 191
Osman bin Tunku Mohd, Gen. 282, P
Oxley P., Maj. 161, 172, 179, P

Pa Bangia 256
Pack, Lt. 103
Pa Dali 256
Pakchon 6
Pakistan 159
Palmer, Gen. 22
Pa Lungan 256
Pa Main 256
Panmunjon 91, 92, 126, 127, 140, 144, 147, 167
Pantai Tanah Merah 283, 286
Papan Gila 191
Parachute Regt 151
Parham J., Lt. Col. 294
Pari 187, 194, 196
Parker J. W., 2lt. 128, 136
Parry, 2lt. 104, P

Parsons, Cpl. 80
Partai Ra'ayat 345
Patch, Cpl. 100
Patterson A. G., Brig. 251
Patterson R. McK., Lt. Col. 92, 118
Pa Umor 256
Pawlett, Maj. 183
Payne K., Sgt. 264, P
Peak 69, 70, 72
Pearce L. A., Lt. Col. 237, 248, 249
Pembroke, Lt. 52, 54–7, 86
Penang 161–6, 170, 171, 181, 182, 223
Pendlebury, Cpl. 43
Peng Hsien-Chieh 70
Pennel, Capt. 105
Pensiangan 250
*People* Newspaper 92
Perak 161, 172, 173, 179, 181, 182, 185, 186, 190–2, 208, 209, 212, 213, 217, 220, 222, 226, 237–9, 242, 261, 265, 276
Perak Communist Party 192
Perlis 243, 259
Perrott B. D., 2lt. 110
Persuaders 63, 92
Peshawar 259
Peterforce 95, 97
*Petrel* 276
P.F.F. 170, 173, 202
Philip, Prince 270, 273, 305, 307, P
Philippines 159, 217
Phillips, Sgt. 73
Phillips, Padre 20
Picasso 88
Pim 195
Pinion A. J., Lt. 258
Pintail 106, 146
Plum Pudding Hill 6
Poananga B., Lt. Col. 276, 291, 292, P
Pollard, Capt. 47
Pollard, Gen. 166, 294
Pontian Kechil 261
Port Louis 293
Port Stanley 58

Post Crown                    290, 294
Potts, Pte.                        153, P
Pountney J. A., Lt. Col.              154
Powell D., Cpl.                        54
Prai                                  171
Pring A., Pte.                         70
Proctor, Cpl.                          47
Province Wellesley      161–3, 168, 170,
                              300, 320
Puckapanyal                           162
Pukhan                     7, 11, 12, 14
Pullen, Sgt.                      222, P
Pun Tung Kwai                         197
Punyer, Pte.                          103
Purves, 2lt.                       69, 70
Pusan                       6, 104, 106
Pyongyang                               6

Queen Elizabeth II   90, 133, 144, 260,
                           305, 307, P
Queenscliffe                          162
Queensland                            162
Quinn D., Capt./Maj.             258, 294

R.A.A.F.           127, 166, 300, 330
R.A.A.S.C.                            297
Radfan                           260, 299
Radio Malaysia                        286
R.A.E.M.E.                            187
R.A.F.              169, 171, 184, 227,
                   129, 252, 256, 259,
                   260, 293, 305, 314
Raison, Sgt.                           22
*Raja Menua*                          246
Rajang River                          249
Ramadu Dan                            256
Ramsay B. M., Capt.                   178
Ramsay, Pte.                          204
R.A.N.                                276
Rangaraj A. G., Lt. Col.       6, 30, 107,
                     114, 115, 148, P
Rangihu, Padre                        149
Ratcliffe E. W., Lt.                  128
Rawlings, Pte.                        136
Rawlinson, Sgt.                        51
Rejek                                 220
Renton T. M., Capt.                   133
Reynolds A. W., Maj.                  274

Reynolds S. M.                        256
Rhee Dr. & Mrs.                       134
Rhodesia                 130, 322, 323
Richardson R., Capt.                  105
Richardson, Cpl.                       19
Rickus, Sgt.                      228, P
Riley, Cpl.                           198
Rimini Line                             4
Rixon, Gnr.                            67
Robertson, Maj. S.A.·            33, 35, P
Robertson-MacLeod, Maj.            46, 61
Robinson, Cpl.                        188
Rockhampton                           287
Rome H. C. I., Lt. Col.               238
Rompin                                260
Rooke, 2lt.                            71
Roper, A. de, 2lt.                    112
Rose, Pte.                        139, P
Rosevear, Lcpl.                       136
Rowe G. C. K., Lt. Col.          277, 294
Royal Australian Marines              243
Royal Canadian Theatre                 87
Royal Dragoons                        239
Royal Engineers            23, 56, 91
Royal Malay Police       169, 201, 208
Royal Malaysian Artillery             275
Royal Marine Commandoes          293, 300
Royal Melbourne Regt.                 138
Royal Navy           239, 265, 276,
                           277, 300
Royal N.Z. Navy                  276, 323
Royal Ulster Rifles                  8, P
Rudd. Sgt.                             27
Russell G. D. G. R., Brig.       319, 320, P

Sabah              245, 246, 250, 252,
                   260, 276, 277, 305
Salamanca Camp                   147, 150
Salmon J. R. Capt./Maj.     114, 231, 244
Saltonstall R. G., Lt. Col.           249
Salvation Army                     33, 35
Samichon              37, 87, 90, 94, 99,
                   105–7, 109, 110, 113,
                   124, 129, 138, 144,
                               154, 157
Sarawak            245–7, 249, 251, 252,
                   256, 257, 260, 269–
                   77, 279, 280, 290

Sarawak Rangers 135, 199, 200, 218
S.A.S. 190, 200, 320
Saunders D. G. B., Lt. Col. 318
Saunders R., Capt. 187
Savage, Pte. 140
Savannakhet 239
Saw 50, 54, 55
Schneider, Pte. 225
Scolley, Pte. 188
Scotland 285
Scott G. 7, 8
Scott W., Col. 194
Scouts 312
Scrase-Dickins S. W., Brig. 3
Seaforth Camp 106
Seaforth Highlanders 29
SEATO 159, 176, 217, 226,
227, 229, 230, 234,
239–41, 245, 251,
274–6, 280, 285,
292, 298, 300, 322
Seddon R. E., Maj. 187
Seewasagur Rangulam, Sir 293
Segamat 239, 265
Selarang 296
Selangor, Sultan of 217, 219
Selepong 249
Sembawang 238, 300, 305
Semengo Camp 270
Senai 294
Seni-oi River 181
Senoi Pra'ak 191
Seoul 14, 127
Sepulot 250
Serangoon 304
Seremban 233, 248, 277, 294
Seria 246
Shaftoe, Cpl. 182
Shanahan P. M., Maj. 161
Shaw-Ball A. S., Lt. Col. 16, 27
Shell Petroleum Co. 246
Shelton, J., Lt. Col./Capt. 37, 41, 290
Sherwood Foresters 197
Shine F., Padre 102
Shoalwater Bay 289
Siegert A. L., Air Comm. 301, P
Sigai anak Jugan, Pte. 197, 199, P
Sihanouk Prince 159

Simanggang 249
Sims, Capt. 229, P
Sinclair, Maj. Gen. 161
Singapore 161, 170, 214, 227,
230, 234, 239–41,
245, 246, 275, 292,
296, 298–301, 303,
304, 314, 315, 318,
320, 322, 323
Singapore Armed Forces 316, 321
Singapore Regt. R.A. 176, 184
Singler J., Gdsm. 171, P
Skelton, Sgt. 104, P
Slim W, Sir F. M. 162
Slim Dusty 232
Slocombe W. S., Maj. 244
Smith Padre 149
Smith, Sgt. 123
Smith F., Lt. 117
Smith M., Capt. 197
Smith P. S. C., Lt. Col. 147
Smyth H. E., Maj. 185
Sockalingam 201
Soerkano, President 255
Soetkino, Lt. 265
Solia, Pte. 226
Solma-Ri 236
Song 249
South Africans 89
South African A. F. 58
South Australian 223
South Vietnam 153, 217, 226, 230,
261, 274, 277
Speakman W., Pte., V.C. 67, 68, P
Special Branch 169, 173, 201–4,
212, 259
Speed F. W., Col. 170
Speer, Lt. Col. 53
*Sri Blalang* 246
Sri Lanka 187
S.S.A.F.A. 221
St. Alban 150
St. Barbara 143
St. Chad 95
St. Clair Morford, 2lt. 91
St. David's School 294
St. George 312
St. Helena 187

| | |
|---|---|
| St. Valery en Caux | 3 |
| *Stars & Stripes* | 35 |
| Steele, Sgt. | 255 |
| Stevens. Lt. Col. | 106, 121, 138, P |
| Steward W., Lt. | 270, 276 |
| Stewart J. | 206 |
| Stewart-Wilson B. A., Maj. | 276 |
| Stone J. R., Lt. Col. | 6, 13 |
| Stratton A. B., Lt. Col. | 231 |
| Suez | 175, 261, 295 |
| Sugden, Gen. | 198 |
| Sui Tit | 181 |
| Sumatra | 261 |
| Sumpner R. I., 2lt. | 189 |
| Sungei Kerbau | 184 |
| Sungei Kuang | 190, 209 |
| Sungei Patani | 165, 166, 223 |
| Sungei Siput | 173, 178, 181, 186, 196, 197, 201, 204, 247 |
| Suparmin W. O. | 265 |
| Suppiah | 200 |
| Surfers Paradise | 287 |
| Sydney | 262 |
| Syn Lee Rubber Co. | 283 |
| | |
| Tadman D. H., Maj. | 64 |
| Taebo-Ri | 20 |
| Taedong River | 6 |
| Taiaha | 311 |
| Taiping | 161, 177, 178, 182, 183, 190, 194, 198, 207, 212, 214, 217, 218, 222, 223, 225, 227, 280, 284, 303 |
| Taitt Maj. | 43, 70 |
| Tanah Hitam | 190, 195 |
| Tancred P. L., Brig. | 281, 292, 295, 296 |
| Tanjong Rambutan | 172, 173, 185, 188, 190 |
| *Taranaki* H.M.N.Z.S | 276 |
| Tapah | 223 |
| Tasker, Lbdr. | 240 |
| Tattersall J., Capt. | 161 |
| Tawau Asslt. Group | 276 |
| Taylor G., Brig. | 7, 10–14, 16, 17, 22, 25, 31, 33, 34, 37, 38, 43, 49, 52, 53, 55, 56, 58–60, 64, P |

| | |
|---|---|
| Taylor, Cpl. | 100 |
| Taylor, Pte. | 185 |
| Teal | 106 |
| Tebedu | 247 |
| Tempasuk River | 245 |
| Templer, Sir G., F. M. | 179, P |
| Tentara Nasional | 246 |
| Terendak | 218, 232, 234–7, 240, 242, 248, 257–61, 265, 267, 268, 270, 272–6, 279–82, 284–6, 290, 292–4, 296, 297, 303, 304, 312, 323 |
| Tetuhi J. H., Sgt. | 311 |
| Thailand | 159, 178, 217, 227, 228, 243, 248, 249, 259–61, 263, 265, 275, 280, 285, 290, 294, 299 |
| Thompson, C. L., Lt. Col. | 182, 195, 206 |
| Thompson, Pte. | 187 |
| Thomson D., Lt. Col. | 100, 276 |
| Thorburn A. M., Capt. | 93 |
| Thornton D., Col. | 318 |
| Tien | 246 |
| *Tiger* | 246 |
| Tofield, Capt. | 260 |
| Tokyo | 32, 88, 115, 252 |
| Trasimene | 4 |
| Trenerry J. B., Lt. Col. | 296 |
| Trengganu, Sultan of | 220 |
| Tresawna J. A., Maj. | 135 |
| Triang | 241 |
| Truell G. D. S., Maj. | 248, 269 |
| Tsei Ko Yin | 206 |
| Tucker, Cpl. | 27, P |
| Tuxworth B. J., Pte. | 192 |
| | |
| Ubon | 227, 228, 230, 248, 249, 275 |
| Uganda | 323 |
| Ulu Kinta | 172 |
| U.N. | 241, 322 |
| Un Dong | 38, 40, 82 |
| United | 65–8 |

Units:
American:
1 U.S. Cavalry Regt. 26
3 U.S.M.C. Regt. 137, 140
5 U.S. Cavalry Regt. 8, 11–13
7 R.C.T. 86, 151
9 R.C.T. 118, 119
19 R.C.T. 14-17
72 Tk.Bn. 7, 12, 13
Australian:
1 R.A.R. 92, 97–9, 103, 106–9,
111–115, 120, 122,
154, 155, 157, 211,
218, 223, 231, 274,
276, 280, 296, 297,
298
2 R.A.R. 122, 125, 129, 132,
135, 137, 138–41,
144, 146, 149, 154,
161, 162, 164, 171,
173, 174, 178, 182,
186, 187, *231, 232,*
238, 241, 244, 248,
249, 294
3 R.A.R. 6, 7, 12–14, 16–21,
23, 25–27, 29, 31,
33–37, 40–7, 49–58,
61, 70, 72, 77, 84–9,
92, 97, 102, 104–7,
109, 115–17, 122,
129–32, 137, 143,
146, 155, 157, 186,
187, 200, 202, 203,
206, 211, 224, 248,
249, 261, 266, 268,
273, 274, 275, 276,
285, 290, P
4 R.A.R. 276, 277, 280–2, 286,
290–2
6 R.A.R. 298, 300, 303, 306,
313–15, 318, 319, P
8 R.A.R. 292–6
1 Fd. Tp. 212, 273,
2 Fd. Tp. 212, 249, 296, 297
4 Fd. Tp. 232, 238, 245, 249
32 Army Dental Unit 238, 286
Belgian:
Belgian Bn 34

British:
8 K.R.I.H. 22, 41, 43, 47, 51,
60, 63, 72, 81, 261
15/19 H 165
16/5 L. 173
4 Lt. Regt. 275
6 Lt. Regt. 277, 294, 296
14 Lt. Regt. 294, 295
25 Fd. Regt. 165
26 Fd. Regt. 236, 238, 240, 248
28 Jungle Fd. Regt. 294
28 ANZUK Fd. Regt. 300, 303, 319
45 Fd. Regt. 248, 249, 251, 257,
259, 266, 269, 270,
273, 274, 275, 277
1 Scots Gds. 265, 266, 268,
270–7, 284, 285
1 R.N.F. 37, 40, 50–5, 58, 60,
72
1 R. Warwicks 148, 149, 152, 157, P
1 R.Fusiliers 103, 106–13, 115,
120, 123–6, 128,
129, 133, 134, 137,
138, 145, 147, P
1 Kings Regt. 139
1 R.Norfolk 64, 81, 82, 87, 88
1 R.Lincoln 164, 172, 178, 179,
181, 183, 184,
186–90
1 R. Leicesters 4, 72, 73, 76, 82, 98
1 R.S.F. 164, 172, 175, 178,
181, 182, 299
2 R.S.F. 3
1 R.H.F. 298–300, 306, 308,
309, 313, 315, 317,
318, P
1 K.O.S.B. 4, 8, 10–21, 31, 33,
36, 37, 40–9, 56, 58,
61, 66, 67, 70–4, 76,
85, 88, 92–4, 98, 99,
102–4, 130, 285, P
6 K.O.S.B. 3
1 Cameronians 4
9 Cameronians 3
1 D of Wellingtons 130–3
1 South Staffs 4
1 Welch Regt. 85, 109
1 Black Watch 110, 123, 130, 134

| | |
|---|---|
| 1 Essex Regt. | 147, 148, 150–3, 155, 157, 212, P |
| 1/3 East Anglian | 212, 214, 217, 218, 222, 232, 238, P |
| 1 Loyals | 182, 184, 189, 192, 194, 196–99, 206, 208, 210, 212, P |
| 1 K.O.Y.L.I. | 238, 240, 242, 246–9, 252, 254, 256, 258, 260, 263, 265, 295, P |
| 2 K.O.Y.L.I. | 259 |
| 1 K.S.L.I. | 4, 16–22, 27–9, 31, 33–7, 40, 41, 43, 45–8, 55, 56, 58, 63, 64, 70, 77, 78, 81–4, 86–92, 94–8, 102–6, 108, 157, 284, 285–8, 292–5, P |
| 1 Middlesex | 4, 6, 12–14, 16, 21, 33, 89 |
| 1 R.G.J. | 252 |
| 2 R.G.J. | 277 |
| 1 D.L.I. | 106, 108, 110, 111, 114–6, 119, 120, 122–4, 127, 130, 133, 135, 136, 138, 140, 141, 145, 147, 148, 229, 295, P |
| 9 D.L.I. | 194 |
| 2 L.I. | 295 |
| 3 L.I. | 295 |
| 10 H.L.I. | 3 |
| 11 H.L.I. | 3 |
| 1 Queens Own Hldrs. | 240, 246, 247 |
| 1 Gordon Hldrs | 275, 276, 317, 318, 320 |
| 1 A. & S.H. | 4, 6–8, 10, 16, 21, 33, 256, 275 |
| 2 Para | 294 |
| 3 Para | 320 |
| 2/2 G.R. | 258 |
| 1/6 G.R. | 165 |
| 2/6 G.R | 4, 188, 190, 197 |
| 1/7 G.R. | 273 |
| 2/7 G.R. | 247 |
| 1/10 G.R. | 263, 266, 274 |
| 2/10 G.R. | 4, 241, 257, 276 |
| 40 Commando R.M. | 247, 251 |
| 28 Engr. Regt. | 164 |
| 9 Fd Sqn. | 298 |
| 11 Fd. Sqn. | 170, 177, 187, 232, 238, 245, 247, 249, 259, 275, 281, 290, 294, 296 |
| 12 Fd. Sqn. | 47 |
| 28 ANZUK Fd. Sqn. | 300 |
| 59 Fd. Sqn. | 230 |
| 28 Sig. Sqn. | 300 |
| 208 Sig. Sqn | 238 |
| 28 Avn. Sqn. | 300 |
| 7 Recce Flt. | 233, 303 |
| 28 O.F.P. | 238 |
| 16 Fd. Amb. | 166, 170, 238, 281 |
| 3 Coy R.A.S.C. | 238 |
| 28 Provost Unit | 138, 238, 242 |
| 2 Inf. Wksps. | 238, 249 |
| 16 Inf. Wksps. | 83, 102 |
| 368 Postal Unit | 238 |
| 22 Int. Pl. | 238 |
| Canadian: | |
| 2 R.C.R. | 20, 95 |
| 2 P.P.C.L.I. | 6, 7, 12, 13, 17, 18, 20, 21, 23, 25, 58, 71, 79, 83 |
| 2 R.22eR. | 20, 26, 28, 104 |
| R Newfoundland Bn. | 3 |
| Chinese: | |
| 569 Regt. | 70, 83 |
| 13/15 Pl. | 173 |
| 31 Pl. | 192 |
| 27 Sect. | 203, 205 |
| French: | |
| French Bn. | 117 |
| Indian: | |
| 60 Para Fd. Amb. | 6, 29, 30, 37, 44, 45, 58, 102, 104, 106, 107, 114, 122, 145, 147, 148, 149, P |
| Korean: | |
| 120 Bn. K.S.C. | 123 |

Malaysian:
1 Fed. Regt. — 172
1 R. Malay Regt. — 284
7 R. Malay Regt. — 240
New Zealand:
1 N.Z.R. — 190, 192, 195, 198, 199, 205, 209, 211, 220, 236–8, 240–2, 244, 247–9, 259, 260, 296, 312
2 N.Z.R. — 212, 216–220, 226–37, 260, 265, 270, P
1 R.N.Z.I.R. — 272, 274–6, 279, 280, 285, 292, 293, 296–8, 300, 304, 305, 307, 310, 311, 313–18, 320, 321, P
16 Fd. Regt. R.N.Z.A. — 6, 7, 13, 19, 20, 29, 32, 57, 60, 71, 86, 89, 92, 98, 102, 104–7, 109, 110, 113, 114, 117–19, 122, 127, 133, 134, 137, 140, 141, 143, 145, 146, 148, 149, 154–8, 216, 231, P
10 Coy R.N.Z.A.S.C. — 89
ANZAC Bn. — 285, 290, 292, 293
Thailand:
Thai Bn. — 118

Van Fleet, Gen — 11, 14–16, 87
Vientiane — 281
Vietnam — 117, 159, 161, 176, 217, 230, 280, 284–7, 290, 292, 293, 295, 296, 298, 299, 303, 304, 314, 320, 322
— 43
Wade, Cpl. — 246, 257, 273
Walker W., Gen. — 186
Walker, Cpl. — 298, 300, 301, 303, 305, 310, 312, P
Walsh M. J. H., Brig. — 
Walter, Capt. — 183–5
Wangjing-Myon — 46

Wan Tui Lui — 184
Warner Jack — 28
Watheram, Maj. — 161
Watt, Sir. A. — 164
Weaver A. C., Lt. — 132
Webb R., Maj. — 15, P
Weir S. P., Lt. Col. — 218
Weir S., Gen. — 242
Wellesley — 313
Wellington — 12, 109, 236, 237, 305, 312
Wells D., R. Admiral — 300, 301, 316, P
Wells, Pte. — 45
Whitamore, Lt. — 22
White D., Capt. — 161
White J., Lt. Col. — 186
White W. F., Lt. Col. — 248–9
Whitelaw F. T., Brig. — 300, 301, P
Whitmore, Cpl. — 63, 84
Whybrow, 2lt. — 90, 91
Widgeon — 106
Wilkinson Sword — 293
Williams R. G., Lt. Col. — 296
Wilson, Sgt. — 70
Wilson S., Pte. — 93
Wilton G. J. N., Brig. — 120, 121, 124, 143, 144, 152–4, P
Wiltshire — 311
Windsor — 312
Wong, Mr. — 223
Wong Sau — 198
Wood, Cpl. — 69
Woodbridge P. H., 2lt. — 128
Woods F. H., Lt. — 199–200
Wright W. G. A., Rev. — 50
Wyoming Line — 36–8

Yacopetti C. P., Lt. — 132
Yang di Pertuan Agong — 217–19
Yang di Pertuan Besar — 217
Yangpyong — 13
Yapp, Lcpl. — 18
Yassin, Effendi — 246, 247
Yeo, Lcpl. — 54
Yeoh Siew-Lye — 223
Yeong Cheong — 192
Yong Dong — 87, 104, 138, 140, 146

Yoong Fan Estate    203
Young, Lt.    50–2
Yugoslavia    193, 323

Zimbabwe    323